STORY
S-T-R-E-T-C-H-E-R-S

Activities to Expand Children's Favorite Books

Shirley C. Raines and Robert J. Canady

gryphon house
Mt. Rainier, Maryland

ACKNOWLEDGEMENTS

Quotations from **A BABY SISTER FOR FRANCES** by Russell Hoban. Text © 1964 by Russell Hoban. Reprinted by permission of Harper and Row, Publishers.

Quotations for **ALFIE GIVES A HAND** by Shirley Hughes. Copyright © 1983 by Shirley Hughes. Reprinted by permission of Lothrop, Lee & Shepard Books (A Division of William Morrow and Company, Inc.)

Quotations from **CAPS FOR SALE** by Esphyr Slobodkina. Copyright © 1940 and 1947 © renewed 1968 by Esphyr Slobodkina. Reprinted by permission of Harper and Row, Publishers.

Quotations from **IF YOU GIVE A MOUSE A COOKIE** by Laura Joffe Numeroff. Text © 1985 by Laura Joffe Numeroff. Reprinted by permission of Harper and Row, Publishers.

Quotations from **MARY WORE HER RED DRESS AND HENRY WORE HIS GREEN SNEAKERS** by Merle Peek. Text and illustrations © 1989 by Merle Peek. Reprinted by permission of Clarion Books, a Houghton Mifflin Company.

Excerpt from **MILLIONS OF CATS** by Wanda Gag, Copyright © 1928 by Coward-McCann, Inc., © renewed 1956 by Robert Janssen. Reprinted by permission of Coward-McCann.

Quotations from **THE RUNAWAY BUNNY** by Margaret Wise Brown. Copyright © 1942 by Harper and Row, Publishers. Text © renewed 1970 by Roberta Brown Rauch. Reprinted by permission of Harper and Row, Publishers.

Quotations from **SARAH'S QUESTIONS** by Harriet Ziefert. Text copyright © 1986 by Harriet Ziefert. Reprinted by permission of Lothrop, Lee & Shepard Books (A Division of William Morrow and Company, Inc.)

Excerpt from **TEENY TINY** retold by Jill Bennett, Text copyright © 1985 by Jill Bennett. Reprinted by permission of G.P. Putnam's Sons.

Quotations from **TEN, NINE, EIGHT** by Molly Bang. Copyright © 1983 by Molly Garrett Bang. Reprinted by permission of Greenwillow Books (A Division of William Morrow and Company.)

Jacket illustration by Holly Keller from **AIR IS ALL AROUND YOU** by Franklyn M.Branley. Illustrations copyright © 1986 by Holly Keller. Reproduced by permission of Harper & Row, Publishers.

Jacket illustration from **COME TO THE MEADOW** Copyright © 1984 by Anna Grossnickle Hines. Reprinted with permission of Clarion Books, a Houghton Mifflin Company.

Jacket illustration from **FIRST COMES SPRING** by Anne Rockwell. Copyright © 1985 by Anne Rockwell. Reproduced by permission of Harper & Row, Publishers.

Jacket illustration from **JAMBERRY** by Bruce Degen. Copyright © 1983 by Bruce Degen. Reproduced by permission Harper & Row, Publishers.

Jacket illustration by John Wallner from **MY FAVORITE TIME OF YEAR** by Susan Pearson. Illustrations copyright © 1988 by John Wallner. Reproduced by permission of Harper & Row, Publishers.

Jacket illustration by Mary Szilagyi from **NIGHT IN THE COUNTRY** by Cynthia Rylant. Illustrations copyright © 1986 by Mary Szilagyi. Reproduced by permission of Bradbury Press, an Affiliate of Macmillan, Inc.

Jacket illustration by Shirley Hughes from **OUT AND ABOUT** Copyright © 1988 by Shirley Hughes. Reproduced by permission of Lothrop, Lee & Shepard (A Division of William Morrow & Co.)

Jacket illustration by Catherine Stock from **SOMETHING IS GOING TO HAPPEN** by Charlotte Zolotow. Illustrations copyright © 1988 by Catherine Stock. Reproduced by permission of Harper & Row, Publishers.

Jacket illustration by Robert Casilla from **THE TRAIN TO LULU'S** by Lisabeth Howard. Illustrations copyright © 1988 by Robert Casilla. Reproduced by permission of Bradbury Press, an Affiliate of Macmillan, Inc.

Jacket illustration from **TRUCK SONG** by Diane Siebert. Illustrations copyright © 1984 by Byron Barton. Reproduced by permission of Harper & Row, Publishers.

Published by Gryphon House, Inc.
3706 Otis Street, Mt. Rainier, Maryland 20712.

Library of Congress Catalog Number: 89–84579

Design: Graves, Fowler & Associates

*To Brian, Lynnette, Scott
and Lark*

PREFACE

THE IDEA OF "STORY STRETCHERS" IS ONE which has been simmering in our minds for many years. When we were teachers and center directors, we used many creative ideas with young children. Now, as professors and consultants, we study language development and emerging literacy, and we observe children becoming interested in literature. We try to find ways to support teachers who develop environments where young children grow to love books, poems, jokes, riddles, songs — the stories of our culture. When we speak about a literature-based early childhood curriculum, teachers often ask if we have a book of these teaching ideas. Finally, we can say, "Yes, STORY S-T-R-E-T-C-H-E-R-S: ACTIVITIES TO EXPAND CHILDREN'S FAVORITE BOOKS."

We are indebted to the students and teachers enrolled in classes at George Mason University in Fairfax, Virginia, and Marymount University in Arlington, Virginia, who field tested many of the ideas with the children they teach. We also appreciate the early childhood educators from a creative teaching course at Northeastern State University in Tahlequah, Oklahoma. They insisted we write our ideas for other teachers to use. In addition, they supplied the initial inspiration for some of the specific story stretchers. Their names are mentioned throughout the book when we adapted ideas from their classrooms. We also must thank the teachers, parents and children at George Mason University's Project for the Study of Young Children for allowing us many hours of observation and probing questions. We would be remiss, however, if we did not thank three of our best consultants, Michelle, Damien and Tina, our grandchildren, who put us onto some of the "hottest" new books which young children enjoy. Finally, our loving thoughts go to Irene and Athel Raines and to the memory of Polly and Bob Canady because they loved us when we were children and taught us to love a good story.

We have been fortunate to work with the fine professionals at Gryphon House. We appreciate Kathy Charner, Sarabeth Goodwin, Leah Curry–Rood and Larry Rood for guiding us in this writing project.

Shirley C. Raines, Ed.D., Associate Professor, George Mason University, Fairfax, Virginia

Robert J. Canady, Ed.D., Professor, Marymount University, Arlington, Virginia

INTRODUCTION

CHILDREN LOVE A GOOD STORY. THEY OFTEN applaud and giggle at happy stories, sniffle at sad ones, and shout, "Read it, again!" whenever they have been delighted, intrigued or charmed by a story. Knowing young children's love of good stories, we devised ways to extend that enthusiasm and better connect children's books and teaching ideas with other areas of the curriculum. This book, then, is a literature-based approach to planning circle time, centers and activities, organized around themes often found in the early childhood curriculum.

The one activity early childhood teachers from across the nation are sure to include in their classrooms on a daily basis is reading to the children. Over the years, teachers have found favorite stories which children request and favorite books which the teachers themselves enjoy. We have written story stretcher ideas to extend children's and teachers' enthusiasm for books.

We selected some old favorites, classics, which have stood the test of time, and we included some new favorites which teachers, librarians and children called to our attention. From the hundreds of new children's books on the market, we selected those suggested by book store owners, and then we asked teachers to read them to their classes and tell us the children's responses. We also verified that the books we selected are currently in print and readily available.

From our research on emerging literacy behaviors and from our experiences in the classroom, we know that children who have an environment at home and at school where they are read to and where they interact with adults about books usually become good readers. Therefore, we encourage you to use story stretchers not only to promote children's interest in books and to increase the likelihood that they will become good readers in later schooling, but also because the activities have immediate value. The children and the teachers enjoy the story stretchers because they are inherently interesting and appealing.

After attending one of our presentations, one Head Start teacher of fours said she began using the term, "story stretchers," regularly after she read to the children at circle time. One day when she described the activity without labeling it, a little boy said, "Teacher, you didn't say 'story stretch.'" A kindergarten teacher related that she used predictable books with patterned language and 'echo' reading, but she worried that she wasn't providing a variety of types of books. She realized how valuable the predictable books were, but she found after using "story stretchers" that children requested a broader variety of books. The active participation appealed to a teacher of threes in a child care center because as she described her children, "They are 'doers' and I look for teaching ideas with a lot of actions.

About The Format Of The Book

Knowing early childhood teachers plan the curriculum around "themes," we have organized each of the eighteen chapters around a common theme or unit taught in preschools, kindergartens and child care centers. For example, there are chapters on the themes of families, counting and friendship. Five books have been selected for each theme, ninety books in all. Each of the ninety books has a suggested way to present the book during circle time followed by five extension activities, four hundred and fifty teaching ideas which have children's literature as their foundation. Story stretchers, then, are teaching ideas based on the stories in children's favorite books.

A photograph of the cover of the book and a description of the storyline introduces each book in the chapter. A brief example of ways to stretch the story during circle time follows the storyline description. A book read at circle time may have a teaching idea based on the story for an art activity, for the block building corner, for cooking and snack time, for music and movement and for the science table. For each story stretcher, we listed "what the children will learn, materials needed, what to do," and in the "something to think about" section, we added pointers about the topic or about guiding children's behavior. A list of additional children's books related to the theme is provided at the end of each chapter. Teachers can read these books at other group times and keep them in the class library.

The materials we recommend are, for the most part, readily available in early childhood classrooms. We suggest inviting parents to contribute "old" dress-up clothes and unusual display items.

The schedule for "STORY STRETCHERS" fits the schedule most teachers of young children already follow. Children participate with their teacher in a large group circle time activity, and then they are free to choose the activities they want during a large block of time, free play. Many teachers have a short circle time which is teacher-directed followed by a long free play time when children choose their activities. This pattern follows throughout the day of alternating brief teacher-directed with long child-choice times. We provide "story stretchers" for the circle times and "story stretchers" for the times when the children are free to choose. None of the "story stretchers" must be done by every child; they are available, if the child chooses to participate. Many of the cooking, creative dramatics and the music and movement activities can be done with small groups or the entire class.

Classrooms for young children are most often divided into learning centers or areas where the same type of activity occurs each day. For example, the easels, a table, paintbrushes, a variety of paints and paper, scissors, tape, staplers are all collected in an area designed for art activity. In addition to the art center,

others areas found in many preschool and kindergarten classes include: block building area, housekeeping and dress-up corner, library corner, an area for puzzles and small blocks — which we call the mathematics and manipulatives center and a science table for nature displays. Often classrooms are equipped with a sand table, water table and work bench. Multi-use tables serve as both the center for cooking activities and for serving snacks. Usually, a large circle time rug is the place to gather children for group story reading, creative dramatics, music and movement.

You will notice, we have expanded the use of several of the centers. We suggest you also use the library corner as a writing center for children to scribble or write on their own, for them to tell stories for the teacher to record or write down, to retell a favorite story using the flannel board or to hear a tape at the listening station. These can be small group or individual language activities.

The books selected for each theme are stretched into different centers or activities which usually take place in an early childhood classroom. We have story stretchers for art activities, block building, creative dramatics, cooking and snack time, the housekeeping and dress-up corner, the mathematics and manipulative center, naptime, the sand table, the science and nature center, the water table and the work bench. Each book is stretched to five activities or centers which best fit that book.

The centers and follow-up activities are listed in alphabetical order for easy reference. The index provides a quick cross-reference for activities, titles of books, authors' and illustrators' names. In addition helpful information is included in the appendix, as tips on book binding, making rebus charts and a recipe for playdough.

How To Use The Book

We suggest you use STORY S-T-R-E-T-C-H-E-R-S: ACTIVITIES TO EXPAND CHILDREN'S FAVORITE BOOKS as a guide and begin to devise story stretchers for your children which best meet their needs. Some teachers select a different book for each day of the week and include all the story stretchers as a base for their curriculum plan for the unit. In some half-day programs, teachers select a book from the five recommended, read the featured book on Monday at the first group time of the day, complete one story stretcher for each day of the week, and read other books related to the theme throughout the unit.

We feel confident that you will begin to notice the children developing a greater interest in books because you relate the books to the very active learning they enjoy in their daily activities. One teacher commented, "I knew the children connected the books and the story stretcher ideas when Marisa who never went into the library corner began carrying THE TEDDY BEARS' PICNIC book under her arm and making a picnic for the dolls and bears in the housekeeping corner. She even took a doll into the library corner and began reading to her."

A student teacher said she was having a problem keeping the children's interests and finding activities related to the theme of the week until we gave her a copy of some of the story stretchers. She found they gave her confidence. New employees in centers may find the story stretchers a valuable resource. However, we have found that, at times, seasoned veteran teachers need creative ideas to stimulate their imaginations. We encourage you to modify the activities and expand them even further, make them your own. We suggest that center directors create a story stretcher file and schedule training sessions for teachers to share their inventive variations sparked from using STORY S-T-R-E-T-C-H-E-R-S: ACTIVITIES TO EXPAND CHILDREN'S FAVORITE BOOKS.

CONTENTS

Preface 7
Introduction 9

---
1 • FAMILIES

A Baby Sister For Frances 24
*by Russell Hoban and Illustrated by
Lillian Hoban*
Storyline
Circle Time Presentation
Story Stretchers:
• For Art: Chalk Drawings
• For Cooking And Snack Time:
  Baking A Cake
• For Creative Dramatics: A Hiding
  Place
• For Housekeeping And Dress-up
  Corner: Playing Frances And Her
  Family
• For Music And Movement: Frances'
  Sad Song Becomes A Happy Song

Me Too! 26
by Mercer Mayer
Storyline
Circle Time Presentation
Story Stretchers:
• For Art: Group Mural
• For Block Building: Tree House
• For Creative Dramatics: Pantomime
• For Science And Nature Center:
  Paper Airplanes
• For Library Corner, Listening
  Station: Me Too! Tape

Whose Mouse Are You? 28
*by Robert Kraus and illustrated by
José Aruego*
Storyline
Circle Time Presentation
Story Stretchers:
• For Art: Yellow And Orange Design
• Another For Art: Mouse Pictures
• For Creative Dramatics: Show What
  We Feel
• For Library Corner, Listening Tape:
  I Want A Brother Mouse
• Another For Library Corner: New
  Family Members

Five Minutes Peace 30
by Jill Murphy
Storyline
Circle Time Presentation
Story Stretchers:
• For Cooking And Snack Time:
  Marmalade Toast
• For Housekeeping And Dress-up
  Corner: Mrs. Large's Household
• For Music And Movement: Relaxing
  To Music
• For Transition Time: Clean-up Time
• For Water Table: Bath Toys And
  Bottles

Titch 32
by Pat Hutchins
Storyline
Circle Time Presentation
Story Stretchers:
• For Art: Blue T-shirts
• For Library Corner, Listening
  Station: TITCH Tape
• For Mathematics And Manipulatives
  Center: Threes, Threes, Threes
• For Science And Nature Center:
  Planting Seeds
• Another For Science And Nature
  Center: Pinwheels

---
2 • FRIENDSHIP

**George And Martha One
Fine Day** 36
by James Marshall
Storyline
Circle Time Presentation
Story Stretchers:
• For Art: Stamp Pictures
• For Creative Dramatics: Tight Rope
  Walking
• For Library Corner: Our Diaries
• Another For Library Corner, Listen-
  ing Station: Surprise, George!
• For Science And Nature Center:
  Nature Walk

Friends 38
by Helme Heine
Storyline
Circle Time Presentation
Story Stretchers:
• For Cooking And Snack Time: The
  Friends Share Cherries
• For Creative Dramatics: Unlikely
  Friends — Mouse, Rooster And Pig
• For Library Corner, Flannel Board:
  I Can Tell A Story
• For Music And Movement: Musical
  Follow The Leader
• For Water Table: Floating On The
  Village Pond

Alfie Gives A Hand 40
by Shirley Hughes
Storyline
Circle Time Presentation
Story Stretchers:
• For Art: Birthday Party Masks
• For Cooking And Snack Time:
  Bernard's Birthday Lunch
• For Library Corner, Listening
  Station: Alfie Gives A Hand
• For Music And Movement:
  Ring-a-ring-o'-roses
• For Water Table: Blowing Bubbles

Best Friends 42
*by Miriam Cohen and illustrated by
Lillian Hoban*
Storyline
Circle Time Presentation
Story Stretchers:
• For Art: Pictures And Compliments
• Another For Art: Friendship Collage
• For Housekeeping And Dress-up
  Corner: Caps And Hats
• For Library Corner: Friendship Chart
• For Science And Nature Center:
  Hatching Baby Chicks

Will I Have A Friend? 44
*by Miriam Cohen and illustrated by
Lillian Hoban*
Storyline
Circle Time Presentation
Story Stretchers

- For Art: Class Mural
- Another For Art: Shape That Clay
- For Block Building: Building In Progress
- For Cooking And Snack Time: Squeezing Orange Juice
- For Music And Movement: Friendship Song

---

3 · FEELINGS

Ask Mr. Bear 48
by Marjorie Flack
Storyline
Circle Time Presentation
Story Stretchers:
- For Art: Birthday Cards For Friends
- Another For Art: An Envelope For An ASK MR. BEAR Card
- For Creative Dramatics: Skip, Hop, Gallop, Trot
- For Library Corner: A Mother's Day/Father's Day Poem
- Another For Library Corner, Flannel Board: Mr. Bear And Friends

William's Doll 50
by Charlotte Zolotow and illustrated by William Pène du Bois
Storyline
Circle Time Presentation
Story Stretchers:
- For Art: A Wish Collage
- For Block Building: A Train Like William's
- For Housekeeping And Dress-up Corner: Dolls And Stuffed Animals
- For Library Corner: Tape Of WILLIAM'S DOLL With Character Voices
- For Music And Movement: Playing Basketball

Where Can It Be? 52
by Ann Jonas
Storyline
Circle Time Presentation
Story Stretchers:
- For Art: Hiding Pictures
- Another For Art: Soft Pictures
- For Library Corner, Listening Tape: The Missing Alphabet
- For Mathematics And Manipulatives Center: Five Lost
- For Music And Movement: Hide The Blanket

Some Things Are Different, Some Things Are The Same 54
by Marya Dantzer-Rosenthal and illustrated by Miriam Nerlove
Storyline
Circle Time Presentation
Story Stretchers:
- For Art: My House, Your House
- Another For Art: Knock, Knock
- For Block Building: Bucket Of Blocks
- For Cooking And Snack Time: Snack With Josh And Stephan
- For Housekeeping And Dress-up Corner: Wagon Ride

My Mama Says There Aren't Any Zombies, Ghosts, Vampires, Creatures, Demons, Monsters, Fiends, Goblins, Or Things 56
by Judith Viorst and illustrated by Kay Chorao
Storyline
Circle Time Presentation
Story Stretchers:
- For Art: Brushes And Feathers
- For Cooking And Snack Time: Cream Cheese And Jelly Sandwiches
- For Library Corner: Tell Me A Story
- For Mathematics And Manipulatives Center: Missing Crayons
- For Music And Movement: Balancing An Egg

---

4 · GRANDMOTHERS AND GRANDFATHERS

Big Boy, Little Boy 60
by Betty Jo Stanovich and illustrated by Virginia Wright-Frierson
Storyline
Circle Time Presentation
Story Stretchers:
- For Art: Watercolors
- For Block Building: Trains, Pegs And Things
- For Naptime: David Takes A Nap
- For Science And Nature Center: Observing A Bird Feeder
- For Work Bench: Our Tool Chest

When I Go Visiting 62
by Anne and Harlow Rockwell
Storyline
Circle Time Presentation
Story Stretchers:
- For Art: Class Photo Album
- For Housekeeping And Dress-up Corner: Packing For A Visit

- For Library Corner: Grandparents Chart Story
- For Music And Movement: Old Mac Donald Had A Farm
- For Science And Nature Center: Seeing Seashells

I Dance In My Red Pajamas 64
by Edith Thacher Hurd and illustrated by Emily Arnold McCully
Storyline
Circle Time Presentation
Story Stretchers:
- For Cooking And Snack Time: Tasting Blueberries
- For Housekeeping And Dress-up Corner: Setting The Table
- For Music And Movement: Dancing In Imaginary Red Pajamas
- For Water Table: Bubble Bath For The Dolls
- For Work Bench: Hammer And Saw

Happy Birthday, Sam 66
by Pat Hutchins
Storyline
Circle Time Presentation
Story Stretchers:
- For Art: Gadget Printed Wrapping Paper
- For Housekeeping And Dress-up Corner: Hanging Up Clothes
- For Library Corner: Story Retelling
- For Mathematics And Manipulatives Center: I Can Reach It
- For Water Table: Sailing Birthday Boats

Come To The Meadow 68
by Anna Grossnickle Hines
Storyline
Circle Time Presentation
Story Stretchers:
- For Art: Yellow, Green And Spring
- For Cooking And Snack Time: No Cooking Picnic
- For Housekeeping And Dress-up Corner: Pretend Picnicking
- For Music And Movement: Ice Cream Clouds
- For Science And Nature Center: Cloud watching and earth watching

---

5 · NAPTIME/BEDTIME

Goodnight Moon 72
by Margaret Wise Brown
Storyline
Circle Time Presentation
Story Stretchers:

- For Art: Bunny's Black And White Pictures
- For Housekeeping And Dress-up Corner: Bunny's Bedroom
- For Library Corner: Hey, Diddle, Diddle
- Another For Library Corner: Rhyming Words
- For Naptime: Saying Goodnight

There's An Alligator Under My Bed 74
by Mercer Mayer
Storyline
Circle Time Presentation
Story Stretchers:
- For Art: Alligator Paw Prints
- For Cooking And Snack Time: Alligator Bait Salad
- For Library Corner: Warning, Story Inside
- For Mathematics And Manipulatives Center: The Alligator Ate It!
- For Music And Movement: Balance Beams

No Jumping On The Bed! 76
by Tedd Arnold
Storyline
Circle Time Presentation
Story Stretchers:
- For Art: Funny Falling Pictures
- For Block Building: Building Dream Houses
- For Library Corner: Listening For Cracking Ceiling
- For Mathematics And Manipulatives Center: Counting Walter's Floors
- For Music And Movement: Ten Little Monkeys Jumping On The Bed

Grandfather Twilight 78
by Barbara Berger
Storyline
Circle Time Presentation
Story Stretchers:
- For Art: Pastel Twilight Pictures
- For Library Corner: Composing A Sequel
- For Mathematics And Manipulatives Center: Stringing Pretend Pearls
- For Music And Movement: Pass The Pearl
- For Science And Nature Center: Oysters And Pearls

Night In The Country 80
by Cynthia Rylant and illustrated by Mary Szilagyi
Storyline
Circle Time Presentation

Story Stretchers:
- For Art: Crayon Etching
- For Cooking And Snack Time: Country Apples
- For Library Corner, Listening Station: A Quiet Retreat
- For Sand Table: Country Geography
- For Science And Nature Center: Animal Babies

6 • PLANTS GROW, ANIMALS GROW AND I GROW

Growing Vegetable Soup 84
by Lois Ehlert
Storyline
Circle Time Presentation
Story Stretchers:
- For Housekeeping And Dress-up Corner: What Gardeners Wear
- For Mathematics And Manipulatives Center: Weighing Seeds
- For Music And Movement: Growing Plants
- For Sand Table: Digging For Potatoes
- For Science And Nature Center: Planting Seeds And Seedlings

The Carrot Seed 86
by Ruth Krauss and illustrated by Crockett Johnson
Storyline
Circle Time Presentation
Story Stretchers:
- For Block Building: Wheelbarrow Lift
- For Cooking And Snack Time: Carrot And Raisin Salad
- For Creative Dramatics: It Won't Come Up!
- For Library Corner, Flannel Board: The Huge Carrot
- For Science And Nature Center: Seeds And Carrot Tops

From Seed To Pear 88
by Ali Mitgutsch
Storyline
Circle Time Presentation
Story Stretchers:
- For Art: Blossoms
- For Cooking And Snack Time: Pear Treats
- For Housekeeping And Dress-up Corner: Fruit Stand
- For Music And Movement: The Pear Tree
- For Science And Nature Center: Nursery Trees

Here Are My Hands 90
by Bill Martin, Jr. and John Archambault and illustrated by Ted Rand
Storyline
Circle Time Presentation
Story Stretchers:
- For Art: Plaster Of Paris Hand Prints
- For Housekeeping And Dress-up Corner: Here Are My Hands To Button, Zip And Snap
- For Library Corner: We Feel Big When We
- For Mathematics And Manipulatives Center: Comparisons, Big And Little
- For Music And Movement: Reaching, Stretching, Growing, Knowing

Whose Baby? 92
by Masayuki Yabuuchi
Storyline
Circle Time Presentation
Story Stretchers:
- For Art: Wildlife Prints
- For Library Corner, Listening Tape: Whose Baby Riddle Tapes
- Another For Library Corner, Listening Station: Riddle Pictures
- For Mathematics And Manipulatives Center: Animal Family Puzzles
- For Science And Nature Center: Farm Babies And Wild Animal Babies

7 • SCIENCE AND NATURE

The Very Hungry Caterpillar 96
by Eric Carle
Storyline
Circle Time Presentation
Story Stretchers:
- For Art: Tissue Paper Designs
- For Cooking And Snack Time: Caterpillar Snack Week
- For Library Corner, Flannel Board: Story Retelling
- For Mathematics And Manipulatives Center: Would You Let A Caterpillar Crawl On Your Hand?
- For Science And Nature Center: Caterpillars In A Terrarium

The Very Busy Spider 98
by Eric Carle
Storyline
Circle Time Presentation
Story Stretchers:
- For Art: Spider Webs
- For Housekeeping And Dress-up Corner: Farmers' Clothes

- For Library Corner, Flannel Board: The Very Busy Spider
- For Music And Movement: Walking The Spider Web
- For Science And Nature Center: Pictures Of Real Spider Webs

Who's Hiding Here? 100
by Yoshi
Storyline
Circle Time Presentation
Story Stretchers:
- For Art: Fabric Painting
- For Library Corner, Listening Tape: Camouflage Riddles
- For Mathematics And Manipulatives Center: Pairing By Color
- For Music And Movement: Who's Hiding Here?
- For Science And Nature Center: Camouflage In Season

Chickens Aren't The Only Ones . . 102
by Ruth Heller
Storyline
Circle Time Presentation
Story Stretchers:
- For Art: Decorating Eggs
- For Cooking And Snack Time: Egg In A Hole
- For Library Corner: Eggcitement Tape
- For Mathematics And Manipulatives Center: Counting Eggs
- For Science And Nature Center: Display Of Eggs

Air Is All Around You 104
by Franklyn M. Branley and illustrated by Holly Keller
Storyline
Circle Time Presentation
Story Stretchers:
- For Art: Fish Pictures
- For Cooking And Snack Time: Orange Air
- For Housekeeping And Dress-up Corner: Astronauts
- For Science And Nature Center: Inverted Glass Experiment
- Another For Science And Nature Center: Fishy Water

---
8 · SEASONS
FOCUS ON FALL

Frederick 108
by Leo Lionni
Storyline
Circle Time Presentation

Story Stretchers:
- For Art: Pictures We Paint In Our Minds
- For Block Building: Old Stone Wall
- For Cooking And Snack Time: Frederick's Granola Log
- For Creative Dramatics: Frederick Tab Puppets
- For Library Corner, Listening Station: Frederick's Poem

My Favorite Time Of The Year . . 110
by Susan Pearson and illustrated by John Wallner
Storyline
Circle Time Presentation
Story Stretchers:
- For Art: Leaf Rubbings
- For Cooking And Snack Time: Pumpkin Bread
- For Music And Movement: Falling Leaves
- For Science And Nature Center: Signs Of Fall Nature Walk
- Another For Science And Nature Center: Carving A Pumpkin

The Tiny Seed 112
by Eric Carle
Storyline
Circle Time Presentation
Story Stretchers:
- For Art: Sponge Painting
- For Cooking And Snack Time: Sunflower Seeds
- For Library Corner, Flannel Board: The Tiny Seed Grows
- For Mathematics And Manipulatives Center: Counting Seeds
- For Science And Nature Center: Seeds And Seed Pods

The Seasons Of Arnold's Apple Tree 114
by Gail Gibbons
Storyline
Circle Time Presentation
Story Stretchers:
- For Art: Flower Arranging
- For Cooking And Snack Time: Baby Apple Pies
- For Housekeeping And Dress-up Corner: Dressing For The Seasons
- For Music And Movement: Here We Go 'round The Apple Tree
- For Science And Nature Center: Sequencing The Seasons

Chipmunk Song 116
by Joanne Ryder and illustrated by Lynne Cherry
Storyline
Circle Time Presentation
Story Stretchers:
- For Art: Sponge Lift-off
- For Creative Dramatics: Pretending To Be Chipmunks
- For Library Corner, Listening Tape: Peaceful Ending
- For Sand Table: Underground Tunnels And Burrows
- For Science And Nature Center: Like A Chipmunk

---
9 · SEASONS
FOCUS ON WINTER

Something Is Going To Happen . . 120
by Charlotte Zolotow and illustrated by Catherine Stock
Storyline
Circle Time Presentation
Story Stretchers:
- For Art: Shaving Cream Snow Pictures
- For Cooking And Snack Time: Breakfast Muffins
- For Housekeeping And Dress-up Corner: Getting Ready For Work
- For Library Corner, Listening Tape: Household Noises
- For Mathematics And Manipulatives Center: Winter Wonderland Village

The First Snowfall 122
by Anne and Harlow Rockwell
Storyline
Circle Time Presentation
Story Stretchers:
- For Art: Snowflake Pictures
- For Cooking And Snack Time: Winter Snacks
- For Mathematics And Manipulatives Center: Circles, Squares, Rectangles
- For Music And Movement: It's Snowing Song
- For Sand Table: Snow Plowing

Sadie And The Snowman 124
by Allen Morgan and illustrated by Brenda Clark
Storyline
Circle Time Presentation
Story Stretchers:
- For Art: Playdough Snowmen
- For Block Building: Tent Play
- For Cooking And Snack Time: Snowmen And Snowwomen Cookies

- For Library Corner, Listening Station: Sadie's Snowman
- For Science And Nature Center: Water In All Its Forms

Chicken Soup With Rice 126
by Maurice Sendak
Storyline
Circle Time Presentation
Story Stretchers:
- For Art: Decorating Soup Bowls
- For Cooking And Snack Time: Cooking Chicken Soup With Rice
- For Library Corner, Listening Station: A Listening Birthday Calendar
- For Music And Movement: Ice Skater's Waltz
- For Science And Nature Center: Magnetic Rice

The Mitten 128
by Alvin Tresselt and illustrated by Yaroslava
Storyline
Circle Time Presentation
Story Stretchers:
- For Art: Decorating Vests
- For Block Building: Gathering Wood
- For Library Corner, Flannel Board: How Many Animals Can Get Inside?
- For Mathematics And Manipulatives Center: Matching Mittens
- For Music And Movement: Mitten, Mitten, Who Has The Mitten?

----
10 · SEASONS
FOCUS ON SPRING

First Comes Spring 132
by Anne Rockwell
Storyline
Circle Time Presentation
Story Stretchers:
- For Art: Spring Photographs
- For Housekeeping And Dress-up Corner: Dressing Bears
- For Library Corner: Favorite Spring Things
- For Mathematics And Manipulatives Center: Easter Egg Mathematics
- For Music And Movement: A Parade

Sleepy Bear 134
by Lydia Dabcovich
Storyline
Circle Time Presentation
Story Stretchers:
- For Art: Add-on Picture

- For Cooking And Snack Time: Sweet Honey
- For Creative Dramatics: Acting Like Sleepy Bear
- For Library Corner, Listening Tape: Follow The Bees
- For Science And Nature Center: Hives And Honeycombs

The Green Grass Grows All Around 136
A Traditional Folk Song illustrated by Hilde Hoffman
Storyline
Circle Time Presentation
Story Stretchers:
- For Art: Paper Bag Masks
- For Library Corner, Flannel Board: The Parts Of A Tree
- For Music And Movement: Singing The Green Grass Grows All Around
- For Outside Play: Playing In The Spray
- For Science And Nature Center: Bird Nests

A House Of Leaves 138
by Kiyoshi Soya and illustrated by Akiko Hayashi
Storyline
Circle Time Presentation
Story Stretchers:
- For Art: Green Leaf Pictures
- For Housekeeping And Dress-up Corner: Rain Wear
- For Library Corner, Flannel Board: Sarah's Visitors
- For Music And Movement: Sarah And The Flying Insects
- For Science And Nature Center: Insects

Sarah's Questions 140
by Harriet Ziefert and illustrated by Susan Bonners
Storyline
Circle Time Presentation
Story Stretchers:
- For Art: Flower Posters
- For Library Corner, Listening Station: Sarah Asks A Lot Of Questions
- For Music And Movement: Musical I Spy
- For Science And Nature Center: Recognizing Flowers
- Another For Science And Nature Center: I Spy Walks

----
11 · TEDDY BEARS
AND OTHER BEARS

Corduroy 144
by Don Freeman
Storyline
Circle Time Presentation
Story Stretchers:
- For Art: Button Pictures
- For Library Corner, Listening Station: Listening With Corduroy
- For Housekeeping And Dress-up Corner: Dressing Teddy Bears
- For Mathematics And Manipulatives Center: Making Sets By Touch
- For Music And Movement: Button, Button, Who Has The Button?

This Is The Bear 146
by Sarah Hayes and illustrated by Helen Craig
Storyline
Circle Time Presentation
Story Stretchers:
- For Art: Talking Pictures
- Another For Art: Hidden Pictures
- For Library Corner: Telling A Lost Teddy Story
- For Mathematics And Manipulatives Center: Checkerboard Patterns
- For Music And Movement: What's Missing?

Jesse Bear, What Will You Wear? 148
by Nancy White Carlstrom and illustrated by Bruce Degen
Storyline
Circle Time Presentation
Story Stretchers:
- For Cooking And Snack Time: Celery Crunchies
- For Housekeeping And Dress-up Corner: JESSE BEAR, WHAT WILL YOU WEAR?
- For Library Corner, Flannel Board: Jesse's Clothes
- For Sand Table: Jesse's Sand Toys
- For Science And Nature Center: Blowing Bubbles

Jamberry 150
by Bruce Degen
Storyline
Circle Time Presentation
Story Stretchers:
- For Art: Silly Berry Jamberry Pictures
- For Cooking And Snack Time: Tasting Berries

- For Music And Movement:
  Berryland Marching Band
- Another For Music And Movement:
  Dancing In The Meadow
- For Science And Nature Center:
  Berry Plants And Berry Bushes

The Teddy Bears' Picnic 152
*by Jimmy Kennedy and illustrated by
Alexandra Day*
Storyline
Circle Time Presentation
Story Stretchers:
- For Art: Decorating For The Teddy
  Bears' Picnic
- For Cooking And Snack Time:
  Picnicking With Our Teddy Bears
- For Housekeeping And Dress-up
  Corner: Dressing Teddy Bears
- For Music And Movement: March-
  ing To The Teddy Bears' Picnic
- Another For Music And Movement:
  Teddy Bears' Picnic Games

- -
12 · CLASSIC STORIES
- -

The Runaway Bunny 156
*by Margaret Wise Brown and illustrated
by Clement Hurd*
Storyline
Circle Time Presentation
Story Stretchers:
- For Art: Bunny's Imaginings
- For Cooking And Snack Time: Raw
  Carrot Crunch
- For Creative Dramatics: Dressed For
  The Part
- For Library Corner, Flannel Board:
  Runaway Bunny And Running After
  Mother
- For Water Table: Runaway Sailboats

Caps For Sale 158
by Esphyr Slobodkina
Storyline
Circle Time Presentation
Story Stretchers:
- For Art: Cap Pictures
- For Creative Dramatics: Caps And
  Monkeys
- For Housekeeping And Dress-up
  Corner: Caps And Hats
- For Mathematics And Manipulatives
  Center: From Concrete To Abstract
  Caps
- For Music And Movement:
  Balancing Caps

Curious George 160
by H.A. Rey
Storyline
Circle Time Presentation
Story Stretchers:
- For Art: Telephone Books
- For Block Building: Fire Trucks
- For Cooking And Snack Time:
  George's Banana Treats
- For Housekeeping And Dress-up
  Corner: A Curious George Visitor
- For Science And Nature Center: Zoo
  Animals

The Three Billy-Goats Gruff . . . 162
by Ellen Appleby
Storyline
Circle Time Presentation
Story Stretchers:
- For Art: Playdough Characters
- For Creative Dramatics: The Three
  Billy-goats Gruff
- For Library Corner, Flannel Board:
  Trip, Trapping Goats
- For Mathematics And Manipulatives
  Center: Sets Of Three
- For Sand Table: Hills And Bridges

Where The Wild Things Are 164
by Maurice Sendak
Storyline
Circle Time Presentation
Story Stretchers:
- For Art: Monster Posters
- Another For Art: Wild Thing Masks
- For Library Corner, Listening Tape:
  Max And The Wild Things
- For Housekeeping And Dress-up
  Corner: Wild Things Costumes
- For Music And Movement: Wild
  Rumpus

- -
13 · Counting
- -

Roll Over! A Counting Song 168
illustrated by Merle Peek
Storyline
Circle Time Presentation
Story Stretchers:
- For Art: A Light In My Picture
- For Housekeeping And Dress-up
  Corner: Alone At Last
- For Mathematics And Manipulatives
  Center: Guesstimate What's Left
- For Music And Movement: Singing
  Roll Over!
- For Sand Table: Digging For
  Dinosaurs

Have You Seen My Duckling? . . . 170
by Nancy Tafuri
Storyline
Circle Time Presentation
Story Stretchers:
- For Art: Pond Pictures
- For Library Corner: Dictated Stories
- For Music And Movement: Quack!
  Quack! Quack!
- For Science And Nature Center:
  Who Lives In The Pond?
- For Water Table: Water Table Pond

Ten, Nine, Eight 172
by Molly Bang
Storyline
Circle Time Presentation
Story Stretchers:
- For Art: Window Pane Pictures
- For Library Corner, Listening Sta-
  tion: Magnetic Counting Tape
- For Mathematics And Manipulatives
  Center: Counting Forwards And
  Backwards
- For Music And Movement: Shoe,
  Shoe, Who Has The Shoe?
- For Science And Nature Center:
  Counting Seashells

The Doorbell Rang 174
by Pat Hutchins
Storyline
Circle Time Presentation
Story Stretchers:
- For Art: Weaving Patterns
- For Clean-up Time: Mopping The
  Floor
- For Cooking And Snack Time:
  Baking Grandma's Cookies
- For Mathematics And Manipulatives
  Center: Counting Cookies
- For Science And Nature Center:
  How Does A Doorbell Ring?

Over In The Meadow 176
*by Olive A. Wadsworth and illustrated by
Mary Maki Rae*
Storyline
Circle Time Presentation
Story Stretchers:
- For Creative Dramatics: "We Move,"
  Said The Children
- For Library Corner, Flannel Board:
  Counting Baby Animals And Insects
- For Mathematics And Manipulatives
  Center: Magnetic Numerals With
  Rhymes
- For Music And Movement: Fireflies
- For Science And Nature Center:
  Insect Habitats

14 · COLORS

Red Is Best 180
by Kathy Stinson and illustrated by
Robin Baird Lewis
Storyline
Circle Time Presentation
Story Stretchers:
- For Art: Painting With Red And
  Music
- For Cooking And Snack Time: Red
  Party
- For Housekeeping And Dress-up
  Corner: Dressing Red
- For Library Corner: Red Is Best
  Caption
- For Mathematics And Manipulatives
  Center: Sorting By Attributes

Mary Wore Her Red Dress And Henry
Wore His Green Sneakers 182
adapted and illustrated by Merle Peek
Storyline
Circle Time Presentation
Story Stretchers:
- For Art: Making Party Hats
- For Cooking And Snack Time: Party
  Cupcakes
- For Creative Dramatics: Dressing
  For Katy's Party
- For Library Corner, Flannel Board:
  Katy Bear's Party Guests
- For Music And Movement: Singing
  What My Friend Is Wearing

Green Eggs And Ham 184
by Dr. Seuss, Theodor Seuss Geisel
Storyline
Circle Time Presentation
Story Stretchers:
- For Art: Silly Cars, Silly Trains,
  Silly Boats
- For Cooking And Snack Time:
  Green Eggs And Ham
- For Housekeeping And Dress-up
  Corner: Funny Seuss Hats
- For Library Corner, Listening
  Station: Sam-I-am Convinced Me
- For Music And Movement:
  Name-I-am

Is It Red? Is It Yellow?
Is It Blue? 187
by Tana Hoban
Storyline
Circle Time Presentation
Story Stretchers:
- For Art: Circle Color Keys
- For Cooking And Snack Time: Red,
  Yellow And Blue Snacks

- For Mathematics And Manipulatives
  Center: Patterns Of Beads
- Another For Mathematics And
  Manipulatives Center: Our Favorite
  Colors Chart
- For Science And Nature Center:
  Mixing Colors

Brown Bear, Brown Bear, What
Do You See? 188
by Bill Martin, Jr. and illustrated by
Eric Carle
Storyline
Circle Time Presentation
Story Stretchers:
- For Art: Strangely Colored Animals
- For Library Corner, Flannel Board:
  Brown Bear Saw
- Another For Library Corner, Listen-
  ing Tape: Group Chanting
- For Mathematics And Manipulatives
  Center: Patterns Of Colors
- For Music And Movement: Old Mac
  Martin Had A Farm

15 · CATS AND OTHER PETS

Cats Do, Dogs Don't 192
by Norma Simon and illustrated by
Dora Leder
Storyline
Circle Time Presentation
Story Stretchers:
- For Cooking And Snack Time:
  Choose Your Fruit
- For Music And Movement: Catching
  Frisbees
- For Sand Table: Cats' And Dogs'
  Hidden Treasure
- For Water Table: Shampooing
  Imaginary Pets
- For Work Bench: Plumber's Tool
  Chest

Where Does My Cat Sleep? 194
by Norma Simon and illustrated by
Dora Leder
Storyline
Circle Time Presentation
Story Stretchers:
- For Art: Rocky's Chair Collage
- Another For Art: Charcoal And
  Chalk Drawings
- For Library Corner: Cat Owners'
  Talks
- For Mathematics And Manipulatives
  Center: Cat Calendars
- For Music And Movement: Cat Chant

Amelia's Nine Lives 196
by Lorna Balian
Storyline
Circle Time Presentation
Story Stretchers:
- For Art: Cat Collage
- For Creative Dramatics: Nora's
  Relatives And Neighbors
- For Mathematics And Manipulatives
  Center: Counting Amelias
- For Music And Movement: Looking
  For Amelia
- For Science And Nature Center:
  Caring For A Kitten

Hi, Cat! 198
by Ezra Jack Keats
Storyline
Circle Time Presentation
Story Stretchers:
- For Art: Fabric Collages
- Another For Art: Silhouettes
- For Cooking And Snack Time:
  Pistachio Ice Cream Or Lime Sherbet
- For Creative Dramatics: Mister Big
  Face
- For Library Corner: Extend The
  Story

Millions Of Cats 200
by Wanda Gag
Storyline
Circle Time Presentation
Story Stretchers:
- For Art: Cat Sculptures
- For Library Corner, Listening Tape:
  Cat Sounds
- For Mathematics And Manipulatives
  Center: Voting For Our Favorite Cat
- For Sand Table: Hills And Valleys
- For Science And Nature Center:
  Observations Of Cats

16 · TRANSPORTATION

The Car Trip 204
by Helen Oxenbury
Storyline
Circle Time Presentation
Story Stretchers:
- For Art: Car Window Pictures
- For Block Building: Traffic Jam
- For Cooking And Snack Time:
  Making Sandwiches
- For Creative Dramatics: A Bus Ride
- For Mathematics And Manipulatives
  Center: Counting Cars, Vans,
  Trucks, Buses

Truck Song 206
*by Diane Siebert and illustrated by Byron
Barton*
Storyline
Circle Time Presentation
Story Stretchers:
- For Art: Painting Trucks
- For Block Building: Loading Docks
- For Library Corner, Listening Station: Truck Sounds
- For Mathematics And Manipulatives Center: How Much Is Too Much?
- For Music And Movement: The Wheels On The Truck Go

The Train To Lulu's 208
*by Elizabeth Fitzgerald Howard and
illustrated by Robert Casilla*
Storyline
Circle Time Presentation
Story Stretchers:
- For Art: Watercolor Scenes
- Another For Art: Milk Carton Train
- For Library Corner, Listening Station: Two Sisters Travel Alone
- For Music And Movement: The Wheels On The Train
- For Science And Nature Center: Physics Experiment

The Train 210
by David McPhail
Storyline
Circle Time Presentation
Story Stretchers:
- For Art: Dream Pictures
- For Block Building: Train Set
- For Creative Dramatics: The Train Ride
- For Housekeeping And Dress-up Corner: Packing For Our Train Trip
- For Work Bench: Matthew's Tool Box

Flying 212
by Donald Crews
Storyline
Circle Time Presentation
Story Stretchers:
- For Art: Cloud Pictures
- For Block Building: Model Airport
- For Cooking And Snack Time: Snacks In Flight
- For Housekeeping And Dress-up Corner: Pilots And Flight Attendants
- For Sand Table: River Traffic

17 • POEMS, JINGLES, CHANTS, AND RHYMES

**Read-Aloud Rhymes For The
Very Young** 216
*selected by Jack Prelutsky and illustrated
by Marc Brown*
Storyline
Circle Time Presentation
Story Stretchers:
- For Art: Animal Squares
- For Library Corner: The Story In The Pictures
- For Mathematics And Manipulatives Center: Counting Rhymes
- For Music And Movement: Animal Moves
- For Science And Nature Center: Poetic Insects And Animals

Hand Rhymes 218
collected and illustrated by Marc Brown
Storyline
Circle Time Presentation
Story Stretchers:
- For Art: Sponge Painting
- For Creative Dramatics: The Snowman
- For Library Corner, Flannel Board: Little Bunny
- For Mathematics And Manipulatives Center: Kittens Hand Rhyme
- For Science And Nature Center: The Caterpillar

Out And About 220
by Shirley Hughes
Storyline
Circle Time Presentation
Story Stretchers:
- For Art: Weather Pictures
- Another For Art: Sand Pictures
- For Housekeeping And Dress-up Corner: Dressing For The Season
- For Library Corner: Action Pictures
- For Sand Table: Sand Poem And Sand Castles

**Honey, I Love And Other
Love Poems** 222
*by Eloise Greenfield and illustrated by
Diane and Leo Dillon*
Storyline
Circle Time Presentation
Story Stretchers:
- For Art: Charcoal Drawings
- For Housekeeping And Dress-up Corner: We Look Pretty
- For Library Corner: Things We Love Tape

- For Music And Movement: I Get Down
- Another For Music And Movement: Jump Rope Chants

**Sing A Song Of Popcorn: Every
Child's Book Of Poems** 224
*edited by Beatrice Schenk de Regniers and
illustrated by nine Caldecott Medal artists*
Storyline
Circle Time Presentation
Story Stretchers:
- For Art: Watercolor Weather
- Another For Art: Funny Pictures
- For Library Corner, Listening Station: Funny Pictures Tape
- For Music And Movement: The Little Turtle
- For Science And Nature Center: Nature Poems

18 • TALL AND FUNNY TALES

If You Give A Mouse A Cookie . . 228
*by Laura Joffe Numeroff and illustrated by
Felicia Bond*
Storyline
Circle Time Presentation
Story Stretchers:
- For Art: Mouse Pictures
- For Cooking And Snack Time: Chocolate Chip Mouse Cookies
- For Creative Dramatics: Pantomiming Mouse
- For Library Corner: If Mouse Came To Our Classroom
- For Mathematics And Manipulatives Center: If Then Sequence

The Giant Jam Sandwich 230
*by John Vernon Lord and verses by Janet
Burroway*
Storyline
Circle Time Presentation
Story Stretchers:
- For Art: Tall Tale Pictures
- For Block Building: The Town Of Itching Down
- For Cooking And Snack Time: Giant Jam Sandwich
- For Housekeeping And Dress-up Corner: Bakery
- For Music And Movement: The Flight Of The Wasps

**Cloudy With A Chance
Of Meatballs** 232
*by Judi Barrett and illustrated by
Ron Barrett*
Storyline
Circle Time Presentation
Story Stretchers:
• For Art: Raining Food Pictures
• For Block Building: A New Town
• For Cooking And Snack Time:
  Snowy Mashed Potatoes
• For Library Corner: Grandpa's Tall
  Tale
• For Water Table: Houseboats

Teeny Tiny 234
*retold by Jill Bennett and illustrated by
Tomie dePaola*
Storyline
Circle Time Presentation
Story Stretchers:
• For Art: Teeny Tiny Puppets
• For Creative Dramatics: Pantomim-
  ing Teeny Tiny
• For Housekeeping And Dress-up
  Corner: Filling Teeny Tiny's
  Cupboard
• For Library Corner, Flannel Board:
  Teeny Tiny's Story
• Another For Library Corner, Listen-
  ing Station: Teeny Tiny Frights

The Bear's Toothache 236
by David McPhail
Storyline
Circle Time Presentation
Story Stretchers:
• For Art: Night Pictures
• For Housekeeping And Dress-up
  Corner: Cowgirl And Cowboy
  Clothes
• For Library Corner: Story Lamp
• For Music And Movement: Who's
  Hiding?
• For Science And Nature Center:
  Animal Teeth And People Teeth

Appendix 239
Index 243

FAMILIES

A Baby Sister for Frances
Me Too!
Whose Mouse Are You?
Five Minutes Peace
Titch

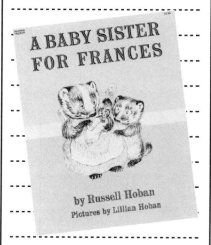

A BABY SISTER FOR FRANCES

By Russell Hoban

Illustrated by Lillian Hoban

Russell Hoban has captured the ambivalent feelings of a child confronted with her jealousy of the new baby in the family and her pride at becoming a big sister. Frances, a badger, reacts by running away to hiding places within the house and waits to see if her parents miss her. The reassuring ending satisfies young listeners. Lillian Hoban's soft pastels and faint line drawings convey a warm family atmosphere in the badger household.

Circle Time Presentation

Introduce the book by having a child who has a baby sister tell what is happening on the cover of the book. Another child can tell what is happening on the title page. After reading the story, have a few children tell about Frances' feelings at the beginning of the story and how she felt at the end. Emphasize the changes by rereading the sad song Frances sang at the beginning of the book. The children can echo the short lines with you. Then reread the song Frances sang at the end of the story and let the children echo those lines in their happy voices.

STORY STRETCHER

For Art: Chalk Drawings

What the children will learn—
To draw happy and sad faces

Materials you will need—
Large sheets of paper, chalk pastels or crayons, large sponge, bowl for small amount of water, hair spray

What to do—
1.   Encourage children to draw pictures with crayons or chalks. When the pictures are done, ask about the happy or sad faces.

2.   For a different variation, lightly wet the paper with a sponge. When the children draw, the pastel chalks will made darker lines.

3.   After they finish their pictures, lightly spray the chalk drawings with hair spray so the chalk will not flake off.

Something to think about—
Some of the older children may wish to write a story on their pictures or to tell a story for you to write. Accept whatever their level of writing might be, from scribbles to actual words.

STORY STRETCHER

For Cooking and Snack Time: Baking A Cake

What the children will learn—
To follow directions for baking a chocolate cake like the one Mother Badger made for Frances

Materials you will need—
Cake mix, water, eggs, mixing bowl, long handled mixing spoon, knife, hand-held mixer or egg-beater, clear baking dish, oven, measuring cups, measuring spoons, poster board, markers, paper doilies and a shaker of powdered sugar (optional)

What to do—
1.   Allow different children to assist in measuring, pouring and mixing the ingredients. Be certain each child has a chance to help.

2.   Bake the cake as directed on the package. Allow it to cool.

3.   Cut the cake into squares and serve as snack with milk.

4.   If you wish to decorate the cake, it can be dusted lightly with powdered sugar. Or place a lacy paper doily over the top of the cake and then shake a little powdered sugar over the doily.

Something to think about—
Make a chart of the basic directions for baking the cake by using rebus symbols (see Appendix), as a picture or a drawing of a cup, of a mixing bowl, of a large wooden spoon, a hand-mixer, a baking dish. The rebus symbols help the children see each step. Have the children tell you which step is next by reading the pictures.

For Creative Dramatics: A Hiding Place

What the children will learn—
To act out scenes from the book

Materials you will need—
Card table, long tablecloth or sheet, backpack, pretend or real snacks

What to do—
1. Make a hiding place with a card table and a long cloth or sheet which reaches the floor. Set it up before reading the story. If the children don't immediately associate it with the book, you can mention to them that the table looks like a place where Frances would hide.

2. Provide a backpack, our modern equivalent to Frances' knapsack, for the children to pack their pretend or real snacks for their "long" running away journey to the spot under the table.

3. Watch for invented dramatizations of other scenes from A BABY SISTER FOR FRANCES.

Something to think about—
While early educators do not tell their children what to play, the props we provide in the classroom often elicit play related to a theme. Careful observations will show the teacher which children make connections between the story and the props.

For Housekeeping And Dress-up Corner : Playing Frances And Her Family

What the children will learn—
To role-play the story using props in the housekeeping and dress-up corner

Materials you will need—
As many of the following as you can find—baby dolls, bottles, rattles, doll clothes, strollers, baby bathtub, highchair, newspaper labeled "Badger News," glasses frames without the lenses, blue and yellow dress-up clothes

What to do—
1. Check the housekeeping corner and place baby dolls and play items associated with babies in clear view.

2. Hang the blue and yellow dress-up clothes in a prominent place. The children can pretend to be Frances getting ready to go to school and deciding what to wear.

3. Paste the label marked "Badger News" over the title of a newspaper. Leave the newspaper and glasses on the table in the housekeeping area. These props will help someone pretend to be Father Badger.

Something to think about—
Children may also dramatize Frances' mother baking the chocolate cake, after they have participated in cooking their own cake for snack. (See the previous activity.)

For Music And Movement: Frances' Sad Song Becomes A Happy Song

What the children will learn—
To respond rhythmically to the songs from the beginning and the ending of the story

Materials you will need—
None

What to do—
1. At a circle time, sing the sad song Frances sang at the beginning of the story. Have the children hit their knees in a slow plodding rhythm. Sing it through once for the children to hear all four lines, then practice echo singing, one line at a time until the children learn it.

2. Sing very slowly and sadly with a low pitch, making up your own tune,

> *"Plinketty, plinketty, plinketty, plink,*
> *Here is the dishrag that's under the sink.*
> *Here are the buckets and brushes and me,*
> *Plinketty, plinketty, plinketty, plee."*

3. Have the children sing rapidly the four lines Frances sang at the end of the story. Sing in a higher, happier pitch and with a light clapping of hands. Follow the same steps you did in teaching the sad song, sing the entire happy song and then have the children echo sing each line.

> *"Big sisters really have to stay*
> *At home, not travel far away,*
> *Because everybody misses them*
> *And wants to hug-and-kisses them."*

4. At the end of the song, have the children hug themselves.

5. Sing the happy song again substituting the word brother for sister.

Something to think about—
For teachers who do not think of themselves as singers, the words can be chanted rhythmically to achieve the same affect. Also, children like to sing and chant rhythms until they know them well, so please continue to practice Frances' songs for several days.

ME TOO!

By Mercer Mayer

Mercer Mayer's comical big brother is hampered in his childhood conquests of skateboarding, playing football, fishing and the like by having a little sister who wants to tag along. She invariably trespasses on his activities. He hates to hear those two little words, "Me, too!" Mayer's trademark is his "little critters," humorous animals with humanized features, almost caricatures with large noses, huge eyes and stringy hair. His ever present tiny mouse will amuse the children who notice him. Through the illustrations, Mayer captures the turmoil of the story and eventual resolution when the little sister wins over the affections of her big brother.

Circle Time Presentation

The little sister says, "Me too," throughout the book. After you read a few pages, the children can hear the language pattern and will begin to shout out, "Me too," whenever they think it is expected in the story. Because of the humor in Mercer Mayer's book, the children will immediately request that your read the book again. Reread the short book, and this time, pause for the children to insert the "Me too" phrase. After the second reading, talk about having a little brother or sister who always wants to tag along. Point out the little sister's generosity at the end of the book when she shares her candy cane with her big brother.

STORY STRETCHER
For Art: Group Mural

What the children will learn—
To create a mural with the children's drawings of the children

Materials you will need—
Large sheet of butcher paper long enough to cover a table, black marker, crayons

What to do—
1. Tape the butcher paper onto the table top so it is secure.

2. Section off the paper by drawing straight lines to create separate work areas. Depending on the age of the children, three or four can work together. Print each child's name at the top of his or her section of the paper.

3. Ask the children to draw a picture. For older preschoolers, you can ask them to draw scenes from the book.

Something to think about—
For young preschoolers who are learning to work with others, have them draw their pictures on individual pieces of paper and paste the pictures onto a large paper to create a mural. For the very young children whose art work is in the scribble stage, ask the child to tell you about his or her picture. Write the story that the child tells you, then arrange the pictures to create a mural effect.

STORY STRETCHER
For Block Building: Tree House

What the children will learn—
To build a block tree house

Materials you will need—
Large hollow blocks like the ones found in the block building corner of most preschools and kindergartens, butcher paper, tape, black, brown and green markers

What to do—
1. Sketch a tree trunk on a large sheet of butcher paper and tape it to the wall. It should be no more than two feet tall.

2. Stack some hollow blocks near the tree trunk.

3. Observe the children during block play to see if they begin building their own tree house with the blocks. If they do not, draw a board a day across the tree trunk. Wait for their reactions and continue adding. Soon you will see them building their tree house like the one you are drawing on the butcher paper.

Something to think about—
As with all creative expressions in art, drama and block building, allow the children to draw, or dramatize or build whatever they want. However, the occasional additional prop from the teacher gives new life and direction to the

learning center or may invite new children into that center.

For Creative Dramatics: Pantomine

What the children will learn—
To perform body movements

Materials you will need—
None for older preschoolers, for young children a full length mirror

What to do—
1. With a small group of children, pantomime some of the actions from the book, as skateboarding and flying paper airplanes.

2. Pair a boy and a girl to be big brother and little sister.

3. Show each pair the action they are to pantomime. As each boy and girl pantomimes, the viewers guess which movement they are pantomiming.

4. Continue with other actions from the book, hiking, playing football, sledding, skating, eating chocolate cake, fishing, building a tree house and, finally, the little sister sharing her candy cane.

Something to think about—
For the younger children, select a few simple actions which are familiar to them, as playing football or eating chocolate cake. Young children may also need to practice their actions before a full-length mirror before showing their pantomime to the group. Pantomime is an activity which becomes more comfortable if practiced often.

For Science And Nature Center: Paper Airplanes

What the children will learn—
To make paper airplanes

Materials you will need—
Heavy typing paper, scissors, yarn or twine

What to do—
1. At free play time, with small groups of children, make paper airplanes. Fold the airplanes one fold a time, with the children duplicating your folds.

2. When finished, conduct test flights in an open area of the classroom.

3. Measure one of the longest flights, by cutting a piece of yarn or twine the length of the flight.

4. Take the paper airplanes outside, and test fly them again.

5. Measure the distance of the outside flight by cutting a piece of yarn or twine the length of the flight.

6. Compare the differences in lengths for the inside and outside flights.

Something to think about—
To avoid competition simply place all the airplanes on the table in a row and have the children select one, rather than the one she made.

For Library Corner, Listening Station: ME TOO! Tape

What the children will learn—
To predict when the recurring phrase, "Me too," will be heard on the tape and to turn the page at the appropriate signal

Materials you will need—
Listening station with several earphones or a cassette recorder, cassette tape, stapler

What to do—
1. With two or three children, make a cassette recording of ME TOO! The book lends itself to a listening station because the children know that when the little sister says, "Me too,"the scene is about to change, and it is time to turn the page.

2. Whenever the story comes to the phrase, "Me too," point to the children so they will say the phrase with you. Practice with the children before taping.

3. Place the stapler near the microphone of the tape recorder and press the stapler when you turn the page; the noise will be the page turning signal.

4. The children can listen to this tape at center time.

Something to think about—
The listening station with earphones can be used by one child or a group of children. Routinely record books that you read during circle time. Then place the book near the listening station as a reminder that the tape of that book is available.

WHOSE MOUSE ARE YOU?

By Robert Kraus

Illsutrated by José Aruego

The question, "Whose mouse are you?," is given delightful answers as a little mouse tells that he is his mother's mouse, his father's mouse, his sister's mouse and, finally, his brother's mouse. Unfortunately, he does not have a brother. The story is whimsical and rhythmic. Young listeners will soon be chiming in with the answers when the story is read a second time. José Aruego's illustrations are bright yellow and orange with delightful decorations.

Circle Time Presentation

Before reading the book, ask, "Whose child are you?" Provide some answers. "I am my mother's child." Extend the idea by having some children use sentences indicating their relationships to brothers and sisters, as, "I am Michael's big brother," or "I am Tina's little sister." Then read WHOSE MOUSE ARE YOU? and the children will understand the basic format of the story, which is to answer the question and to answer the longing of one mouse for a baby brother. When you reread the book, you can have the children finish phrases you begin, such as "Whose mouse are _____," or "Find my sister and bring her _____." Soon the children will be saying the words along with you as you read. The rhythmic flow of the language in the story makes it a good "reading with the teacher" book.

STORY STRETCHER

For Art: Yellow And Orange Design

What the children will learn—
To make simple designs

Materials you will need—
Yellow and orange tissue paper, white construction paper, glue

What to do—
1. Simply place the art supplies out onto a table and display the book.

2. Encourage the children to use the bright orange and yellow paper to create a picture. Be certain to emphasize that their pictures can be different than José Aruego's. They are designing their own pictures.

3. Often the children doing this activity want to draw a mouse and surround it with the tissue pieces.

Let each child select his own design inspired by Aruego's use of orange and yellow.

Something to think about—
The bright orange and yellow illustrations convey a lighter tone to even the serious scenes of the cat and the mousetrap; the children know that no harm will come to the mother and father mouse. They sometimes will comment on the orange cat decorated with yellow flowers. Somehow a flower bedecked cat does not seem so mean, even if it has caught a mouse. To further connect the illustrations with the children's own art, provide orange, yellow, gray and a little bit of rosy pink tempera paints at the easel and watch for other WHOSE MOUSE ARE YOU? pictures to take shape.

ANOTHER STORY STRETCHER

For Art: Mouse Pictures

What the children will learn—
To draw their favorite scene from the book or a scene from their family

Materials you will need—
Manilla or light construction paper, pencils, crayons

What to do—
1. Make the supplies available. If the children need a suggestion about what to draw, ask the children to tell you about their favorite scene from the book.

2. Some children will want to draw a scene from the book. Other children could be encouraged to make a picture about their family.

3. Have the children write something they want to recall about the book, even if their writing is scribbles. Or, the teacher can

write the caption of the story, as stated by the child.

Something to think about—
It is important to accept the children's scribbles or their actual writing, as well as to accept whatever the child tells the teacher to write. From the children's first attempts at writing and at composing, their work should be valued. Even for the twos and threes whose writing is mostly scribbles, one can see that their drawings and their scribbles for writing look quite different from each other.

STORY STRETCHER

For Creative Dramatics: Show What We Feel

What the children will learn—
To express feelings through dramatic movements

Materials you will need—
For younger preschoolers, a full length mirror; for older preschoolers, hand-held mirrors will suffice

What to do—
1. Leaf through the book, demonstrating the little mouse's gestures and movements. For example, at the beginning, he is walking upright with his hands (paws) behind his back looking distraught and worried. Then, later, he covers his eyes with his hands looking scared. As he wishes for a brother, he places one hand on a cheek. As he comments about his mother who loves him so his arms are stretched up in delight. At the end, he is so happy to have a little brother, he hugs himself.

2. Have the children mimic the little mouse's gestures and facial expressions as you turn to specific scenes. Partners can hold mirrors for children to check their expressions.

3. After a practice session, read the story as the children use their faces and bodies to express the mouse's feelings.

Something to think about—
To further extend the creative dramatics of WHOSE MOUSE ARE YOU?, ask the children to come up in pairs and role-play the scene you show them from the book. Ask the other children to guess what scene is being portrayed.

STORY STRETCHER

For Library Corner, Listening Tape: I Want A Brother Mouse

What the children will learn—
To hear the voice of the narrator and of the little mouse

Materials you will need—
Cassette recorder, cassette tape

What to do—
1. Read the book onto the tape with a friend, preferably someone of the opposite sex or with an older child who has a very different voice than yours. There are only two voices in the story, the narrator's and the little mouse. If you are good at varying your vocal expressions, make the tape yourself, but emphasize the differences in the voices.

2. Make a "turn the page" signal by lightly tapping a fork onto a glass or clicking a stapler.

3. The children can "read" the book at free play time.

Something to think about—
Children's literature is filled with stories where a narrator's voice is implied. The narrator is the one telling the story. For this type of book, try telling the story instead of reading it.

ANOTHER STORY STRETCHER

For Library Corner: New Family Members

What the children will learn—
To talk about family relationships

Materials you will need—
Cassette recorder, tapes, posterboard, glue

What to do—
1. At free play time, invite the children who have new babies in their families to come over to the library corner and tell you about their sisters and brothers.

2. After the discussion, ask the children to bring a picture of the babies to school the next day.

3. On the following day, meet the children in the library corner during free play time and have each child tell about his or her baby brother or sister. Record a sentence or two from each child.

4. Make a poster of the babies' pictures.

5. Let the other children listen to what the children with new babies had to say.

Something to think about—
At this age, there will be many only children in your class, and many families with new babies. For the children with a new sibling, hearing their classmates describe the babies can be helpful. For the only children, encourage them to talk about the babies in the pictures or to tell you about babies of family friends or relatives.

FAMILIES

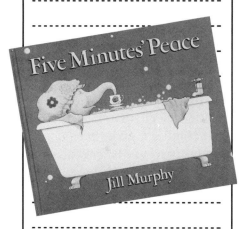

FIVE MINUTES PEACE

By Jill Murphy

Young children enjoy both comedy and stories which remind them of their families. FIVE MINUTES PEACE accomplishes both. Jill Murphy follows the actions of an elephant mother, Mrs. Large, as she attempts to escape her rowdy children, Laura, Lester and the baby. All she wants is five minutes peace, but wherever she attempts to find it, the children want to join her, too. Jill Murphy's illustrations are colorful, charming and witty.

Circle Time Presentation

Ask the children to tell you where their mothers go when they want to rest. After a few responses, show the cover of FIVE MINUTES' PEACE and ask what Mrs. Large is doing. Be prepared for giggles about an elephant sitting in a bathtub with a shower cap over her head and drinking through her trunk from a teacup. During the reading, pause after the scene where Mrs. Large is taking her tray up to the bathroom and ask the children to predict what will happen next. After each scene and prediction confirm whether the children's guesses are correct. Then reread the entire story from start to finish without an interruption.

STORY STRETCHER

For Cooking And Snack Time: Marmalade Toast

What the children will learn—
To make their own snacks

Materials you will need—
Toaster, knives, whole-wheat bread, margarine or cream cheese, marmalade or jelly, milk

What to do—
1. In small groups, have the children toast bread, select a spread of margarine or cream cheese and top with marmalade or jelly.

2. Select children who need practice with small muscle control to make the snacks for the entire class.

Something to think about—
While snack time in most preschools and kindergartens is often prepared by the teacher's aide or a cafeteria worker, children can learn a great deal by preparing their own snacks, often with

surprising results. For instance, teachers who have difficulty getting certain children to eat raw vegetables will find that if the child prepares the vegetables from package to serving dish, the reluctant eater will at least try a bite or two.

STORY STRETCHER

For Housekeeping And Dress-up Corner: Mrs. Large's Household

What the children will learn—
To role-play Mrs. Large and her three rambunctious children

Materials you will need—
The usual dress-up corner clothes, including pajamas, robe, nightgown. Add some large bath towels, and a few props to remind the children of Mrs. Large's household.

What to do—
1. Supply the props and the inventiveness of the children will supply the storyline. For the children who need help getting started, you can tell them that the bathrobe and towels remind you of Mrs. Large.

2. Watch the play unfold and intervene only to help a child who is having difficulty being accepted into the group.

Something to think about—
Early childhood teachers who are concerned about germs, clean the toys and learning materials regularly. Dress-up clothes also should be washed often and any play objects which get a lot of use should be thoroughly cleaned. Inexpensive articles may be replaced rather than attempting to clean them.

For Music And Movement: Relaxing To Music

What the children will learn—
To relax while responding to music

Materials you will need—
Record player or cassette tape player, relaxing record or tape

What to do—
1.   All Mrs. Large wanted was five minutes peace to relax. Tell the children that if Mrs. Large could come to preschool, she could learn how to relax.

2.   Play some soft relaxing music while the children simply sit in a circle and listen.

3.   Ask the children how the music makes them feel.

4.   Have the children take deep breaths in response to the music. Signal when it is time for them to breathe by taking deep breaths yourself and using hand signals to let them know.

5.   Gradually get up from your seated position and move slowly in time with the music. Model how to move first.

6.   Have the children join you and pretend they are limp rag dolls, like a limp Raggedy Ann or Andy. Practice light flowing movements. Have the children gradually drop down onto the floor.

Something to think about—
Children often have difficulty relaxing before naptime. Practice the musical relaxation and limp Raggedy Ann and Andy routine on a regular basis until the children are able to use the deep breathing exercise for relaxation without the music.

For Transition Time : Clean-up Time

What the children will learn—
To clean up their play or learning centers

Materials you will need—
None

What to do—
1.   At the end of free play, the housekeeping corner will invariably look like Mrs. Large's house from FIVE MINUTES' PEACE.

2.   Show the children in the housekeeping corner the picture of Mrs. Large's kitchen, and have them put their housekeeping corner back in order.

3.   At circle time, comment on how the children in the housekeeping corner and the dress-up corner found their house looking like Mrs. Large's until they cleaned it up.

Something to think about—
Children enjoy playing, but often balk when asked to clean up. Regularly scheduled clean-up times, five minutes at the end of free play or learning center time, can alleviate the problem. Establish the clean-up time routine by using the same signal each day, a simple song — "It's clean-up time, It's clean-up time, Everyone must help, It's clean-up time," or a flick of the light switch, or have a child carry around a clean-up time sign for everyone to see. Most importantly, have a routine and keep the same signal each day until clean-up time goes well. Then, you can change the signal for variety.

For Water Table: Bath Toys And Bottles

What the children will learn—
To sort the water toys

Materials you will need—
Water table, large plastic tubs, floating bath toys, variety of sizes of plastic bottles with caps

What to do—
1.   Remind the children of the little elephant in FIVE MINUTES' PEACE who dumped his bath toys in the tub where his mother was relaxing.

2.   Provide some bath toys for the water table. Then, add extra items which are not toys, as a variety of sizes of plastic bottles some clear and some opaque.

3.   For young preschoolers, have them separate the toys from "non-toys." Place each category in a plastic tub. For older preschoolers, encourage them to compare how much water the different sizes of bottles contain.

Something to think about—
While the water table has much potential for mathematics and science learning, it also needs to be left out and available just for fun. The filling, pouring, comparing, floating and warmth of the water helps to relax even the most rambunctious children. Limit the number of children at the water table, usually only one or two.

TITCH

By Pat Hutchins

Children who are the youngest in the family will identify with the plight of Titch who is always left behind or has the smallest of everything. Then, one day, Titch plants a seed which grows and grows and is the envy of his family. Pat Hutchins tells a humorous story which encourages the youngest and the smallest to take heart. The author/illustrator uses primary colors of yellow, blue and red. She draws the characters with quite large heads and gives each an appealing munchkin expression.

Circle Time Presentation

When reading the book, pause and show the picture of Titch on the tricycle and have the children finish the phrase, "And Titch had a little . . . . " Pause whenever this recurring phrase appears. After reading the book, make a chart with three columns on the chalkboard or a tablet. Head the columns Peter, Mary, Titch. Begin with the tricycle and ask the children in which column should you write tricycle. Then ask them to say what Peter had that was like Titch's tricycle (a great big bike) and what Mary had (a big bike). List the bikes under Peter's and Mary's column on the chart. Continue with Titch's pinwheel compared to Peter's kite that flew above the trees and Mary's kite that flew above the houses. Finish the chart with asking about the flowerpot. Mary had the flowerpot; Peter had the spade, but Titch had the seed that grew and grew and grew.

STORY STRETCHER

For Art: Blue T-shirts

What the children will learn—
To decorate T-shirts on the front and back

Materials you will need—
Large sheets of blue construction paper, stapler, markers

What to do—
1.   For each child, cut two large sheets of blue construction paper in the shape of a T-shirt.

2.   Staple them together at the shoulder.

3.   Ask the children to decorate the front and back of their Titch T-shirt. You can talk about Titch's blue shirt, and show the children the front and back of the book.

Something to think about—
Allow children freedom of expression. Many children will want to decorate their T-shirts like ones they have at home.

STORY STRETCHER

For Library Corner, Listening Station: Titch Tape

What the children will learn—
To follow the story and turn the pages at the appropriate signal.

Materials you will need—
Listening station with several earphones or a cassette tape recorder; cassette tape, onto which you have recorded the story of TITCH; tap a glass lightly with a fork for the signal of when to turn the page

What to do—
1.   In a small group of three or four children, introduce the tape to the children.

2.   Practice turning the pages at the signal. Allow several children to have a turn. After the practice sessions they should be able to function on their own.

3.   Encourage the children to listen for the different things that Peter, Mary and Titch had.

Something to think about—
TITCH is a wonderful book for beginning users of the listening station or a cassette recorder because it is short and contains predictable phrases. Younger preschoolers may remember to turn the page at the signal. Older preschoolers will begin reading along with the tape. You should vary the size of the group depending upon their needs.

For Mathematics And Manipulatives Center: Threes, Threes, Threes

What the children will learn—
To count three items to form a set of three and recognize the numeral 3

Materials you will need—
Three flowerpots or large cups, three index cards or small pieces of paper with the numeral 3 printed on them, a collection of items from around the room, as tape, chalk, blocks, pencils, paper cups; collect any item if you have three of them

What to do—
1. Have the children count the characters in the book, Titch, Mary and Peter (3).
2. Count the characters' possessions in sets of three. There were three bikes, but Titch's was a tricycle. Three things which move with the wind, Mary's and Peter's kites and Titch's pinwheel. Three items needed to plant a seed, Mary's flowerpot with soil in it, Peter's spade and Titch's seeds.
3. Count the set of three pictures on the front cover of the book, the tricycle, Titch holding a pinwheel and the huge plant.
4. Count the set of three pictures on the back cover of the book, which is a back view of the front cover. There is a tricycle, a picture of Titch showing the back of his head and the huge plant.
5. Count small items making sets of three. Collect items from around the room and place them on a table — chalk, paper cups, spools of thread, crayons, paper clips, pencils, spoons, popsicle sticks, rolls of tape.
6. Place three flowerpots in a row on the table. Print the numeral 3 on index cards. Tape the index cards onto the flowerpots. Have the children find a set of three items, three crayons, three paper clips, three spoons and drop them in the flowerpots.

Something to think about—
Younger preschoolers can count out three of the same item, as three pieces of chalk or three crayons. For older preschoolers, the three items can belong to a general category. For instance, a crayon, a piece of chalk and a pencil would all go in one flowerpot because they are used for writing. Another set which could be formed are knife, fork and spoon, or hair brush, comb and hair barrette.

For Science And Nature Center: Planting Seeds

What the children will learn—
To observe the growth of a plant

Materials you will need—
Rye grass seeds or other fast germinating seeds, paper cups, potting soil, spade or large spoon for shoveling the soil into the cups, water, plastic tub to hold the potting soil, optional salt shakers, popsicle stick, markers, scissors

What to do—
1. Demonstrate planting the seeds by filling a cup with potting soil, leaving a little space at the top. Sprinkle about ten rye grass seeds on the top. For young preschoolers, place the seeds in a clean, empty salt shaker; one good shake is enough seeds. Moisten the seeds with a little water. Salt shakers also can be used for watering. This avoids the problem of overwatering.
2. Let the children plant their seeds following your directions.
3. Place the seed cups on a sunlit window sill. If planted in the summer, avoid a sill which is too hot.
4. Observe the plants each day. Measure the growth of a few sample plants by placing a popsicle stick in the cup. Each day, place a mark at the top of the growth. Alternate colors of markers for the children to notice the different days.
5. Trim the rye grass in a few cups and notice the difference in growth. Cut one down to the top of the cup; barely trim another. Have the children notice the differences.

Something to think about—
Children delight in Titch's final triumph at having a tiny seed which grows into a huge plant to the amazement of his sister and brother. Planting seeds with preschoolers can be exciting, but it is often hard to wait many days for the seeds to grow. For threes and fours, we recommend purchasing rye grass seeds which germinate quickly and cut down on the children's waiting time. The seeds will grow about an inch a day on a bright sunlit sill. After they are successful at growing rye grass seeds, graduate to lima bean seeds and others which take longer to germinate.

For Science And Nature Center: Pinwheels

What the children will learn—
To make a pinwheel and watch how it works

Materials you will need—
Brightly colored construction paper cut into five inch squares, tape, scissors, a straw and straight pin per child

What to do—

1. Cut a diagonal straight line from each corner of the five inch square of construction paper to within 1/2 inch of the center. Fives will be able to do this task after you model it, but younger children will probably need assistance with this step.

2. Fold the outside corner of each flap into the center of the square and tape into place.

3. The teacher should place a straight pin through the construction paper and the tape in the center of the square.

4. Then, the teacher should stick the pin with the attached paper pinwheel into a plastic straw.

5. The teacher then bends the straight pin down and places tape over the sharp end so that it will not puncture the child's finger. Remember to leave the pinwheel loose enough so it can move in a breeze. Test to see if it is too tight by blowing on the pinwheel.

6. The children can blow on the pinwheels to move them. Also, place them near an air vent in the room, or go outside and watch the wind spin the pinwheels.

Something to think about—
Make some large pinwheels as decorations for the room. Place them in flowerpots filled with rocks. Arrange flowerpots of large pinwheels on a window sill or near an air conditioner or blower for the children to observe.

REFERENCES

Hoban, Russell. (1964). Illustrated by Lillian Hoban. **A BABY SISTER FOR FRANCES.** New York: Harper and Row Publishers.

Hutchins, Pat. (1971). **TITCH.** New York: Macmillan Publishing Company.

Kraus, Robert. (1970). Illustrated by José Aruego. **WHOSE MOUSE ARE YOU?** New York: Macmillan Publishing Company.

Mayer, Mercer. (1983). **ME TOO!** New York: A Golden Book.

Murphy, Jill. (1986). **FIVE MINUTES' PEACE.** New York: G.P. Putnam's Sons.

Additional References for Families

Hines, Anna Grossnickle. (1986). **DADDY MAKES THE BEST SPAGHETTI.** New York: Clarion Books. *Not only does Corey's father make the best spaghetti, but he also dresses up like Bathman and barks like a dog.*

Johnston, Tony. (1985). Illustrated by Tomie dePaola. **THE QUILT STORY.** New York: G.P. Putnam's Sons. *A pioneer mother lovingly stitches a beautiful quilt which warms and comforts her daughter Abigail; many years later another mother mends and patches it for her little girl.*

Quilan, Patricia. (1987). Illustrated by Vlasta van Kampen. **MY DAD TAKES CARE OF ME.** Toronto: Annick Press. *A little boy tries to explain to his friends why his father doesn't have a job. He learns to appreciate the fact that his father is there to take care of him.*

Thompson, Richard. (1988). Illustrated by Eugenie Fernandes. **FOO.** Toronto: Annick Press. *One of a series of Jesse books. A little girl's habit of blowing kisses comforts her when she blows a kiss to her mother who is away for the evening.*

Ziefert, Harriet. (1987). Illustrated by Mavis Smith. **HURRY UP, JESSIE.** New York: Random House. *Jessie prepares for a trip to the beach as her mother hurries her along.*

FRIENDSHIP

George and Martha One Fine Day
Friends
Alfie Gives a Hand
Best Friends
Will I Have a Friend?

FRIENDSHIP

GEORGE AND MARTHA

ONE FINE DAY

By James Marshall

George and Martha are hippopotamuses who share a day together. The books is divided into five brief stories: "The Tight Rope," "The Diary," " The Icky Story," "The Big Scare" and "The Amusement Park." Children love the humor and relate to the outrageousness of two hippos with friendship problems. Each story has a clear moral, cleverly and kindly exposed. For example, in "The Tight Rope," George's comments make Martha lose her confidence when she is walking the tightrope, but as soon as he realizes his words are making her shaky, he compliments her and she does some fancy footwork for George to see.

Circle Time Presentation

All five short stories about George and Martha can be read at one circle time, or each can be read separately. The moral of each is that friends treat each other kindly and respectfully. Show the children the cover of the book and ask them to tell you what is funny; George and Martha, the two hippos, are swinging in a hammock. Ask how the children know that George and Martha are friends. Then, have the children tell what friends do together. Read the book and compare what the children said friends do together with what George and Martha did.

STORY STRETCHER

For Art: Stamp Pictures

What the children will learn—
To design a picture with a stamp

Materials you will need—
Crayons or markers, construction or manilla paper, moistened sponge, glue, cancelled stamps, or stamps from magazine advertisements

What to do—

1.   Have the children select a stamp and place it at random on their paper.

2.   Then have them draw a picture using the stamp as part of it. For example, one child might place a stamp in the upper section on the paper on the right side, then draw a little girl flying a kite. The stamp is a kite. Another child might place a stamp near the bottom of the page, draw wheels on it and it becomes a truck. The children are also inspired by each other's creations.

3.   Young preschoolers enjoy the simple activity of moistening the stamps (cancelled stamps will need glue) and placing them on the paper. Their stamp pictures can be a collage of stamps.

Something to think about—
Invite a parent who is a stamp collector to bring her or his books to school. Also, the post office has information on stamp collecting.

STORY STRETCHER

For Creative Dramatics: Tight Rope Walking

What the children will learn—
To pretend to be George and Martha

Materials you will need—
The usual dress-up clothes found in a preschool or kindergarten classroom, a jump rope, an umbrella

What to do—

1.   Tape a jump rope to the floor. Place the umbrella nearby so the children can pretend to be Martha, the hippo, balancing on the tight rope.

2.   Play some lively music while the children are performing their tight rope act.

Something to think about—
James Marshall has written a series of George and Martha books, beginning with simply GEORGE AND MARTHA, GEORGE AND MARTHA ENCORE and GEORGE AND MARTHA RISE AND SHINE. If you find that George and Martha stories are often requested for rereading, then consider adding the entire series to your collection of books. Teachers also find the short stories are good time fillers because of the humor and completeness of each single story.

For Library Corner: Our Diaries

What the children will learn—
To write in their diaries like Martha

Materials you will need—
Notebooks, or diaries, or several sheets of paper stapled to make a notebook, pens, pencils, crayons

What to do—
1. At free play time, have a writing table set up in or near the library corner.

2. Construct the notebooks which will become the diaries. Have the children assist you in counting out the pages, stapling, and then have them decorate the cover so they can distinguish between the diaries. If you already have notebooks, let the children decorate the covers.

3. Write the date at the top of the first page. Let the children write or draw whatever they wish.

4. On the next day when children come to the writing table in the library corner, write the date at the beginning of the next page in the diary.

Something to think about—
Children with older brothers and sisters may know about diaries, but most preschoolers will think of the diary as a notebook. Expect some children to pretend to be writing letters to grandparents or notes to friends.

For Library Corner, Listening Station: Surprise, George!

What the children will learn—
To anticipate when Martha will scare George

Materials you will need—
Listening station with earphones or cassette recorder, tapes

What to do—
1. The fourth and fifth stories of GEORGE AND MARTHA, ONE FINE DAY are particularly good ones for a listening station because the children hold their breaths with anticipation trying to figure out when Martha will scare George.

2. Tape record the story, using a page-turning signal.

3. Place the tape of the story and the book in the library corner.

Something to think about—
Children who have heard the story several times, enjoy listening again because they know when Martha is going to get George. Be prepared that for a few days there will be several Georges and Marthas who like to surprise each other. The book makes an excellent selection for Halloween.

For Science And Nature Center: Nature Walk

What the children will learn—
To sort natural objects

Materials you will need—
Paper bags, crayons or markers, index cards for signs or labels, display table from the science center

What to do—
1. Discuss that Martha enjoys collecting as a hobby. Have the children volunteer information about things they like to collect. Tell the children that today you will take a walk around the school or center and find rocks, or leaves, or acorns, or signs of the season for a class collection.

2. Ask the children to decorate their paper bags so they will know which is theirs.

3. Take the nature walk. Have the children collect things in their bags.

4. After returning to the classroom, have the children select three objects they want to place on display. Place these on the science table.

5. Put an index card with the child's name near each collection of three.

6. Allow the children to dictate some observations about their nature collection of rocks, or leaves, or signs of the season. A parent volunteer, the aide or teacher can write the dictations on the index card near each child's collection. One little girl dictated, "This rock was dirty. I rubbed it off and now it is pretty." A boy said, "This leaf has a hole in it. A hungry caterpillar ate it."

Something to think about—
The collections of natural objects for the science table have many other possibilities. Children can order the rocks from the smallest to the largest. Begin by taping the rocks to index cards, then have children place them in order of size. For young children, begin with five rocks. Leaves can be grouped according to type. Create an attractive display which encourages manipulation and exploration of the objects. The display should be a "Please Touch" one.

2
FRIENDSHIP

FRIENDS

By Helme Heine

Three unlikely friends, a mouse, a rooster and a pig, spend the day together in the wonderfully unlikely pursuits of riding a bicycle, playing hide-and-seek, pretending to be pirates while sailing a boat on the village pond and trying, quite unsuccessfully, to spend the night together. Their sworn oath to stay friends and stay together forever is met with a few obstacles. Helme Heine's illustrations are bright, light watercolors which tease the imagination.

Circle Time Presentation

Talk with the children about some of the things they like to do with their friends. Ask the children to think about some things a mouse, a rooster and a pig, who are friends, might do together. Accept their wildest exaggerations. Read FRIENDS and talk about how friends want to be together all the time, and even though friends have to go home, they still think about each other when they are apart.

STORY STRETCHER

For Cooking And Snack Time: The Friends Share Cherries

What the children will learn—
To compare fresh or frozen cherries with the cherry taste in snacks

Materials you will need—
Fresh cherries, if available, or frozen cherries, cherry toaster pastries, toaster, napkins, milk

What to do—
1. Show the children the fresh or frozen cherries as they are packaged in the grocery store.
2. Have one or two children assist you in preparing the cherries for snack, wash the fresh cherries or separate the frozen ones.
3. Toast the cherry flavored toaster pastries.
4. Serve the fresh or frozen cherries and talk about how they taste. Point out that the pit in the middle, which Charlie Rooster ate, is the seed for a cherry tree.
5. Serve the cherry toaster pastries and compare the tastes of fresh or frozen cherries with the sweetened taste of the pastry.

Something to think about—
Compare other cherry tastes as cherry jelly, cherry pie filling and candied cherries.

STORY STRETCHER

For Creative Dramatics: Unlikely Friends — Mouse, Rooster And Pig

What the children will learn—
To act like mouse, rooster and pig

Materials you will need—
None

What to do—
1. Select three children to be Johnny Mouse, Charlie Rooster and Percy Pig. Have the children who are assigned the roles act them out and the other children do the same by following the leader.
2. First, Charlie Rooster pretends he is going to the barn to wake the other animals. The other children "cock-a-doodle-doo" with Charlie.
3. Then, have the children follow their leader Percy Pig as he rides the bicycle.
4. Let Charlie Rooster lead the children in pretending to be a sailboat.
5. After a practice session, reread the story and the children act out the scenes. The actors role-play the scenes and the other children follow their leads. Tell the children a hand signal you will use for them to know when to stop acting and listen.

Something to think about—
In early childhood education, we encourage children to use their bodies and facial expressions to role-play the characters in a story, instead of speaking the lines. Forgetting lines and getting embarrassed can make the child self-conscious.

For Library Corner, Flannel Board : I Can Tell A Story

What the children will learn—
That a story has a certain order

Materials you will need—
Flannel board, flannel board pieces of Charlie Rooster, Johnny Mouse, Percy Pig, a barn, a bicycle, a sailboat, mousehole, fence for the pigsty, board for the roost, moon and stars

What to do—
1. Construct the flannel board pieces. This book is particularly adaptable as a flannel board story.
2. Model retelling the story with the flannel board at another circle time.
3. Place the book near the flannel board in the library corner for the children to use.

Something to think about—
After the children are familiar with the story, encourage them to tell the story from the perspective of a farmer watching these three animals. If you have young threes and fours, you tell the story and then leave the flannel board out and see if they retell your new version. For late fours and fives, just get them started pretending to be the farmer, they they will pick up on your cue and continue telling the tale.

For Music And Movement: Musical Follow The Leader

What the children will learn—
To follow the musical and movement clues

Materials you will need—
Recording of marching music, record player or cassette player; if you play the piano, select a good marching tune

What to do—
1) Select one child who will be good at inventing movements and have the child march around the room. The other children imitate her movements while saying, "Friends forever," in time with the music. Some of the possible movements are: waving arms, tapping waist with hands, hands to shoulders, pointing fingers, strutting like a drum major.
2. Then select a new leader for the children to follow while saying, "Friends forever" in time to the music.
3. Continue the sequence with several leaders.

Something to think about—
Vary the activity by having the children do animal movements. They can pretend to be different animals waking up in the barnyard or different actions from the story. Doing the actions in time with the music makes the activity even more enjoyable.

For Water Table: Floating On The Village Pond

What the children will learn—
To see whether objects float

Materials you will need—
Plastic detergent bottles with caps, plastic margarine tubs, plastic cups or bowl with lids, rocks, pebbles, bolts, bath toys

What to do—
1. Fill the water table with warm water; cool water if the weather is hot. Supply the items for floating.
2. During free play time, circulate around to the water table and encourage the children to find out which objects float like the boat Johnny Mouse found on the village pond.
3. Then, have the children place rocks or pebbles into some of the containers and see if they still float. Then put the bolts into the containers and see if they still float.

Something to think about—
Warm water makes the water table more inviting for a child who is not quite sure it is alright to play in the water. Also, try encouraging a reluctant participant by starting the activity with him or having the child be your helper. For example, he could change the color of the water by adding food coloring or a diluted mixture of tempera paint. Also, be certain that the child who is reluctant to participate has old clothes to wear. Some teachers use boots for young preschoolers, as they invariably spill water onto their shoes.

ALFIE GIVES A HAND

By Shirley Hughes

Alfie receives his first invitation to a birthday party from his best friend, Bernard. He wants to go if he can take his security blanket along. No amount of persuasion can convince Alfie to leave his blanket at home. He clings to it during the party games and even lunch, until he sees Min who is frightened by a mask Bernard is wearing. Then he bravely places his blanket in a safe place and runs to hold Min's hand. When Mom and baby sister pick-up Alfie from the party, Bernard's mother thanks Alfie for being a good friend to Min. Alfie feels quite grownup and decides that next time he may leave his blanket at home. Shirley Hughes' illustrations are filled with details. The children's realistic expressions tell the story as charmingly as the dialogue. The author/illustrator has other Alfie stories which are equally appealing, ALFIE'S FEET and ALFIE GETS IN FIRST.

Circle Time Presentation

Talk with the children about their "security" blankets or toys. Mention that Alfie, the little boy in the story, had a special blanket he liked to have with him, even at his friend Bernard's birthday party. Read ALFIE GIVES A HAND, have the children recall how Alfie made Min feel more comfortable and what happened to Alfie's feelings about his blanket.

STORY STRETCHER
For Art: Birthday Party Masks

What the children will learn—
To make a mask

Materials you will need—
Grocery bags, crayons, scissors, yarn and stapler (optional)

What to do—
1. Talk about the tiger mask Bernard was given for a birthday present and ask the children what masks they might like to make.

2. Place a grocery bag over a child's head and mark the position of the eyes and mouth by drawing a line with the crayon on the outside of the bag.

3. Remove the bag from the child's head and cut eyes and a mouth. Continue until each child has a grocery bag with the eyes and mouths cut.

4. Assist the children in stapling on yarn to make a mane or hair for the animals, or have them use their crayons to draw all of the features.

Something to think about—
Bernard is overly excitied and overly stimulated by many of the activities of the party. His mother keeps correcting him and trying to get him to be a good host to the other children. Teachers often must help parents understand that too much celebration can cause

their child to act in a disruptive manner. Establish guidelines for the length of birthday parties in your classroom, as the last few minutes of the day or at snack time.

STORY STRETCHER
For Cooking And Snack Time: Bernard's Birthday Lunch

What the children will learn—
To assist in preparing and serving lunch

Materials you will need—
Hot dogs, buns, potato chips, lemonade, birthday cake, plates, napkins, knives, forks, spoons, three small packages of Jell-O mix, hot water, mixing bowl, gelatin molds

What to do—
1. Prepare the hot dogs, lemonade and birthday cake ahead of time.

2. Working in three small groups, have the children assist you in preparing the Jell-O. Use a small package of Jell-O mix for each group. Follow the directions on the package. Involve children in each step. For example, one child opens the package. Another child pours the mix in the mixing bowl. Then another child measures the hot water. Someone else pours it into the mixing bowl. Another child mixes up the water and the gelatin. Still another child pours the mixtures into the gelatin mold.

3. Repeat the process with each new group of children.

Something to think about—
Have each group add different fruits to their Jell-O mixture after it begins to set. Also, consider molding the Jell-O in a clear glass bowl so the children can see how the fruit is suspended in the

gelatin. At snack or lunch time, the children can compare the tastes.

For Library Corner, Listening Station : Alfie Gives A Hand

What the children will learn—
To operate the tape recorder or listening station by oneself

Materials you will need—
Listening station or cassette recorder and tapes

What to do—
1.   Have the children who are least proficient at using the listening station or the tape recorder help you make the tape of ALFIE GIVES A HAND.

2.   Have one child in charge of turning on the recorder and another one responsible for making the signal for turning the page, as tapping a glass with a fork or clicking a stapler near the microphone.

3.   Rehearse the story once and record the rehearsal. Let the children decide if they want to do the tape again.

4.   Make this listening station for one child only so that the student who wants to listen to the tape must know how to operate the cassette player and earphones, as well as coordinate the turning of the pages of the book at the signal.

Something to think about—
One of the major goals of early education is for children to develop as independent learners. There may be children in your class who seem to wait for you or another child to help them with starting the tapes, setting up the materials for art or other tasks. Help these children become independent by involving them in the preparation of the materials or the activity. Often they do not know how something is done or they have become so accustomed to older brothers and sisters or parents doing things for them that they simply do not think of themselves as capable. You can change their self-concept by teaching them how to be more independent, just as Alfie learned to be more independent without his blanket.

For Music And Movement: Ring-a-ring-o'-roses

What the children will learn—
To play the game

Materials you will need—
None

What to do—
1.   Have the children join hands in a circle. Let one child pretend to be Bernard and wear a birthday mask.

2.   Sing the song,

*"Ring-a-ring-o-'roses
A pocket full of posies
A-tishoo, a tishoo,
We all fall DOWN!" (Hughes, p. 26)*

3.   Have the children dance around in a circle, singing the song and falling down.

Something to think about—
If you have a large group of children, divide them into two groups and ask the aide to lead one group. If you have no one else to assist you, then divide the children into two groups and take turns with each group.

For Water Table: Blowing Bubbles

What the children will learn—
To blow bubbles

Materials you will need—
Either commercially prepared bottles of bubble blowing liquid and a wand or large bars of soap, sponges, bowls of water, spools

What to do—
1.   With a small group of children at a time, play with the bubbles over an empty water table. If you use the commercial bubbles, show the children how to blow gently through the wand to make the bubbles.

2.   If you use the bars of soap, wet each bar of soap and place it on a sponge. Position the bowls of water nearby.

3.   Have the children take their spools, dip them in the water and then lightly rub one end of the spool across the bar of soap.

4.   Demonstrate how to gently blow through the end of the spool that does not have soap. Bubbles will come out of the end with the soap on it.

Something to think about—
Consider having the commercial bubbles one day and the old-fashioned soap bar bubbles on another day. On another day, fill the water table and let the children float their bubbles on the surface of the water.

BEST FRIENDS

By Miriam Cohen

Illustrated by Lillian Hoban

Miriam Cohen expresses the anxiety of many young children who wonder if they will have friends. Jim wants Paul to be his best friend, but their friendship is tested by a problem in the class. The light in the incubator goes out and Jim and Paul come to the rescue of the soon-to-hatch eggs. By the end of the day, the chicks are hatched and the friendship is secure as Paul and Jim know they are best friends. The children in the preschool class are from a city neighborhood and several ethnic groups are represented in the illustrations. Lillian Hoban's line drawings are washed over with warm, muted colors to complement the feelings of the dilemma in BEST FRIENDS.

Circle Time Presentation

Ask the children to tell you some of the things they like doing with their friends. Mention that the little boy in the story is Jim and he wants Paul to be his best friend. After reading the book, have the children tell you how they know Jim and Paul are best friends. Then, compare the activities of the children in BEST FRIENDS with the activities in your classroom. Activities from the book include: building with blocks, painting at the easel, cleaning up the block corner, eating snack and playing outdoors.

STORY STRETCHER

For Art: Pictures And Compliments

What the children will learn—
To create a self-portrait and to accept compliments

Materials you will need—
Butcher paper, scissors, crayons or tempera paints and paint brushes, paper, glue

What to do—
1. Discuss with the children that in the BEST FRIENDS book, there is a scene of a little girl who has painted two girls "stuck together." She says, "They're best friends."

2. To extend the friendship theme, make full-body sketches of children by having one child lie down on some butcher paper and let a friend draw the outline around him.

3. After the outline drawing is completed, the child paints his self-portrait with tempera paints or colors with crayons.

4. After the painted versions have dried for a day, the children can cut them out.

5. Complete the self-portrait activity by selecting two or three children a day to highlight. Place the self-portraits of those children in a prominent spot. Explain what a compliment is. Then, lead the children in complimenting the highlighted children.

6. Write the compliments on a sheet of paper titled, "Children's compliments about _____." Glue the sheet of compliments to the back of the child's self-portrait. When the self-portraits are sent home, parents will be delighted to read how their children are perceived by the friends at preschool.

Something to think about—
Select the less popular children to begin both the self-portrait and the compliment sessions. Model giving compliments and make certain children understand that they are only to tell the "nice things."

ANOTHER STORY STRETCHER

For Art: Friendship Collage

What the children will learn—
To make pictures about friendships

Materials you will need—
Yellow construction paper, old magazines or catalogs, glue, scissors

What to do—
1. Call the children's attention to the way Lillian Hoban, the illustrator, emphasized Jim and Paul's friendship on the cover of BEST FRIENDS. She shows them standing together on a yellow background.

2. Give the children yellow construction paper and ask them to create a friendship collage by finding pictures of children from the magazines or catalogs, cutting them out and pasting the pictures on the yellow background in a way

that we will know they are friends. Young children may need help cutting.

3. Display the friendship collages on a bulletin board labeled, "Friends like Jim and Paul."

Something to think about—
When constructing the friendship collage, some children may want to make a pair of friends, while others will show many children as friends. Emphasize that we can have many friends, just like Miriam Cohen emphasized throughout BEST FRIENDS.

For Housekeeping And Dress-up Corner: Caps And Hats

What the children will learn—
To play the different roles represented by caps and hats

Materials you will need—
A variety of caps and hats, as nurses' caps, letter carriers' hats, soft canvas hats, baseball caps, straw hats, felt hats, sunvisors, women's hats, men's hats,

What to do—
1. Talk about the cap that Jim wears to school. In one of the scenes two children argue over a hat.

2. Make a collection of the caps and hats in the classroom and hang them in a prominent place.

3. Be certain to include a cap like Jim's in the collection.

4. Observe the changes in roles, as children begin to play and relate to each other differently based on the hats or caps the players are wearing.

Something to think about—
Add to the cap and hat collection by asking parents to send ones from home. As a reminder of your request, place a cap and hat table

near the classroom door, and they will see the display when they deliver and pick up their children.

For Library Corner: Friendship Chart

What the children will learn—
To think about and appreciate the other children in the class

Materials you will need—
Chart tablet or butcher paper, or backs of old computer paper, markers

What to do—
1. Extend the compliments on the back of the self-portraits by making Friendship Charts.

2. Take a small group of children (up to five) to the library corner to make pages for the Friendship Chart.

3. Highlight two to three children a day. Select one and have the children in the library corner dictate an ending to this sentence, "I like (Michelle) because _____." Write at least three positive sentences about each child.

4. Turn the chart tablet to the next sheet and have the children dictate sentences about the next child to be highlighted.

Something to think about—
Keep this Friendship Chart in the library corner. The chart can stay in the library corner for many weeks. You will soon observe children looking at their friends' charts, as well as their own.

For Science And Nature Center: Hatching Baby Chicks

What the children will learn—
To watch baby chicks hatch and learn about the beginning of the baby chick's life

Materials you will need—
Incubator, fertilized eggs, food and water, habitat for after the chicks are hatched, paper, pen

What to do—
1. Set up an incubator, available from school supply stores. They can direct you to a source in your community for fertilized eggs.

2. Introduce the incubator to the children with very specific rules for what they can and cannot do. Go over the rules each day until the children are familiar with them.

3. Make a calendar to record the days and mark the days when the eggs should hatch.

4. Alert the custodian and secure his or her assistance in taking care of the eggs and the chicks if they should hatch over the week-end.

Something to think about—
At the preschool age, children have seldom seen baby chicks and will have little idea as to their needs. Carefully instruct the children about how to handle the chicks. Have a plan in mind as to what you will do with the chicks when they are a week to two weeks old. From the beginning, be certain you inform the children of where the chicks will go. Often children think of them as classroom pets, like the gerbil, which will always be there. Prepare the children for the birth and the departure of the chicks.

43

FRIENDSHIP

WILL I HAVE A FRIEND?

WILL I HAVE A FRIEND?

Story by Miriam Cohen · Pictures by Lillian Hoban

WILL I HAVE A FRIEND?

By Miriam Cohen

Illustrated by Lillian Hoban

Jim's worry on the first day of school is whether or not he will have a friend. His father reassures him and Jim spends the day looking at the different children in his class trying to decide if they will be his friends. The story takes the listener through a day of activities in a preschool or kindergarten, free choice time, playing with clay, listening to stories, snack time and naptime. Finally, at the end of the day, Jim shares a special moment with Paul and thinks of him as his friend. Lillian Hoban's illustrations of this city preschool or kindergarten shows children from different ethnic groups. She uses line drawings colored over with warm pinks, reds and peach tones.

Circle Time Presentation

At the beginning of the year or whenever a new child enters the group, discuss how new children worry about whether or not they will have any friends at school. Tell the children that Jim is the boy on the cover of the book who is building with blocks. Ask them to predict whether or not Jim will find a friend in this story. Read the story. After reading the book, have the children tell all the things they saw in the illustrations that are like what happens in their classroom.

STORY STRETCHER

For Art: Class Mural

What the children will learn—
To create a class mural

Materials you will need—
Butcher paper, crayons or markers, long table, tape

What to do—

1. Tape a long piece of butcher paper onto a table.

2. Discuss again all the things that the children at Jim's school did.

3. Have each child make a picture, using an idea from the book — blocks, snack, naptime, a book, painting, puzzles, dolls, clay, a workbench, a little red car — or an idea of her own.

4. Hang the mural on the wall.

Something To Think About:
After each child has drawn a picture, let the child dictate a sentence to you about her part of the mural. If the child wants to write, let her write and then you can write below the writing interpreting what is said.

ANOTHER STORY STRETCHER

For Art: Shape That Clay

What the children will learn—
To explore ways to shape clay

Materials you will need—
Clay or playdough, storage containers

What to do—

1. Simply supply the clay or the playdough and let the children work with it on their own.

2. Give each child two "oranges" of clay (about two handfuls).

3. Avoid emphasizing finished products. Manipulating the clay or playdough is the object of this activity.

Something to think about—
Often teachers choose playdough and do not have children work with clay. Potters' clay is available from school and art supply stores. It is messier, but it also has other properties children enjoy. Children enjoy molding the clay, having it dry out a bit, feeling the clay dust on their hands and the sensation of the cool, wet surface of the clay. Natural clay can be fired when children make things for special occasions. (Avoid the modeling clay which has an oil base and is not easily malleable with young fingers.) A large plastic jar is a good storage container. When the children finish with the clay, have them shape it back into large "oranges" and place them into the plastic jar. Then, place a wet paper towel over the clay and put the lid on tightly. Clay washes off the tables easily because it is just dirt and water.

For Block Building: Building In Progress

What the children will learn—
To manipulate and build with blocks

Materials you will need—
Large hollow blocks like those found in many preschools and kindergartens, paper, markers or crayons, yarn

What to do—
1. After reading the book, point out that there are several pictures of Jim with the blocks in WILL I HAVE A FRIEND?

2. Encourage the children who are block enthusiasts to tell why they like to build with the blocks.

3. At free play time, when the block builders are making their creations, visit the block corner and listen to what is being built. Just before clean-up time have the builders tell you about their construction. Have them think of a name for their design and then make a sign for the block construction. Print, "Do Not Disturb, Building in Progress." Add their name for the structure. Stretch a piece of yarn across the area, roping it off so others will not disturb the building, then the children can return the next day to add to or reconstruct their building.

4. At circle time at the end of the day, have the children recall that Jim liked block building and that we have friends in our class who especially like block building. Then have all the children go over and look at the block builders' creation, and have the builders tell about their construction.

Something to think about—
Early childhood educators often wonder about the children who spend so much time in the block building area. Sometimes, other children cannot negotiate their way into the block building group, and, perhaps, the block builders are missing out on some other important activities. If a child or a group of children shows no other interests, the teacher should interest them in other activities. For example, have the block builders begin with another activity and finish it before going on to the blocks. When a small group begins to monopolize the block area, the teacher may need to intervene. Suppose there are four children who always choose blocks at free play time, the teacher can have two of the four begin a different activity for their first part of free play time. This allows new children to enter the group.

For Cooking and Snack Time: Squeezing Orange Juice

What the children will learn—
To prepare orange juice from the whole orange

Materials you will need—
Juice oranges, cutting board, knife, juicers, spoon or strainer for removing the seeds, pitchers and glasses

What to do—
1. With a small group of children, demonstrate how to roll the oranges by pressing them with your hands against the table to make them softer. This helps to release the juice.

2. Slice the oranges in half.

3. Demonstrate for the children how to place the orange over the top of the juicer and turn it round and round to make the juice come out. Remove the seeds with a spoon or strain them. Straining also removes the pulp. The younger children may need help squeezing all the juice out of the oranges.

4. Show the children how to pour their juice into the pitcher and then into their cups or glasses.

5. Let each child squeeze at least one orange and drink the juice he has prepared.

Something to think about—
Encourage independence. Let the children pour their own juice. If you use small pitchers and allow the child to stand while pouring, it will be easier. Also, have a clean-up sponge nearby for spills.

For Music And Movement: Friendship Song

What the children will learn—
To sing a short song about friendship

Materials you will need—
None

What to do—
1. Sing this friendship song to the tune of "Here We Go Round the Mulberry Bush."

"Today, I'm going to meet a friend,
meet a friend, meet a friend.
Today, I'm going to meet a friend and
we'll be friends together."
Today, I'm going to play with my
friend, play with my friend, play with
my friend,
Today, I'm going to play with my friend
and we'll be friends forever."
(Raines)

2. Arrange the children into pairs of friends for the motions of the song.

3. When the song says, "Today," turn hands over with the palms up, then the child points to herself for "I," waves "hi" back and forth for the "meet a friend" phrase and ends with two fingers held up for

the "together" phrase. Repeat the "Today" and "I" motions for the second verse, then wave arms as if calling someone over for the "play with my friend" phrase. End by hugging oneself for the "friends forever."

4. Sing the song (with or without hand motions) at several transition times throughout the day, including while cleaning up the room.

Something to think about— Teachers often feel inhibited about singing. To get over those inhibitions, learn a few songs to sing with a record or cassette tape, then simply burst into song whenever you feel like singing. Or hum the tune and let the children guess what it is. It is amazing how a few good songs can brighten a rainy day or can calm the most rambunctious child.

REFERENCES

Cohen, Miriam. (1971). Illustrated by Lillian Hoban. **BEST FRIENDS.** New York: Macmillan Publishing Company.

Cohen, Miriam. (1967). Illustrated by Lillian Hoban. **WILL I HAVE A FRIEND?** New York: Macmillan Publishing Company.

Heine, Helme. (1982). **FRIENDS.** New York: Margaret K. McElderry Books.

Hughes, Shirley. (1983). **ALFIE GIVES A HAND.** New York: Lothrop, Lee and Shepard Books.

Marshall, James. (1978). **GEORGE AND MARTHA ONE FINE DAY.** Boston: Houghton Mifflin Company.

Additional References for Friendship

Aliki. (1982). **WE ARE BEST FRIENDS.** New York: Greenwillow Books. *When Robert's best friend Peter moves away, both are unhappy, but they learn that they can make new friends and still remain best friends.*

Iwamura, Kazuo. (1980). **TON AND PON: BIG AND LITTLE.** Scarsdale, NY: Bradbury Press. *Two friends compare the advantages of being big and little and being friends.*

Malone, Nola Langner. (1988). **A HOME.** New York: Bradbury Press. *Molly does not feel comfortable in her new home until she makes friends with a girl named Miranda Marie.*

Marshall, James. (1984). **GEORGE AND MARTHA, BACK IN TOWN.** Boston: Houghton Mifflin Company. *Though their friendship is often tested, George and Martha survive with a sense of humor.*

Wilhelm, Hans. (1986). **LET'S BE FRIENDS AGAIN!** New York: Crown Publishers, Inc. *A boy overcomes his anger and learns to forgive his sister who is also his friend for setting his pet turtle free.*

FEELINGS

Ask Mr. Bear

William's Doll

Where Can It Be?

Some Things Are Different, Some Things Are the Same

My Mama Says There Aren't Any Zombies, Ghosts, Vampires, Creatures, Demons, Monsters, Fiends, Goblins or Things

3
FEELINGS

ASK MR. BEAR

By Marjorie Flack

Danny is trying to find the perfect birthday present for his mother. He consults with several of his animal friends for their suggestions. The hen offers him some eggs; the goose some feathers; and the sheep some wool. But Danny's mother already has those things. Then the cow sends Danny to ask Mr. Bear for a suggestion. The wonderful gift Mr. Bear suggests is one that only Danny can give. The illustrations are clear and charming, and the style is an exemplary one for the era in which it was first published, 1932.

Circle Time Presentation

Have the children name the animals on the cover. As they list the animals, hen, goose, goat and sheep, write them on the chalkboard. Then, as you read the story, point out the names of the animals as they appear. The cow and the bear are not shown on the cover. After the reading, have the children tell you which animals were in the story but not on the cover. Add their names to your list. Discuss why the book is called ASK MR. BEAR. Talk about the significance of the best present to give mother for her birthday, the bear hug.

STORY STRETCHER
For Art: Birthday Cards For Friends

What the children will learn—
To create an inexpensive birthday card

Materials you will need—
Construction paper, tempera paint, straws

What to do—
1. Fold construction paper in half to form a card.

2. Place small drops of tempera paint onto the front of the paper.

3. Give each child a straw, and let her place the straw near the drop of paint, then gently blow air through the straw. The paint will fan out into a nice pattern. Let it dry for a day. This can be the cover for the greeting card. On the following day, have the children write a message on the inside. If it is in scribbles, the teacher can write an interpretation or leave it for the child to interpret. For children who write by inventing spellings, the same process can apply.

Something to think about—
Make birthday cards, or Mother's day cards, or "thinking of you" cards, or party invitations using the same idea. Always place the emphasis on expressing affections, not on bringing gifts. ASK MR. BEAR helps to set the tone.

ANOTHER STORY STRETCHER
For Art: An Envelope For An Ask Mr. Bear Card

What the children will learn—
To decorate envelopes for their special greeting cards

Materials you will need—
Scraps of construction paper, envelopes for younger children, typing paper for older pre-schoolers, paste or glue, scissors, hole punchers (optional), tape

What to do—
1. Show the children some greeting cards you have received. Comment on the cards and the pretty envelopes.

2. Have the children decorate pieces of typing paper or large envelopes for their greeting cards (see the previous activity). The children can cut bits of scrap construction paper, or punch holes in it.

3. Glue the bits and circles of construction paper onto the typing paper in a random design.

4. Allow the collage envelope to dry over night. Then, place the card in the envelope or demonstrate how to fold the typing paper around the card and tape it to hold it in place.

Something to think about—
Cutting and pasting help develop fine muscle control. The design of the envelope engages the children, and the many movements neces-

sary to glue each little piece in place refines the coordination.

For Creative Dramatics: Skip, Hop, Gallop, Trot

What the children will learn—
To practice skipping, hopping, galloping, trotting, running and walking

Materials you will need—
None needed

What to do—
1. Have the children form a circle and at the teacher's signal, hop, then gallop, then trot, then run, then walk.

2. Include a "freeze" direction after each movement.

3. After the children demonstrate these movements, then reread the story and have them move like the characters moved from scene to scene.

Something to think about—
Some young preschoolers will not be able to skip, gallop and trot. However, the activity can still be successful for them when they see the movements and learn there is a special word to describe the actions. When you say skip, gallop and trot, even if the children only vary their rhythm of movement a bit, it will be a beginning step to learning these actions.

For Library Corner: A Mother's Day/Father's Day Poem

What the children will learn—
To recite an easy verse to accompany their Mother's Day or Father's Day cards

Materials you will need—
Typing paper, colorful small markers, glue, scissors

What to do—
1. Make a card using the technique described in the birthday card activity. It becomes a Mother's Day card when the children glue a poem inside the card. The poem could be:

> *"Open your arms and you will see just how sweet I can be. Here's a Big Mother's Day Bear Hug just from me."* (Raines)

2. Provide a copy of the poem for each child. Glue the poem on the inside of each card.

3. Teach the children to recite the poem by saying a phrase at a time and having them echo it after you. Practice the poem several times throughout the day, especially just before the children take their cards home.

Something to think about—
For other occassions, as Father's Day, substitute the phase, "Here's a Big Father's Day Bear Hug," or for Valentine's Day, "Here's a Big I Love You Bear Hug." Often children want to add their own private messages under the pasted one.

For Library Corner, Flannel Board: Mr. Bear And Friends

What the children will learn—
The order of the events in the story of ASK MR. BEAR

Materials you will need—
Flannel board, felt pieces, tracing paper or thin typing paper

What to do—
1. Create flannel board pieces of the animals in ASK MR. BEAR by tracing the hen, goose, sheep, cow and bear. Create the little boy and his mother as well. Simply place tracing paper or thin typing paper over the pictures in the book if you cannot draw them. Remember, flannel board pieces need only have the outline shape, the details are not needed.

2. Place the paper with the traced patterns of the animals over different colored felt. Pin in place.

3. Cut out the pattern and the felt piece at the same time.

4. Danny and his mother can be made in the same way or cut out a picture of a little boy and a mother from a magazine or a catalog and glue them onto some felt to represent the two human characters.

5. Introduce the flannel board pieces after you have read ASK MR. BEAR at circle time.

6. Place a copy of the book and the flannel board pieces in the library corner for the children to use at free play time. After the children have had time to explore the flannel board pieces on their own, introduce the idea of telling the story in the order that it happened.

Something to think about—
Consider changing many other stories into flannel board pieces when they have a few characters and there is an easy sequence. Making flannel board pieces is a task parents or volunteers can do for you. If felt is too expensive for your program, consider making the pieces out of tagboard or poster board and gluing a felt strip onto the back. Old emery boards can also be used on the back. They provide just enough friction to stick the piece onto the flannel. Avoid using velcro which sticks too hard and pulls the flannel away from the board.

3
FEELINGS

WILLIAM'S DOLL

By Charlotte Zolotow

Illustrated by

William Pène du Bois

William would like a doll so that he could play with it like his friend Nancy does with her doll. At the very thought of a little boy with a doll, his brother and his friend call him creep and sissy. William's father buys him a basketball and a train, instead of a doll. William becomes a very good basketball player and he enjoys the train set, but he still longs for a doll. Finally, when William's grandmother comes for a visit, she buys him a doll and explains to his father that having a doll will be good practice for him when he grows up and has a real baby to love. The illustrations which capture the mood of the story are soft sketches, with warm colors, effective use of white space and a blue outline around all the pictures.

Circle Time Presentation

Talk about dolls and stuffed animals and how much we enjoy playing with them. Have several children tell about their favorite doll or stuffed animal at home and at preschool. Read WILLIAM'S DOLL and discuss that playing with dolls is good practice for how to take care of a baby. If some boys tease other boys who want to play with dolls, emphasize that is all right for boys to play with dolls because someday they will be fathers.

STORY STRETCHER
For Art: A Wish Collage

What the children will learn—
To practice cutting out pictures and pasting them onto paper

Materials you will need—
Old catalogs with pictures of toys and books, paper, scissors, glue

What to do—
1. Talk with the children about William's wish for a doll. Ask them to cut out pictures of toys or books that they wish to have. Young children may need help.

2. Let the children paste the pictures onto the paper to create a Wish Collage.

Something to think about—
Young preschoolers need a lot of practice to develop the abilities to use scissors skillfully. Often they become lost in the act of cutting out the pictures and are not as concerned about their finished product. Accept the different skill levels that the children bring to the task.

STORY STRETCHER
For Block Building: A Train Like William's

What the children will learn—
To set up a train and tracks and to make trees for the train

Materials you will need—
Train set, tracks, short limbs or branches of trees, clumps of clay

What to do—
1. Provide assistance if the children who choose block building need help setting up the train.

2. After they have played with the train for a while, introduce the tree limbs and the clay. Have the children recall that in WILLIAM'S DOLL, the father helped William make trees for his train set by pressing clumps of clay onto the floor and then sticking the branches into the clay.

3. Make trees with the children.

Something to think about—
If you do not have a train set available, children enjoy making their own train with the long hollow blocks. You can make a train track by drawing a large figure 8 onto butcher paper. The block and butcher paper train set can be used on the floor or on a table top. The trees can still be added.

STORY STRETCHER
For Housekeeping And Dress-up Corner: Dolls And Stuffed Animals

What the children will learn—
To take care of the dolls and stuffed animals

Materials you will need—
Baby dolls, stuffed animals, bathtubs, soap, towels, high chairs, strollers, baby clothes

What to do—

1. Place the baby dolls out in a prominent place, along with their play accessories.

2. During one of the center times, have bathtubs and warm water available for the children to bathe the dolls.

Something to think about—
Encourage all the children to participate in the bathing of the doll babies. If there are children who show little interest in the dolls or who have difficulty expressing tenderness, start the activity with those children and stay nearby to encourage their play.

For Library Corner: Tape Of William's Doll With Character Voices

What the children will learn—
To distinguish the voices of the different characters of the book

Materials you will need—
Cassette tape and recorder

What to do—

1. Involve several of your family members or friends in producing a tape of WILLIAM'S DOLL. You will need a voice for William, for his brother, the boy next door, his father, the grandmother and you can be the narrator.

2. Rehearse, then tape the reading of WILLIAM'S DOLL.

3. At a circle time, share the tape for the entire class to hear, and then place it at the listening station in the library corner.

Something to think about—
This book is a good book to recommend to parents who are anxious about the roles their children are playing. Point out that children of both sexes often play both mothers and fathers.

For Movement: Playing Basketball

What the children will learn—
To develop muscle coordination

Materials you will need—
Basketballs (the soft kind can also be used), goal

What to do—

1. Set up the basketball and goal outside on the playground. Adjust the height to fit young children.

2. Basketball also can be played inside by placing a plastic wastebasket on a chair.

Something to think about—
For young children, the object is to give them practice in lifting the ball, throwing it and sharing it. Various games can be played with balls, as sitting in a circle on the floor with legs spread wide apart. When the teacher calls out a child's name, the child with the ball must roll it to the other child. It's best to avoid having children choose someone to roll it to because then the popular children are chosen and the others are left out.

WHERE CAN IT BE?

By Ann Jonas

The little girl in the story goes around her house looking for something which is very important to her. The story is the search for this special item with the little girl repeating, "Where can it be?" The child searches through her clothes, toys, cupboard and even in the refrigerator. Finally, the door bell rings, and it is her friend Deborah with the lost possession, her blanket. The pictures are brightly colored, full-page illustrations with the bold print imposed on the picture. The pages are cut so that as the child searches a place in the house, the next page shows the inside. For example, when the little girl decides to search for her blanket in the refrigerator, first we see the outside, and when the page is turned, the inside of the refrigerator is shown.

Circle Time Presentation

Read the book, WHERE CAN IT BE? Ask the children to tell you about their special soft blankets or soft toys that they sleep with to make them feel secure. Some children may have none and some may have several. Discuss how it feels when something special is lost. Reread WHERE CAN IT BE? a second time for the children to enjoy the way the illustrations show the insides of the closets, cupboards, refrigerator, and under the covers of the bed and under the table.

STORY STRETCHER

For Art: Hiding Pictures

What the children will learn—
To fold paper and create a surprise picture inside

Materials you will need—
Construction paper or manilla paper, crayons or markers or chalks

What to do—
1. Show the children several different ways to fold paper to create a hidden area. One way to fold the paper is to bring both ends to the middle. Another is to fold the paper like a greeting card, but not exactly in the middle, leaving about an inch on one side.
2. Show the outside-inside pictures in the book. Have the children draw an outside-inside picture on their folded papers.

Something to think about—
Some younger children who do not relate making the folded pictures to the idea of inside and outside, may draw the inside and outside of a house. Accept each child's level of interpretation. The fun is creating a hidden picture.

ANOTHER STORY STRETCHER

For Art: Soft Pictures

What the children will learn—
To design a picture or collage using cotton balls

Materials you will need—
Construction paper, crayons or markers or chalks, cotton balls, glue

What to do—
1. Remind the children that the little girl in the story liked her blanket so much because it was soft and cuddly.
2. Show the children the cotton balls, feel and stretch them and notice the changes. Then, ask the children to name some other soft, cuddly things.
3. Let the children create their pictures or collages on their own using the cotton balls.
4. Place the pictures or collages flat until the glue can dry to hold the cotton balls in place.

Something to think about—
Sometimes teachers are tempted to provide patterns of soft, cuddly things, as a ditto of a rabbit for the children to color and to stick a cotton ball on the tail. Avoid providing patterns for children's art. It takes away their inventiveness and imagination.

STORY STRETCHER

For Library Corner, Listening Tape: The Missing Blanket

What the children will learn—
To appreciate the illustrator's use of page cuts to show the inside and outside of spaces

Materials you will need—
Cassette tape recording you have made of WHERE CAN IT BE?

What to do—

1. Select one child who has shown little interest in books and read WHERE CAN IT BE? to her. Be sure to point out the illustrator's unique page designs of inside and outside of spaces.

2. Encourage this same child to listen to the book at the listening station.

3. Demonstrate the use of the recorder and earphones so that the child can learn to use them independently.

Something to think about—
WHERE CAN IT BE? is an excellent book for a child who shows little interest in books because the pages are an interesting experience, and the recurring sentence patterns make it easy for the child to follow the text. In addition, this story is about two little girls, and teachers often look for books with girls as the main characters. Many more boys than girls are the main characters in children's books.

STORY STRETCHER

For Mathematics And Manipulatives Center: Five Lost

What the children will learn—
To count five objects in a set and recognize when something is missing

Materials you will need—
Several groups of five things which are easily found in the classroom, as five puzzle pieces, five crayons from a box, five missing snacks, five hiding children

What to do—

1. Play "Where can it be?" with sets of five things. Throughout the day, hide five things. For example, when you place a puzzle out on the table, have five pieces missing. At the art table, have five crayons missing from the box. At circle time, hide five children behind a room divider. At outdoor play time, hide five coats. At snack time, leave five snacks off the table.

2. Then have different children search for the missing objects by going round and asking, "Where can they be?" just like the little girl in the book.

3. Give hints to the child by using the old ploy of "You're getting hot," when the child is close and "You're getting cold," when the child is far away from the hidden objects.

4. After the child finds the missing five, have her count them and return the objects to their proper places.

Something to think about—
For a young preschooler, hide the items or children in obvious places and direct the child to the area where she is to look. For older preschoolers, let them take turns hiding five objects and playing the game throughout the day. Remember to keep the element of surprise going by suddenly having five things missing throughout the day.

STORY STRETCHER

For Music And Movement: Hide The Blanket

What the children will learn—
To listen for musical clues

Materials you will need—
A soft blanket, a cassette or record of music

What to do—

1. Play musical hide and seek by having one child hide the blanket while the others close their eyes. The child must hide the blanket before the teacher stops the music.

2. Another child is chosen to be the seeker and he must find the blanket before the teacher stops the music.

Something to think about—
For a variation, have the children sing a song while the children are hiding and seeking the blanket and keep singing it until the teacher gives a signal, as ringing a bell. This occupies the children who are waiting for their turns.

3
FEELINGS

Some Things Are Different,
Some Things Are the Same
Marya Dantzer-Rosenthal *pictures by Miriam Nerlove*

SOME THINGS ARE
DIFFERENT,
SOME THINGS ARE
THE SAME

By Marya Dantzer-Rosenthal

Illustrated by Miriam Nerlove

Josh and Stephan are friends. When Josh visits Stephan's house, he compares their houses, including the playrooms, the bedrooms, the bathrooms and the family junk room. He compares their kitchens and the snacks they eat. He compares their favorite toys, their pets and even how their families handle arguments about sharing toys. This tone of this warm story is set through Miriam Nerlove's realistic line drawings that are washed with color and pattern. The pictures are large enough to share the book at circle time and rich enough in detail for a child to discover on her own or his own.

Circle Time Presentation

Show the pictures of Josh's and Stephan's houses. Explain that you want the children to listen for what is different when Josh visits Stephan and what is the same. Read the book. Make a chart on the chalkboard or a large piece of paper by drawing a line down the middle of the area. Label one side, "Different," and the other side, "Same." Have the children recall what was different and the same and write their answers on the chart. Reread the book and then add to the chart to make it complete.

STORY STRETCHER

For Art: My House, Your House

What the children will learn—
To compare their homes with their friend's homes

Materials you will need—
Drawing paper, crayons or markers

What to do—
1. Have the children draw "house" pictures. Younger pre-schoolers will recall features of their houses and their friends' without trying to separate like-nesses and differences.

2. After the children have completed their pictures, ask if it is their house or their friend's house. Note their responses on their papers.

3. Older preschoolers can make two drawings, one for the things which are the same, and one for the things which are different.

Something to think about—
If your children have had little experience visiting friends' homes, then encourage comparisons of "My Home" and "My School."

ANOTHER STORY STRETCHER

For Art: Knock, Knock

What the children will learn—
To design a picture (symbol) for their cubbyhole

Materials you will need—
Index cards, tape, crayons or markers, scissors, magazines or catalogs

What to do—
1. Discuss the whale's tail door knocker Josh used when he knocked on Stephan's door.

2. Have the children think of a picture (symbol) which they like. For instance, a favorite toy, a favorite activity, a favorite wild animal or a pet. Some children will choose a teddy bear, others cars, others a wild animal. If this activity is done near the end of the year, let the children choose a favorite storybook character.

3. The children then draw and color or decorate their index card with their own private symbol.

4. Younger preschoolers can cut pictures from magazines or catalogs to make their door knocker.

5. Tape the index cards to each child's cubby.

Something to think about—
Consider designing a door knocker symbol for your classroom door. If your name is one that suggests a symbol, use it. For example, for our names Raines and Canady, the former could be an umbrella, and the latter a can with a "D" painted on.

For Block Building: Bucket Of Blocks

What the children will learn—
To construct houses

Materials you will need—
Small building blocks (a variety of types if possible). plastic bucket, butcher paper, crayon or marker

What to do—
1. In a plastic bucket, collect blocks like the ones which are Josh's favorite toys.

2. Cover a table top with butcher paper.

3. Ask the children to construct a village of houses. Some can be made of plastic blocks and some of wooden logs.

4. Draw lines for streets when several of the village houses are built.

5. Leave the village on display for several days, and the children will devise ways to make it look more like a town.

Something to think about—
Younger preschoolers can add small trucks, cars and buses. Older preschoolers can add construction paper trees, held up by popsicle sticks glued onto them, road signs, street lights and other features.

For Cooking And Snack Time: Snack With Josh And Stephan

What the children will learn—
To prepare nutritious snacks

Materials you will need—
For Josh's snack — muffin mix, milk, mixing bowl, mixing spoon, muffin tins, vegetable oil, liquid measuring cup, oven; for Stephan's snack — variety of types of apples, graham crackers

1. For Josh's snack — prepare the muffin mix with several children helping at each stage of the preparation. Because each package makes only six to eight muffins, use several groups of children and prepare several batches. Those muffins not eaten for this snack time can be frozen for later.

2. For Stephan's snack — involve the children in the washing and paring of the apples. If possible, have a variety of types of apples for the children to taste.

3. After the apples are washed, have a small group of children sit with you at a table and cut the apples. Plastic knives can be used for paring; however, real paring knives can be used under close supervision. Using real knives gives you an opportunity for a safety lesson.

Something to think about—
Construct a rebus chart (see Appendix) of the directions for preparing the muffins. Simply turn the directions on the muffin mix package into rebus directions. For example, when the directions say, "Add one-half a cup of milk," draw a cup half filled with milk. For the directions to mix, draw a bowl with a long-handled mixing spoon. Keep your rebus charts. A variety of types of muffins can be made with the same directions and your rebus chart can fit all of them. If differing amounts of milk or water are added to the mixture in the different recipes, simply place a large "Post-it" note over the old recipe amount, and write the new one on the note. (See the Appendix for an example.)

For Housekeeping And Dress-up Corner: Wagon Ride

What the children will learn—
To practice taking turns and asking for turns

Materials you will need—
A wagon, stuffed animals, dolls, timer

What to do—
1. Discuss how Stephan's mother helped Josh and Stephan take turns pulling the wagon of dolls and stuffed animals. She set a timer and when they heard the "ding," they knew it was time for the other person to have a turn.

2. Model asking for a turn. "Tina, may I have a turn pulling the wagon." Tina replies, "Yes, Damien, when the timer dings, you can have a turn."

3. Limit the number of children who are waiting for turns. For young children who need extra help taking turns, supervision may be necessary. Older preschoolers and kindergartners may be able to negotiate and control the timer on their own. Eventually, we hope the timer will not be necessary.

Something to think about—
For very young children and those who simply take toys without asking, have them practice asking to take turns before you set the timer. Stay nearby to compliment the child. Use the timer in other settings for turn-taking with these children. Do not use it as a punishment, but simply as a means to solve the problem of how long a turn should be before we must share with others.

3
FEELINGS

MY MAMA SAYS THERE AREN'T ANY ZOMBIES GHOSTS, VAMPIRES, CREATURES, DEMONS MONSTERS, FIENDS, GOBLINS , OR THINGS

By Judith Viorst

Illustrated by Kay Chorao

Nick has a vivid imagination, but when he tells Mama about all the creatures he fears, she tells him there is no such thing. Throughout the story, he tries to decide whether to believe Mama or not, after all, she has been wrong before. The story alternates between Nick's descriptions of creatures which his mother says do not exist and his recalling instances when his mother was wrong. In the end, he finally decides that sometimes mamas make mistakes, but "sometimes they don't." Kay Chorao's black and white illustrations of the creatures have just a touch of fright, but clearly are figments of the child's imagination.

Circle Time Presentation

Ask the children if anyone ever tells them, "Oh, it is just your imagination." Read MY MAMA SAYS THERE AREN'T ANY ZOMBIES, GHOSTS, VAMPIRES, CREATURES, DEMONS, MONSTERS, FIENDS, GOBLINS, OR THINGS. Comment on how much fun it is to imagine scary things and then to remember that they are not real. Talk about what children do when they get scared.

STORY STRETCHER

For Art: Brushes And Feathers

What the children will learn—
To use familiar paint and brushes with some new art tools

Materials you will need—
Tempera paint, paper for painting, construction paper, stapler, feathers — if available, scissors, glue

What to do—
1. Review the illustrations in the book and have the children notice the funny ways the artist showed all the imaginary creatures. For instance, the mean-eyed monster scritchy-scratching is really a tree branch. Point out the way the artist used lines to make the textured look in most of the pictures.

2. On a table and at the easel have the paint and paper available. Take a six inch strip of construction paper and fold it into several thicknesses. Secure with a staple. Make a paper brush by cutting one end, making a fringe. Encourage the children to make their own brushes and then to experiment with the brushes.

3. Have feathers available and demonstrate how to float the feather on top of the paint, then gently lift it up and pull the feather lightly across the paper to paint with it.

Something to think about—
After the experimentation and exploration stage, the children can create their own zombies, ghosts, vampires, creatures, demons, monsters, fiends, or goblin paintings using the paper brush or the feathers.

STORY STRETCHER

For Cooking And Snack Time: Cream Cheese And Jelly Sandwiches

What the children will learn—
To make a sandwich for snack

Materials you will need—
Cream cheese, jelly, toaster, wholewheat bread, knives, napkins

What to do—
1. Place the cream cheese and jelly out on the snack table until it reaches room temperature. They are easier to spread when warm.

2. With a small group of children at a time, toast the bread. Place each slice flat on a napkin.

3. Show the children how to spread the softened cream cheese on the bread. Spread the jelly on the second slice of bread.

4. Discuss with the children whether or not they like cream cheese and jelly better than peanut butter and jelly.

Something to think about—
While teachers usually serve snack to all the children at the same time, vary the routine occassionally and have a small group make their snack and enjoy it casually with you. The smaller group may prompt more social conversations.

For Library Corner: Tell Me A Story

What the children will learn—
To recall the story and interpret the pictures

Materials you will need—
Book, and later a tape recorder

What to do—
1.   Invite a child or two who shows little interest in books to come to the library corner with you. Have the child retell MY MAMA SAYS THRE AREN'T ANY ZOMBIES, GHOSTS, VAMPIRES, CREATURES, DEMONS, MONSTERS, FIENDS, GOBLINS, OR THINGS by Judith Viorst or another book of the child's choice. Listen attentively and do not correct the child.

2.   After a few sessions of retelling books, tape record the story retelling and then listen to the tape together.

Something to think about—
Research has shown that we can increase children's interest in books by having them interact more with books. Of course, reading to children in the group and being available to read to individuals and small groups of children in the library corner is something every early childhood educator does routinely. However, some children need additional help to stimulate their interest in books. Story retelling is one way we can encourage their interest.

For Mathematics And Manipulatives Center: Missing Crayons

What the children will learn—
To determine what is missing

Materials you will need—
Boxes of crayons

What to do—
1.   With a small group of children who choose the mathematics and manipulatives center during free play time, discuss that today you are going to look for Nick's missing crayons.

2.   Place crayons in a crayon box or other small box. Have the children arrange their crayons in the same order you have arranged the crayon's in a box you call Nick's box of crayons. For example, red, blue, yellow, purple, green, orange. Continue until all the crayons in each box are in exactly the same order.

3.   Have the children close their eyes and remove one of the crayons from Nick's box. Ask the children to open their eyes, look at their boxes, compare them to yours and decide which crayon is missing.

4.   After a few turns with you removing the crayons, put a child in charge of Nick's box of crayons.

Something to think about—
Vary the activity by having a child add a crayon. For younger children, use fewer crayons. For older preschoolers, use a long pattern of crayons and sometimes take a crayon away and other times add a crayon.

For Music And Movement: Balancing An Egg

What the children will learn—
To walk in time to the music while balancing an egg on a spoon

Materials you will need—
Four to six tablespoons or soup spoons, four to six hard boiled eggs or plastic eggs which will fit in the bowl of the spoon, cassette tape or record of peppy music, tape or record player

What to do—
1.   Talk about Nick's mishap of dropping the grocery bag and seeing the scrambled eggs on his shoes, on a lady's coat and on his mother's slacks.

2.   Hold up an egg and ask the children what they think would happen if you dropped the egg.

3.   Balance the egg on a spoon and walk around the room almost, but not dropping it.

4.   Give the tablespoons to a group of children, place an egg in each of the tablespoons. Start the record or tape and have the children walk around the circle time rug in step with the music.

5.   Then give other children a chance to balance the eggs.

Something to think about—
For older preschoolers, place teams of two childen each on either side of the circle time area. Give the children on one side of the room eggs for their spoons. Have them place their eggs in their spoons and walk to the other side of the room and transfer their eggs from spoon to spoon without touching the eggs.

REFERENCES

Dantzer-Rosenthal, Marya. (1986). Illustrated by Miriam Nerlove. **SOME THINGS ARE DIFFERENT, SOME THINGS ARE THE SAME**. Niles, IL: Albert Whitman and Company.

Flack, Marjorie. (1932). **ASK MR. BEAR**. New York: Macmillan Publishing Company.

Jonas, Ann. (1986). **WHERE CAN IT BE?** New York: Greenwillow Books.

Viorst, Judith. (1973). Illustrated by Kay Chorao. **MY MAMA SAYS THERE AREN'T ANY ZOMBIES, GHOSTS, VAMPIRES, CREATURES, DEMONS, MONSTERS, FIENDS, GOBLINS, OR THINGS**. New York: Aladdin Books, Macmillan Publishing Company.

Zolotow, Charlotte. (1972). Illustrated by William Pène duBois. **WILLIAM'S DOLL**. New York: Harper and Row Publishers.

Additional References for Feelings

Carle, Eric. (1977). **THE GROUCHY LADYBUG**. New York: Thomas Y. Crowell. *A grouchy ladybug who is looking for a fight challenges everyone she meets regardless of their size or strength.*

Keller, Holly. (1984). **GERALDINE'S BLANKET**. New York: Greenwillow Books. *When her mother and father insist that Geraldine get rid of her baby blanket, she finds a new way to keep it with her all the time.*

Kline, Suzy. (1984). Illustrated by Dora Leder. **SHHHH!** Niles, IL: Albert Whitman and Company. *Constantly hushed by all the older people around her, a little girl finally goes outside and lets loose with all the noises she knows.*

Preston, Edna Mitchell. (1969). Illustrated by Rainey Bennett. **THE TEMPER TANTRUM BOOK**. New York: Penguin Puffin Books. *Relates in rhyme several issues between parent and child that provoke temper tantrums.*

Wilhelm, Hans. (1985). **I'LL ALWAYS LOVE YOU**. New York: Crown Publishers, Inc. *A child's sadness at the death of a beloved dog is tempered by the remembrance of saying every night, "I'll always love you."*

GRANDMOTHERS AND GRANDFATHERS

Big Boy, Little Boy
When I Go Visiting
I Dance in My Red Pajamas
Happy Birthday, Sam
Come to the Meadow

BIG BOY, LITTLE BOY

By Betty Jo Stanovich

Illustrated by

Virginia Wright-Frierson

Betty Jo Stanovich has written a warm, inviting story of an afternoon shared by a little boy and his grandmother. He is busy with his activities and she is busy with hers. They meet together in a cozy discussion of how big he has gotten. He tries to remember what he was like when he was little. Virginia Wright-Frierson's watercolor washes over realistic line drawings enrich the text. The mood of the book is captured in the delicate shading of shadows from the afternoon sun. The grandmother is dressed in slacks and a sweater, has gray hair cut in an easy style, not the stereotypical old woman with a long dress, bun on her head, and glasses.

Circle Time Presentation

Talk with the children about their grandmothers, the ones who live far away, the ones who live near them and the ones who live with the children. Ask the children who have grandmothers nearby to tell some of the things they do together. After reading the book, ask the children if they can remember when they were little. Discuss all the things David does well that his grandmother noticed, as building a train from blocks, hammering pegs into a pegboard, drawing a picture and standing on his head. Discuss the things that the children do well. Have children who show less confidence than others tell what they do well.

STORY STRETCHER

For Art: Watercolors

What the children will learn—
To make a watercolor painting

Materials you will need—
Watercolor paper, if none is available, construction paper or butcher paper, small brushes, pencils, watercolors, small bowls for water

What to do—
1. At the art center, allow the children to experiment with watercolors for a few days.

2. Display BIG BOY, LITTLE BOY in a prominent area near their art work.

3. Encourage the children to make line drawings like the illustrators and wash (paint lightly) them over with watercolors. Show several scenes from the book so they will understand the term "wash."

Something to think about—
The watercolor illustrations are so appealing that they will inspir young artists. For the younger preschoolers, experimenting with the

watercolors may be the extent of their involvement. The older preschoolers are more likely to go through the experimenting stage quickly and then draw a picture and enhance it with watercolors. As with all activities, give choices and allow the children who are not interested in relating their art work to scenes from the book to draw or paint whatever they choose.

STORY STRETCHER

For Block Building: Trains, Pegs And Things

What the children will learn—
To create their own block and peg designs

Materials you will need—
Small blocks, pegboard and pegs, peg hammer

What to do—
1. Because the child in the book made a long train with blocks, undoubtedly, many of the children will enjoy making a train like David's. Encourage children who do not usually choose the block corner to spend some time there.

2. David was also proud of hammering pegs into his pegboard. Have the pegs, pegboards and hammers available for children who prefer them.

Something to think about—
An important point to remember is to have these items visible and available for the children to make the connections between what they heard in the book and the manipulatives they see before them.

STORY STRETCHER

For Naptime: David's Nap

What the children will learn—
To relax and get ready for naptime

Materials you will need—
None needed

What to do—

1. Have the children go to their cots for naptime. Follow your usual routine.

2. Reread BIG BOY, LITTLE BOY in your most relaxing, warm tone of voice.

Something to think about—
At the end of the book, David falls asleep in his grandmother's arms. The slowing down of his activity and his grandmother's leads the listeners to a relaxed mood. Rereading this book at naptime is a quiet, comfortable interlude between play and rest.

STORY STRETCHER

For Science And Nature Center: Observing A Bird Feeder

What the children will learn—
To feed and observe the birds

Materials you will need—
Bird feeder, purchased or homemade, seeds, chart tablet or poster board, markers

What to do—

1. Hang a bird feeder just outside your classroom window.

2. If possible, station the science and nature center near the bird feeder.

3. Prepare a chart of the days of the week. Ask the children to tell you about the birds that came to the feeder. What color were they? How big were they? How many came to the feeder? Were seeds added to the feeder today?

Something to think about—
One of the things the grandmother does in BIG BOY, LITTLE BOY is fill the bird feeder with seeds. The simple charting of statements the children make about the birds and the notations of when the seed tray was filled are comparable to a scientist's observations. Continue this project throughout a season if possible, so that the children's observations will become routine.

STORY STRETCHER

For Work Bench: Our Tool Chest

What the children will learn—
The names and uses of common household tools

Materials you will need—
Tool box, hammer, screwdriver, several different sized wrenches, nuts and bolts, large headed screws and nails

What to do—

1. Prepare a tool box for the classroom.

2. Invite the custodian to show his or her tool box to the class.

3. If some of the children's parents use tool boxes in their work, invite the parents to drop by and show their tool boxes.

4. Set up a place to use the tools.

5. Use a vice to secure wood in place for hammering nails into it.

6. To practice with the screw driver, have some of the screws already started into soft wood. Use large head screws, and a large screw driver.

7. A variety of sizes of nuts and bolts make wonderful small muscle manipulatives.

Something to think about—
Many children have little exposure to tools. The work bench supply of tools can be changed every week. Some weeks the hammering may be the activity, using the screwdriver may be another week, and the nuts and bolts still another. Sawing takes extra supervision, but should also be included. Purchase small sized adult saws, rather than the ones in a child's tool chest. They are much safer because they saw easily. Scrap wood can be saved by one of the parents who is a carpenter or a parent who is having something built. Also, the tool box itself is an excellent prop for creative dramatics.

(Adapted from Kathryn Durrett's classroom.)

WHEN I GO VISITING

By Anne and Harlow

Rockwell

WHEN I GO VISITING is a story told by a little boy who spends the night with his grandmother and grandfather in the city. He enjoys the differences in his home and theirs. He explores their seashell collection and enjoys the family photo album. From singing with Grandfather and reading with Grandmother, he delights in the warmth of their affectionate attention. Anne and Harlow Rockwell tell the story with realistic drawings and clear, crisp colors.

Circle Time Presentation

Place a small duffel bag or child's suitcase packed with overnight clothes near you. Discuss visiting grandparents. Have children tell you whether their grandmothers and grandfathers live nearby or far away. Read WHEN I GO VISITING. The children will notice your overnight bag is like the one in the story. Have them guess what might be inside. Compare their guesses with the contents pictured in the book.

STORY STRETCHER

For Art: Class Photo Album

What the children will learn—
To tell about their past, present and future

Materials you will need—
Photo album, drawing paper the size of the pages of the album, instant print camera, film

What to do—
1. Ask the children to bring photographs of themselves when they were babies.

2. Place the pictures in an album and write the children's names underneath. Be sure there are many additional pages in the album.

3. Make instant print photographs of the children in their favorite classroom activity and include them in the album.

4. Have the children draw pictures of themselves all grown-up to put in the album.

Something to think about—
The photograph album can be part of a family unit by having the children bring in pictures of their families. If there are children who do not have pictures of themselves as babies, have the children draw what they think they were like.

Also, the families will appreciate receiving the pictures you took of their children at school.

(Adapted from Janice Elam's clas room.)

STORY STRETCHER

For Housekeeping And Dress-up Corner: Packing For A Visit

What the children will learn—
To pack a bag

Materials you will need—
Duffel bag or child-sized suitcase, toothbrush, toothpaste, comb, pajamas, change of clothing for both girls and boys

What to do—
1. After circle time, move the packed bag over to the housekeeping and dress-up corner.

2. Provide a variety of clothes for both boys and girls so the children may choose which outfits to pack for their visit.

Something to think about—
Young children are accustomed to having their parents or teachers plan for them. Throughout the day, encourage the children to plan and to tell you what they will need ahead of time. For example, when a child is painting at the easel, have him tell you all the supplies needed — a smock or painting shirt, brushes, paints, paper, even a pencil for the teacher to print the child's name.

STORY STRETCHER

For Library Corner: Visiting Grandparents

What the children will learn—
To compose a story about visiting grandparents

Materials you will need—
Chart tablet, markers

What to do—

1. With a small group of children, compose a story about a girl visiting her grandparents.

2. For a few minutes, discuss grandparents and visits to set the stage for composing a story.

3. Have each child dictate a sentence until the story is completed.

4. As you print what the child dictates, say each word. Then, reread the sentence fluently, making it sound like language.

5. At the end of the story, reread it in its entirety.

6. If the children are able to recall their sentences, have each child read her dictation.

Something to think about—
WHEN I GO VISITING is the story of a little boy. We composed the chart story about a little girl to insure that the girls feel connected with the book. Try balancing boys and girls as main characters in books you select. There are many more children's books with boys as main characters than girls.

STORY STRETCHER

For Music And Movement: Singing Ole' Macdonald Had A Farm

What the children will learn—
To sing a favorite standard song of childhood

Materials you will need—
None needed

What to do—

1. In the book, WHEN I GO VISITING, one of the activities the little boy enjoys is singing with his grandfather. If possible, invite a grandfather to sing with the children.

2. After the children know the song well, vary the song by insert-

ing storybook characters' names. For instance, "and on this farm, he had a Donald," or "and on this farm, he had an Eyeore," or "and on this farm, he had a Roo, with a Roo, Roo, here and a Roo, Roo, there."

3. Another variation is to sing "Ole' MacDonald Had a Zoo," and use wild animals and their sounds.

Something to think about—
The the majority of preschool teachers are women. Whenever possible, invite males into your classroom. If there are males working in the center or school in any capacity, invite them in your classroom often.

STORY STRETCHER

For Science And Nature Center: Seeing Seashells

What the children will learn—
To observe similarities and differences in seashells

Materials you will need—
A collection of seashells, magnifying glasses, shoe boxes or plastic tubs for sorting, children's reference books on seashells (optional)

What to do—

1. If your collection of seashells is limited, ask parents to donate them.

2. Let the children help you arrange the seashells appealingly. Have them invite other children to touch and explore the display.

3. Add sorting boxes and let the children decide which seashells are similar in form.

4. Display a children's reference guide to seashells and invite comparisons with the classroom collection and the illustrations.

5. Label some of the children's favorites with the proper name for the shell.

Something to think about—
As a guide for young preschoolers, tape a sand-dollar or another flat shell to one of the boxes. Tape a conical shell to another sorting box. For older preschoolers, avoid organizing for them. Encourage their exploration of differing ways to group and regroup the shells, including ordering by size and shading.

4
GRANDMOTHERS
AND
GRANDFATHERS

I DANCE IN MY RED PAJAMAS

By Edith Thacher Hurd

Illustrated by

Emily Arnold McCully

A mother worries that visiting grandparents will not interest her daughter and that her daughter will be too noisy at their house. However, the child recalls all the busy and noisy reasons she likes visiting her grandparents. The highlight of the evening is when Grandmother plays the piano and the little girl dances in her red pajamas. Emily Arnold McCully's realistic drawings and warm colors express the child's delight in this loving relationship with her grandparents.

Circle Time Presentation

Place some folded pajamas, red if possible, on a chair near you or inside a child-sized suitcase. Read I DANCE IN MY RED PAJAMAS. When you read about the red pajamas, unfold the pajamas or take them from the suitcase. After the reading, ask the children if the book reminds them of any others. They will recall WHEN I GO VISITING in which a little boy was the main character. End circle time by having a little girl take the red pajamas to the housekeeping and dress-up corner.

STORY STRETCHER
For Cooking And Snack Time: Tasting Blueberries

What the children will learn—
To compare the tastes of fresh and frozen blueberries

Materials you will need—
Fresh blueberries and frozen ones, if possible; if fresh ones are not available, let children compare sweetened and unsweetened blueberries

What to do—
1. During free play time, invite a few children to help prepare snack for the class by washing the blueberries, rinsing the frozen ones and spooning out servings.
2. Discuss differences in tastes between fresh and frozen or between sweetened and unsweetened.

Something to think about—
As a snack for another day of the week, bake blueberry muffins or serve blueberry pie like Granny did in I DANCE IN MY RED PAJAMAS.

STORY STRETCHER
For Housekeeping And Dress-up Corner: Setting The Table

What the children will learn—
To set the table with the proper placement of plate, glass, napkin and eating utensils

Materials you will need—
Construction paper, markers, clear contact paper

What to do—
1. Make a place-setting pattern with each child by using a permanent marker and drawing around the plate, the base of the glass, the outline of a folded napkin, the outline of a knife, fork, and spoon. Draw the pattern onto a plastic placemat or onto construction paper and then laminate the construction paper or cover it with clear contact paper.
2. Provide patterned placemats of the place settings for the housekeeping corner on a permanent basis.
3. Use the place-setting placemats at snack time until the children know the arrangement.
4. Send the patterned placemats home with a note encouraging parents to let their children help set the table at home.

Something to think about—
Practice good manners and proper use of utensils at snack time. Whenever possible, use real silverware instead of throw-away plastics. If plastics are used for snacks, at least place real utensils in the housekeeping center.

(Adapted from Mary Legan's classroom.)

For Music And Movement: Dancing In Imaginary Red Pajamas

What the children will learn—
To move in response to the music

Materials you will need—
Piano, if you have none, cassette or record player, recording or tape of waltz music

What to do—

1. Have the children remove shoes so they can glide more easily.

2. Begin by having the children simply sway in response to the music.

3. Then begin moving slowly around the room, stopping periodically to allow the children to listen and sway, then move again.

Something to think about—
If you have a child who has difficulty moving rhythmically, take both of the child's hands, and sway back and forth until he seems to feel the music.

For Water Table: Bubble Bath For The Dolls

What the children will learn—
To bathe a "baby" gently

Materials you will need—
Water table or baby bathtubs, dolls, towels, bath cloths, bubble bath

What to do—

1. With a group of three or four children, pretend one of the dolls is a baby. Bathe the doll, holding it carefully and talking lovingly to the doll.

2. Leave the children to bathe the baby on their own.

Something to think about—
Treat the bathing of the dolls differently than simply playing at the water table. If the children begin water play, remove the dolls and add the water toys. If possible, invite a mother or father to come to class and give their baby a bath.

For Work Bench: Hammer And Saw

What the children will learn—
To handle tools safely

Materials you will need—
Vice, hammer, nails, saw, scrap wood pieces, screws, screw driver, large nuts and bolts

What to do—

1. Set up the work bench with small hand tools. Avoid toy versions and instead choose small real tools. They are safer because they are balanced and designed for actual use.

2. Secure any wood to be sawed with a vice.

3. Limit the number of children at the work bench to one or two at a time.

4. Remind the children that the little girl and Grandpa built a house for Catarina, the cat. However, they can build anything they choose.

Something to think about—
Often, the work bench, like the blocks, becomes the center of attention for the boys. Encourage the girls to work with you. Remind them that the little girl in the story enjoyed building at the work bench with Grandpa. Sometimes, it is fun just to hammer and nail, to thread nuts and bolts and to screw in screws with the screwdriver without making anything special.

4
GRANDMOTHERS
AND
GRANDFATHERS

HAPPY BIRTHDAY, SAM
By Pat Hutchins

Sam expected to be much taller when he awoke on his birthday, but he still couldn't reach his clothes hanging in the closet, the light switch, the sink to brush his teeth or sail his birthday sail boat, until Grandpa came to the rescue with a present. The present, a little chair, came in the mail. When Grandpa came to Sam's birthday party, Sam used the chair to stand on to open the door. Pat Hutchins' illustrations are brightly colored and capture festive scenes from Sam's birthday.

Circle Time Presentation

Ask the children, "Who has grandparents who live far away?" Discuss whether the grandparents come to the children's birthday parties. Discuss how the children know when they have grown. Select one child to try to reach a toy truck you have placed out of reach. Read HAPPY BIRTHDAY, SAM. After the reading, ask the children how the child you selected could reach the truck. They will say, "Stand on a little chair like Sam's in the story." Show the children how to place a chair with the back against the wall for safety. Label one of your safe chairs for reaching, "Sam's Birthday Chair from Grandpa." Let the child who could not reach the toy truck try again and stand safely on Sam's chair to reach it.

S T O R Y S T R E T C H E R
For Art: Gadget Printed Wrapping Paper

What the children will learn—
To decorate wrapping paper

Materials you will need—
Butcher paper or plain paper bags, tape, ribbon, tempera paints, plastic bowls, liquid soap, gadgets such as assorted small blocks, old puzzle pieces, spools or cookie cutters

What to do—
1. Mix thick tempera paints by stirring in some liquid soap instead of the usual amount of water.

2. Place tempera paints in plastic bowls.

3. Demonstrate how to decorate wrapping paper by making gadget prints. Dip items or gadgets (puzzle pieces, spools, small blocks) into paint and press onto paper.

4. Allow printed wrapping paper to dry overnight. If your program is a full-day program, allow about an hour for drying.

Something to think about—
Often children whose grandparents live far away communicate only briefly over the phone and through presents for birthdays and holidays. The children will relate to HAPPY BIRTHDAY, SAM and Grandpa's knowing just the right present.

S T O R Y S T R E T C H E R
For Housekeeping And Dress-up Corner: Hanging Up Clothes

What the children will learn—
To hang up and store clothing properly

Materials you will need—
The usual dress-up clothes, hangers, chest of drawers or shelves

What to do—
1. Place the book, HAPPY BIRTHDAY, SAM, in the housekeeping center and open it to the page where Sam is getting dressed.

2. Hang up some clothes on hangers, but not all of them.

3. Fold some of the clothes nicely and place them in the chest of drawers or shelf, but not all of them.

4. Encourage the children to try hanging up or folding the remainder of the clothes.

5. Just before clean-up time, after the clothes are in disarray, go over to the area and ask the players to make their clothes as neat as Sam's. Assist again with the folding and hanging up of the clothes.

Something to think about—
Encourage the use of the dress-up corner by periodically changing

the dress-up clothes. When children see different items in a new place, they are more likely to practice taking care of them. Also, include both boys' and girls' clothes.

For Library Corner: Story Retelling

What the children will learn—
To recall the sequence of events in HAPPY BIRTHDAY, SAM

Materials you will need—
Book, optional cassette tape recorder and tapes

What to do—
1. Point out the predictability of the story. HAPPY BIRTHDAY, SAM is a good story for retelling because it is a predictable book. The child realizes that all the things Sam could not reach before he receives his present from Grandpa are repeated as "reach-ables" after he has his little chair to stand on.

2. With a small group of children, record the story of HAPPY BIRTHDAY, SAM so they can listen at a later time.

3. Use this opportunity to work with the reluctant story retellers so they will become more confident in their interactions with books.

Something to think about—
Pat Hutchins' illustrations are matched perfectly to the text. Younger preschoolers will rely upon the pictures for their retelling clues. Some older preschoolers will read parts of the book because it is so predictable, or they will "pretend read" by recalling it from memory.

For Mathematics And Manipulatives Center: I Can Reach It

What the children will learn—
To reach things by safely standing on a chair or stool

Materials you will need—
Strips of construction paper, approximately one inch wide, glue or paste, construction paper, safe stepping stool or chair

What to do—
1. Place some objects at three different levels. For instance, put five objects on the table within reach, place three items on a shelf within the reach of some children and put two or three objects out of the reach of all the children but within sight.

2. Let the children take turns reaching for the objects.

3. Rearrange the comparison area and repeat the process, except this time, let the children use "Sam's chair" to reach objects.

Something to think about—
For younger preschoolers, use fewer objects to reach and place them on two levels only. Older preschoolers may enjoy helping to rearrange the comparison area. Try repeating the activity for several days and use different types of objects as all red things, or blue things, or soft things, or transportation things.

For Water Table: Sailing Birthday Boats

What the children will learn—
To make a boat move without touching it

Materials you will need—
Water table, plastic boats, styrofoam or wooden flat pieces, straws, hole puncher, paper, stapler, tape, cardboard pieces

What to do—
1. Have the water table available during free play time. Place some plastic floating toys on the water.

2. Encourage the children to experiment with how they can make the boats move without touching them. They probably will make waves by splashing the water with their hands.

3. Help the children construct small birthday sailboats by using a flat piece of styrofoam or wood about the size of your hand for a base. Cut a piece of paper about the same size for a sail. Punch two holes in the paper. One near the center of the top and one near the center of the bottom. Insert a straw through the holes. Fold the lower end of the plastic straw down onto the base and staple it into place. Push the paper down a bit from the top of the straw until the paper sail billows out. Tape the top of the sail in place.

4. Soon the youngsters will be blowing to create a breeze. Provide the cardboard pieces, and see if the children fan them to make a breeze for the sailboats.

Something to think about—
We often provide answers too quickly. Try setting up a problem, staying available to stimulate thinking, but avoid solving the problem for the children.

4
GRANDMOTHERS
AND
GRANDFATHERS

COME TO THE MEADOW

By Anna Grossnickle Hines

Mattie has discovered spring in the meadow, but she is having difficulty finding anyone to appreciate her discoveries until she invites Grandmother. Then, packing a picnic hamper of bread and cheese, apple juice, bananas and cookies, Mattie and Grandmother set off for the meadow. As they pass by with their loaded picnic basket, Mother stops planting her garden and joins them, Father stops putting up the storm windows and joins them, Sister stops repairing her kite and Brother stops untangling his fishing line. They follow Mattie and Grandmother over to the meadow to see the signs of spring. Hines' line drawings are colored with shades of green and yellow to emphasize spring.

Circle Time Presentation

Ask if anyone has a grandmother living with them. Continue the discussion by exploring some special things a live-in grandmother could do with children. Read COME TO THE MEADOW. Ask the children to tell you how Grandmother helped Mattie to get the entire family to the meadow to see the signs of spring. At another reading, focus on Mattie's discoveries of the signs of spring, "the monkey flowers, tiny buttercups, a toad, a turtle, the field mice tunnels and ice-cream clouds," to name a few.

STORY STRETCHER

For Art: Yellow, Green And Spring

What the children will learn—
To make yellow, green and pastel pictures of spring

Materials you will need—
Shades of green and yellow tempera paints, brown tempera paint, easel, paper, brushes, painting shirts or smocks

What to do—
1. Bring in budding branches and branches with little green leaves, or take a nature walk with the children and make a few cuttings to place in the classroom.
2. Place the branches in a vase near the easel so the children can view them while painting.

Something to think about—
Do not instruct the children to paint the arrangement, but provide tempera paints in the same colors as the budding branches. Simply placing a lovely arrangement of the branches within view of the painters will inspire them.

STORY STRETCHER

For Cooking and Snack Time: No Cooking Picnic

What the children will learn—
To prepare a "no-cooking" picnic

Materials you will need—
Bread, cheese, apple juice, bananas, cookies, plates, napkins, picnic basket, tablecloth

What to do—
1. Have some children assist you in packing a picnic lunch like Mattie's and Grandmother's.
2. Since all these items would be too much for one snack, cut the sandwiches and bananas into bite-sized pieces. Plan for a cup of juice and a whole cookie per child.
3. Serve snack outside on a picnic tablecloth.

Something to think about—
Have the picnic basket nearby for any beautiful day when snacking outside would be a treat. The spontaneity of a picnic cheers teachers and children.

STORY STRETCHER

For Housekeeping And Dress-up Corner: Pretend Picnicking

What the children will learn—
To role-play the preparations for a picnic

Materials you will need—
Picnic basket, plates, plastic glasses, eating utensils, checkered tablecloth and napkins, plastic models of fruits and other food items

What to do—
1. Simply supply the props for the role-playing.
2. Watch the children role-play a COME TO THE MEADOW picnic or their own family picnics.

3. Assist children who may have difficulty getting into an on-going play group by pretending to bring in a special guest or a cousin who stopped by.

Something to think about—
Consider having the picnic basket with you as you read COME TO THE MEADOW. If possible, manage some of the other props associated with the story as Mother's gardening hat and gloves, Dad's work gloves, Brother's fishing pole and Sister's mended kite. Rereading the story with the props brings the story alive again.

STORY STRETCHER

For Music And Movement: Ice Cream Clouds

What the children will learn—
To observe the clouds

Materials you will need—
Blankets, tape player with cassette of slow, waltz music

What to do—
1. On a bright day with fluffy clouds, reread Mattie's description of the ice cream clouds.

2. Take blankets outside onto the playground area. If the ground is still cold, stretch out on the blankets, if not, on the grass. Watch the clouds.

3. Point out some changing ones and what they make you think of, a rabbit, an elephant, Mattie's ice cream clouds.

4. After cloud watching for a while, when the imagining dies down, put on the music and have the children listen and relax as they watch the fluffy clouds floating by.

Something to think about—
Time to wonder, to gaze in amazement, to discover on one's own are precious experiences which our hurried children often miss. Help children to grow in their love and appreciation of nature, and do not hurry exploration.

STORY STRETCHER

For Science And Nature Center: Cloud Watching And Earth Watching

What the children will learn—
To recognize the signs of spring

Materials you will need—
Note-pad, pencil

What to do—
1. Read the passages from COME TO THE MEADOW which describe the signs of spring which Mattie saw, including how the clouds look different.

2. Talk about what close observation means.

3. Go outside to the playground "meadow" or an open field within walking distance.

4. Encourage both cloud watching and earth watching for signs of spring.

5. Ask the aide and volunteers to take notes of the comments the children make while exploring their "meadow" and making close observations.

6. Return to the classroom and ask the children to recall the signs of spring they saw in their meadow.

7. Have the aide or volunteers check their notes and read some of the things the children said were signs of spring when they were outside exploring and observing.

Something to think about—
Your own curiosity about nature and your appreciation of living things will inspire the children. Be prepared to get down on your hands and knees to search for the insect tunnel, and don't be squeamish about the wiggly worms and strange looking bugs.

(Adapted from Ruth Plaster's classroom.)

REFERENCES

Hines, Anna Grossnickle. (1984). **COME TO THE MEADOW.** New York: Clarion Books.

Hurd, Edith Thacher. (1982). Illustrated by Emily Arnold McCully. **I DANCE IN MY RED PAJAMAS**. New York: Harper and Row, Publishers.

Hutchins, Pat. (1978). **HAPPY BIRTHDAY, SAM**. New York: Greenwillow Books.

Rockwell, Anne & Rockwell, Harlow. (1984). **WHEN I GO VISITING**. New York: Macmillan Publishing Company.

Stanovich, Betty Jo. (1984). Illustrated by Virginia Wright-Frierson. **BIG BOY, LITTLE BOY**. New York: Lothrop, Lee and Shepard Books.

Additional References for Grandmothers and Grandfathers

Mayer, Mercer. (1985). **JUST GRANDPA AND ME.** New York: A Golden Book. *One of Mayer's "little critters" characters goes shopping for a suit with his grandfather with hilarious results.*

dePaola, Tomie. (1981). **NOW ONE FOOT, NOW THE OTHER.** New York: G.P. Putnam's Sons. *When his grandfather suffers a stroke, Bobby teaches him to walk, just as his grandfather had once taught him.*

Douglass, Barbara. (1982). Illustrated by Patience Brewster. **GOOD AS NEW.** New York: Lothrop, Lee and Shepard Books. *When Grady's young cousin ruins his teddy bear, Grandpa fixes his toy just like he fixes everything else around the house.*

Kroll, Steven. (1977). Illustrated by Lady McCrady. **IF I COULD BE MY GRANDMOTHER.** New York: Pantheon Books. *A young girl describes all that she would do if she were her grandmother.*

Williams, Vera B. (1982). **A CHAIR FOR MY MOTHER.** New York: Greenwillow Books. *A child, her waitress mother and her grandmother save dimes to buy a comfortable armchair after all their furniture is lost in a fire.*

BEDTIME/NAPTIME

Goodnight Moon
There's An Alligator Under My Bed
No Jumping on the Bed
Grandfather Twilight
Night in the Country

GOODNIGHT MOON

By Margaret Wise Brown

This classic book is the story of a little rabbit who is having difficulty going to sleep and begins a ritual of saying goodnight to everyone and everything in sight. The goodnights even extend to the moon shining in the window. Clement Hurd's bright colors on facing pages and his alternate black and white pages lull the viewer into the mood of the story. The dying flame in the fireplace and the gradually darkening room assure the listener and the viewer that indeed the little rabbit finally will go to sleep.

Circle Time Presentation

Ask the children who they say goodnight to before they go to bed. After a few brief responses, have the children listen and try to remember all the things the little bunny says goodnight to in GOODNIGHT MOON. After the reading, have the children recall the list of things the bunny told goodnight. (If desired, write each on a chalkboard or a chart tablet. When there is a pause in the listing, reread the list.) Complete the circle time by having the children tell you things they would like to say goodnight to in their classroom when they take a nap today. (Write their list beside the bunny's list.)

STORY STRETCHER

For Art: Bunny's Black And White Pictures

What the children will learn—
To make black and white pictures

Materials you will need—
Black construction paper, white and colored chalk, damp sponge, bowl of water

What to do—
1. Call the children's attention to the way the illustrator of GOODNIGHT MOON showed us the bunny was falling asleep. He alternated black and white pages with the colorful ones. Have the children close their eyes and notice the color is gone. Call attention to the fact that the little bunny's room was dark, but he still could see the outlines of things in his room.

2. Place the art supplies on the table in the art center.

3. Demonstrate how to dampen the paper and make the chalk lines look different when the paper is wet.

4. Allow much time for exploration. Suggest that some children draw scenes from the little bunny's room or from their own classroom for a GOODNIGHT PRESCHOOL bulletin board.

Something to think about—
Allow young preschoolers to experiment with the difference between using chalk on wet and dry construction paper.

STORY STRETCHER

For Housekeeping And Dress-up Corner: Bunny's Bedroom

What the children will learn—
To role-play naptime routines

Materials you will need—
The bedroom area of the housekeeping corner with bed, dolls, blankets, stuffed animals

What to do—
1. Turn the housekeeping corner bedroom area into a place for the dolls and stuffed animals to nap.

2. Discuss with the children who choose that center during free play how they can make this a good nap area.

3. Encourage any child who is having difficulty napping to come to the housekeeping corner and help make the nap area.

4. Use the baby blankets and soft pillows to create a comfortable spot.

Something to think about—
If the children in your program must nap in the classroom, place the cot of the child who is having difficulty napping near the napping area he created for the dolls and the stuffed animals. Make sure the cot is visible so you also can reassure the child with a smile. Your nearness is comforting.

For Library Corner : Hey, Diddle, Diddle

What the children will learn—
To recite "Hey, Diddle, Diddle"

Materials you will need—
A copy of a nursery rhyme book, chart tablet or poster board, markers

What to do—

1. Create a poster of "Hey, Diddle, Diddle."

2. For the children who come to the library corner during free play time, point out to them that in GOODNIGHT MOON there was a picture on the little bunny's bedroom wall of a cow jumping over the moon. They will think that is funny.

3. Then, read to them the nursery rhyme you have printed on a chart tablet or poster board, "Hey, diddle, diddle, the cat and the fiddle, and the cow jumped over the moon." Print the entire rhyme.

4. Teach them the nursery rhyme and let them enjoy the absurdity of a cow jumping over the moon and a cat playing a fiddle.

5. Let the children decorate the poster with their own drawings.

6. Leave the nursery rhyme poster in the library corner as a reminder of the rhyme they learned.

Something to think about—
Many of the story stretchers can be used for a small group of children or for the entire class. After hearing the children reciting the rhyme, others will want to learn it.

(Adapted from Kathy Carter's classroom.)

For Library Corner: Rhyming Words

What the children will learn—
To pair rhyming words heard in GOODNIGHT MOON

Materials you will need—
None needed

What to do—

1. For the children who visit the library corner, reread the section of GOODNIGHT MOON where the little bunny is trying to fall asleep and he begins saying rhyming words, "kittens and mittens, toyhouse and mouse, mush and hush, room and moon, bears and chairs, clocks and socks, house and mouse, brush and mush, air and everywhere."

2. After reading the rhyming section once, pause and let the children supply the words which rhyme.

Something to think about—
The rhyming exercise in the library corner also can be a follow-up activity in another circle time. Some of the children who enjoy rhyming words may not choose the library corner because they are attracted to other activities. Reading to the children in small groups allows them to enjoy the pictures at a more intimate distance than in a large circle. Observe the children during free play, and if an opportunity arises, ask a few children to come to the library. Afterwards, they can return to the activity of their choice .

For Naptime : Saying Goodnight

What the children will learn—
To prepare for naptime

Materials you will need—
None needed

What to do—

1. Help the children remember the things Bunny said goodnight to. Then, have them to whisper to you what they want to say goodnight to in their classroom at naptime.

2. Let each child say goodnight to one thing by going over and gently touching the object and whispering, "Goodnight."

3. Have the children tiptoe back to their cots.

4. Darken the room a bit and sit within view of any child who seems to need reassurance.

5. Reread GOODNIGHT MOON in your most relaxing and warm voice.

Something to think about—
Young children who have difficulty napping need clear expectations that regardless of whether they are sleepy or not, naptime will be a rest time with everyone on their cots. However, if you play some relaxing music or read a relaxing book, then the children who are having difficulty falling asleep at least have something to occupy their thoughts.

THERE'S AN ALLIGATOR UNDER MY BED

written and illustrated by MERCER MAYER

THERE'S AN ALLIGATOR UNDER MY BED

By Mercer Mayer

A little boy imagines an alligator under his bed, but his parents don't believe him. Determined to get the alligator out of his room, the child invents an elaborate trail of alligator bait leading to the garage where he will close the door behind the creature. Safe at last, the little boy now worries that his father may be in danger the next morning when he goes to get in the car. Finally, he decides to write a warning sign. Mercer Mayer's illustrations are witty and sensitive. His drawings of the facial expressions of the little boy translate the humor and imagined fears most effectively.

Circle Time Presentation

Children enjoy the intrigue of what will happen, the eventual success of the child tricking the alligator and the resolution of the nightmare. Read with anticipation in your voice, wait for the listeners' reactions to his success and pretend the story ends with the little boy safely in his bed. Some children may even applaud when the boy traps the alligator in the garage. Close the book, then say, "But wait, there's more." Open the book and read the final sequence about the warning sign.

STORY STRETCHER

For Art: Alligator Paw Prints

What the children will learn—
To print a pattern of paw tracks

Materials you will need—
Green construction paper, thick tempera paint, small plastic animals and plastic dinosaurs, plastic trays (or use meat trays from the grocery) as containers for the paint

What to do—
1. For each child, cut a large paw print of green construction paper. Tell the children these are the alligator's footprints.

2. Fill plastic trays or meat trays with tempera paint.

3. Stand a plastic animal in each color of paint.

4. Show the children how to make paw prints of each animal by taking it from the paint tray and standing it on the large alligator paw print.

5. Instruct the children to return the plastic animal to the same color paint it came from.

6. When the prints are dry, display them as an alligator trail and end the trail with a picture of an alligator and a warning sign just as the little boy did in THERE'S AN ALLIGATOR UNDER MY BED.

Something to think about—
For older children who are adept at cutting, allow them to draw and cut out their own paw print. Also, if you are using plastic dinosaurs, talk about the similarities between the alligator and the ancient reptilian dinosaurs.

STORY STRETCHER

For Cooking and Snack Time: Alligator Bait Salad

What the children will learn—
To prepare and eat salad

Materials you will need—
A variety of vegetables seen on the stairs as the trail for the alligator to follow, tomatoes, squash, lettuce, broccoli, carrots, corn, peas, or make up your own alligator bait salad with your own ingredients; vegetable brushes, peelers, knives, cutting boards, large salad bowls, large serving fork and spoon, salad bowls, forks, napkins

What to do—
1. Bring in a grocery bag filled with the vegetables and tell the children it is for alligator bait.

2. Have a small groups of children work with you to clean the vegetables and others help cut the ingredients.

3. At snack time or lunch time, place a large bowl of salad on each table. Tell the children that snack today is "alligator bait salad."

4. Teach the children how to serve themselves salad. Place the large salad bowl in front of the child, have the child stand up and use the salad serving spoon and fork, one in each hand. You guide the salad bowl under the serving utensils.

Something to think about—
Use hinged serving utensils for younger preschoolers.

For Library Corner: Warning, Story Inside

What the children will learn—
To look for different forms of the story

Materials you will need—
Tape, paper, crayons, tape recorder, cassette tapes, chart tablet, markers, flannel board and pieces for the bed, alligator, refrigerator, fruits, vegetables, soda, cookies, car, sign

What to do—
1. Ask several children to draw alligator pictures, tape them over the tape recorder, on the front of a chart tablet, over the flannel board and on the cover of the book.
2. Make warning signs which read, "Warning, Story Inside." Tape the signs under the alligator pictures for each story form.
3. Have some children assist you in creating a listening tape of THERE'S AN ALLIGATOR UNDER MY BED. The children can make the page turning signals by saying, "Uh, OH!" or by saying, "Hurray," depending on what the scene on the page dictates.
4. Create the flannel board pieces and let the children retell the story. Leave your "Warning, Story Inside!" sign over the package of pieces where the flannel board story is stored.

Something to think about—
Continue the "Warning, Story Inside" signs with characters and activities from other favorite children's books.

For Mathematics And Manipulatives Center: The Alligator Ate It!

What the children will learn—
To create sets and to observe changes

Materials you will need—
Plastic vegetables and fruits from the housekeeping corner, cookies, bag, three trays, large sheet of construction paper

What to do—
1. Place all the items at random on the table.
2. Have children create sets of the items by placing objects that go together on separate trays. One for the fruits, one for the vegetables and one for the cookies.
3. Then have the children close their eyes or place a sheet of construction paper in front of one of the trays. Remove a piece of fruit or a vegetable, lift the paper and say, "What did the alligator eat?"
4. For the cookie tray, have the children count how many cookies there are. When you lift the paper ask, "How many cookies did the alligator eat?" Afterwards, let the children be alligators and eat the cookies.

Something to think about—
Younger preschoolers can associate the cookies by one-to-one correspondence. Say, "One for Michelle, one for Tina, one for Brian and one for Damien." Then when the cookies are uncovered they redo the one-to-one association and decide whose cookie the alligator ate. Be sure there are enough cookies for everyone.

For Music And Movement: Balance Beams

What the children will learn—
To practice balancing on a low beam

Materials you will need—
Low balance beams, the type that are just a few inches from the floor, or masking tape, cassette or record player, music

What to do—
1. Show the illustration of the little boy walking up a board balanced from the floor to his bed to avoid the alligator he imagined was lurking there.
2. Ask some children to help you set up the balance beam, or walking boards, or make a balance strip of masking tape.
3. Let the children practice walking and balancing on the beam. After a few practice sessions, add music to the balancing. When the music starts, the balancer performs by walking back and forth on the beam and continues until the music stops.

Something to think about—
In some supply catalogs, the low balance beams are also called walking boards. As an alternative use several strips of wide masking tape to look like a balance beam. Have children who lack good balance help you set up the boards or the tape strip. Let these children practice a few extra times before involving others. Often the children with more physical prowess are eager to demonstrate their skills, and the children who need the extra practice do not assert themselves.

NO JUMPING ON THE BED

By Tedd Arnold

Walter's father warned him a million times, "No jumping on the bed!" Walter jumped on the bed one time too many, and it went crashing down through the floors of his building. When he opened his eyes and realized he was dreaming, he said, "No more jumping on the bed." Tedd Arnold's full color pictures capture the humourous expressions, and the astonishing surprises as Walter falls through each floor will turn the preschoolers into hilarious gigglers.

Circle Time Presentation

Ask the children if their parents ever tell them not to jump on the bed. Read what Walter's father said about jumping on the bed and then continue reading the entire story. Expect a lot of laughs. The children will want you to reread the story and will enjoy examining the funny illustrations more closely.

STORY STRETCHER

For Art: Funny Falling Pictures

What the children will learn—
To express humor in their artwork

Materials you will need—
Easel, tempera paints, paper, brushes, drawing paper, crayons, construction paper

What to do—

1. Discuss the funny pictures from NO JUMPING ON THE BED!

2. Point out the ways Tedd Arnold shows us that Walter was falling. His feet are up in the air, there is a torn hole in the floor and then one in the ceiling, he is landing "splat" on the building blocks, he is in midair with all the things floating around him from each floor of the apartment building.

3. Staple two pieces of construction paper together along the left hand side of the artwork, then tear a hole in the construction paper cover to represent the "torn ceiling hole."

Something to think about—
Some children may enjoy cutting out pictures from magazines and catalogs to paste on their drawings to show all the furniture and toys floating around in midair as Walter is falling. Always provide a variety of art options for children.

The variety supports their creative options.

STORY STRETCHER

For Block Building: Building Dream Houses

What the children will learn—
To make and sustain a large building project

Materials you will need—
Large hollow building blocks, small manipulative building blocks

What to do—

1. Show Tedd Arnold's illustration of Patty and Natty's dream house they worked on for three days.

2. Ask the children to build different houses out of as many different blocks as they can.

3. Leave the blocks set up for three days, if possible. Then let the builders become "Walters" and tear them done. Have two rules. One is that the house must be completely built before Walter can "fall through the ceiling on it," and, two, that only the people who built the house can tear it down.

Something to think about—
Extend the activity by having children create apartment buildings with several floors from their blocks. They can look at the backs of two story doll houses and see how they might be constructed inside. Also, shoe boxes can be stacked and held together with pipe cleaners to create different floors. Children with good fine motor skills may build entire towns or city blocks. Tiny toy people can be added. Landscape around the apartment buildings by standing twigs in playdough for trees. Place the buildings on butcher paper with streets marked for cars and buses.

For Library Corner: Listening For Cracking Ceiling

What the children will learn—
To make the sound effect at the appropriate cue

Materials you will need—
Kindling or balsa wood or twigs, recorder, cassette tapes

What to do—
1. Ask the children what the sound might be like when Walter was crashing through the ceiling.

2. Reread NO JUMPING ON THE BED! and have the children break a piece of kindling wood or twigs each time Walter falls through a different floor of the apartment building. Practice and then record your reading and their breaking the twigs as sound effects.

3. Display the tape, the book and some of the "falling" pictures to create an inviting listening center.

Something to think about—
Make another tape where the sound effects are different. Ask the children to think of what they would need for each picture, as water splashing for Walter falling in the aquarium, blocks falling, pots and pans falling when Aunt Batty is unpacking. Another tape could be made with expressive children providing the sound effects verbally, as "Crash, bam, bang."

For Mathematics And Manipulatives Center: Counting Walter's Floors

What the children will learn—
To count events, people, toys they hear mentioned in a funny story

Materials you will need—
Paper, crayons

What to do—
1. Tell children about using tally marks. Use a concrete example and demonstrate with paper and pencil. For instance, if you wanted to count and remember how many children are sitting at the mathematics table, you could make a tally mark for each child and count the marks.

2. Ask each child to listen as you read the story and each time Walter falls through a different floor to make a mark on the tally sheet and then when the story is over, count the tally marks and see how many floors in the apartment building Walter fell through.

3. Continue the activity by rereading the story and this time have children listen for something different. They can make a tally mark each time they hear a person's name. They can make a mark for the different rooms, for the toys mentioned, or even for all the surprises they hear.

Something to think about—
Complicate or simplify the listening task depending on the experiences and the abilities of the children. Show them how you use tally marks to keep track of attendance, snacks and who completed special art projects and other classroom activities.

For Music And Movement: Ten Little Monkeys Jumping On The Bed

What the children will learn—
To sing this favorite childhood counting song

Materials you will need—
None needed

What to do—
1. Teach the children the tune and hand motions. "Ten little monkeys, jumping on the bed, one fell down and broke his head, called for the doctor and the doctor said, 'That's what you get for jumping on the bed.' Nine little monkeys, jumping on the bed, one fell down and broke his head, called for the doctor and the doctor said, 'That's what you get for jumping on the bed.'" Continue the counting song until there are no little monkeys jumping on the bed.

2. Improvise motions holding up fingers for the number of monkeys, for the falling, holding head, dialing the phone to call the doctor, and pointing finger for the doctor talking.

3. Resing the song and substitute, "Ten little Walters" and called for his father and his father said, "That's what you get for jumping on the bed."

Something to think about—
For younger children, shorten the song and use five little monkeys. If the song is familiar to the children, tell them you are going to try to trick them and call out the wrong number. When you are supposed to count down to nine, say four instead. Continue the tricky counting and let the children correct you.

GRANDFATHER TWILIGHT

By Barbara Berger

This gentle story is the tale of how Grandfather Twilight, a kindly old man with long white hair and a beard, brings twilight at the end of every day. The old man takes a glowing pearl from an endless strand of pearls locked away in an old chest. He holds the pearl carefully in his hand and walks through the woods bringing twilight along his path. The pearl grows in his hand, and when he reaches the ocean it rises up into the silent sky. Then, the old man returns to his cottage in the woods and lies down to sleep. Barbara Berger spins the quiet spell of the story with very few words, but with pages filled with transfused pastel drawings to create the mood. The luminous magic of the pearl lulls the listener and the viewer into a sleepy trance.

Circle Time Presentation

Read GRANDFATHER TWILIGHT at a morning circle time, and reread it just before naptime. At circle time, go back through the book and let the children tell you how each scene made them feel. Recall all the animals they saw in the pictures, the dog who walked with Grandfather Twilight, the little bird, the cat and the rabbits. Have them think of other animals that might be hidden in the forest. Ask the children to close their eyes and visualize the pictures as you reread the story.

S T O R Y   S T R E T C H E R

For Art: Pastel Twilight Pictures

What the children will learn—
To shade their drawings using pastel chalks

Materials you will need—
Light colored construction paper, white and pastel chalks, wet sponge, white construction paper circles about the size of a dime, nickel or quarter, glue

What to do—
1. Show the children several scenes from GRANDFATHER TWILIGHT where he is changing the way the world looks as he walks trailing the light from the pearl behind him.

2. Let the children select a piece of construction paper and then a pearl (construction paper circle), one per child.

3. Have the children glue their pearls on their pictures.

4. Dampen the construction paper by going over it lightly with the wet sponge.

5. Ask the children to create GRANDFATHER TWILIGHT pictures or any picture they would like using the pearl and the pastel chalks.

Something to think about—
For older preschoolers, you can have the children draw their own pearls without gluing on the pearl circles. Younger preschoolers may enjoy creating a collage of pearl circles rather than drawing a twilight picture. If you have pictures of beautiful sunsets, display them along with the book of GRANDFATHER TWILIGHT.

S T O R Y   S T R E T C H E R

For Library Corner: Composing A Sequel

What the children will learn—
To make up a story which is a sequel to GRANDFATHER TWILIGHT

Materials you will need—
Chart tablet, marker, drawing paper, crayons

What to do—
1. Review the scenes in GRANDFATHER TWILIGHT.

2. Ask the children to imagine that instead of a grandfather, there was a grandmother and instead of the time being twilight, it was just before sunrise. What kind of jewel might Grandmother Sunrise get from the chest? Some child will say a golden one.

3. Then have the children pretend that Grandmother Sunrise is waking up the world with her golden bead.

4. Ask the children to draw a picture of Grandmother Sunrise. After the drawing is completed, have the children tell you their stories of Grandmother Sunrise. Write the stories they dictate on the chart tablet.

5. Glue each child's picture at the top of his chart tablet page.

Something to think about—
Reread the chart tablet stories whenever you are in the library corner reading with children. As they become more comfortable storytellers, the length and complexity of their stories will increase. The young preschoolers can tell you captions to go with their drawings or dictate sentences for the three sets of wordless pages in GRANDFATHER TWILIGHT.

STORY STRETCHER

For Mathematics And Manipulatives Center: Stringing Pretend Pearls

What the children will learn—
To create a pattern with the beads

Materials you will need—
Beads of varying sizes, shoelaces or yarn

What to do—
1. Discuss how Grandfather Twilight took a pearl from an endless string of pearls.

2. Ask the children how we might create a long string of beads like Grandfather's Twilight's pearls.

3. Give each child some beads. Have him create a pattern with the beads, completely filling his string.

4. Tie the strings together end to end and see how long they are. Decide if these are enough strings of pearls or whether the group wants to make it even longer.

Something to think about—
To count the number of days in the month string thirty or thirty-one beads on a string. Each day during circle time, a child can take a bead from the string and place it in a treasure chest like Grandfather Twilight's. The children can then count the beads on the string to see how many days are left in the month, or they can count the beads in the chest to know how many days have passed in the month.

STORY STRETCHER

For Music And Movement: Pass The Pearl

What the children will learn—
To follow the rules of a game

Materials you will need—
Quiet, restful music, record player or cassette player, playdough pearl

What to do—
1. Have the children sit in a circle.

2. Darken the room and pretend it is nearly twilight time.

3. Explain the rules of the game in a hushed tone.

4. Play the music at a low volume. Have the children place their hands behind their backs and close their eyes. You be Grandfather Twilight and put the pearl in someone's hands. Stop the music and call on someone to guess who has the pearl. It doen't matter if the child is right or wrong. After the child guesses, the one with the pearl says, "I'm Grandfather Twilight." The child who is Grandfather Twilight now goes around the circle while the music is playing and drops the pearl in someone's hand. Grandfather Twilight keeps pretending to drop the pearl until the music stops. You stop the music and call on someone to guess. The new Grandfather Twilight then begins the process all over again.

Something to think about—
After the children have played the Grandfather Twilight game, have them play the game with a golden bead for Grandmother Sunrise

based on their stories in the library corner.

STORY STRETCHER

For Science And Nature Center: Oysters And Pearls

What the children will learn—
To recognize oyster shells and know pearls come from oysters

Materials you will need—
Oyster shells, children's reference book on food from the sea, Costume jewelry pearl, magnifying glasses

What to do—
1. Discuss oysters, where they live and how they are caught from the ocean. Show the oyster shells. Use live oysters if possible.

2. Tell how the pearl is created from a tiny grain of sand.

3. Hide a costume jewelry pearl inside or under an oyster shell.

4. Have the children find the pearl and then examine the inside and outside of the oyster shell. Use the magnifying glasses and look at the inside of the shell. Compare their descriptions of the inside of the shell to how a pearl looks.

Something to think about—
Children who live near the seacoast may be familiar with a variety of shellfish; however youngsters from other areas of the country may know little about them. Whenever possible, create a display of many kinds of shells, or living shellfish, and extend the real display with pictures and reference books.

(Adapted from Korey Powell's classroom.)

NIGHT IN THE COUNTRY

By Cynthia Rylant

Illustrated by Mary Szilagyi

"There is no night so dark, so black as night in the country," and with this opening line the mood is set for the night observer to see and hear. The sights and sounds of the night carry the visitor through the countryside. In addition to Cynthia Rylant's sensitive wording, Mary Szilagyi's dark, but not scary, illustrations make the listener and viewer want to linger in the scene and enjoy the almost silence and the almost stillness of a country night. The drawings look like layered crayons with just enough of the darkness scrapped away to expose an animal or a scene from the night.

Circle Time Presentation

Talk with the children about their experiences visiting or living on a farm. Have the children try to recall what night was like in the countryside. Read NIGHT IN THE COUNTRY. Discuss the night sounds they would like to hear if they were living on a farm.

STORY STRETCHER
For Art: Crayon Etching

What the children will learn—
To etch a design in multiple layers of colors

Materials you will need—
Crayons, paper, plastic knives

What to do—
1. Show the children Mary Szilagyi's illustration of NIGHT IN THE COUNTRY. Discuss the way she used colors on top of colors. See if they can find any places where it looks like the crayons are scraped away. Look at the lines on the tree and the raccoon.

2. Have the children completely cover their papers with different colors of crayon. To speed the process along, have them place the crayons sideways and color using the entire length of the crayon. Encourage them to use many different colors.

3. Then using black or another dark color, deep purple or blue, color over the entire first layer of crayons.

4. Take the plastic knife and demonstrate how to use it to etch out a pattern in the crayons. When a line is scraped, it exposes the colors underneath.

5. Leave the book in the art area for continued inspiration of crayon etchings.

Something to think about—
Younger preschoolers can create a similar effect using fingerpaints and multiple colors. Their fingers create the etching. Avoid using too many colors or the paints turn muddy.

STORY STRETCHER
For Cooking And Snack Time: Country Apples

What the children will learn—
The names and tastes of different kinds of apples

Materials you will need—
Golden delicious apples, red delicious apples, green cooking apples, knives, cutting boards, baskets

What to do—
1. If possible, let the children help you shop for the apples. If not, bring the apples to the classroom in a grocery bag. Let interested children help you wash the apples.

2. Have other children arrange a variety of apples in a basket for each snack table.

3. During snack, cut slices from the kind of apple the child says he likes best. Then ask him to try at least one other kind and to tell you how it tastes.

4. Remember to use descriptive words as sweet, tart, tangy.

Something to think about—
You can extend the apple tasting snack by polling the children and deciding which apple is the class favorite. You also can do a simple mathematical graph by having the child select a strip of construction paper the same color as the type of apple he likes. Each child then glues the strips onto a poster and the class can compare visually or count and decide what their

favorite flavor of apple is. This graph is both a pre-number and a numerical graph.

(Adapted from an activity in Penny Clem's classroom.)

For Listening Station: A Quiet Retreat

What the children will learn—
To appreciate a quiet story

Materials you will need—
Tape recorder, cassette tape

What to do—

1. At a quiet interlude in the activity in the library corner, ask children to tell you how different books make them feel.

2. Show the children NIGHT IN THE COUNTRY and ask them to tell you how they felt after you read the book at circle time.

3. Discuss how the illustrations make them feel that it is night without being scared. Elicit their understanding that it is a peaceful and relaxing book that someone can enjoy alone.

4. Read NIGHT IN THE COUNTRY to the group of children in the center, and record it as you read.

5. After the reading, tell the children that anytime they want a quiet and peaceful book to help them relax, they can come and get the tape and listen along while looking at the pictures of the book.

Something to think about—
In full-day programs where young children are active all day, it is important to design activities which alternate between being quite active and those that are relaxing. Also, it is imperative that we show individual children ways to relax on their own.

For Sand Table: Country Geography

What the children will learn—
To shape the sand and dirt to simulate the countryside

Materials you will need—
Sand table, shovels, small watering can, small blocks, twigs, grasses, playdough, small plastic animals, small toy truck, tractor

What to do—

1. Refer to NIGHT IN THE COUNTRY and the way it seemed you were looking over hills and valleys to see the countryside at night.

2. Suggest that the children form and shape the sand to look like hills, valleys and fields in the country. Show them how to sprinkle water from the watering can to get just enough moisture to shape the sand.

3. On their own, children will think of building houses and barns. Then someone will think of the plastic farm animals.

4. If they do not think of how to make the trees and fields, provide the playdough, twigs and grasses, and let them improvise.

Something to think about—
Depending upon their experiences in the country, older preschoolers may remember to plow the fields and create the rows. Younger preschoolers will enjoy driving the tractor and the truck and rearranging the sand more than they will enjoy creating scenes.

For Science And Nature Center: Animal Babies

What the children will learn—
To associate the names of animals and their young

Materials you will need—
Pictures of baby animals and their mothers

What to do—

1. Show the pictures of the baby animals and their young found in NIGHT IN THE COUNTRY. There are raccoons, rabbits and cows with their young.

2. Collect pictures of other farm and wild animals and tell the names for each one. Go beyond the usual baby cow is a calf, dog is a puppy, cat is a kitten. Include unusual ones as a baby goose is a gosling. Baby foxes and wolves are also called pups.

Something to think about—
Many of the books for young children humanize animals as the main characters. In science and nature study, it is important to separate the real and the imaginary. Include in your displays for the science and nature center only pictures and illustrations of real animals. For instance, do not place a copy of the RUNAWAY BUNNY in a display of mother animals and their young, even though the story is about a mother rabbit and her son. Avoid combining the humanized animal stories and real animal information. Check with a reference librarian at the school or a community library for many excellent sources about real animals and their young.

(Adapted from Darlene Cobb's classroom.)

REFERENCES

Arnold, Tedd. (1987). **NO JUMPING ON THE BED!** New York: Dial Books for Young Readers.

Berger, Barbara. (1984). **GRANDFATHER TWILIGHT.** New York: Philomel Books.

Brown, Margaret Wise. (1947). **GOODNIGHT MOON.** New York: Harper and Row, Publishers.

Mayer, Mercer. (1987). **THERE'S AN ALLIGATOR UNDER MY BED.** New York: Dial Books for Young Readers.

Rylant, Cynthia. (1986). Illustrated by Mary Szilagyi. **NIGHT IN THE COUNTRY.** New York: Bradbury Press.

Additional References for Naptime/Bedtime

Bourgeosis, Paulette. (1986). Illustrated by Brenda Clark. **FRANKLIN IN THE DARK.** New York: Scholastic, Inc. *A little turtle is afraid to go inside his shell and sleep until his friends help him conquer his fear.*

Freedman, Sally. (1986). Illustrated by Robin Oz. **DEVIN'S NEW BED.** Niles, IL: Albert Whitman and Company. *Devin is reluctant to give up his crib and accept his new grown-up bed, until he discovers how much fun the new bed can be.*

Koide, Tan. (1983). Illustrated by Yasuko Koide. **MAY WE SLEEP HERE TONIGHT?** New York: Atheneum Press. *Many animals become lost in a dense fog and as each finds the log cabin, they ask, "May we sleep here tonight?" Finally, the bear owner returns to tell them he has been out looking for anyone who might be lost in the fog and that everyone may sleep here tonight.*

Rice, Eve. (1980). **GOODNIGHT, GOODNIGHT.** New York: Greenwillow Books. *Goodnight comes to all the people in the town and to the little cat as well.*

Stoddard, Sandol. (1985). Illustrated by Lynn Munsinger. **BEDTIME FOR BEAR.** Boston: Houghton Mifflin Company. *Small bear uses every excuse to avoid going to bed much to the exasperation of Big bear.*

PLANTS GROW, ANIMALS GROW, AND I GROW

Growing Vegetable Soup
The Carrot Seed
From Seed to Pear
Here Are My Hands
Whose Baby?

GROWING VEGETABLE SOUP

By Lois Ehlert

This boldly colored book, with a red cover, blue and purple end pages and full-color, full-page graphics inside, is the story of growing vegetable soup. The seeds, sprouts, plants, tools and gardening activities are sometimes displayed in fluorescent colors. The story is told from the planting of the vegetables through the eating of the soup.

Circle Time Presentation

When you read the book, linger for a while for the children to see each page and make comments about what they see. If you live in an area where families often have gardens, ask the children to share some of their gardening experiences. Read the book a second time and pause to read the labels on the packages of seeds and the markers on the rows of plants. Then, have the children recall the vegetables the family grew to make their soup, green beans, peas, zucchini, carrots, potatoes, onions, peppers, cabbage, tomatoes, corn and broccoli. Think of all the tools the gardeners used, rake, shovel, hoe, their fingers, trowel, watering can, hand grubber and spading fork. Try to think of all the containers basket, pail, bucket and bushel basket. Finally, at the end, ask what were the cooking tools needed to make and eat the soup?

STORY STRETCHER

For Housekeeping And Dress-up Corner: What Gardeners Wear

What the children will learn—
To pretend to be gardeners

Materials you will need—
Gardening gloves, hats, bandannas, loose coveralls or overalls, tools as watering can, trowel, spade

What to do—
1. Pretend you are Dad in GROWING VEGETABLE SOUP and you announce that we are going to grow vegetable soup.

2. Have the gardeners get ready for their work. Start the pretending and then as the opportunity allows, leave the gardeners to go on with their play.

Something to think about—
Knowing when to initiate play is much easier to determine than knowing when to leave. Give a good reason for leaving, as I'm going over to my neighbor's house to help her with her garden. You can ask a child who has been on the fringes of the play to step in and pretend to be Dad. This legitimizes the child's taking over the role, and he doesn't have to negotiate his way into the group.

STORY STRETCHER

For Mathematics And Manipulatives Center: Weighing Seeds

What the children will learn—
To use the balance to determine which seeds weigh the most

Materials you will need—
Balance, small plastic covered containers, measuring cups, seed corn, bean seeds, pea seeds, sunflower seeds

What to do—
1. Demonstrate how to use the balance by having someone pour a cup of corn seed in one side and a cup of bean seeds in the other. Tell the children how to tell which weighs more. The side which is lower indicates it is heavier.

2. Have the children make other comparisons and decide which seeds weigh the most.

3. Ask them questions and then write down their observations. For example, "Joey, which seeds did you weigh and which one weighed more?" Write their answers on index cards. As other children come to the mathematics center to weigh seeds, you can have them investigate and find out if they get the same answer as Joey.

Something to think about—
It is easier to make gross comparisons than to make finer ones. For example, the children can easily see that sixteen peach seeds would weigh more than sixteen bean seeds. For younger children, try these more obvious distinctions.

(Adapted from Linda Larmon Ragsdale's classroom.)

For Music And Movement: Growing Plants

What the children will learn—
To pretend to be tiny seeds which grow into plants

Materials you will need—
Tape or record of calming instrumental music

What to do—
1. Have the children seated in a circle. Talk with them about the growing process while demonstrating growth movements. First, a seed is a tiny thing (close the fingers of your hands very tightly), then it begins to send out tiny roots under the ground (begin opening the fingers), then the sprouts begin to push their way through the ground (move your fingers upward), then the warm sun hits the plant, the rain sprinkles down and it begins to stretch upward (reach your hands and arms up), then a breeze comes along and the branches of the plant are blown gently (sway your hands and arms above your head), until finally you are ripe.

2. Ask the children to pretend to be growing plants, as you tell them their stage of growth and repeat the actions from above.

3. At the end, select one child to be the gardener, have her tap the

plants signaling that they have been picked and can stop growing.

Something to think about—
You can make the movements of the growing plants even more dramatic by having each child use her entire body to express the growing process. Start from the fetal position, then stretch legs for underground sprouts and arms for growing above ground.

(Adapted from an idea by Pat Hubbard.)

For Sand Table: Digging For Potatoes

What the children will learn—
To plant and dig for potatoes

Materials you will need—
Sand table, change to soil if possible, a dozen potatoes or more, trowels, gardening gloves, bucket or pail

What to do—
1. Explain that potatoes grow under the ground, but their green plants grow above the ground. If possible, show a picture, or draw a diagram of above and underground growth.

2. Have a few gardeners hide the potatoes by making up rows in the sand or soil, and making little hills the way potatoes are planted.

3. Then, have other gardeners use the trowels and dig up the potatoes. Children can take turns being the planters and the diggers.

Something to think about—
Use the watering cans to sprinkle the sand and keep it moist. It will be easier to shape into rows and hills for the planting (hiding) of the potatoes. Also, if you have a vegetable garden within walking distance, take a walking field trip there.

For Science And Nature Center: Planting Seeds And Seedlings

What the children will learn—
To plant and care for some growing vegetables

Materials you will need—
Vegetable seeds or seedlings, potting soil, window box or patio planter, plastic glasses, trowels

What to do—
1. Select seeds which germinate well based on the advice from the seed store or garden shop owner. Also, purchase some seedlings, as tomato plants and pepper plants.

2. Have the children plant seeds in plastic glasses so they can see the root system beginning. Fill the glass with potting soil, then place some seeds in the middle of the glass and some near the edge.

3. Continue planting and caring for the seeds. Line up the plastic glasses in rows with like seeds together.

4. With the help of some of the children who are most interested, plant the window box or the patio planter. Place the pepper plants and tomato plants in this area.

Something to think about—
Keep the plants at school as long as there is enough nutrition in the soil to maintain them. Give one plastic glass with a plant to each child. Give the remaining plants to someone who has a garden. Also, consider growing herbs which take up little space. Chives grow quickly, but some herb varieties grow too slowly.

6

PLANTS GROW
ANIMALS GROW
AND I GROW

THE CARROT SEED

By Ruth Krauss

Illustrated by

Crockett Johnson

A little boy planted a carrot seed, but no one in his family believed it would come up. His mother, his father and his big brother repeated to him each day, "I'm afraid it won't come up," but the little boy watered it and weeded it anyway. Finally, a huge carrot grew, "just as the little boy had known it would." Crockett Johnson's wonderfully simple illustrations of this classic simple story by Ruth Krauss is a favorite of children whose attempts often are criticized by adults and brothers and sisters.

Circle Time Presentation

Bring a package of carrot seeds to circle time. Without showing the outside of the package, shake one tiny seed into each child's hand. Ask the children to guess what this seed might grow to become if it were planted in some rich soil, had enough bright sunlight and were watered each day. Read the book without reading the title. Near the end of the book the seed is identified when Krauss wrote, "a carrot came up," and Johnson shows a carrot top taller than the little boy. The children will delight in comparing their tiny seed to the carrot which is so big the little boy must transport it from the garden in a wheelbarrow. Reread the book and let the children join you in the repeated phrase, "I'm afraid it won't come up."

STORY STRETCHER

For Block Building: Wheelbarrow Lift

What the children will learn—
To use a wheelbarrow

Materials you will need—
Wheelbarrow, hollow blocks

What to do—
1. After a particularly busy block building session where all the blocks from the storage shelves are out, have a child or two try to carry too many blocks at once. When the blocks come tumbling out of their arms, ask if there is an easier way to get the blocks from one area to the other.

2. Introduce the wheelbarrow as an efficient way of collecting the blocks, rolling them over to an area, and then unloading one's cargo.

3. Find other practical uses for the wheelbarrow. For example, a

teacher asks for help carrying two large gallons of apple juice. A child could not manage a gallon, but with the wheelbarrow the juice is delivered to the snack area. Perhaps it is time for all the library books to be packed up and returned to the library for new ones, another appropriate wheelbarrow delivery.

Something to think about—
Any job where the teacher or the children have to carry many items might be a good wheelbarrow task.

STORY STRETCHER

For Cooking And Snack Time: Carrot And Raisin Salad

What the children will learn—
To prepare a nutritious snack

Materials you will need—
Carrots, one per child, raisins, vegetable peelers, paper towels, bowls

What to do—
1. Ask some children to help wash the carrots.

2. Demonstrate how to hold the carrot to use the vegetable peeler to make slivers of carrots.

3. Let each child take a carrot and using the vegetable peelers make a mound of carrot "slivers."

4. Place the shredded carrots into a bowl and sprinkle in the raisins.

5. Place the carrot and raisin salad in the refrigerator to chill. Serve at snack time.

Something to think about—
If the carrot and raisin salad is not moist enough, add a teaspoon of French dressing to the salad; however, we find most children enjoy the salad without the dressing. Also, vary the recipe by adding chopped apples or nuts. Make different recipes and let the children decide which they like best.

For Creative Dramatics: It Won't Come Up!

What the children will learn—
To reenact the scenes of THE CARROT SEED

Materials you will need—
Water can, wheelbarrow, four children

What to do—

1. Review the sequence of events in THE CARROT SEED.

2. Select four characters to play the little boy, his mother, his father and his big brother.

3. Reread the book and let the children pretend to be the characters.

Something to think about—
If you have young preschoolers, let the audience say the one repeated line each character says, "I'm afraid it won't come up," and the characters can concentrate on their actions. If you have kindergartners, let them improvise more dialogue, since the little boy never said anything. Also, extend the story and think of what the little boy is going to do with such a huge carrot. If you find the children hesitant to extend the story, ask the child playing the little boy, "Hey, little boy, what are you going to do with that huge carrot?" In his play role, he probably will think of something to say. When we tried this activity, a five year old said, "Feed 'bout a million rabbits." If you have already made the carrot and raisin salad for snack time, ask how much salad they think this carrot would make.

For Library Corner, Flannel Board: The Huge Carrot

What the children will learn—
To retell THE CARROT SEED using flannel board pieces

Materials you will need—
Felt pieces of the little boy, mother, father, brother, tiny seed, watering can, carrot top, wheelbarrow and huge carrot

What to do—

1. Read THE CARROT SEED and let a child put up the felt pieces on cue. Have the other listeners join in with the repeated phrase, "I'm afraid it won't come up."

2. After reading the book through once, leave the children on their own to retell the story.

Something to think about—
THE CARROT SEED is an excellent book to select as a flannel board story because the sequence is very clear and predictable. Each character tells the little boy the carrot won't come up, and after each person tells him, he continues to water the seed and weed the garden. The phrases and actions are repeated three times so they become predictable. The simplicity of the story and the surprise ending are satisfying to children to hear and satisfying to retell in a flannel board story. Young children who show little interest in books often will respond to flannel board stories which can become a bridge to their interest in stories in books.

For Science And Nature Center: Seeds And Carrot Tops

What the children will learn—
To plant carrot seeds and to watch carrot tops grow

Materials you will need—
Packages of carrot seeds, carrots with tops on them, plastic glasses, paper towels, potting soil, bowls

What to do—

1. Germinate some carrot seeds by placing them in a wet paper towel, inside a plastic sandwich bag. Put the bag on a sunny window sill and the seeds should germinate quickly.

2. Compare the carrot seeds from the package and the germinated seeds.

3. Plant the seeds by just making a thumb print in the soil.

4. Also plant the germinated seeds by lightly covering them with soil. Mark each set of plantings to compare the growth. Let the children predict which set of seeds will grow faster.

6. Cut carrots so that about one inch of carrot is still attached to the carrot top.

7. Place the bottom of the carrot in a bowl which has about a half inch of water in it. Place the carrots tops where they can get some sunlight and watch them grow.

Something to think about—
Seldom does a classroom seed become a fully grown edible vegetable. In the spring, consider having a container or patio garden and the children can see their seeds grow into vegetables.

6

PLANTS GROW
ANIMALS GROW
AND I GROW

FROM SEED TO PEAR

By Ali Mitgutsch

This simple book shows a gardener planting pear seeds and tending the tree until it grows large enough to produce fruit. The book is simply and charmingly illustrated, but contains enough information for young readers to understand the growth process. The watercolor illustrations are simple and graphic, but are bright enough to be easily seen in a large group.

Circle Time Presentation

Cut a large juicy pear down the middle and show the children the seeds. Ask them how long they think it will take for the seeds to grow into a tree. Read FROM SEED TO PEAR. Pause and emphasize the illustrations of the white blossoms turning into little hard green pears and then into yellow ripe juicy ones. If possible, show a green pear from the grocery and one which is ripened. Cut some green pears into small bite-sized pieces and some ripe pears. Have the children eat them and compare the tastes and textures. Place the FROM SEED TO PEAR book in the science and nature center for future reference.

S T O R Y   S T R E T C H E R
For Art: Blossoms

What the children will learn—
To decorate with things from nature, as pear blossoms in vases

Materials you will need—
Real blossoms from a pear tree or a flowering fruit tree, or silk blossoms, vases

What to do—
1. If you have flowering fruit trees in your play area or within walking distance of the center, go and observe the flowering trees.

2. Cut small branches from flowering trees or use silk blossoms and let the children arrange them for the housekeeping corner and for the snack tables.

3. Discuss how the blossom is the beginning of the fruit.

Something to think about—
The classroom needs to be a place of beauty for the children and their teachers to enjoy. A flower arrangement makes the snack tables special, but it also lets the children

know how society values beautiful things from nature. Even the silk reproductions are an attempt to keep alive the beauty of the fragile blossom.

S T O R Y   S T R E T C H E R
For Cooking and Snack Time: Pear Treats

What the children will learn—
To prepare a variety of snacks with pears

Materials you will need—
Fresh ripe pears, canned pear halves, raisins, coconut, mixed nuts, baskets, large serving bowls, large serving spoons, small bowls, spoons and napkins

What to do—
1. Invite several children to assist with the preparation of the special snack time. Have them wash the ripe pears and arrange them in baskets for the snack table.

2. Cut some of the fresh ripe pears in halves for the children to see the seeds. Then cut slices from the fresh pears for everyone to taste.

3. Open the canned pears and let other children pour them into large serving bowls. The children then serve themselves from the large bowl.

4. Have everyone compare the tastes of the fresh pears with the canned ones.

5. Let the children sprinkle a variety of toppings onto their canned pear halves (for example, coconut, raisins, mixed nuts), then compare the tastes.

Something to think about—
Vary the toppings and on other days have brown sugar or nutmeg, grated cheese or cottage cheese, but let the children choose whether

to have their pears plain or with toppings.

For Housekeeping And Dress-up Corner: Fruit Stand

What the children will learn—
To role-play fruit sellers and customers

Materials you will need—
Real, plastic or playdough fruit, paper bags, scales, apron, poster-board, markers, cash register, play money

What to do—
1. Have several children help you create a fruit stand by using a table from the housekeeping corner. With the children's assistance, name the fruit stand and create a sign telling what fruits are for sale.

2. If the children are unaccustomed to the scales, practice weighing and bagging a few items.

3. Interact with the children until the play gets started and then leave them to improvise their roles. If they sell all their fruit, suggest making some of playdough.

Something to think about—
Children who do not live in communities with roadside stands or green grocers on the sidewalks may think of the fruit stand as the produce section of a supermarket.

For Music And Movement: The Pear Tree

What the children will learn—
To perform the motions of the poem

Materials you will need—
None

What to do—
1. Teach the children the poem with motions, as arms in a circle showing how big the hole was for the seed, fingers pinched together showing the tiny seed, creating a circle with hands stretched overhead and fingertips touching to show the sun, arms outstretched for the branches and making a circle with thumb and index finger to show the size of the blossom.

2. Recite:

"This is the hole I dug so round
This is the seed I put in the ground.
This is the sun shining so
This is the pear tree starting to grow.
These are the limbs stretching up high
These are the blossoms, so pretty, oh my.
I think I see a green one there
Just wait, it will ripen into a pear."
(Raines)

3. Practice the poem and movements several times.

Something to think about—
Build your repertoire of finger plays, songs, poems and chants not only to help children recall information, but also to fill those moments when children have to wait before a new activity can begin.

For Science And Nature Center: Nursery Trees

What the children will learn—
That small trees grow into larger ones

Materials you will need—
Trees from a nursery

What to do—
1. If possible, visit a nursery and see trees in a variety of sizes.

2. Invite a nursery owner to bring in small trees in various stages of growth. If you have a wooded area nearby, have the children walk in the woods and observe the growing trees.

3. Compare other objects from the classroom which are about the same height as the small trees from the nursery. For example, this tree is about the height of this library book. This tree is about as tall as this block is long. This tree is twenty unifix cubes tall.

Something to think about—
Vary the activity to fit the background experiences of your children. Most children think of the fruits they eat as coming from the supermarket, rather than trees in an orchard. If you live in an area where there are many trees, plan several walking field trips to let children make first hand observations. A trip to the orchard to pick fresh fruit will be a memorable experience. Take advantage of whatever is around you.

6

PLANTS GROW
ANIMALS GROW
AND I GROW

HERE ARE MY HANDS

By Bill Martin, Jr. and

and John Archambault

Illustrated by Ted Rand

A charmingly simple verse which captivates the feelings of young children noticing all the different parts of their bodies, from "hands for catching and throwing" to the "skin that bundles me in." The rhymes and illustrations combine to make a lovely book which children will begin reading on their own because they will remember the lines of the poem. The book is a particularly good one for reading in circle time because the illustrations extend across both pages of the open book. Children from different ethnic backgrounds are warmly and sensitively depicted through chalk drawings.

Circle Time Presentation

Ask the children what are some things we do with our hands, with our feet, with our head, with our nose, with our knees, with our neck. Read HERE ARE MY HANDS. Have the children point to the part of the body mentioned as you reread the verse. Discuss the changes in their bodies by talking about the things they can do now that they couldn't do when they were little.

STORY STRETCHER

For Art: : Plaster Of Paris Hand Prints

What the children will learn—
To make hand prints

Materials you will need—
Plaster of Paris mix available from craft stores, measuring cup, water, large mixing bowl, one meat tray per child, pencil, paper towels, newspaper

What to do—

1. During free play at the art center, cover the tops of the table in the art center with newspaper for easy clean-up after the activity.

2. Mix the plaster of Paris as directed on the package, usually one part water to two parts plaster.

3. Pour the plaster into three or four meat trays at a time.

4. When the plaster begins to harden, usually in about ten minutes, make the hand print. Hold the child's hands loosely and guide the child in making the hand print.

5. Before the plaster hardens, carve the child's name and the date in the plaster with a pencil with no lead in it.

6. Continue mixing and making the hand prints a few at a time.

Something to think about—
The hand prints make excellent Mother's Day or Father's Day presents.

STORY STRETCHER

For Housekeeping And Dress-up Corner: Here Are My Hands To Button, Zip And Snap

What the children will learn—
To button buttons, zip zippers and snap snaps

Materials you will need—
Variety of clothes for both boys and girls with buttons, zippers and snaps, chest of drawers from housekeeping corner

What to do—

1. Show the children in the housekeeping and dress-up corner some of the extra pieces of clothing you brought.

2. Have them find all the pieces that have buttons and sort them into one drawer of the chest of drawers. Save another drawer for snaps and another for zippers.

3. Discuss that as we grow we learn to use our hands to dress ourselves.

4. Encourage the children to try on some of the clothing and decide whether or not it fits.

Something to think about—
Dressing and undressing are wonderful fine motor activities for young children. Starting zippers on winter coats is often quite a trick for little fingers. Encourage children to help each other with zippers by telling them some are easier to start than others. Also, it is difficult to see the front of their own coats. Make helping each other routine and then children will not feel frustrated by having

to wait for all the coats to be fastened by the teacher.

For Library Corner: We Feel Big When We

What the children will learn—
To associate their feeling big with the fact that they are growing and learning how to do much more for themselves

Materials you will need—
Chart tablet, marker

What to do—
1. With a few children during free play, discuss what makes them feel they are growing up.

2) Continue the discussion for a few minutes until everyone has contributed. Help the children to associate that as they grow they are able to do more things and need less help.

3. After the discussion, tell the children you want to remember what they said so you are going to write it down. Have one child repeat when she feels big. Begin the sentence with, "I feel big when." Continue with the sentences in this pattern until everyone has stated when they feel big.

4. Read the chart tablet and inform the children that when other boys and girls come over to the library center you will be making a chart of what makes them feel big.

Something to think about—
At the last circle time of the day, or at the end of the week, read all the charts.

For Mathematics And Manipulatives Center: Comparisons, Big And Little

What the children will learn—
To compare the attributes of a variety of objects

Materials you will need—
Small manipulative blocks, large hollow blocks, small and large pictures, yardstick, ruler, rock, cotton ball, playdough

What to do—
1. Ask the children to describe the objects; then have them make comparisons, as this is a **big** building block in comparison to this little or **small** one. This is a **long** yardstick in comparison to this **shorter** ruler. This rock is **heavy** in comparison to this **light** cotton ball.

2. With the playdough, have the children make things to compare. One child may make a tall person and the other a short person. Let the children pair up and decide what they want to make. Compare their sculpting.

Something to think about—
Young preschoolers may not be able to work in conjunction with another child but may prefer to make both of the objects. The fat snake and the thin playdough snake, the foot long playdough hot dog and the one almost all eaten, the heavy ostrich egg and the light hummingbird playdough egg are a few examples they may decide to make. Seek comparisons from them. Whenever possible, provide just a few ideas to get them started. Often teachers say too much and the children do not get to think on their own.

For Music And Movement : Reaching, Stretching, Growing, Knowing

What the children will learn—
To chant with the motions

Materials you will need—
None

What to do—
1. Use motions of reaching up with arms, pointing to self, indicating short and tall with hands, and tapping temple to show remembering.

"Reach-ing, stretch-ing, grow-ing, know-ing,
I'm not little, I'm so big.
I'm the growingest one of all.
Reach-ing, stretch-ing, grow-ing, know-ing,
I'm not short, I'm so tall.
I'm the growingest one of all.
Reach-ing, stretch-ing, grow-ing, know-ing,
I didn't forget, I remembered
I'm the growingest one of all." (Raines)
(Repeat first stanza)

Something to think about—
Make-up your own tune to the chant and sing it for a song. Record your chant and let the children take the tape home to play.

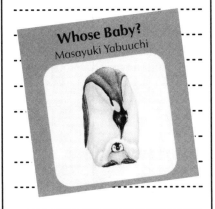

Whose Baby?
Masayuki Yabuuchi

WHOSE BABY?

By Masayuki Yabuuchi

Animal babies and their mothers interest young children. This beautifully il-lustrated book includes the pictures of the babies and on the following pages are the babies' mothers and fathers, along with the proper names of the animals. For example, the baby peacock is called a chick, the father is a peacock and the mother is a peahen. The baby seal is called a pup, while the father is a bull seal and the mother is a cow seal. The collection includes the dear, the peacock chick, the fox cub, the lion, the seal and a bison. Yabuuchi's illustrations are life-like and brightly colored.

Circle Time Presentation

Ask the children, whose baby is a kitten? a puppy? a calf? a chick? a colt? a piglet? Many children will already know these animals and their mothers. Read WHOSE BABY? and then discuss any knew information they learned. Review matching the baby animal's name to the name of the mother and father. Ask what two animals were mentioned which have a bull and a cow for their parents? Show the illustrations again for the children to describe where these animals live. Use the word, habitat. Then ask the children whose baby is a pup, a calf, a lion, a cub, a chick and a dear. They will incorporate their new learnings with the old.

STORY STRETCHER

For Art: Wild Life Prints

What the children will learn—
To name wild life animals and their babies

Materials you will need—
Wild life magazines, as Ranger Rick, calendar prints of wild life, drawing paper, choice of media — crayons, markers, watercolors, tempera paints

What to do—
1. Show the illustrations from WHOSE BABY? Then, show some of the wild life pictures, either photographs or drawings, from wild life magazines and old calendars. Ask the children what these animals' babies are called. Many will not have babies in the pictures.

2. Each child selects a wild life photograph and draws a picture of the animal's baby. The child is free to choose the media he likes best — crayon, markers, water-colors or tempera paints.

3. Display the chosen wild life prints and the child's drawings together with a caption indicating the name of the baby and of the parents.

Something to think about—
Use the drawings for an art dis-play, but retain them to use in the science and nature center as well. Encourage children who may have sculptures or figurines of favorite animals to bring them to school for an art display. Say the names of the animal babies and their parents so the children will also begin to use them.

STORY STRETCHER

For Library Corner, Listening Tapes: Whose Baby Riddle Tapes

What the children will learn—
To solve the animal babies riddles

Materials you will need—
WHOSE BABY? book, cassette recorder, tape

What to do—
1. Read WHOSE BABY? and tape record it.

2. At the end of the tape, ask the children the following questions and suggest they answer them by finding the pictures in the book. Whose baby is a pup?

Whose father is a buck?

Whose baby is a cub?

Whose mother is a peahen?

Whose baby is a calf?

Pause after each question to allow time to find the answer.

Something to think about—
If you have young preschoolers, do this activity with the children in the library corner before you leave them to do it on their own with the tape. Some kindergartners, with your assistance, may ask the

questions on the tape, and other children can answer them on the tape. Because the text of the book is such a simple one with patterned questions and patterned responses, many children will be able to record the book on their own, reading the words and the pictures.

ANOTHER STORY
STRETCHER

For Library Corner, Listening Station : Riddle Pictures

What the children will learn—
To select the picture which answers the riddle

Materials you will need—
Animal pictures, large index cards, rubber cement, tape recorder, tape

What to do—
1. Rubber cement some pictures of animals onto index cards.

2. Tape record some riddles. For example, "I am called a pup. My father is a fox, and my mother is a vixen. Turn the tape off and find my picture." (Fox) "I live in the water and on the shore. My father is called a bull, and my mother is a cow. Find my picture." (Seal) "My father is also called a bull, and my mother is a cow, but I live on land and eat grass. Find my picture." (Bison)

3. Also, insert some picture riddle cards that the children already know, as the farm animals and pets.

4. Record the instruction, "When you find the picture, turn the tape back on for the next riddle."

Something to think about—
Young preschoolers may need you to present the riddles at first, but after they become accustomed to the activity, then they can use the recorder. Although early childhood educators must be collectors, seek assistance from the parents and your friends. Calendars are treasures for science and art lessons. Remember to write in your December and January parent newsletters that you want the families' old calendars for their children's projects.

STORY STRETCHER

For Mathematics And Manipulatives Center : Animal Family Puzzles

What the children will learn—
To match the shapes to form puzzles

Materials you will need—
Animal pictures from wild life magazines and calendars, cardboard or posterboard, rubber cement, marker, scissors, large envelopes

What to do—
1. Rubber cement the animal prints onto a sheet of cardboard or posterboard. Older children can help with this step.

2. On the back of the picture, draw squiggly puzzle piece lines. Make the puzzles simple or complex depending upon the age of your child. Mark a code on the back of each puzzle piece, as F for fox; then, when you are sorting puzzle pieces they are easy to find.

3. Cut the print into puzzle pieces.

4. Store in heavy duty large envelopes, large zip-lock top freezer bags or find boxes of the same size.

Something to think about—
Show parents how to make these simple puzzles and encourage them to make them at home as inexpensive alternatives to wooden puzzles. Whenever possible, match the shape of the puzzle to the lid of a box. For example, cut one print the same width as a shoe box cover, then the child can complete the puzzle in the lid during car trips. If a print is not quite large enough to match the lid, glue it onto construction paper before rubber cementing it onto the posterboard.

STORY STRETCHER

For Science And Nature Center: Farm Babies And Wild Animal Babies

What the children will learn—
To classify the animals as farm or wild animals and to recall the names of their babies

Materials you will need—
Plastic models or pictures of farm animals and wild animals

What to do—
1. At the table in the science and nature center, mix up the models of the farm animals and the wild animals.

2. During free play, have some children sort them into categories. Some children may place all the babies together and some may place all the yellow ones together. If they do not naturally begin classifying the animals by where they live, then suggest the category.

3. After the animals are categorized as either farm animals or wild animals, try and recall the names of the babies and their mothers and fathers from WHOSE BABY? and the other activities.

Something to think about—
Since early childhood classrooms seldom have models of Arctic animals, as polar bears and seals, use pictures for these animals. The school and city libraries often have excellent wild life pictures to circulate. Of course, whenever possible, see the real animals by making trips to a farm and to a zoo. However, plan several short trips rather than long exhausting ones where the children's routines are interrupted.

(Adapted from Lisa Tuder's classroom.)

REFERENCES

Ehlert, Lois. (1987). **GROWING VEGETABLE SOUP.** San Diego: Harcourt Brace Jovanovich, Publishers, Inc.

Krauss, Ruth. (1945). Illustrated by Crockett Johnson. **THE CARROT SEED.** New York: Harper and Row Publishers.

Martin, Bill, Jr. and Archambault, John. (1987). Illustrated by Ted Rand. **HERE ARE MY HANDS.** New York: Henry Holt and Company.

Mitgutsch, Ali. (1971). **FROM SEED TO PEAR.** Minneapolis, MN: Carolrhoda Books, Inc.

Yabuuchi, Masayuki. (1985). **WHOSE BABY?** New York: Philomel Books.

Additional References for Plants Grow, Animals Grow, and I Grow

Hines, Anna Grossnickle. (1985). **ALL BY MYSELF.** New York: Clarion Books. *One night, for the first time, Josie has to cross the dark bedroom to go to the bathroom all by herself.*

Hoban, Tana. (1976). **BIG ONES, LITTLE ONES.** New York: Greenwillow Books. *Photos without text depict the mature and young of various animals, both domestic and wild.*

Krauss, Ruth. (1987). Illustrated by Mary Szilagyi. **BIG AND LITTLE.** New York: Scholastic, Inc. *Brief text and illustrations describe some of the little things that big things love.*

Le Tord, Bijou. (1984). **RABBIT SEEDS.** New York: Four Winds Press. *A gardener's work begins in spring when the sun warms up the earth and ends when the leaves turn yellow in autumn.*

Rylant, Cynthia. (1984). Illustrated by Mary Szilagyi. **THIS YEAR'S GARDEN.** Scarsdale, NY: Bradbury Press. *Follow the seasons of the years as reflected in the growth, life and death of the garden of a large rural family.*

7

SCIENCE AND NATURE

The Very Hungry Caterpillar
The Very Busy Spider
Who's Hiding There?
Chickens Aren't the Only Ones
Air Is All Around You

THE VERY HUNGRY CATERPILLAR

By Eric Carle

This favorite children's book is destined to become a classic. Eric Carle follows the metamorphosis of a caterpillar from the day of his birth when he was a small egg on a tiny leaf until he becomes a beautiful butterfly. Carle's illustrations are ingenious because of the way he uses vibrant rich colors, the effective use of white space, his inventive changing of page sizes to represent what the caterpillar ate, even the tissue paper design of the end paper pages. The sharp images help the children recall the book long after the cover is closed.

Circle Time Presentation

Without showing the cover of the book, ask the children, "Would you let a caterpillar crawl on your hand?" Read THE VERY HUNGRY CATERPILLAR. Encourage the children to say the recurring phrase with you, "But he was still hungry." This book is another one that the children will request you read again as soon as you have finished it. Honor their request and pause slightly for them to recall with you what the caterpillar ate each day. Because Carle uses counting and the days of the week the children can easily recall the phrases.

STORY STRETCHER

For Art: Tissue Paper Designs

What the children will learn—
To create tissue paper designs like the end paper pages of THE VERY HUNGRY CATERPILLAR

Materials you will need—
Tissue paper, scraps and whole sheets of construction paper, white paper, glue, scissors, hole punchers

What to do—
1. Call attention to the end paper pages of the book and the way the illustrator used paints to look like torn colored tissue paper with little round holes in it.

2. Let the children tear pieces of tissue paper to create the same effect. If they want to make holes in the paper, construction paper works better.

3. Glue the torn pieces of tissue or construction paper onto white paper for clear color contrast.

Something to think about—
The colorful tissue paper may remind the children of the butterfly wings. If you want to make butterflies, cut out the shape of a large butterfly. The children can then paste tissue paper on it by overlapping the pieces. The design of the butterfly then becomes their own, rather than the pattern the teacher provided. Remember with art that children should be told about the art project for the day, but have other art materials and supplies available in case they want to make something else.

STORY STRETCHER

For Cooking And Snack Time: Caterpillar Snack Week

What the children will learn—
To prepare and eat a variety of fruits

Materials you will need—
Apples, pears, plums, strawberries, oranges

What to do—
1. Announce the caterpillar snack week, minus the nice green leaf he ate on Sunday and the junk food he ate on the week-end. Serve apples on Monday for the one apple he ate. On Tuesday, serve pears. On Wednesday, serve plums. On Thursday, serve strawberries and on Friday, serve oranges.

2. At the sink in the classroom, have a small group of children assist you or the aide in washing the fruit, cutting it and serving it to the children.

3. Assign different children as snack preparers each day.

Something to think about—
You will find the children checking the book to predict what their snack will be for the next day. A discussion of good fruit snacks versus junk food snacks is also a logical extension of the story.

For Library Corner, Flannel Board : Story Retelling

What the children will learn—
To retell a story in sequence with the book and flannel board pieces

Materials you will need—
Flannel board and felt pieces

What to do—
1. Carle's bold illustrations are easy to design as flannel board pieces. The caterpillar can be made of overlapping green circles and the fruit he ate can be made by drawing an outline on the appropriate colored felt. Also, include a bright yellow sun, a big green leaf and a brown cocoon. The scraps of felt cut from making the different colored fruit can be used to make the butterfly wings. Or have a child draw and color a butterfly.

2. Provide the flannel board and pieces at free play time for the children to retell the story. Also, place the book near the flannel board story in case a child wants to refer to it.

Something to think about—
After children become familiar with the use of the flannel board by your modeling it during circle time, there is no need for you to supervise the library corner when they are using the flannel board. It is helpful to have the same type of storage of the flannel board pieces for each story. For instance, many teachers use large zip lock plastic bags to store each set of story pieces.

For Mathematics And Manipulatives Center: Would You Let A Caterpillar Crawl On Your Hand?

What the children will learn—
To make a simple graph and to compare the numbers of yes's and no's

Materials you will need—
Construction paper, posterboard, glue or tape, pencils or crayons, scissors

What to do—
1. Ask who would let a caterpillar crawl on their hand. Have these children draw around each other's hands, cut out the hand shapes and then draw a caterpillar on their hands. For the children who answered no, leave the hand blank.

2. Construct a chart with a yes and no column.

3. Have the children place the hands with the caterpillar in the "yes" column and the hands without the caterpillar in the "no" column.

4. Compare the simple graph and determine which column has more responses.

Something to think about—
Young preschoolers will count a few hands and simply say this one has "more" than the other chart. The older children will be able to count and actually make the numerical comparison.

For Science And Nature Center: Caterpillars In A Terrarium

What the children will learn—
To observe the movements of the caterpillar and compare what a real caterpillar looks like, rather than THE VERY HUNGRY CATERPILLAR

Materials you will need—
Caterpillars, terrarium, magnifying glasses

What to do—
1. The natural extension of the book is to have a terrarium in the class and place caterpillars in it. The caterpillars are easy to find at certain times of the year, but rarely are teachers able to keep them through the entire metamorphosis.

2. If you find the caterpillars in a wooded area, observe their natural habitat. Reproduce the caterpillar's habitat as closely as possible in the terrarium.

3. Have the children observe the caterpillars by looking through the side of the terrarium. Place magnifying glasses nearby.

4. Working with small groups of three or four children, take one caterpillar from the terrarium and let it crawl on the backs of their hands. Teach them to be very gentle with the caterpillar.

5. After a few days, take the caterpillars outside to a similar habitat as the one where you found it and set it free.

Something to think about—
Reconstruct the hand shape chart again and compare the children's answers now that they have really experienced a caterpillar.

(Adapted from Penny Patterson's classroom.)

7
SCIENCE AND NATURE

THE VERY BUSY SPIDER

By Eric Carle

A little spider ignores the farm animals' requests to join them in their activities and silently proceeds to spin her web of silky thread. The book ends with a lovely night scene and the owl calling, "Who built this beautiful web?" Eric Carle's illustrations are creative collages with raised lines tracing the spider's web. At the beginning of the book, there is just the outline of the web hanging from the fencepost, but as each animal approaches the busy spider, we see and can feel the pattern of the web growing.

Circle Time Presentation

Ask the children if they have heard the phrase, "busy as a bee?" Suggest that after hearing this book, we should say, "busy as a spider." Read THE VERY BUSY SPIDER. Recall all the animals who talked to the spider and what each animal said to the spider. Let the children feel the spider's web. Then place the book in the library corner for children to look at and feel during free play.

STORY STRETCHER

For Art: Spider Webs

What the children will learn—
To draw lines which look like a spider's web

Materials you will need—
Black construction paper, cotton swabs, lids or small bowls, thick white school glue, scissors

What to do—
1. Show the children the illustrations of the spider's web and have them talk about how the design changed. Then, look at the beginning of the web, the middle and the finished, beautiful web the owl saw at night.

2. Cut a sheet of black construction paper lengthwise into three sections.

3. Pour thick white school glue into large jar lids or into small bowls.

4. Demonstrate for the children how to dip the cotton swab into the glue, load the glue like paint on a paint brush, then use the glue to paint the lines of a spider's web.

5. Ask the children to think about the differences they want to show in the beginning, middle and end of their webs.

Something to think about—
Display the black spider web prints against white paper on a bulletin board. If possible, do this activity after you have examined real spider webs through magnifying glasses.

STORY STRETCHER

For Housekeeping And Dress-up Corner: Farmers' Clothes

What the children will learn—
To dress in farmers' work clothes

Materials you will need—
Overalls, coveralls, western hats, shirts with snaps, jeans and boots

What to do—
1. Talk about the animals in THE VERY BUSY SPIDER being farm animals. Ask the children what other animals they would expect to see on a farm. Discuss how the farmer cares for these animals, as the cow must be milked, must have a green pasture to graze or be fed hay in the winter, needs a barn for shelter. Ask why farmers like to have spiders in their barns. They catch flies which bother the animals.

2. Mention that children who live on farms help their parents care for the animals. Discuss the chores they might like to do.

3. Place the work clothes out in the dress-up corner and observe the play associated with dressing like farmers.

Something to think about—
If you live in a farming community, the children's play will be more elaborate because they have firsthand knowledge of a working farm. If many of your children lack information about farms and farm animals, plan a visit to a small working farm which still has a variety of stock. In some areas, farmers grow crops, but keep few farm animals.

(Adapted from Virginia Sindle's classroom.)

For Library Corner, Flannel Board : The Very Busy Spider

What the children will learn—
To retell the animals' attempts at dialogue with the silent, but busy spider

Materials you will need—
Flannel board, felt pieces for the horse, cow, sheep, goat, duck, rooster, fly, spider, owl, web at three different stages

What to do—
1. With the children who choose the library corner during free play, tell the story, letting each child add a felt animal.

2. Pause during the telling for the children to add dialogue whenever they can recall what the animals said.

3. Supervise one retelling with a child as the teller and the audience participating by handing him the felt animals to place on the flannel board.

4. Suggest that two children can work together or a child can tell the story alone.

Something to think about—
Encourage groups, pairs and individual enjoyment of a story. You can use white yarn and let each child add a piece of yarn onto the flannel board creating a pattern for the web as each scene of the animals approaching the very busy spider unfolds. This book also is an excellent one to tape record for the listening station.

For Music And Movement: Walking The Spider Web

What the children will learn—
To balance while walking on a narrow strip

Materials you will need—
Masking tape, scissors, cassette tape or record with violin, flute or light instrumental music, tape player or record player

What to do—
1. With several children's assistance, create a huge spider's web pattern of masking tape on the floor.

2. Gather the children on the rug and have them pretend to be spiders, talk about how the spider must balance on the threads, but must walk lightly or the thread will snap and the spider will be caught in its own web.

3. Station two or three children around the edges of the spider web, start the music and have them tiptoe on the lines of the masking tape web. When they meet on a strand of thread, they must talk with each other and decide how they can get around each other without leaving the thread of the web.

4. For the next group, who have seen the children solve the web problem, add four or five children.

Something to think about—
It is often difficult for young children to wait their turns. Have the children who are waiting practice their tiptoeing by going around the outside of the circle time rug moving in step with the music.

For Science And Nature Center: Pictures Of Real Spider Webs

What the children will learn—
To appreciate different kinds of spiders and the intricacies of their webs

Materials you will need—
Children's reference books on spiders, pictures of picture webs, magnifying glasses

What to do—
1. With a small group of children, walk onto the playground in the spring and early fall while the dew is still on the ground. Look in the tops of shrubs for spider webs. The dew makes the webs more visible. Have the children look at them through magnifying glasses.

2. Check with a librarian in the children's section and select some reference books which have big colorful pictures of spiders and their webs.

3. Spend some time in the science center discussing the pictures with the children. Have them compare the pictures of the real spider webs with the one in Carle's THE VERY BUSY SPIDER.

Something to think about—
It is important to help children separate reality and fantasy. Discuss with them how we know the story of THE VERY BUSY SPIDER is not real. The animals talk. However, spiders do make webs and can catch flies in their webs. For more reference materials, check with your local library about nature filmstrips for young children.

7

SCIENCE AND NATURE

WHO'S HIDING HERE?

By Yoshi

This magnificently illustrated book of riddles is about animals, fish and insects which use camouflage to protect themselves. We will see a rabbit, frog and snake, butterfly and beetle, moth and caterpillar, one big fish and two little fish, an owl and a black cat. Each riddle is written in poetry form and ends, "Who's hiding here?" At the end of the book, there are two pages of information written for adults about how animals protect themselves. These notes are helpful as reference for questions children may ask or to extend discussion of the book after reading. The full-color, full-page illustrations of beautiful batik paintings are large enough for a group story time.

Circle Time Presentation

Place a small red car, a red wooden block and a red plastic number one on a red sheet of construction paper or against a red swatch of fabric or a red sweater. Then place white objects against the red and let the children compare how easy or difficult they are to see. Use the word camouflage in your discussion. Read WHO'S HIDING HERE? pausing after each riddle for the children to think and make a few guesses, before turning the page for the answer. Show the illustrations a second time for the sheer visual pleasure.

STORY STRETCHER

For Art: Fabric Painting

What the children will learn—
To experiment with how paint works on a fabric canvas

Materials you will need—
Swatches of fabric at least as large as a half sheet of construction paper, newspaper, stapler, painting rocks, crayons, tempera paint, brushes, watercolor brushes, scissors

What to do—
1. Ask the parents for any left over swatches of plain, not print fabric, in cotton or a cotton blend, or purchase a yard of fabric.

2. Have the children examine Yoshi's illustrations and notice the background looks like fabric.

3. Cover a table with several thickness of newspaper. Secure the fabric in place by either stapling it to the thick newspaper or placing painting rocks, just heavy rocks, to hold the corners.

4. Experiment with crayons and paints on practice swatches.

5. Have the children make heavy waxy lines on their fabric with crayons, then paint over them using a variety of colors.

6. Remove the staples from the corners, hang the fabric taunt across a clothesline to dry. Let it dry thoroughly.

7. Send the fabric painting home by cushioning it between layers of newspaper. They are quite lovely and will be treasured.

Something to think about—
Ask the children to think who could be hiding in their pictures?

STORY STRETCHER

For Library Corner, Listening Tape: Camouflage Riddles

What the children will learn—
To answer the riddles on cue

Materials you will need—
Cassette tape, tape recorder

What to do—
1. Select a few children to assist you with making the listening tape of WHO'S HIDING HERE?

2. At the beginning of the tape, record the instructions, "When you hear the children's voices, turn the page."

3. After you read each riddle poem, have the children say, "You'll be surprised," as the page turning signal.

4. When you complete the tape recording of the book, let the children listen and decide if they want to tape it again.

Something to think about—
Young children are developing their listening abilities. The listening tape is valuable for both the children who assist in making it and those who listen for the page turning cues. We recommend routinely taping every book you read so the children can go to the

library corner and find the tape. Label the tapes with printed titles and matching sticker pictures on the cover of the book and the cassette tape and organize in an inexpensive cassette tape storage box.

For Mathematics And Manipulatives Center: Pairing By Color

What the children will learn—
To create camouflage by pairing objects of like color

Materials you will need—
Sheets of different colors of construction paper, random objects of like colors from around the classroom

What to do—
1. Show the pictures from WHO'S HIDING HERE? and discuss what camouflage means. Note that except for the first and last illustrations in the book, Yoshi showed pairs of animals.

2. Spread the different colors of construction paper out on the table.

3. Ask the children to select a color. Then instruct them to look around the room and find a pair of objects the same or nearly the same as the color of the construction paper. Ask them to find two different types of things, for example a blue bead and a blue block.

4. Display the camouflage pairs, then as other children come to the center, have them collect more objects for the display.

Something to think about—
Also use printed fabric and let children try to find pairs of things they could hide on the material, as little scraps of construction paper, pieces of yarn, broken crayons and

chalk. Help the children see that the camouflage works because of the distraction of the pattern.

For Music And Movement: Who's Hiding Here?

What the children will learn—
To pace their hiding and seeking in time with the music

Materials you will need—
Cassette tape or record of lively music, tape or record player

What to do—
1. Discuss with the children that animals must learn to run and hide quickly when they are being chased. Tell them the music is going to chase them and when it stops they must be hidden.

2. Select five children to hide. Tell the remaining children to close their eyes.

3. Start the music and have the five "hiders" find their hiding places quickly. Direct them to stay hidden until someone finds them.

4. Stop the music just as you see the last one duck into a place.

5. Instruct the "seekers," all the remaining children, to look for those hidden. Tell them they must find the "hiders" before you stop the music. Start the music for the search.

6. Stop the music. Have the children return to the circle. If someone has not been found, go to the place where you saw the child hide and say, "Who's hiding here?"

Something to think about—
For young children, divide the class, half are "hiders" and half are "seekers." For one of the sessions, you go looking for all of the hidden children and ask, "Who's hiding here?"

For Science And Nature Center: Camouflage In Season

What the children will learn—
To recognize how the colors of different seasons hide insects and animals

Materials you will need—
For spring and summer, green and brown twigs, leaves and grasses; for fall and winter, brown dry leaves, branches and grasses, small grocery bags

What to do—
1. Turn to the pages of WHO'S HIDING HERE? which correspond to the season of the year. For example for fall, show the pages of the snake and frog hidden among the leaves and grasses.

2. Discuss what the children could collect from a nature walk which they could display as good camouflage materials.

3. With a few children at a time or the whole group with other adults assisting, take the children on a walk around the school to collect some of the rocks, leaves, twigs, branches and grasses.

4. Have the children look carefully to see any insects which might be hiding there now.

5. Return to the classroom and have children arrange their examples of nature's camouflage on the table in the science and nature center.

Something to think about—
The following day hide some items from the classroom among the camouflage materials and have the children search for them.

SCIENCE AND NATURE

CHICKENS AREN'T THE ONLY ONES

By Ruth Heller

This wonderfully illustrated science and nature book is told in rhyme and has many surprises. Heller begins with a concept children usually know "that chickens lay eggs" and expands the idea to every wild or tame bird, to snakes, lizards, crocodiles, turtles and dinosaurs. She continues with amphibians, frogs, toads and salamanders. The fish, including seahorses, sharks, rays and the octopus, are set on watery deep blue and green pages. She adds the spiders, snails and insects in glowing, beautiful detail. The ending of the book refers back to the beginning and gives the children a new word to say, "Everyone who lays an egg is O VIP A ROUS."

Circle Time Presentation

Discuss where we get eggs. Then, ask if other animals lay eggs. Read CHICKENS AREN'T THE ONLY ONES. Read it through first for the information, then read it through a second time for the children to enjoy the beautiful illustrations. Practice saying, "Oviparous" together. Ask children to tell you what surprised them, which animals lay eggs that they did not know and did they know about insects. Tell the children you learned a lot from reading this book, also. Then, ask several girls and boys to tell you which pictures they liked best. Give the book to a very interested child and ask her to place it in the science and nature center for others to see during free play.

STORY STRETCHER

For Art: Decorating Eggs

What the children will learn—
To color and dye eggs

Materials you will need—
Boiled eggs, egg dyeing kit, large tablespoons or soup spoons, egg carton or plate for drying, crayons

What to do—

1. Boil the eggs ahead of time.

2. Follow the directions on the egg dyeing kit. Depending on the age of children you are working with, you may want to have the dye colors already mixed.

3. Write each child's initials on the bottom of an egg.

4. Have the children draw designs on their eggs using different colored crayons.

5. Demonstrate how to place the egg on the spoon, to hold it under water until the shell absorbs the amount of the dye you want.

6. Let the children dye their eggs, then help them place the eggs on a plate or in an egg carton to dry.

Something to think about—
Often the egg dyeing kits contain a wire to fit around the egg and dip into the dye. From my experience, seldom does the flimsy wire last through a session. If you want to use the wire idea, substitute a heavier gage and form enough dippers to have one for each child at the table.

STORY STRETCHER

For Cooking And Snack Time: Egg In A Hole

What the children will learn—
To eat an egg prepared in a different way

Materials you will need—
Skillet, bread, vegetable oil, eggs, spatula

What to do—

1. With a few children assisting at a time, prepare "Eggs in a Hole." The child takes a slice of bread and pinches a circle about the size of a half dollar out of the center of the bread to make a hole. The old recipe was to fry an egg and drop it in the hole in the middle of the bread. We give the children a choice.

2. Ask the child if he wants a scrambled egg or a fried egg.

3. Prepare the egg, but use the spatula to contain it in a small area.

4. When the egg is cooked, drop it into the hole in the bread.

Something to think about—
For variety, use different types of bread or toast the bread. Encourage the children to try a different variety of bread—pumpernickel, rye, oat bran, cinnamon raisin.

For Library Corner: Eggcitement Tape

What the children will learn—
To recall the new information which "eggcited" and surprised

What to do—
1. Make a listening tape of CHICKENS AREN'T THE ONLY ONES. Introduce the tape by telling the listeners that you were excited about the new facts and new words you learned when you read this book. Mention a few and emphasize the word, excitement, by saying it as "eggcitement."

2. Tell them when they finish listening to the tape to turn the cassette tape over and record at least one new thing which "eggcited" them.

3. For the page turning signal, cluck or cackle like a chicken. Instruct the children to turn the page when they hear the sound the chicken makes.

Something to think about—
For young preschoolers, have just one child listening to the tape at once and you assist with the child's recording one new bit of information she learned from the book. You might let older preschoolers assist you in making the tape. They can make the clucking or cackling sounds for the page turning signals. Also, they can be the first children to record their new learnings.

For Mathematics And Manipulatives Center: Counting Eggs

What the children will learn—
To count the number of objects inside a plastic egg

Materials you will need—
five plastic eggs that hosiery is packaged in, a crayon, two small puzzle pieces, three pennies, four paper clips, five jelly beans

What to do—
1. Fill the different plastic eggs with little objects. For example, place the one crayon in one egg, two puzzle pieces in the second egg, three pennies in the third egg, four paper clips in another and five jelly beans in the fifth egg.

2. Mix up the eggs.

3. Have a child pick up an egg, shake it and guess what is inside.

4. Then the child opens up the egg and counts the contents. She then places the eggs in order according to the number of objects inside.

Something to think about—
Complicate the activity by adding more eggs with more objects for the child to count and then place in order.

For Science And Nature Center: Display Of Eggs

What the children will learn—
To compare the sizes and colors of eggs

Materials you will need—
Real eggs or models you make from clay, tempera paint, glue

What to do—
1. Show the children Ruth Heller's illustration comparing the size of the ostrich egg to the hummingbird's egg.

2. If it is possible to find them, bring in eggs from different fowl. Order them by size and tell about the wild and tame birds which laid the eggs.

3. Discuss how we might make some eggs which look like the ones in Ruth Heller's illustration. Use clay or playdough and let it harden, then paint them. Talk about how to create speckled eggs by taking a toothbrush, loading it with paint, then rubbing your thumb across it to make the paint spray out and land in speckles. Encourage and accept the children's own ideas as to how they might create the models.

4. Paint the eggs, let them dry, then brush over with a very watery glue. Let the glue dry and it will keep the paint from rubbing off.

Something to think about—
To simplify the activity for young children, have them shape their playdough eggs out of the same color as the real eggs. They also will enjoy making playdough nests for their eggs. To add "eggcitement" to their display, bring in straw for nests.

AIR IS ALL AROUND YOU

By Franklyn M. Branley

Illustrated by Holly Keller

AIR IS ALL AROUND YOU is a book describing the properties of air and how to do some simple experiments to prove it. The experimenter is a little girl. Each step of the experiments is explained in the pictures and in words. How fish breathe air dissolved in water is illustrated, and why divers and astronauts need tanks of air is explained. Holly Keller's illustrations are bright, the stylized drawings of the children appealing and the match with the text makes children confident they can do the experiments.

Circle Time Presentation

Talk with the children about how they know where air is. They will mention the wind blowing and some may mention blowing out air on a cold morning and seeing a little cloud. Read AIR IS ALL AROUND YOU. Then discuss again how they know air is all around them after having heard the book. Assure the children that they will have a chance to do the science experiments. Tell the children you will place the book in the science center and during free play you will be there to help anyone who wants to do the experiments.

STORY STRETCHER

For Art: Fish Pictures

What the children will learn—
To recognize where the fish's gills are and to incorporate this into their picture

Materials you will need—
Brightly colored construction paper, scissors, easel, fluorescent tempera paints, variety of sizes of brushes

What to do—
1. Cut the construction paper into giant fish shapes.
2. Cut a half-circle flap where the fish's gills should be.
3. Encourage the children to use many different colors to paint their fish like the ones in the class aquarium.

Something to think about—
Children respond to new information and will incorporate their new learnings into their art work. If possible, display many pictures of fish near the art area and you will see more variety in the paintings.

STORY STRETCHER

For Cooking And Snack Time: Orange Air

What the children will learn—
To recall the analogy of how the peel of the orange is like the air around the earth

Materials you will need—
Whole oranges

What to do—
1. Read the analogy from the book, "Air is all around you, and it is all around the earth. Air covers the earth like peel covers an orange."
2. Cut thin stripes down the orange peel from top to bottom without cutting through to the inside of the orange. Cut stripes all around the orange so the children can peel their oranges more easily.
3. Let the children peel their own oranges.

Something to think about—
It is difficult to know when to provide assistance to children. Often volunteers in the classroom will quickly take over for the child and peel the orange. However, encourage them to wait and only provide assistance after the child is having a great deal of difficulty. Then, do not peel the entire orange, but get some of the sections started. Many children will persist and need more time to finish their snacks. Do not hurry them; let them enjoy peeling the orange and savor eating it.

STORY STRETCHER

For Housekeeping And Dress-up Corner: Astronauts

What the children will learn—
To pretend to be astronauts

Materials you will need—
Football helmets or bike riding helmets, large expandable hoses from a dryer connection, earphones from the listening station, down-filled jackets

What to do—
1. Show the picture of the astronaut in AIR IS ALL AROUND YOU.

2. Ask the children how they might use the dress-up materials you have collected to dress up like astronauts. If possible, have several of each. If this is impossible, explain that there is only one astronaut outside the spaceship at a time and the others have their air supply inside the spaceship.

Something to think about—
Every time I see children playing astronauts, I am amazed at their inventiveness. The puffy down-filled coats reminded me of the air in the space suits; however, the idea of using the dryer air hose connection came from a child, as well as using the earphones for communication. Do not be concerned if you only have a few of the supplies, your astronauts will find what they need.

(Adapted from classroom at George Mason University's Project for the Study of Young Children.)

STORY STRETCHER

For Science And Nature Center: Inverted Glass Experiment

What the children will learn—
To follow the directions of the experiment and observe what happens

Materials you will need—
Large clear mixing bowl, food coloring, paper napkins, glass

What to do—
1. Follow the directions in the book, which are:

   a. put water in a big bowl;

   b. color the water with a little bit of good coloring;

   c. stuff a paper napkin into the bottom of a glass;

   d. turn the glass upside down;

   e. keep the glass upside down, make sure it is straight up and down, do not tip it;

   f. push it all the way under the water;

   g. lift the glass out of the water; and

   h. turn it right side up and take out the napkin.

2. Have the children observe that the napkin is dry.

3. Let all the children who want to do the experiment have a turn.

Something to think about—
Remember that young children are hands-on learners. They will learn more if they do the experiment themselves. Many of the children will not understand what the experiment demonstrates, but they enjoy following the directions and getting the same results as the teacher. Also, avoid referring to this experiment as magic or as a trick. While it may seem phenomenal, it is natural.

ANOTHER STORY STRETCHER

For Science And Nature Center: Fishy Water

What the children will learn—
To observe the air bubbling in an aquarium and the air bubbling in water

Materials you will need—
An aquarium, two glasses filled with water, magnifying glasses

What to do—
1. For the children who are interested, reread the section of the book about the air dissolved in the water for fish. Show the pictures of the fish and point out the fish's gills.

2. Have the children look at the fish in the aquarium with their magnifying glasses and see if they can see the fishes' gills moving as the water passes through them.

3. Do the science experiment where you fill a glass with water, wait an hour and then look with the magnifying glasses for tiny bubbles of air.

4. After an hour, fill another glass with water, and have the children search for any air bubbles in this glass.

Something to think about—
While an aquarium requires a great deal of attention, it is worth it to have living things in the classroom. Before spending school supply money on an aquarium, check with parents, often there is one in storage or one in operation that a family will donate complete with fish. Get specific instructions about its operation from the owners.

REFERENCES

Branley, Franklyn M. (1986). Illustrated by Holly Keller. **AIR IS ALL AROUND YOU.** New York: Thomas Y. Crowell.

Carle, Eric. (1981). **THE VERY HUNGRY CATERPILLAR.** New York: Philomel Books.

Carle, Eric. (1984). **THE VERY BUSY SPIDER.** New York: Philomel Books.

Heller, Ruth. (1981). **CHICKENS AREN'T THE ONLY ONES.** New York: Grosset and Dunlap.

Yoshi. (1987). **WHO'S HIDING HERE?** Saxonville, MA: Picture Book Studio Ltd.

Additional References for Science and Nature

Heller, Ruth. (1982). **ANIMALS BORN ALIVE AND WELL.** New York: Grosset and Dunlap. *A beautifully illustrated book filled with facts about mammals.*

Heller, Ruth. (1984). **PLANTS THAT NEVER EVER BLOOM.** New York: Grosset and Dunlap. *Horticultural book of interesting facts and lovely illustrations of plants that never bloom.*

Reidel, Marlene. (1974). **FROM EGG TO BUTTERFLY.** Minneapolis, MN: Carolrhoda Books, Inc. *Describes the metamorphosis of a butterfly through its stages of egg, caterpillar, pupa and finally butterfly.*

Udry, Janice May. (1956). Illustrated by Marc Simont. **A TREE IS NICE.** New York: Harper and Row Publishers. *Some of the many wonderful and funny reasons why trees are nice to have around.*

Wildsmith, Brian. (1975). **SQUIRRELS.** New York: Franklin Watts, Inc. *A beautifully illustrated book about the life of squirrels.*

SEASONS
FOCUS ON FALL

Frederick
My Favorite Time of Year
The Tiny Seed
The Seasons of Arnold's Apple Tree
Chipmunk Song

FREDERICK

Leo Leonni

Frederick, a field mouse, lives with his family in an old stone wall near a deserted barn and granary. While the other field mice are busy in the fall, Frederick sits quietly. When the four mice ask him why he does not work, Frederick tells them he gathers "sun rays for the cold dark winter days." Later, he gathers colors because the winter will be gray. When they find him looking half asleep, Frederick tells them he is gathering words they will need when they run out of something to say on those long winter days. When winter does arrive, Frederick rescues them from the cold, helps remember the beautiful colors in the meadow and cures their boredom with his poetry. Leo Lionni's illustrations are cleverly crafted, simple designs.

Circle Time Presentation

Talk with the children about how each person in the class helps when there is work to be done, as at clean-up time. Ask how they would feel if someone was not helping. Read FREDERICK. Discuss how Frederick's family thought he was not helping in the fall, but when winter came, Frederick shared the sun rays, the beautiful colors and his lovely poetry he had gathered.

S T O R Y S T R E T C H E R

For Art: Pictures We Paint In Our Minds

What the children will learn—
To visualize the colors in a scene they like

Materials you will need—
Crayons, paper

What to do—
1. With a small group of children who choose the art center during free play, talk about how Frederick helped his family recall the beautiful colors of the flowers in the meadow.

2. Have the children close their eyes and think of something they think is beautiful.

3. Then, ask them to open their eyes and find a crayon which is the color of the thing they thought of which was beautiful and have them make some marks on the paper with that crayon.

4. Repeat the visualizing, finding the crayon and marking the color two more times.

5. When the children have at least three colors of crayons on their papers, ask them to talk about the three beautiful things they remembered.

6. Ask the children to draw a picture of something which is beautiful that they want to remember during the gray days of winter.

Something to think about—
The charm of FREDERICK is the inventive way Leo Lionni allowed Frederick to be different from the other field mice and yet, he was appreciated for his contribution. As teachers, we can allow our children to be different, unique, true individuals and still contribute to the group.

S T O R Y S T R E T C H E R

For Block Building: Old Stone Wall

What the children will learn—
How to stack blocks to build a sturdy wall

Materials you will need—
Large hollow blocks

What to do—
1. Demonstrate how to stack the blocks, alternating each level in a brick wall design.

2. Ask the children to build an "old stone wall" for the place where Frederick and his family of field mice could live.

3. Tell the children that later the wall will be the stage for a puppet play, so they are not to tear it down at the end of free play.

Something to think about—
Whenever possible, tie one activity of the day to something which will occur later.

S T O R Y S T R E T C H E R

For Cooking and Snack Time: Frederick's Granola Bars

What the children will learn—
To mix their own granola treats

Materials you will need—
A variety of grains, wheat, oats, cornflakes, honey, brown sugar,

peanuts or almonds, bowls, tablespoons, teaspoons, waxed paper, milk, napkins

What to do—

1. Place bowls of the different ingredients onto the snack table, along with tablespoons for each bowl.

2. Give each child a sheet of waxed paper to mix the ingredients on and to roll the granola log.

3. Have each child take a tablespoon of each of the grains and nuts. Sprinkle a little brown sugar over the top of the mixture.

4. Let the children use their fingers and mix all the dry ingredients together.

5. Drizzle about a teaspoon of honey over the ingredients on each child's sheet of waxed paper.

6. Have the children mix in the honey with the teaspoons, and then let them shape the log with their hands.

7. Place each child's granola log onto a clean sheet of waxed paper, wrap it, place it in the refrigerator to harden.

8. Serve the granola logs with milk for snack.

Something to think about—
If you do not have all of the ingredients, make substitutions. You can use peanut butter instead of honey. You can leave out the nuts and substitute a crunchy ready mixed cereal.

STORY STRETCHER

For Creative Dramatics: Frederick Tab Puppets

What the children will learn—
To act out the story of Frederick

Materials you will need—
Two inch wide and six inch long strips of construction paper,
stapler, scissors, tape, glue, crayons, construction paper

What to do—

1. Ask the children to draw and cut out field mice that are about as tall as crayons. Leo Lionni's field mice are shaped like eggs lying on their sides. The children will be able to construct the field mice easily.

2. Fold the strips of construction paper in half and staple the ends together.

3. Flatten the center of the strip and attach the field mouse to the tab by stapling, gluing or taping it in place.

4. Divide the children into groups of five to take turns acting out the story. Select one child's tab puppet to be Frederick and the other four will be his family.

5. Have the puppeteers position themselves behind the "old stone wall" the block builders built. Add some nuts and straw for props.

6. As you read the story, let the field mice act it out.

Something to think about—
If you have older preschoolers, let them act out the story in their own words, rather than you reading it. Younger preschoolers may enjoy just pretending to be Frederick through the puppet.

STORY STRETCHER

For Library Corner, Listening Station: Frederick's Poem

What the children will learn—
To turn the pages at Frederick's signal

Materials you will need—
Cassette tape, recorder, listening station, earphones, fork, glass

What to do—

1. With a small group of children, make a tape recording of FREDERICK for the listening station.

2. Assign one child the responsibility of making the page turning signal by lightly tapping a fork against a glass.

3. Rehearse by reading the book through and at your signal have the children say, "Frederick, why don't you work?"

4. Tape record the story with the children's lines and the page turning signal.

5. Let the children hear the tape and decide if they want to do it again.

6. Place the tape and the book at the listening station with the earphones.

Something to think about—
If you notice a child who shows more interest in Frederick than the other children, consider letting the child tell the story of Frederick in her own words. Tape record the story as the child tells it while looking at the pictures. You provide the page-turning signal. Provide the child's version of the story on one side of the tape and the teacher reading the story on the other.

SEASONS

FOCUS ON FALL

MY FAVORITE TIME
OF THE YEAR

By Susan Pearson

Illustrated by John Wallner

Susan Pearson presents all four seasons of the year beginning with October through December as fall scenes. The main characters are Kelly, her mother and her baby brother, Patrick. The scenes follow the changes in nature and in the family's activities during each season. The characters are a modern family who live in an old two story frame house. Each season's changes can be seen on the lawn of their house and their neighbors. The cheerful, colorful illustrations are framed, and the text is printed in a frame below them.

Circle Time Presentation

Ask the children to tell you what season it is. Some may say the month instead of the season. Reply, "You are right, it is October and that means, it's fall." Read the pages in MY FAVORITE TIME OF YEAR which describe fall. Ask the children to compare fall as it is happening at Kelly's house to what is happening where they live. Is it the same, or is it different? Are the leaves turning? Are people raking leaves and fixing up their houses? Have they seen geese flying south? Have they already decorated for Halloween? When the discussion is over, summarize the signs of fall in the area of the country where you live. Read the entire book.

S T O R Y   S T R E T C H E R

For Art: Leaf Rubbings

What the children will learn—
To observe the shapes and veins in the leaves

Materials you will need—
Typing paper, newspaper, crayons in fall colors, construction paper, tape, stapler, leaves of a variety of kinds and sizes

What to do—
1. Let the children collect leaves from the playground or bring some interesting ones from home. Tell them the names of the trees their leaves came from.

2. Have the children arrange their leaves on top of several thickness of newspaper. Roll a piece of tape and place it under each leaf to hold it in place. Tape the leaf so that the veins are up. Tape the sheet of typing paper over the leaf to hold it place.

3. Demonstrate how to hold the crayon lengthwise, press down on the paper and move the crayon back and forth. The imprint of the leaf will appear.

4. Assist with arranging the second leaves for their prints and help the children select a variety of types and sizes of leaves.

5. Create a border for the leaf rubbings by stapling the paper onto a sheet of construction paper in one of the fall colors.

Something to think about—
Completely dry leaves are difficult to use because they crumble easily. Use leaves which still have some moisture in them.

S T O R Y   S T R E T C H E R

For Cooking And Snack Time: Pumpkin Bread

What the children will learn—
To taste a different kind of bread

Materials you will need—
Pumpkin bread, bread knife, optional cream cheese or margarine

What to do—
1. If possible, bake the bread at the school, substituting pumpkin for bananas in a banana nut bread recipe. If not, ask a parent who is a baker to bring in an already-baked pumpkin bread.

2. Slice the bread from a whole loaf and ask the children to guess what kind of bread it might be based on its color. Some will say, carrot bread or banana bread.

3. Give each child a slice and ask them to try it. Most children enjoy the taste because it is not too sweet.

4. Let children who want a spread on their pumpkin bread top it with cream cheese or margarine.

Something to think about—
If you have a microwave in your classroom, wrap the bread in a

plastic wrap and heat it for just a minute or two. The aroma and the warmth will make it even more appetizing.

For Music And Movement: Falling Leaves

What the children will learn—
To move like leaves drifting down and swirling in the wind

Materials you will need—
A recording of the song, "Autumn Leaves" or a waltz tune, cassette tape or record player

What to do—
1. Observe the ways the leaves are falling from the trees, swirling, drifting, some landing nearby and others far away.

2. Play the music, "Autumn Leaves," and begin to sway, move around the room in the way you want the children to move.

3. Then, tell the children you are the tree and they are the leaves. At first, all the leaves are attached to the tree. So, they must all stand near you or touching you. Then, pretend a little wind is beginning to rustle the leaves. Have a few leaves blow away and begin to dance on the wind. Then, a large gust of wind comes along and blows most of the leaves from one side of the tree, but the others remain. Continue the slow gentle winds and the gusts of wind until all the leaves are dancing on the breeze.

4. Sway to the music with your arms outstretched. When the music stops all the leaves are on the ground ready to be raked.

Something to think about—
Children who are reluctant to move in response to the music can be your last little leaves. Hold

their arms and sway with them until the music stops.

For Science And Nature Center: Signs Of Fall Nature Walk

What the children will learn—
To recognize the signs of fall, as fallen leaves, acorns, brown dry grasses, tunnels where insects and little animals are burrowing

Materials you will need—
Small grocery bags, one with each child's name on it

What to do—
1. On a lovely fall day, take a nature walk around your center and, if possible, into a wooded area.

2. Ask the children to be good scientists, meaning good observers, and notice the changes in nature. Point out a few of the changes.

3. After you have hiked for a while, distribute the small bags with the children's names on them.

4. Have the children collect some of the signs that it is fall by picking up leaves, acorns, twigs and placing them in their bags.

5. Return to the classroom and discuss some of the signs of fall.

6. Open up the bags and let the children tell you something special about their signs of fall collection. One child may say, "The is a maple leaf." Another person will report, "I found five acorns." Someone else may observe, "I have a leaf just like hers."

Something to think about—
Teachers are botanists, biologists and naturalists. If you are unsure of some of the common trees, insects, rocks and shells, start a collection of children's reference books which have good illustra-

tions and are easy guides for you to use.

For Science And Nature Center: Carving A Pumpkin

What the children will learn—
To identify the parts of a pumpkin — shell, pulp, seeds, stem

Materials you will need—
Carving knife, tray, mixing bowls, large serving spoons

What to do—
1. While the children will be excited that you are carving a jack-o'-lantern, you will be excited that they will be exploring a pumpkin first hand.

2. Let several of the children try to lift the pumpkin. Hold your hands under theirs so the pumpkin doesn't drop.

3. Cut the stem and crown out of the top of the pumpkin.

4. Have the children observe the inside of the pumpkin at every step in the process.

5. Scrape out the pulp and the seeds onto the tray. After the children have tasted and touched them, scoop them up into the mixing bowl.

6. Proceed to cut the eyes and mouth of the jack-o'-lantern.

Something to think about—
While it is a messy job, you can have the children pull the seeds loose from the pulp and wash them. Then you can roast them in the oven. Explain that the jack-o'-lantern still has the meat of the pumpkin that we use to make pumpkin bread and pumpkin pies. If possible, on another day, carve a pumpkin and put it into a food processor to make the filling for a real pumpkin pie.

THE TINY SEED

By Eric Carle

It is autumn and the wind blows the seeds far away. The seeds' journey is told in the voice of a tiny seed which is swept along with the bigger seeds. When the wind stops blowing, the seeds fall to the ground. It spends the winter under the snow and when spring comes the snow melts and the little seed begins to grow into a little plant. The little seed which is now a flower keeps on growing and growing, and growing. It is a huge sunflower and provides food for the insects and birds all summer long until fall comes and the leaf pod forms. The flight of the tiny seed begins again. Eric Carle's bright collages and spatter painted backgrounds are most appealing.

Circle Time Presentation

Place a sunflower seed in each child's hand to hold while you read the story. Ask the children to imagine that this tiny seed is being blown by the wind. Read THE TINY SEED and pause to ask the children what will happen to the little seed when the big foot is about to step and when the petals are being blown away.

STORY STRETCHER

For Art: Sponge Painting

What the children will learn—
To create a painting using a sponge

Materials you will need—
Tempera paints, sponges, bowls, brushes, paper

What to do—
1. Show Eric Carle's illustrations which look like sponge painting and spatter painting.

2. Fill small bowls or margarine tubs with thick tempera paint.

3. Cut sponges into irregular, but manageable sizes. Place one sponge in each color of paint.

4. Demonstrate how to use the sponges to create the "pebbly" effect on the paper.

5. Provide some practice paper and some paper for their pictures they want to keep.

6. Some children will also want to paint with the brushes for a multi-media effect.

Something to think about—
Give children a variety of media and teach them many artistic techniques for painting. When they begin to search for collage materials and combine them with watercolors or tempera paints, then you know you have created an environment where children feel free to express themselves and do not have preconceived ideas of what is appropriate and inappropriate as a medium for self-expression.

STORY STRETCHER

For Cooking And Snack Time: Sunflower Seeds

What the children will learn—
To eat sunflower seeds

Materials you will need—
Toasted sunflower seeds without hulls, sample of seeds with hulls, unsalted mixed nuts, small paper cups, napkins, apple juice

What to do—
1. Have the children recall the flight of the tiny sunflower seed.

2. Discuss how huge the sunflower grew and that there were hundreds of seeds in the middle of its seed pod. Show the seeds with hulls, noting hundreds of these come from one sunflower.

3. Distribute the toasted sunflower seeds and let the children enjoy them. After they have described the taste as crunchy and nutty, add servings of unsalted mixed nuts.

4. Teach the names of the different kinds of nuts.

5. Serve the apple juice to accompany the nuts.

Something to think about—
Create a centerpiece for the snack table by filling wooden bowls or baskets with a variety of unshelled nuts. Add small packages of the sunflower seeds and help the children compare the sizes of the nuts, which also are seeds to grow, with the size of the tiny sunflower seeds.

For Library Corner, Flannel Board: The Tiny Seed Grows

What the children will learn—
To remember the order of the flight and growth of the tiny seed

Materials you will need—
Flannel board, felt pieces representing the tiny seed, sun, mountain, ocean, desert, bird, snow, mouse, big foot, hand, small plant, larger plant with leaves, big sunflower, petals and leaf pod, cassette tape, tape player

What to do—
1. Tell the story of THE TINY SEED using the flannel board.

2. Place a tape of you reading the story in the library corner with the flannel board and as they hear you read the story, the children can place the pieces on the board.

3. After the children know the story well, let them retell the story in their own words with the flannel board and refer to the book if needed.

Something to think about—
Often the same children use the flannel board and develop their skills so well that others let the good storytellers do all the flannel board stories. Have the reluctant storytellers assist you while you are telling the story with the flannel board, then have them practice right after you have finished. Often, with a little encouragement, these children will develop as good "re-tellers" of stories.
(Adapted from Mary Eckert's classroom.)

For Mathematics And Manipulatives Center: Counting Seeds

What the children will learn—
To count to ten

Materials you will need—
Ten acorns, ten leaves, tray

What to do—
1. With five children at the table, explain that acorns are the seeds from the oak trees which fall in the autumn.

2. Display a pile of ten acorns piled up on a bed of brightly colored fall leaves. Have the children guess how many acorns are in the pile. Accept any of their guesses, then ask how we can find out how many there are.

3. Count the acorns by moving them from the bed of leaves onto a tray, but pile them again in the center of the tray.

5. Recount another time by rearranging them into a counting pattern where there is one-to-one correspondence. For example, place one in each hand of the children and then ask how many acorns do we have. The children then will count ten hands, not acorns.

6. Rearrange the counting pattern again by placing ten leaves out on the table and have the children place an acorn under each leaf. Ask the children how we can know how many acorns we have now without looking at them. We count the leaves instead.

Something to think about—
Encourage children to think of other hidden ways to count, but retain the one-to-one correspondence.

For Science And Nature Center: Seeds And Seed Pods

What the children will learn—
To recognize that seeds come in many different sizes and shapes

Materials you will need—
Pumpkin seeds, sunflower seeds, pine cones, acorns, pumpkins, gourds, acorn squash, corn stalks, seed pods from a variety of plants, fall leaves

What to do—
1. Have several children assist you and arrange the science and nature area with brightly colored leaves, small pumpkins, gourds, acorn squash, corn stalks and a variety of seed corn and other seeds.

2. Have the children look at the display and decide which are seeds.

3. Examine the fall foods and the seeds from the harvest display.

4. Cut one of the pumpkins, one gourd, one acorn squash and look for the seeds. Leave them open so the seeds are exposed.

Something to think about—
Helping children develop their powers of observation and description is the basis of all scientific teaching. Whenever possible use the real objects instead of pictures and involve children in the work of creating the science exhibits. When you do not know the answers to children's questions, tell them you will find out. Then find the answer and write it on an index card to keep. Over the years, children ask many of the same questions.

THE SEASONS OF ARNOLD'S APPLE TREE

By Gail Gibbons

Arnold's special place is his apple tree. The story follows Arnold through the seasons and the many activities he enjoys because his apple tree is there. In the spring Arnold watches the buds develop into blossoms, the bees collecting nectar, and he enjoys the swing he made for the tree. In the summer, he builds a tree house, eats his snack up there, finds shelter from a shower and watches the small green apples grown bigger. By the fall, Arnold's tree now has red apples to eat and decorate, as well as golden leaves which have to be raked. In the winter, Arnold builds a snowman to keep his tree company, hangs popcorn and berries from the branches for the birds, and waits for spring for the process to begin again.

Circle Time Presentation

Ask the children to listen and when they hear you reading about fall say, "It's fall now." Read the book, pause for the children to know it is their cue at the fall scenes. Have the children recall all the things Arnold did in the fall. Reread the fall section and discuss some of the things Arnold did that they will do in class as making a flower arrangement, baking apple pies and, of course, eating delicious red apples.

STORY STRETCHER

For Art: Flower Arranging

What the children will learn—
To make a flower arrangement

Materials you will need—
Real branches of apple blossoms or silk flowers, vases, styrofoam pieces, styrofoam wreaths

What to do—
1. Discuss the part of the book where Arnold made wreaths of the apple blossoms and also where he took some of the branches covered with blossoms home for the family to make flower arrangements. In the illustration, Arnold, his father and his mother are arranging the flowers in a lovely tall blue vase.

2. With a few children at the art table, bring out the real or silk flowers and a variety of vases. For some arrangements just place the branches in the vases. For others, put styrofoam in the bottom of the vase to hold the flowers in place.

3. With another group of children, show them how Arnold made the apple blossom wreaths by intertwining the branches. Use the real apple tree twigs or flexible silk flower stems. The children can push the stem into the styrofoam to create the wreaths.

4. Display the flower arrangements and wreaths in the housekeeping corner, on the snack tables and in the reception area for parents to appreciate.

Something to think about—
Invite a florist to demonstrate simple flower arranging.

STORY STRETCHER

For Cooking and Snack Time: Baby Apple Pies

What the children will learn—
To prepare apple pies for snack

Materials you will need—
Pre-mixed pie crusts, knife, flour, saucepan, wooden spoon, rolling pin, muffin tins, shortening, apple pie filling, toaster oven

What to do—
1. Turn the muffin tins upside down. Grease and flour lightly the bottoms of the cups of the muffin tins.

2. Cut circles from the pie crusts just the size to fit over the bottoms of the muffin tin cups.

3. Let the children take the pie crust circles and shape them over the bottom of the muffin tin cups.

4. Bake the baby pie crusts following the directions on the pie crust package, but shorten the baking time briefly.

5. Remove the baby pie crusts from the oven, take them off the bottoms of the tins to cool.

6. Heat the apple pie filling in a saucepan. Fill the baby pie crusts. An optional step is to add a topping.

Something to think about—
On another day, invite a parent who enjoys baking to come to class and prepare an apple pie from scratch. The parent can work at a table and children can come and go during free play, but be cer-

tain each child participates in some step of the preparation. (Adapted from Lisa Lewis's classroom.)

For Housekeeping And Dress-up Corner: Dressing For The Seasons

What the children will learn—
To sort clothing according to its appropriateness for the season

Materials you will need—
Appropriate clothing for each season of the year for girls, boys and adults, full length mirror, four grocery bags

What to do—
1. Call attention to the many different ways Arnold dressed, from the long sleeved red checked shirt in spring, the shorts and tee shirt in summer, sweat shirt and jeans for fall and bundled up in coat, boots, mittens, scarf and hat for winter.

2. Tell the children you have added some different clothes to the dress-up area, but they are all mixed-up. If Arnold came today to this class, he wouldn't know where to find his fall clothes.

3. Ask the children to help organize the clothes by putting them in the bags. Ask them for suggestions as to how you can label the bags. Accept their suggestions and leave them organizing.

4. There will be different opinions about where the jeans and other items belong. Listen for their solutions.

5. After the clothes are distributed in the season bags, ask the children to decide how to store them in the chest of drawers.

Something to think about—
Have a fashion show of clothes for fall with the dress-up clothes from the housekeeping corner. The audience can suggest what fall activities the models are dressed for doing.

For Music And Movement: Here We Go 'round The Apple Tree

What the children will learn—
To sing "Here We Go 'Round the Apple Tree" to the tune of "Here We Go 'Round the Mulberry Bush"

Materials you will need—
None

What to do—
1. Sing "Here We Go 'Round the Mulberry Bush." Then teach the children the words you want to substitute.

2. Sing,

> "Here we go 'round the apple tree, the apple tree, the apple tree
> Here we go 'round the apple tree, so early in the morning.
> Here we go arranging flowers, arranging flowers, arranging flowers,
> Here we go arranging flowers, so early in the spring.
> Here we go building a tree house, building a tree house, building a tree house,
> Here we go building a tree house, just in time for summer.
> Here we go picking apples, picking apples, picking apples,
> Here we go picking apples, so late in the fall."
> Here we go baking pies, baking pies, baking pies,
> Here we go baking pies, all winter, all winter long." (Adaptation by Raines)

Something to think about—
Let the children suggest hand motions and body movements to accompany the song.

For Science And Nature Center: Sequencing The Seasons

What the children will learn—
To arrange pictures of the seasons in their sequence

Materials you will need—
Pictures depicting the various seasons, large index cards, rubber cement, hole puncher, long shoe laces or yarn

What to do—
1. From magazines, catalogs and calendars, have the children cut out pictures depicting the seasons. Rubber cement their pictures to index cards.

2. Ask the children to arrange their cards in the order of the seasons. Do not tell them where to begin. If they begin in fall, have them place the winter card next, and so on.

3. After they have practiced arranging the season sequence cards, punch a hole at the top in the center of the card. Then, punch one at the bottom in the center of the card.

4. Demonstrate how to lace the cards together. Tie a shoe lace or yarn with a big knot in one end and lace it through the fall card at the top, put the lace on the back side of the card, then lace through the hole at the bottom of the fall card. Next lace the top of the winter card, then the bottom, and so on. Tie a knot in the lace at the end. Hold it up and see the season pictures in order.

Something to think about—
You can laminate the cards and make them durable for a lot of practice. Also try the lacing cards for other sequencing tasks.

CHIPMUNK SONG

By Joanne Ryder

Illustrated by Lynne Cherry

The beautiful pictures are two-page illustrations of scenes from nature with a little child imagining the life of a chipmunk. Each is filled with detail and natural colorings. The story begins with, "under the trees, under the grass, deep in the ground, small ones live in darkness." The little child, who could be either a boy or a girl, follows the activities of a chipmunk. The underground scenes show the tunnels and burrows of the little animals and an above the ground view. The story continues to hibernation. Many of the scenes take place in fall when the chipmunk is finding acorns, storing them, burrowing and creating a bed of leaves.

Circle Time Presentation

Show the cover of CHIPMUNK SONG and have the children describe the coloring and markings of the little chipmunk. Point out how the child is pretending to be a chipmunk. Read CHIPMUNK SONG and let the children make any appreciative comments about the story or the illustrations they would like to make. Then give the book to a child who seemed quite interested in the story to place it in the library corner. Emphasize that the book will be available for anyone to look at the beautiful pictures during free play.

STORY STRETCHER

For Art: Sponge Lift-off

What the children will learn—
To create the effect of the underground soil with sponge and paint

Materials you will need—
Paper, tempera paints, brushes, sponges, easel, bowls

What to do—

1. Look again at Lynne Cherry's beautiful illustrations in the CHIPMUNK SONG. Point out the way she made the underground look like soil and tiny rocks.

2. Demonstrate one way to create this effect — by using a sponge to lift off some of the paint. Use brown tempera paint and brush on a thick coat of paint across the bottom of a piece of paper. Take a sponge and press it down over the top of the paint. Lift it off and some of the paint will be absorbed in the sponge and will leave behind a "pebbly" effect.

3. After the children create their "pebbly" effects, they can finish the pictures as they desire.

4. Children can use the sponges at both the easel and for table top art.

5. Encourage experimentation and leave the materials out for several days for the children to practice the lift-off technique.

Something to think about—
Teachers are often hesitant to teach new art techniques for fear that the technique will take the place of the child's self-expression. We have found the opposite. The more techniques and variety of media the children know how to use, the more expressive they become.

STORY STRETCHER

For Creative Dramatics: Pretending To Be Chipmunks

What the children will learn—
To improvise actions as inspired by the story

Materials you will need—
None

What to do—

1. Read CHIPMUNK STORY. At the end of the story, discuss how the child was pretending to be a chipmunk. Ask the children what actions they would do to be like a chipmunk. Let a few children volunteer some answers, as, "Puff out my cheeks like they had acorns in them." "Turn on my tummy and stretch my head up like I'm looking out of a hole." "Dig with my hands to find nuts."

2. Tell the children you want them to act like chipmunks while you read the story.

3. Read the story and pause briefly, looking expectantly at your pretenders when the story seems to indicate an action. For example, when you read, "Imagine you are someone small sleeping on a bed of leaves," expect the children to curl up in a little ball. When some child makes the action, say, "I see Nicholas is pretending to be a little sleeping chipmunk." Others will follow.

Something to think about—
Give specific observations of actions instead of just complimenting, "Good job, Nicholas." Try phrasing your observations in genuine tones, which do not overly excite the children, but continue the mood of the story.

STORY STRETCHER
For Library Corner, Listening Tape: Peaceful Ending

What the children will learn—
To coordinate their page turning with the illustrations they see and the story they hear on tape

Materials you will need—
Cassette tape, tape recorder

What to do—
1. Make the cassette tape of CHIPMUNK SONG without any assistance from the children. Use a hushed page turning signal, as simply saying, "Turn now," in a low voice.

2. Record the story leaving a bit of time after you have read each page for the child to look at the pictures, then say your "turn now" signal.

3. Leave the tape and the book in the library corner for the children who choose it for science information and also for the children who need a nice quiet place to relax and enjoy a peaceful story.

Something to think about—
CHIPMUNK SONG is a good selection for nature study and is quite appropriate for a naptime book. The chipmunk's moves as he unwinds from his busy

activities of gathering and storing nuts to preparing for hibernation invite comparisons to the busy activities at preschool or kindergarten and the time when everyone relaxes and enjoys a peaceful ending to all the activities.

STORY STRETCHER
For Sand Table: Underground Tunnels And Burrows

What the children will learn—
To create burrows and tunnels

Materials you will need—
Sand table, sand — mix in potting soil if possible, watering can

What to do—
1. Fill the sand table with a mixture of sand and potting soil. If potting soil is not available, the sand will do. Have the children help with this step.

2. Moisten the sand and soil by sprinkling water from the watering can.

3. Demonstrate how to make a tunnel in the sand by pointing your fingers, holding them together tightly, then pushing down under the surface. They can create mounds by packing the soil around their hands, then slowly withdrawing their hands.

Something to think about—
Children who are allowed to play outside in the sand and the dirt already know many ways to make tunnels and mounds. Since the mud-pie era of child's play is less appreciated today, some children may not know about making the soil soft with water, letting it dry out to harden, and creating burrows and tunnels. Keep the sand table out and available for extensive play. Encourage parents to dress their children in old clothes and compliment the children for

remembering to wear work clothes for the sand table. Keep big shirts handy for needed cover-ups.

STORY STRETCHER
For Science And Nature Center: Like A Chipmunk

What the children will learn—
To compare the behaviors of the class pet — a gerbil, hamster or white rat — to the behaviors of the chipmunk

Materials you will need—
Appropriate cage or habitat, animal, food, water, chart tablet, marker

What to do—
1. Have the children who visit the science and nature center during free play discuss with you what they recall about the chipmunk's behaviors from your reading of CHIPMUNK SONG. For example, some child will recall, "The chipmunk eats acorns." Another child will remember, "The chipmunk tunnels under the ground." Someone else will say, "It lives in a burrow."

2. Then point out the classroom pet and ask, "Is our gerbil like a chipmunk?" Give the children time to think and answer. Do not rush them. One child will say, "No, because he doesn't eat acorns." Another will say, "Yes, he makes tunnels in the shredded newspaper we have in his cage, and the chipmunk makes tunnels."

Something to think about—
For older preschoolers, continue the comparisons of how the chipmunk is like the class pet and write their comments on a chart tablet, then read their comments as a summary of the discussion.

117

REFERENCES

Carle, Eric. (1987). **THE TINY SEED**. Saxonville, MA: Picture Book Studio, Ltd.

Gibbons, Gail. (1984). **THE SEASONS OF ARNOLD'S APPLE TREE**. San Diego: Harcourt Brace Jovanovich Publishers, Inc.

Lionni, Leo. (1967). **FREDERICK**. New York: Pantheon.

Pearson, Susan. (1988). Illustrated by John Wallner. **MY FAVORITE TIME OF YEAR**. New York: Harper and Row, Publishers.

Ryder, Joanne. (1987). Illustrated by Lynne Cherry. **CHIPMUNK SONG**. New York: Lodestar Books, E.P. Dutton.

Additional References for Seasons: Focus on Fall

Balian, Lorna (1983). **SOMETIMES ITS TURKEY - SOMETIMES ITS FEATHERS**. Nashville: Abingdon Press. *When she finds an egg, Mrs. Gumm decides to hatch it and have a turkey for Thanksgiving dinner.*

Goss, Janet L. and Harste, Jerome C. (1985). Illustrated by Steve Romney. **IT DIDN'T FRIGHTEN ME**. Worthington, Oh: Willowisp Press, Inc. *A patterned language book where a child sees some delightfully scary animals outside his window on one pitch black night.*

Miller, Edna. (1985). **MOUSEKIN'S THANKSGIVING**. New York: Prentice Hall Books for Young Readers. *Mousekin and his forest friends struggle to survive with the help of a wild turkey.*

Testa, Fulvio. (1980). English text by Naomi Lewis. **LEAVES**. New York: Peter Bedrick Books. *A story of some leaves from the beginning of the fall as they drop from their tree.*

Williams, Linda. (1986). Illustrated by Megan Lloyd. **THE LITTLE OLD LADY WHO WAS NOT AFRAID OF ANYTHING**. New York: Thomas Y. Crowell. *A little old lady who is not afraid of anything must deal with a pumpkin head, a tall black hat, and other spooky things that follow her through the dark woods trying to scare her.*

SEASONS
FOCUS ON WINTER

Something Is Going to Happen
The First Snowfall
Sadie and the Snowman
Chicken Soup With Rice
The Mitten

SOMETHING IS GOING TO HAPPEN

By Charlotte Zolotow

Illustrated by Catherine Stock

As the family members wake up, they each say to themselves, "Something is going to happen." The mother feels it as she dresses and starts breakfast. The father thinks it as he shaves and dresses for work. The brother says it as he stretches and thinks of the bleak clouds he saw the day before. The little sister thinks, "Something is going to happen," as she pulls on her fuzzy bedroom slippers and bathrobe. The little girl comes downstairs to say good-bye to her father and her brother. Just as they open the front door, the father says, "Look what happened!" Catherine Stock's illustrations are line drawings washed over with soft watercolors to create the quiet of the waking hours and the wonder of the beautiful snow.

Circle Time Presentation

Ask the children, "Who gets up first at your house?" Tell them to think about how quiet it is in the morning when everyone is just waking up. Have the children sit quietly and pretend they are being very quiet so as not to wake their families. In a whispering voice say, "Something is going to happen." Read the book with low, but warm intonation. Express the families' delight at seeing the snow.

STORY STRETCHER

For Art: Shaving Cream Snow Pictures

What the children will learn—
To draw and make designs in the shaving cream snow

Materials you will need—
Shaving cream, paint shirts, sponge and clean-up pail of water

What to do—
1. Have the children put painting shirts on to protect their clothing.

2. Place a puff of shaving cream about the size of the palm of your hand in front of each child.

3. Talk about how the shaving cream is like the snow and how it is different than the snow.

4. Let the children enjoy drawing in the shaving cream and when one child is finished, smooth out the shaving cream, add a bit more and let another child begin.

Something to think about—
For variety, add some coloring to the shaving cream by using dry tempera paint. Place the dry paints in salt shakers, then the children can shake out some color, work it into the shaving cream and create still different pictures inspired by their new colors. A white snow scene can turn into an underwater scene with fish designs inspired by adding blue paint to the shaving cream.

STORY STRETCHER

For Cooking And Snack Time: Breakfast Muffins

What the children will learn—
To taste breakfast muffins

Materials you will need—
A variety of wheat muffins, bran muffins, banana-nut muffins, any of the fruit muffins recommended for breakfast, apple juice, napkins

What to do—
1. The best activity would be to bake the muffins with the children helping you. However, if this isn't possible, another good beginning is to involve some of the children in helping you select the muffins at the bakery. If neither step is possible, you choose a wide variety of breakfast muffins.

2. Have several children help you arrange them on serving dishes or in baskets. Cover the snack surprises with colorful napkins.

3. Tell the children what kinds of muffins you have brought them and tell them where you purchased them.

4. Have them select their muffin and pour their own apple juice.

Something to think about—
Large muffins may need to be cut in half for young children. When they choose the fruit muffins, talk about whether they like the fresh fruit better or the muffins. Warm the muffins in a microwave for more appealing taste and aroma.

For Housekeeping And Dress-up Corner: Getting Ready For Work

What the children will learn—
To role-play their parents getting ready for work in the mornings

Materials you will need—
Both men's and women's clothing, blazers or suit coats, ties, briefcases, high heel shoes, full length mirror, razor with no blade, empty shaving cream can

What to do—
1. Discuss how the little girl in SOMETHING IS GOING TO HAPPEN heard all the household noises and knew everyone was getting ready for the days' activities.

2. Point out that the father dressed in a suit and tie and was getting ready to go to an office. Discuss some other places people work that are not in offices. Mention some of their mothers and fathers workplaces and what they wear to work.

3. Place the new items for the dress-up corner on the chest of drawers and on the bed. The children will begin role-playing the getting ready scenes from the book and from their own experiences.

Something to think about—
The housekeeping and dress-up corner is almost always an appropriate center for a story stretcher activity. It is just as important to change the items in this center as it is to rotate the science display. Involve the children in making the changes, but also surprise them sometimes with the changes you have made.

For Library Corner, Listening Tapes: Household Noises

What the children will learn—
To identify common household sounds

Materials you will need—
Cassette tape, tape recorder

What to do—
1. Tape record some of the everyday sounds of your household waking up. Make a list of the sounds in order.

2. Experiment with the volume and the distance you need to record some of the noises so they sound like ordinary household sounds.

3. Play the tape and erase any sounds which may be too difficult to understand.

4. With the children who come to the library corner during free play, discuss all the sounds the little girl heard as she was waking up in SOMETHING IS GOING TO HAPPEN.

5. Tell the children that you recorded the sounds at your house when everyone was waking up, having breakfast and getting dressed for work or school.

6. Have them listen to the tape and try to figure out each sound.

Something to think about—
Ask parents to record some of the sounds from their work. The office worker can record the keyboard sounds, the telephone ringing, the sound of shoes walking in the hallway. A mechanic can record garage sounds. Also, record sounds from different areas of the preschool, as the kitchen, the office and on the bus.

For Mathematics And Manipulatives Center: Winter Wonderland Village

What the children will learn—
To create a village from the small manipulative blocks

Materials you will need—
Small manipulative building blocks, cotton batting, cotton balls

What to do—
1. Show the children the illustrations at the end of the book in SOMETHING IS GOING TO HAPPEN where there was a surprise snow fall.

2. Ask the children to build a village for the snow that has fallen on the table in the mathematics and manipulatives center.

3. Spread cotton batting over the table top and let the children construct their village by placing houses in the "snow."

4. Leave the snowy scene up for several days for the children to stretch their imaginations and add cars and trucks.

Something to think about—
If you live in an area of the country where children have not seen snow, then construct a village, but without the emphasis on the snow and the wintry scene.

9

SEASONS
FOCUS ON WINTER

The First Snowfall

Anne & Harlow Rockwell

THE FIRST SNOWFALL

By Anne and Harlow

Rockwell

A little girl tells the story of the first snowfall from the time she observes the first snow flakes. The snow covered the houses and streets as it fell all through the night. The next morning, she dressed in her warmest clothes, including her new ski jacket, and went outside. She shoveled a path in the snow, built a snowman and helped her father brush the snow from the car. They loaded her sled and her mother's skis and poles into the car and went to the park to play in the snow. She returned home to hot cocoa to warm her up so she could go out in the snow and play again. The Rockwells' illustrations with their bright colors and simple lines of child-like drawings are cheerful reminders of a young child's delight at the first snowfall of the season.

Circle Time Presentation

Ask what children do when they play in the snow. Do grown-ups play in the snow? Show the children the cover of THE FIRST SNOWFALL and ask them what they think the little girl will do on the day of the first snowfall. Read the book and comment on whether their predictions where in the story. After the reading, ask the children if there were any surprises. Did they know that adults like to play in the snow? Turn to the pages of the children and adults at the park and let the children discuss all the activities they see happening.

STORY STRETCHER

For Art: Snowflake Pictures

What the children will learn—
To make a picture showing the snow falling

Materials you will need—
Salt, shakers, paper, markers, damp sponges

What to do—

1. Ask the children to draw a winter scene of anything they would like.

2. When the drawing is finished and is dry, use a damp sponge and go over the paper lightly.

3. Then have the child shake salt over the picture. When the salt touches the damp paper, it will crystalize and look like snowflakes.

Something to think about—
For older preschoolers, have a multi-media approach to snow scenes. Ask some children to paint with watercolors and just before the paint is dry, shake the salt onto the picture. They can experiment with the tempera paints and the salt pictures; however, it is harder to create the same effect with the

thicker paints. Also, flaked detergent, like the kind recommended for washing baby clothes, can be used. Place it in a shaker with larger holes and as it falls onto the damp paper, it sticks. Let it dry thoroughly with the paper lying flat.

STORY STRETCHER

For Cooking and Snack Time: Winter Snacks

What the children will learn—
To mix and eat oatmeal

Materials you will need—
Packages of instant oatmeal, hot water, bowls, spoons, toppings as applesauce, apple butter, cinnamon, brown sugar or dried fruits

What to do—

1. Demonstrate for the children how to mix the oatmeal.

2. Let them mix their own oatmeal with the teacher assisting with the hot water.

3. If the children want toppings for their oatmeal, provide applesauce, brown sugar, apple butter, cinnamon or dried fruits.

Something to think about—
Usually one of the first foods children learn to prepare for themselves is dry cereal with milk. Emphasize that hot cereal requires an adult's or older child's help. However, putting the topping on the cereal is something that they can do for themselves. Tell them they know a good winter snack for the family to try.

STORY STRETCHER

For Mathematics And Manipulatives Center: Circles, Squares, Rectangles

What the children will learn—
To recognize the shapes in the illustrations from THE FIRST SNOWFALL

Materials you will need—
None

What to do—

1. Show the cover of THE FIRST SNOWFALL and have the children count how many different circles they can see, the three for the snowman, the little girl's eyes, the snowman's eyes and the birds' eyes.

2. Continue throughout the book looking for circles or circular objects on each page. Every page in the book has circles in the illustrations.

3. Repeat the process with squares by turning to the pages showing the houses and those with trucks and cars. Also notice the blade on the little girl's snow shovel.

4. Continue again through the book looking for rectangles. Help the children to see that some of the rectangles may have long horizontal sides and some have long vertical sides.

Something to think about—
If you have children who are unsure of the shapes, use templates and let the children trace their fingers around the edges before you begin.

STORY STRETCHER

For Music And Movement: It's Snowing Song

What the children will learn—
To chant and sing a simple song about snow

Materials you will need—
None

What to do—

1. Chant and sing:

"It's snowing, it's snowing,
I'm going to play in the morning.
It's snowing, it's snowing,
I'm shovel-ing this morning.
It's snowing, it's snowing,

I'm going to sled this morning.
It's snowing, it's snowing
I'm freez-ing this morning.
It's snowing, it's snowing,
I'm coming in this morning." (Raines)

2. After you teach them the words, let the children make up movements to accompany each verse.

Something to think about—
The children may be able to think of other verses, as one for building a snowman or one for ice skating.

STORY STRETCHER

For Sand Table: Snow Plowing

What the children will learn—
To clear the highways in their sand table winter landscape

Materials you will need—
Sand table, sand representing the snow, watering can, dump trucks, road graders, snow plows, and other cars and trucks to be stuck on the highways

What to do—

1. Show the children the Rockwells' illustration of the little girl waving to the driver of the snow plow. Discuss how the snow plows, dump trucks with sand and road graders clear the highways for people to get to work and to school.

2. Ask the children to collect all the vehicles from around the room which would be good for the sand table play which represents a landscape covered with snow and ice.

3. Leave the snow removers to their play and visit them periodically to discuss what they are doing.

Something to think about—
Encourage sustained play by introducing a new toy to the sand table or give them a new problem to solve. For example, have them pretend that a car has skidded off the road and is stuck in a snow bank. How could they get the car unstuck? They can not simply lift the car out with their hands, they must devise a way with one of their trucks.

SEASONS
FOCUS ON WINTER

SADIE AND THE SNOWMAN

By Allen Morgan

Illustrated by Brenda Clark

Sadie is a persistent little girl who delights in making a snowman, but there are problems, the animals keep stealing the food she uses to make his face and he keeps melting. Yet Sadie doesn't get discouraged. She waits for the next snowfall, takes whatever little bit is left from the first snowman, and rolls it in the snow to make the balls for her next snowman. Finally, when he is almost melted, Sally has an idea. She places the now tiny snowman in a large plastic bowl, he melts into water, she pours him into a freezer bag and keeps him frozen until next winter. Then at the first snowfall of the season, she brings out the ice, rolls it in the snow to start her first snowman of the season. Brenda Clark's drawings of Sadie and the snow scenes are brightly colored and detailed enough to prompt several sessions with this delightful story.

Circle Time Presentation

Discuss the steps in building a snowman. Get several suggestions for what makes good eyes, a nose and a mouth. Read SADIE AND THE SNOWMAN. Have the children join you in saying the predictable phrase, "He was a really good snowman and he lasted for a long time." Recall the different foods Sadie used to make her snowmen's faces. Discuss what happened each time to the faces.

STORY STRETCHER
For Art: Playdough Snowmen

What the children will learn—
To be persistent like Sadie in building a playdough snowman

Materials you will need—
Large mixing bowl of white playdough, variety of colors of playdough in smaller quantities to make the faces and hats

What to do—
1. Look at the illustrations of all the different faces Sadie made for her snowman. Suggest that the children make a lot of different snowmen to represent the ones Sadie made.

2. Give each child small pinches of the white playdough and ask them what they will need to make it into a snowman. Discuss that they will need to start with a small amount and roll it into a ball, just like Sadie did for her snowman.

3. Suggest that they make several different sizes of snowmen like Sadie did.

4. Leave the snow playdough sculptors to work on their own. Check with them periodically.

Something to think about—
To encourage the less persistent children to complete their snowmen plan a display of all of their snowmen. When children finish their snowmen, fold pieces of index cards and print their names on them, as "Derrick's Snowman" or "Teresa's Snowman."

STORY STRETCHER
For Block Building: Tent Play

What the children will learn—
To improvise play activities centered around a tent

Materials you will need—
Clothesline and a blanket or a small tent which is real

What to do—
1. Stretch a clothesline across one corner of the block building area. Place the blanket across the clothesline to create a tent.

2. Discuss how Sadie used the tent to protect the snowman and we use tents when we go camping to protect us from the hot sun and from the rain.

3. The children in the block building area will play with the tent in many ways. Some children will think of Sadie and the tent, while those who have been camping will relate the tent to their own experiences.

Something to think about—
If you have a family who has a real tent, a small one, have a parent come and set it up in the classroom, preferably when the children are present to watch and assist. Often teachers change the creative play centers in their classrooms when the children are not there and miss valuable opportunities for the girls and boys to see how things are done.

For Cooking And Snack Time: Snowmen And Snowomen Cookies

What the children will learn—
To decorate sugar cookies

Materials you will need—
Ingredients for sugar cookie recipe or prepackaged rolls of cookies, rolling pin, cookie sheet, waxed paper, spatula, oven, variety of decorations as sprinkles, raisins, peanuts, licorice twirls

What to do—
1. Roll out or flatten the cookie dough, leave the dough a bit thick, use different sized cookie or biscuit cutters to cut out the three balls for the snowman's and the snowoman's bodies.

2. Bake the cookies following the recipe or package directions being careful not to over bake.

3. Tear one sheet of waxed paper per child.

4. Remove the cookies from the over, lift each one onto the separate sheets of waxed paper to cool.

5. Place the decorations on the snack table and let the children decorate their snowmen or snowomen. Discuss how theirs look like Sadie's.

Something to think about—
Create a large version of Sadie's snowman by making a sheet cookie snowman and snowowoman for the snack tables. Use half the cookie dough for each. Improvise large cookie cutters from mixing bowls. Let the children assist in decorating.

For Library Corner, Listening Station: Sadie's Snowman

What the children will learn—
To cooperate in listening and viewing the book

Materials you will need—
Listening station, headphones, tape recorder, cassette tape

What to do—
1. Record yourself reading SADIE'S SNOWMAN to the children at circle time. Reread the book for the recording with the children joining you in saying the recurring phrase, "He was a really good snowman and he lasted for a long time." Have one child clap her hands as a signal to turn the page. Have her sit near the tape recorder.

2. Model how to operate the listening station. You hold the book and turn the pages.

3. Select a child to hold the book and turn the pages for the other children to see while they are listening with their earphones.

Something to think about—
Make the listening station and tape recorder regular extensions of each book you present to the class. Children will soon learn to depend on being able to follow up a good story from circle time by going to the library corner. However, the taped versions never replace the need for the teacher to spend time in the library corner sitting with a child, reading and loving a good storybook together.

For Science And Nature Center: Water In All Its Forms

What the children will learn—
To associate water in its solid, liquid and vapor forms

Materials you will need—
Snow, if available, ice, water, plastic mixing bowl, sealable large plastic freezer bags, tea kettle, cups, hand mirrors

What to do—
1. Discuss how Sadie kept part of her snowman all through the summer.

2. Bring some snow in from outside, place it in a bowl and leave it out on the science table. With the children, check it periodically throughout the day and see how much it has melted.

3. Finally when it is all melted, with the children watching, pour part of it into a freezer bag and place it in the refrigerator. Again, check it periodically with the children to notice that it is beginning to freeze.

4. Take the other half of the water and pour it into a tea kettle and boil the water. Have the children notice that the steam is rising from the tea kettle. Pour some of the hot water into cups for the children to see that it is steaming. Place a hand mirror over their cups and let them observe the water vapors.

5. Talk about the liquid, frozen and vapor forms of water.

Something to think about—
Throughout the science experiments with water, associate what you are doing with what happened to Sadie's snowman.

9

SEASONS
FOCUS ON WINTER

CHICKEN SOUP
WITH RICE

By Maurice Sendak

Maurice Sendak, author and illustrator, has written a deliciously amusing calendar of rhymes which begins with January and a little boy skating across the ice sipping chicken soup with rice. The rhyme for each month ends with a recurring phrase and a wonderful use for chicken soup with rice. Sendak's comic drawings help the children interpret the calendar rhymes.

Circle Time Presentation

Ask the children to imagine a cold, windy wintry day. Have them tell you what they would like to eat to warm up. Then read CHICKEN SOUP WITH RICE. Soon the children will be chiming in the recurring phrase which ends the rhyme for each month. Because the book is a funny one, the children will want to hear it again. Reread the rhymes of the winter months, January, February and March.

STORY STRETCHER
For Art: Decorating Soup Bowls

What the children will learn—
To decorate an everyday object with their own designs

Materials you will need—
A plastic margarine bowl for each child, a variety of colors of permanent markers, large rocks or beanbags to place in the bowls to hold them in place

What to do—
1. With a small group of children at the art table, discuss how the little boy in CHICKEN SOUP WITH RICE had a special soup bowl.

2. Talk about some ways bowls and other dishes are decorated to make them more attractive.

3. Turn the bowls right side up and place a rock or heavy beanbag in the bottom of each bowl to hold it still while the child is decorating it.

4. Ask the children to draw pictures or a design to make their special bowl for chicken soup with rice. Explain how the permanent markers dry slowly so it is best not to touch what they have just drawn. It is easier for the child to stand and move around the bowl while decorating it, rather than trying to turn it.

Something to think about—
Provide a few extra bowls for the children to experiment making their designs. Drawing on a curved surface is more difficult. Avoid showing them how to decorate their bowls, but encourage their own designs without adult models.

STORY STRETCHER
For Cooking And Snack Time: Cooking Chicken Soup With Rice

What the children will learn—
To prepare canned chicken soup with rice

Materials you will need—
Enough canned chicken soup with rice for the entire class, water, can opener, long wooden mixing spoon, heat source — electric crock pot, hot plate with saucepan, or a bowl-shaped popcorn popper will do — bowls from the art project, soup spoons, crackers or bread to accompany the snack

What to do—
1. During free play, have a few children assist you in collecting the supplies.

2. Let that small group of children open the first can of chicken soup with rice, add water and mix. While each child is stirring, repeat the rhyme from the book,

3. Continue with small groups of children until all have participated in adding to the class batch of soup.

Something to think about—
If possible, prepare home-made chicken soup with rice. Invite a parent to lead the activity. Include the children in each step of the preparation. They can even help

with cutting up the vegetables. For safety sake, work with only two children at a time when using real paring knives.

STORY STRETCHER

For Library Corner, Listening Station: A Listening Birthday Calendar

What the children will learn—
To recite a poem about their birthday month

Materials you will need—
Tape recorder, blank cassette tape

What to do—
1.   Have the children who have birthdays in January come to the listening area of the library corner.

2.   Teach them the ten line rhyme for January. For younger preschoolers, you can have the children repeat each line after you instead of learning all ten lines.

3.   Before recording them saying their January rhyme, have the children tell their names and their birthdays by saying, "Hi, I'm _____ and my birthday is January _____.

4.   Record the children who have birthdays in February saying the February rhyme and continue for a full-year listening calendar of birthdays.

Something to think about—
Include a few surprise voices on the tape. Invite the teacher's aide, a parent volunteer, the custodian, any adult who is familiar to the children to record their birthdays as well. Of course, the teacher must be included.

STORY STRETCHER

For Music And Movement: Ice Skater's Waltz

What the children will learn—
To move like ice skaters

Materials you will need—
Tape or record of the "Skater's Waltz" or any waltz music, tape or record player, plastic soup bowls

What to do—
1.   Have the children sit in a circle and take off their shoes so they can glide more easily like ice skaters.

2.   Show them the first picture for January in CHICKEN SOUP WITH RICE where the boy is skating while balancing a bowl of hot soup.

3.   Start the music and have the children stand in place and sway back and forth to feel the movement of the skaters.

4.   Give the children empty plastic bowls and ask them to pretend they are skating while sipping hot chicken soup with rice.

Something to think about—
For younger preschoolers, the task of skating and balancing the bowl may be too difficult. Allow them a few practice rounds on the imaginary ice before giving them the bowls. When children do drop their bowls, help them not to feel embarrassed by saying,

> *"It's all right,*
> *It's so nice*
> *Now the ice has*
> *Chicken soup with rice."* (Raines)

Undoubtedly, the silly rhyme will produce more pretend spills.

STORY STRETCHER

For Science And Nature Center: Magnetic Rice

What the children will learn—
To locate objects which are attracted by the magnet

Materials you will need—
Large sheet cake baking pan, two or three pounds of rice, small metal objects — toy car, screw, nuts and bolts, scissors, other non magnetic objects — puzzle pieces, chalk, plastic blocks, large magnet

What to do—
1.   Place the objects in a random pattern in the bottom of the cake pan.

2.   Pour enough rice over the top to just cover the objects.

3.   When children come to the science corner during free play to investigate what has been added to the area, demonstrate how the magnet will pick up an object hidden under the rice. Find one object by moving the magnet just barely over the surface.

4.   Have the children find the other objects which are magnetic.

Something to think about—
After the children have experience with the magnets, select new objects and have the children predict which ones will be attracted to the magnet. Then have them test their predictions by burying the objects in the rice and using the magnet to search.

(Adapted from Suzanne Gray's classroom at George Mason University's Project for the Study of Young Children.)

THE MITTEN

By Alvin Tresselt

Illustrated by Yaroslava

THE MITTEN is an adaptation of an old Ukrainian folktale. A little boy is out in the snowy woods gathering firewood for his grandmother. He loses his yellow mitten edged with fur and lined with red wool. The tale is the story of what became of the mitten when animals from the forest crawled inside it to keep warm. First there was the field mouse, then a frog, an owl, a rabbit, a fox, a wolf, a wild boar and a bear. Finally when a tiny cricket comes inside, the tiny mitten explodes. Yaroslava illustrates the book charmingly with alternating pages of crystal clear snow scenes with just line drawings followed by double page scenes of the mitten.

Circle Time Presentation

Place a warm pair of children's mitten on your lap. Ask a child to put them on and describe how they feel inside. Have the children imagine that they lost one of their mittens out in the woods. Do they think any little animals or insects might crawl in the mitten to keep warm? Read THE MITTEN and build up the excitement with each new animal's plea to be let into the warm mitten. After the reading, ask the children when they thought the mitten would split. Ask them how the author of the folktale surprised us at the end.

STORY STRETCHER
For Art: Decorating Vests

What the children will learn—
To decorate a paper bag to make it look like a vest

Materials you will need—
Paper grocery bags, markers, scissors

What to do—
1. If possible, bring in some vests, skirts or blouses with a lot of embroidery or fancy stitchery for the children to examine and appreciate.

2. Show the illustrations of the clothing the animals and the little boy was wearing in THE MITTEN. The bear has on a particularly colorful vest, edged with fur and stitched with elaborate designs.

3. Cut the paper bags by cutting out a neck hole and and two arm holes on the sides. Then cut it down the center to make it open like a vest.

4. Display the book and the embroidered clothing for the children to see, but tell them their colorful designs can be different than these.

5. For some of the vests, cut a fringe around the bottom.

6. Let the children wear their vests throughout the day.

Something to think about—
Invite parents who have examples of folk costumes or fancy stitchery items to bring them in and discuss their culture with the children. However, ask the parents to only bring items which children can try on and which are not too delicate.

STORY STRETCHER
For Block Building: Gathering Wood

What the children will learn—
To load and stack wood so it can be hauled easily

Materials you will need—
Wagon, wheelbarrow, sled, any other toys from the block building or outside play area which can be used to haul as wood, large building blocks, walking boards

What to do—
1. Discuss that the little boy in THE MITTEN was gathering firewood for his grandmother. Have them discuss why he chose a sled and not a wagon or a wheelbarrow.

2. If playing inside, have the children haul their building blocks and try to stack as many as they can onto their haulers.

3. If playing outside, let the children load the walking boards and use outside building blocks for their imaginary firewood.

Something to think about—
Often the simplest repetitive physical activity, as loading the imaginary firewood, will consume children's interests when they are playing a role. What is drudgery when they have to pick up and put away the blocks at clean-up time,

is sheer pleasure when they are genuinely involved in playing a role. Children need to be able to engage in sustained activity of their own design. We do not advocate teachers ringing bells every twenty minutes for children to change their activity. It does not allow for sustained play which leads to cooperative play.

STORY STRETCHER

For Library Corner, Flannel Board: How Many Animals Can Get Inside?

What the children will learn—
To retell the folktale of THE MITTEN

Materials you will need—
Flannel board, felt pieces for the little boy, the mitten, mouse, frog, owl, rabbit, fox, wolf, boar, bear, cricket

What to do—
1. Tell the folktale in your own words using the flannel board pieces. Include some of the polite wording of the animals' requests to come in from the cold.

2. Retell the story for those children who would like to hear it again and have them help you with the felt pieces.

3. Let the storytellers work with the flannel board pieces on their own, but leave the book as a reference for the children to sequence the animals correctly.

Something to think about—
Many of the folktales have patterns which are predictable because originally they were passed on from generation to generation orally. The predictable sequence of events and the repeated patterns of language allowed the storyteller to remember the story easily.

They also help the child using the flannel board to remember it easily.

STORY STRETCHER

For Mathematics And Manipulatives Center: Matching Mittens

What the children will learn—
To observe similarities and differences in the patterns of mittens

Materials you will need—
The children's real mittens and gloves or construction paper ones with similar designs colored on them

What to do—
1. Mix up the mittens and gloves. Display them at the mathematics table. Have some mittens and gloves which have no mates. For younger preschoolers, use fewer pairs of mittens.

2. Count the mittens and gloves one by one, not in pairs.

3. Have the children work pairing the mittens.

4. As they work, ask them to describe what they are looking for. "I'm looking for one with a red thumb." "I'm looking for one that's quilted inside." "I'm looking for a pink one with squiggly lines."

5. When the mates are all found, count the number of pairs of mittens and gloves. Count the number which do not have mates. Maybe their mates are lost in the woods for animals to find.

6. Decide whether there are enough pairs of gloves and mittens for all the children in the classroom.

Something to think about—
If you make construction paper mittens, the children can decorate them for art projects. Have the children make identical patterns on each mitten. For younger

children, simply have them color each mitten the same color.

STORY STRETCHER

For Music And Movement: Mitten, Mitten, Who Has The Mitten?

What the children will learn—
To recall their character when playing the game

Materials you will need—
A yellow mitten, lively music on a tape or record, tape or record player, sled or wagon

What to do—
1. Have the children seated in a circle on the floor. Place the sled or wagon in the center of the circle.

2. Ask the children to recall the animals from THE MITTEN.

3. Assign each child an animal from the story.

4. For the first turn, you be the little boy who looses his mitten. Start the music and pretend to be picking up firewood and putting it on the sled or in the wagon. Walk in front of a child and accidentally drop the mitten.

5. Stop the music and look all around the wagon or sled for your mitten, then ask, "Mitten, mitten, who has my mitten."

6. Instead of the child answering, "I do," he must answer with his animal name, "The rabbit has the mitten."

7. The child who has the mitten gets to be the mitten "dropper."

Something to think about—
To avoid some children not being chosen, whisper in the "dropper's" ear the name of the person you want to get the mitten.

REFERENCES

Morgan, Allen. (1985). Illustrated by Brenda Clark. **SADIE AND THE SNOWMAN**. New York: Scholastic, Inc.

Rockwell, Anne and Rockwell, Harlow. (1987)**. THE FIRST SNOW-FALL**. New York: Macmillan Publishing Company.

Sendak, Maurice. (1962). **CHICKEN SOUP WITH RICE**. New York: Harper and Row.

Tresselt, Alvin. (1964). Illustrated by Yaroslava. **THE MITTEN**. New York: Scholastic, Inc.

Zolotow, Charlotte. (1988). Illustrated by Catherine Stock. **SOMETHING IS GOING TO HAPPEN**. New York: Harper and Row.

Additional References for Seasons: Focus on Winter

Goffstein, M.B. (1986). **OUR SNOWMAN**. New York: Harper and Row, Publishers. *The snowman two children build looks so lonely when night comes that the little girl and her father go out and make a snowman to keep him company.*

Gregory, Valiska. (1987). Illustrated by Jeni Bassett. **RIDDLE SOUP**. New York: Four Winds Press. *When Scamp complains that they never have interesting suppers, Mr. Poggle decides to make Riddle Soup. Recipe is included at the end of the story.*

Keats, Ezra Jack. (1962). **THE SNOWY DAY**. New York: The Viking Press. *The adventures of a little boy in the city on a very snowy day.*

Lobe, Mira. (1984). Illustrated by Winfried Opgennoorth. Translation by Peter Carter. **THE SNOWMAN WHO WENT FOR A WALK**. New York: William Morrow Company. *A snowman becomes mobile, and in his wanderings, decides to seek a place where he can live and never melt.*

McCully, Emily Arnold. (1985). **FIRST SNOW**. New York: Harper and Row, Publishers. *A timid little mouse discovers the thrill of sledding in the first snow of the winter.*

SEASONS
FOCUS ON SPRING

First Comes Spring
Sleepy Bear
The Green Grass Grows All Around
A House of Leaves
Sarah's Questions

FIRST COMES SPRING

By Anne Rockwell

When Bear Child looks out of the window of his house, he notices the changes in how people are dressed and in the things they are doing. When he walks around the town, he sees many kinds of spring activities. He sees the daffodils, tulips and apple blossoms. He also dresses differently because it is spring. Anne Rockwell's illustrations continue with Bear Child in the summer, fall and winter. The text is simple and the drawings are child-like and colorful but filled with enough detail to invite several private explorations of the pages.

Circle Time Presentation

The book is the story of Bear Child and all the seasons, but it begins and ends with spring. Read the entire book, then return to discuss all the spring activities Bear Child saw in his town. Count how many different activities they can see. Some of the things we see the bears doing are: planting, fishing, hiding Easter eggs, marching in a parade, holding a balloon, seeding the lawn, making a birdhouse, fixing a car, looking through binoculars, eating breakfast, potting a plant, painting a picture, pruning a tree, planting a garden, digging in the dirt, riding a bicycle, seesawing, jumping rope, swinging, washing windows, sleeping, flying a kite, hiking and taking pictures.

STORY STRETCHER

For Art: Spring Photographs

What the children will learn—
To take a picture of something they think is a spring beauty

Materials you will need—
Instant print camera and film, spring photos, pastel colored construction paper

What to do—
1. From your own photo collection, show the children some of the pictures you have taken of beautiful spring flowers or flowering trees and shrubs.

2. Take a spring appreciation walk around the school and notice all the spring beauties, the grass turning green, the azaleas, the green buds and leaves on the trees. Call these things Nature's Spring Beauties.

3. Let each child take a picture of one thing he thinks is a Spring Beauty. Assist the child with aiming the camera and holding it steady. Since there are no people in the pictures, you are certain to get at least some of the Spring Beauty in the photo.

4. Fold a sheet of pastel colored construction paper in half. Glue the instant print photo to the outside cover.

5. Open the cover and on the inside, print a sentence or two which the child dictates to you about the Spring Beauty photo.

Something to think about—
This activity is an excellent one to have help from grandparents or volunteers.

STORY STRETCHER

For Housekeeping And Dress-up Corner: Dressing Bears

What the children will learn—
To role-play dressing the teddy bear according to the season

Materials you will need—
Four teddy bears, baby clothes

What to do—
1. Show the four different pictures of Bear Child as he was dressed for the seasons. Have the children tell you all the things he was wearing.

2. Ask one child to start dressing one of the teddy bears for spring. Give another bear to a child to dress for summer, one for fall and give the fourth bear to a child to dress for winter.

3. At a later circle time when you reread FIRST COMES SPRING, place a small chair beside your chair. As you read about spring have the child who dressed the spring teddy bear come and sit in the chair beside you. Continue with the other seasons as well.

Something to think about—
Other children can dress and hold the bears when they are listening to the tape of the book in the library corner.

For Library Corner: Favorite Spring Things

What the children will learn—
To state the activities they like to do best in the spring

Materials you will need—
Teddy bear dressed in his spring clothes, chart tablet, marker

What to do—

1.   Look at the illustration of Bear Child and all the things he sees going on in Anne Rockwell's FIRST COMES SPRING.

2.   Have a child who dressed one of the teddy bears in spring clothes bring him over to the library corner. Let the other children tell what activities he could do dressed as he is.

3.   Talk with the children about favorite spring activities.

4.   After a brief discussion, tell the children you want to remember all the things they said they liked to do, so you are going to write them down on the chart tablet. Also, when other children come to the library corner, you will read to them what this group said about spring.

5.   Ask each child to tell you a favorite spring activity and write, "Marty said, 'I like to fly a kite.' Christy said, 'I like to plant the flowers.' Becky said, 'I like to pick the flowers.'"

Something to think about—
As children see you print the words they begin to associate that spoken words can be written down and read by other people. When

you reread the sentences, read them fluently, not word by word, but make the reading sound like real language.

For Mathematics And Manipulatives Center: Easter Egg Mathematics

What the children will learn—
To count the Easter eggs and their contents

Materials you will need—
Five large plastic eggs which open, various small objects — paper clips, hair barrettes, tiny car, buttons, jelly beans — basket

What to do—

1.   Fill the large plastic eggs with the objects. Place the objects in different colored plastic eggs. Put the tiny car in one, two hair barrettes in another, three paper clips in another, four buttons in another egg, and five jelly beans in the last egg.

2.   Have a child rattle the egg and try to guess how many things are inside. Continue picking up eggs and shaking them to try to find the egg which has only one thing inside.

3.   When the child has found the egg with one item inside, let her open it and check. Then, she places the egg in the basket.

4.   The next child shakes the other eggs and tries to find the one that has two things inside and so forth to five.

5.   When the last child finds the egg with five things inside, then she opens it and eats the jelly beans.

Something to think about—
Vary the activity by having up to ten eggs. To make the task even more complex, place the same thing (in different amounts) inside each egg. Also include one egg which has zero items in it. This

activity is a popular one with preschoolers.

For Music And Movement: A Parade

What the children will learn—
To march with each other in a parade

Materials you will need—
Rhythm band instruments, baton, recording of march music, tape or record player

What to do—

1.   Mention that springtime is the perfect time for a parade. Show the illustration in FIRST COMES SPRING of the bears marching.

2.   Play the march music and show the children how to march by making exaggerated movements of lifting your knees and swinging your arms with your head held back.

3.   Have the children join you and march for a while to the music.

4.   Distribute the rhythm band instruments around the circle and have the children try out their instruments, then hold them still until the music begins.

5.   March with the rhythm band instruments for your spring parade.

Something to think about—
After children are comfortable with playing their instruments and marching at the same time, plan a parade out onto the playground. Take a portable tape player outside and play the march music there. It feels like a different experience when the children are parading in the spring sunshine. On another day, parade two by two and see if they can march together. This may be too difficult for some young threes to coordinate.

SLEEPY BEAR

A UNICORN PAPERBACK

by Lydia Dabcovich

SLEEPY BEAR

By Lydia Dabcovich

The book follows Sleepy Bear from the late fall, through his winter hibernation until he emerges hunting for honey again in the spring. The illustrations are charming, showing Sleepy Bear's facial expressions and body movements as he yawns, lumbers off to his cave, snuggles in for the winter, and his wonderful delight at the sights and sounds of spring. The children especially like his scratching when the bugs comes back, but the bees remind bear of honey and now he really knows it is spring. The words of the text are simple and the drawings bright enough and large enough for young children to see in a group story session.

Circle Time Presentation

Show the cover of the book and ask the children what they think the bear is thinking about. He looks like he is almost asleep with his eyes half closed. Ask the children to show you what they look like when they are sleepy. Read SLEEPY BEAR and discuss the illustrations which begin with springtime. Let the children tell you all the signs of spring they see in the illustrations. Which animals know it is spring before Sleepy Bear? The rabbits, birds and squirrels are all awake before Sleepy Bear ventures from his cave. Ask the children which illustration they think is the funniest?

STORY STRETCHER

For Art: Add-on Picture

What the children will learn—
To examine the picture and decide what to draw as their additions

Materials you will need—
Large sheet of butcher paper, about the size of the art table top, crayons, markers, chalk, scissors, construction paper, glue stick, hair spray

What to do—
1. Discuss Lydia Dabcovich's illustration of Sleepy Bear where he goes off looking for honey. The picture is filled with signs of spring.

2. Draw a large brown bear in the center of the butcher paper with brown chalk and then edge him in black crayon.

3. Spray the drawing of the bear with hair spray so the chalk will not smear.

4. Ask the children to "add-on" to the picture so it shows Sleepy Bear in the spring. Let them know that they may choose any medium or they may cut and paste some items for the group mural.

Something to think about—
Encourage experimentation. Some children can cut tiny pieces of construction paper and glue them on for apple blossoms or for other flowering trees and shrubs. When they are running out of ideas, have them check the SLEEPY BEAR book for other possibilities. Also, let them know you want many flowers, trees, butterflies, birds, rabbits and insects, not just one or two.

STORY STRETCHER

For Cooking And Snack Time: Sweet Honey

What the children will learn—
To taste honey

Materials you will need—
Toaster, bread, honey, margarine, knives for spreading, honey jars

What to do—
1. Ask the children what Sleepy Bear loved to eat. What brought him out of his cave in the spring?

2. Serve the toast, and if they want margarine, they can spread it.

3. Show the children a variety of honey jars, a plastic squeezable one that you snip the top off to squeeze the honey out, a pottery jar with a wooden honey server that you twirl and honey in clear glass jars where you can see the honeycomb inside.

4. Ask the children to select one kind of honey. Let the children serve themselves.

Something to think about—
Discuss with the children that honey is a natural sweetener. The bees make it and store it in honeycombs, which we collect. Place the honey with the honeycomb in the jar on the

science table for children to look at with their magnifying glasses.

For Creative Dramatics: Acting Like Sleepy Bear

What the children will learn—
To act like Sleepy Bear when they hear the story

Materials you will need—
None

What to do—

1. Go through the book looking at the way Sleepy Bear is moving and what he is doing.

2. Discuss how we might show some of Sleepy Bear's actions, as a stretch and yawn, swatting flies, licking lips for honey.

3. Ask the children to act like Sleepy Bear, but there is only one rule, they may not speak, only move and act.

4. Read the book from beginning to end.

5. Pause occasionally to state observations of what you see different children doing. "I see Paul walking on all fours like Sleepy Bear looking for a cave." "I see Melissa scratching like Sleepy Bear when the bugs come back."

Something to think about—
Do not call attention to a child who is participating poorly. With practice and self-assurance, many of the children will become more involved in the creative dramatics. Help them to enjoy it and encourage even their smallest attempts. Do not have an audience; everyone is Sleepy Bear.

For Library Corner: Follow The Bees

What the children will learn—
To learn that the buzzing bees mean it is time to turn the page

Materials you will need—
Cassette tape, tape recorder

What to do—

1. Have the children who select the library corner for their free play activity assist you in making a tape of SLEEPY BEAR for the rest of the class to hear.

2. Ask them to buzz like bees. After they have practiced their buzzing, explain that you will read SLEEPY BEAR and every time you point to them you want them to buzz like bees. Have them practice how long their buzzing should last.

3. Introduce the book on the tape as a part of the class spring unit. Ask the children to follow the sounds of the buzzing bees and they will hear a story about Sleepy Bear and his spring awakening.

4. Tape record yourself reading SLEEPY BEAR with the bees buzzing as the signal to turn the page.

Something to think about—
Listen to the tape and see if the children are satisfied with their performances. The book is a short one and they may want to do it again. If other library corner visitors want to make buzzing tapes, then make others; however, only incorporate the children who are interested.

For Science And Nature Center: Hives And Honeycombs

What the children will learn—
To know that bees make honey and store it in the honeycomb inside the hive

Materials you will need—
Jar of honey with comb inside, magnifying glasses, an old beehive from the woods and a man-made hive (optional), children's reference book on bees, honeycomb small linking blocks if available

What to do—

1. Recall the toast and honey served for snack.

2. Discuss that bees collect pollen from flowers and turn it into honey.

3. Have the children examine the honeycomb closely with their magnifying glasses and notice the way each little cells links together. If you have small manipulative blocks which link together in a honeycomb design, show the blocks as a larger model of the honeycomb.

4. If you are able to secure an old beehive from the woods, cut it open on one side, leaving the other side intact. Compare what they see to the honeycomb in the jar of honey.

5. If you have a beekeeper in the community, ask that person to bring in a beehive without the bees and explain how it works.

Something to think about—
Often naturalists with the local park service and nature centers will bring beehive exhibits to the school.

SEASONS
FOCUS ON SPRING

THE GREEN GRASS GROWS ALL AROUND

A Traditional Folk Song

Illustrated by Hilde Hoffman

Hilde Hoffman illustrated this traditional folk song as the story of a little boy's city back yard and what happens in the spring when he plants a tree in the ground. The recurring refrain, "and the green grass grows all around, all around" is used to signal the time to turn the page. The story begins with a hole in the ground and ends with a backyard celebration of the boy's tree and the mother bird living there. The bright yellow and green illustrations are of gleeful children of different ethnic backgrounds frolicking, singing and playing.

Circle Time Presentation

Read the book with an easy rhythmic cadence. You may find yourself singing it before you finish. Invariably, the children request that you read this book a second time so that they can join in by repeating the green grass refrain. Emphasize the cumulative pattern of the folk song. First, there is a hole in the ground, roots in the hole, then tree on the roots, then a limb on the tree, then a branch on the limb, then a twig on the branch, then a nest on the twig, then eggs in the nest, then birds on the nest, and it ends with a feather on the bird. You can end with a promise to read the story often until the children can learn the sequence.

STORY STRETCHER

For Art: Paper Bag Masks

What the children will learn—
To use an everyday object and make it something to play with

Materials you will need—
Paper bags, crayons or markers, scissors

What to do—
1. Show the picture in THE GREEN GRASS GROWS ALL AROUND where a child visiting the little boy's backyard plays with a paper bag mask over his head.

2. Draw the eyes on the mask and cut out the eye holes, then the children can decorate around them.

Something to think about—
For variety, have a happy mask on one side and a scary mask on the other side. Let the children decide the personality of their masks. Some young children do not enjoy role-playing feelings they are not yet comfortable with, as being a scary person, a wicked witch or a hungry wolf. The happy mask lets them participate securely.

STORY STRETCHER

For Library Corner, Flannel Board : The Parts Of A Tree

What the children will learn—
To listen for the cues for when to add the flannel board pieces of the tree

Materials you will need—
Flannel board pieces to represent a patch of green grass, a hole in the ground, tree roots, limb, branch, twig, nest, egg, bird, feather

What to do—
1. Demonstrate THE GREEN GRASS GROWS ALL AROUND by reading the folk song or singing it while putting up the parts of the tree at the appropriate cue.

2. Read or sing again and have a child place the flannel board pieces on.

3. Leave the flannel board pieces and the book on display in the library corner as a part of your spring emphasis.

Something to think about—
For variety, try a backwards version of the song, "There was a feather, the prettiest little feather you ever did see, and with this feather there was a bird," etc.

STORY STRETCHER

For Music And Movement: Singing The Green Grass Grows All Around

What the children will learn—
To sing all the verses to the song

Materials you will need—
Chart tablet or posterboard

What to do—
1. Make a chart picturing the green grass, the hole, the roots, the tree, the limb, the branch, the twig,

the nest, the egg, the bird and the feather.

2. Practice singing the book until you are comfortable with the words.

3. Teach the folk song to the children by talking through the words and giving visual clues by pointing to pictures on the poster.

Something to think about— Children feel a sense of accomplishment when they learn a long song. Also, when we teach our children traditional folk tunes, many of their parents will know the songs as well. It keeps alive some of the connections between the childhoods of the parents and their children.

STORY STRETCHER

For Outside Play: Playing In The Spray

What the children will learn— To enjoy cool water on a warm or hot day

Materials you will need— Water hoses, children's swim suits, towels

What to do—
1. Inform the parents that you plan a "play in the water day" for outside play. Then, watch the weather forecast and the day before your special day, send notes home requesting that tomorrow the parents send their children's swim suits.

2. Connect sprinklers to a couple of water hoses.

3. Plan to be involved in the play and dress appropriately.

Something to think about— Young children can become over stimulated easily and may need an alternative. Also, some children will not want to continue just running through the sprinklers. For

alternatives, use many forms of water play. Move the water table outside. Fill the "pretend house paint cans" with water for children to imitate house painters with their big brushes.

STORY STRETCHER

For Science And Nature Center: Bird Nests

What the children will learn— To observe bird nests

Materials you will need— Collection of various types of bird nests, playdough; ask the families of the children for bird nests, chances are older brothers and sisters have them stored away somewhere

What to do—
1. Write a note in the newsletter requesting bird nests for a science and nature display and ask for information about where the nest was found and what bird built it. If the owners do not know the information, ask them to send the nest for the display, anyway.

2. Arrange the bird nests and label each nest.

3. By referring to a child's reference guide, determine the size of the eggs for the birds nests you have.

4. Have the children shape eggs for the nest out of playdough.

Something to think about— Be certain to teach the children not to disturb any bird's nests they might find when out walking and playing. Talk about the importance of letting the egg remain undisturbed so that the little bird can grow inside.

10

SEASONS
FOCUS ON SPRING

A HOUSE OF LEAVES

By Kiyoshi Soya

Illustrated by Akiko Hayashi

A little girl, Sarah, is caught out in a gentle spring shower. She ducks under some plants with big leaves and waits for the rain to stop. While she is waiting, some insects also fly in for protection from the rain. A praying mantis, a cabbage butterfly, a beetle and a ladybug fly into Sarah's house of leaves. Sarah and the insects are quiet and still and wait for the rain to stop. Through the leaves she can see the sky get lighter; the rain has stopped and Sarah hurries home to her real house. The delicate illustrations and innocent expressions will help any child to imagine a house of leaves.

Circle Time Presentation

Talk about the differences between a thunderstorm and a light spring shower. Ask if anyone has ever been caught out in a gentle spring shower? After a little discussion, show the picture of Sarah on the front cover of the book and tell the children this is the story of what happened to Sarah when it began to rain. Read A HOUSE OF LEAVES in a calm, reassuring voice. This book often ends with a request to read it again. Ask the children to listen during the second reading and recall all the insects Sarah shared her house of leaves with. At the end of the story, discuss whether they would like to find a house of leaves like Sarah's if they were caught out in a spring shower.

STORY STRETCHER

For Art: Green Leaf Pictures

What the children will learn—
To paint a spring leaf

Materials you will need—
Easels, green construction paper, brushes, painting shirts, stapler

What to do—
1. Cut large green leaf shapes, one per sheet of construction paper.

2. Hang up the large green leaves at the easel for the children to paint.

3. Tell the children that you want to make a house of leaves like Sarah's for the bulletin board.

Something to think about—
When assisting the children with their painting shirts, or printing their names on their leaves, talk with them about Sarah and A HOUSE OF LEAVES and the bulletin board you are making.

STORY STRETCHER

For Housekeeping And Dress-up Corner: Rain Wear

What the children will learn—
To dress in the clothing needed when it is raining

Materials you will need—
Rain boots, rain slickers, umbrellas

What to do—
1. Discuss Sarah and A HOUSE OF LEAVES. Sarah did not have an umbrella or a rain coat. How did she keep dry?

2. Have the children collect all the things they would need if they were going out into the rain.

3. Leave the children to role-play on their own in the dress-up corner.

Something to think about—
If you have parents bring in umbrellas for your dress-up corner, do not accept any umbrellas which have sharp points on the ends. Most of the children's umbrellas and many of the women's umbrellas no longer have the sharp points. Children delight in umbrellas whether it is raining or not.

STORY STRETCHER

For Library Corner, Flannel Board: Sarah's Visitors

What the children will learn—
To retell their own versions of the HOUSE OF LEAVES story

Materials you will need—
Flannel board, Sarah picture, laminating material, sand paper, felt pieces for the praying mantis, the cabbage butterfly, the beetle, and the ladybug

What to do—
1. Use a large paper doll, a large picture of a child from a magazine or sketch Sarah. Laminate the pic-

ture or cover it in clear contact paper. Attach a little strip of sand paper to the back of the picture to hold it in place on the flannel board.

2. Make the insects from brightly colored pieces of felt.

3. Model the flannel board story of A HOUSE OF LEAVES, feeling free to improvise any dialogue along the way.

4. Give the flannel board story to a child to tell and be certain to tell them it is alright to think of things Sarah and the insects might have said to each other.

Something to think about—
Often when children retell an interesting story, they add something to the story which they have imagined. Encourage these story extensions and do not correct the children.

STORY STRETCHER

For Music And Movement: Sarah And The Flying Insects

What the children will learn—
To move in response to the music

Materials you will need—
Cassette tape or recording of calm gentle music, triangle and drum from the rhythm instruments, tape of weather sounds (optional)

What to do—
1. Have the children imagine that the center of their circle time rug is Sarah's house of leaves.

2. Set the stage for their imagining by lowering your voice and telling them that it is getting very quiet outside and if they listen very closely they might hear a tiny raindrop.

3. Very gently tap the triangle making tiny pinging sounds.

4. Pause and make the pinging sound again, then make it more

rapidly. Switch to the drum and very lightly thump it.

5. Continue faster until the Sarahs decide they need to come inside their house of leaves.

6. Repeat the exercise and have different children pretend to be the different insects. Show them how to hop like the praying mantis, flutter like a butterfly and fly like the beetle and the ladybug.

7. This time create the mood with a weather recording or a slow gentle selection of music.

Something to think about—
After the spring rain, enjoy the calm and have everyone relax.

STORY STRETCHER

For Science And Nature Center: Insects

What the children will learn—
To recognize the real-life pictures of the insects mentioned in A HOUSE OF LEAVES

Materials you will need—
Children's guides to insects, magnifying glasses

What to do—
1. Recall with the children the insects which flew into Sarah's house of leaves.

2. Show the children pictures of how these insects look from drawings in children's guide books or from nature photographs.

3. Look at the pictures through the magnifying glasses to see more details.

4. With a few children at a time, go out into a grassy area and look for insects. When you find some, have the children look at them through their magnifying glasses.

Something to think about—
Create a terrarium and let children bring in a variety of insects to add to the terrarium. Teach the children how to keep the insects alive while transporting them to school.

SEASONS
FOCUS ON SPRING

SARAH'S QUESTIONS

By Harriet Ziefert

Illustrated by Susan Bonners

Sarah is an inquisitive young child who talks her mother into taking a walk and playing "I Spy." The two share their delights in the many beautiful things they see, as a fluffy cloud, a little bird, dogs napping in the sun, a rabbit hidden in the brush and a lovely view of the valley from the hillside. On their walk home Sarah asks many questions which often puzzle young children, such as, "Why do squirrel have bushy tails?, Do dogs dream?, Why do cats purr?, Why do bees buzz?, How does a baby duck know who its mother is?, Why do birds sing?," and many more questions. The wonderful mother and daughter relationship is illustrated beautifully by Susan Bonners in realistic drawings.

Circle Time Presentation

Recall with the children that you have already read a book about a girl named Sarah in A HOUSE OF LEAVES, but this is a different Sarah. Show the beautiful cover of the book and ask the children what they think Sarah might be pointing out to her mother. Tell the children that Sarah asks her mother lots of questions and that some of the questions she asked may be ones they have thought about as well. Read SARAH'S QUESTIONS and discuss the answers.

STORY STRETCHER
For Art: Flower Posters

What the children will learn—
To name some of the more common flowers

Materials you will need—
Seed catalogs, gardening magazines, posterboard or construction paper, scissors, glue

What to do—
1. Discuss that Sarah saw jonquils and hyacinths growing near the pond. Tell them that in some areas of the country jonquils are called buttercups or daffodils.

2. Show them some of the pictures from the seed catalogs of jonquils and hyacinths. Notice that there are many different varieties.

3. Spend some time with the children exploring the pictures and commenting on the ones they like.

4. Ask them to make posters of the flowers they like. They can select many different flowers and arrange the poster like a collage, or they may select one or two and make frames for those pictures. Let the children decide.

5. Assist them in making their collage posters or in framing some pictures for their poster.

Something to think about—
If you have art posters of famous paintings of flowers, display the posters near the art center for this unit of study on spring. Also, display attractive photographs of flowers.

STORY STRETCHER
For Library Corner, Listening Station: Sarah Asks A Lot Of Questions

What the children will learn—
To recall the answers to Sarah's questions by hearing the book read again

Materials you will need—
Cassette tape, tape recorder, listening station, earphones

What to do—
1. Record yourself reading SARAH'S QUESTIONS. Whisper "I Spy" as the page turning signal. Make your voice much lower than when you are reading.

2. Place the tape recording and the book at the listening station with the earphones.

3. Give SARAH'S QUESTIONS to one of your most inquisitive young girls and have her be the page turner while she and her friends listen to the tape of the book.

Something to think about—
Research has shown that teachers answer boys' questions more thoroughly than they do girls'. Think back to the activities of the day and make certain you are not one of those teachers. Find ways to let the children know that you want them to ask lots of questions, but just like Sarah's mother, sometimes you do not know the

answers. You will find out the answers to their questions or you will help them to answer the questions themselves. Some of the children's questions like, "Why is the sky blue?" are just things they wonder about, they really don't want an answer.

For Music And Movement: Musical I Spy

What the children will learn—
To describe what they see

Materials you will need—
Cassette tape or record of light instrumental music, tape or record player

What to do—
1. Explain to the children how to play musical "I Spy."

2. When the music begins, they move in any way which the music inspires them. If they can't think of a way to move, they can skip, hop, jump or march, but they must move.

3. When the music stops, they turn around once and freeze, then stare at something straight in front of them.

4. The teacher then calls on someone and the person says, "I Spy," and describes something that is seen.

5. The listeners have three chances to guess what the person spies, then the person tells the answer.

6. The music starts again and everyone moves however the music makes them feel, until the teacher stops the music, then the process of "I Spy" begins all over again.

Something to think about—
Young children may play "I Spy" by just giving colors and then everyone guesses. There are no winners and losers. The children enjoy moving to the music, freezing when it stops, describing what they see and hoping they will be called on next.

For Science And Nature Center: Recognizing Flowers

What the children will learn—
To name the common flowers

Materials you will need—
Live flowers if possible, if not large beautiful pictures of flowers

What to do—
1. Have the children examine the flowers carefully. Ask them to describe their colors, their stems, their fragrances.

2. After they have learned the names of the flowers, play a variation of "I Spy" at the science and nature center.

3. Teach the children this chant,
Teacher asks:

"Sarah, oh Sarah, what do you see?
Child replies:

I see a little purple violet
That's what I see." (Raines)

4. Substitute different children's names and let them pick up the plant or the picture of the plant they will say in their response.

5. Continue with the rest of the plants.

Something to think about—
Using a chant or a rhyme helps to make the learning of the names of the plants more enjoyable.

For Science And Nature Center: I Spy Walks

What the children will learn—
To state their observations

Materials you will need—
None

What to do—
1. With two or three children at a time, take a nature walk around the center and have the children tell you what they spy.

2. Try to make this time a very special event. Linger for a time over a pretty flower or investigate an insect tunnel or listen to the breeze rustling the new young green leaves.

3. Encourage the children to describe what they are seeing so completely that when they return to the classroom, if they want to tell someone about it, they can remember.

Something to think about—
Practice the "I Spy" nature walks with a grandparent or a parent volunteer observing quietly in the background. Try to recreate the mood you felt when reading SARAH'S QUESTIONS. Then encourage the volunteer to take another small group of children out for "I Spy" walks. In our busy hurried schedules where the classroom is so active and noisy, the "I Spy" walks become a treat for the children and for the volunteers.

REFERENCES

Dabcovich, Lydia. (1982). **SLEEPY BEAR**. New York: E.P. Dutton.

Hoffman, Hilde. (1968). **THE GREEN GRASS GROWS ALL AROUND**. New York: Macmillan Publishing Company.

Rockwell, Anne. (1985). **FIRST COMES SPRING**. New York: Thomas Y. Crowell.

Soya, Kiyoshi. (1986). Illustrated by Akiko Hayashi. **A HOUSE OF LEAVES**. New York: Philomel Books.

Ziefert, Harriett. (1986). Illustrated by Susan Bonners. **SARAH'S QUESTIONS**. New York: Lothrop, Lee and Shepard Books.

Additional References for Seasons: Focus on Spring

Clifton, Lucille. (1973). Illustrated by Brinton Turkle. **THE BOY WHO DIDN'T BELIEVE IN SPRING**. New York: E.P. Dutton. *Two boys look everywhere for spring which they hear is just around the corner until finally it is found in a most unexpected place.*

Hoban, Lillian. (1987). **SILLY TILLY AND THE EASTER BUNNY**. New York: Harper and Row Junior Books. *Silly Tilly Mole is so forgetful and silly on Easter morning that she cannot find her bonnet and nearly fails to let the Easter Bunny into the house.*

McMillan, Bruce (1986). **COUNTING WILDFLOWERS**. New York: Lothrop, Lee and Shepard Books. *A counting book with photographs of wildflowers illustrating the numbers one through twenty.*

Moncure, Jane Belk. (1975). Illustrated by Frances Hook. **SPRING IS HERE!** Elgin, IL: Child's World. *A little boy celebrates all the things he can do because it is spring, play baseball, visit the meadow and watch the birds, plants and insects.*

Tafuri, Nancy. (1985). **RABBIT'S MORNING**. New York: Greenwillow Books. *When the sun come up a baby rabbit goes exploring and sees many other animals.*

TEDDY BEARS AND OTHER BEARS

Corduroy
This is the Bear
Jesse Bear, What Will You Wear?
Jamberry
The Teddy Bear's Picnic

TEDDY BEARS AND OTHER BEARS

CORDUROY

By Don Freeman

Corduroy is an adventuresome toy bear who wanders around in a department store at night. One night while he is looking for a button to replace the one missing from his overalls, the night watchman discovers him and takes him back to the toy display. When he awakes the next morning, a little girl is there to buy him with the pennies she had saved. She takes him home and the first thing she does is sew a new button on his overalls. Don Freeman's expressive illustrations and the bright red cover of the book capture the attention of young children. Corduroy captures their affections. Many teachers already count CORDUROY among the classics.

Circle Time Presentation

Read the story of how Corduroy came to his new home. Have the children think about how Corduroy went looking for his lost button. Where were all the places he went in the department store? Then, ask the children how Corduroy got his name. We are not told in the story. Ask several children to tell you the names of their favorite stuffed animals. Discuss how their favorite toys came to be theirs. Were they presents or "saved for" toys? What makes the animal special? On a chart tablet, write Corduroy and then write the names of some of the children's favorite stuffed animals.

STORY STRETCHER

For Art: Button Pictures

What the children will learn—
To incorporate a button into a picture

Materials you will need—
Assorted buttons, construction paper, glue, crayons or markers

What to do—

1. Discuss Corduroy's missing button which was never found. Ask the children where they think it might be.

2. Have children select a button and some paper. Place a button on one child's paper near the top center of the paper and say, "Here's Corduroy's button, where do you think it is?" The child might reply, "It is in an airplane flying in the sky?" Try some other placements on the paper. When the button was placed at the bottom of the paper, one girl told her teacher, "A dog took Corduroy's button and 'hideded' it."

3. Encourage the children to use their imaginations and think of

places to "hide Corduroy's button" in their pictures.

Something to think about—
With younger preschoolers, you can ask them to glue the button on their papers and then make a picture using the lost button. The button can lose its "Corduroy identity" and becomes one of wheels on a car or any pretation.

STORY

M_____d—
Cas_____ recorder and play____y bear who is dressed like Corduroy

What to do—

1. Tape record yourself reading CORDUROY. Include a gentle sound for a page turning signal, as a light thump with your finger on a tabletop.

2. Place the tape, the book and Corduroy teddy bear at the listening station for cuddling while listening to the story.

Something to think about—
A young preschooler may want to listen to the tape while holding Corduroy, without looking at the book. Older preschoolers may take turns, one child holds Corduroy while the other turns the pages of the book. This satisfying story is an excellent quiet time retreat into a good book.

For Housekeeping And Dress-up Corner: Dressing Teddy Bears

What the children will learn—
To manipulate small buttons and snaps

Materials you will need—
Baby clothes and doll clothes (often baby clothes fit the stuffed animals best); be certain to have some overalls with buttons on the straps like Corduroy's; variety of sizes of teddy bears

What to do—
1. Discuss how fathers and mothers often help us or our baby brothers and sisters get dressed in the mornings.

2. Show the children some of the special clothes you have collected for them to use to dress their teddy bears.

3. Dress a teddy bear who looks like Corduroy and see if the children make the connection. One teacher even had overalls with a missing button. Then she sewed the button on so the children could see how a button was sewn.

4. Leave the children to proceed on their own.

Something to think about—
Encourage more boys to participate in this excellent small muscle coordination activity by suggesting that they pretend to be fathers who are helping their children get dressed.

For Mathematics : Making Sets By Touch

What the children will learn—
To make sets of swatches of fabric which feel alike or are similar

Materials you will need—
Three swatches of fabric which are the same — three of corduroy, three of cotton, three of tweedy wool, three of satin or silk, 5 x 8 index cards, stapler

What to do—
1. Ask parents to contribute scraps of fabric.

2. Cut the fabric into rectangles the size of the large index cards. Have at least three samples of each type of fabric.

3. Staple each swatch of fabric onto an index cards.

4. Have the children find the fabric which feels the same and place these cards together to make a set.

Something to think about—
For very young preschoolers, allow them to use their hands and eyes. Then, use a blindfold or dark sunglasses and have the child do the activity by just concentrating on feeling the similarities. Also, to challenge the young pre-schooler, have some fabric which feels the same, but is a different color. For example, use brown and green corduroy. For older pre-schoolers, use the blindfold and have more types of fabric for them to sort into sets. This activity can also be used for ordering from roughest to smoothest.

For Music And Movement: Button, Button, Who Has The Button?

What the children will learn—
To follow the simple rules of a game

Materials you will need—
A large button, recording of lively music, tape or record player

What to do—
1. Have the children sit in a circle.

2. Explain the rules of "Button, Button, Who Has the Button? When the music starts, everyone puts their hands behind their backs, making cups for the button. The person who is "it" moves around the circle pretending to drop the button, but we don't know where. The person drops the button in someone's hand and then keeps pretending to drop it until the music stops. When the music stops the teacher chooses a child who guesses who might have the button by saying, "Button, button, who has the button? I think Brian has the button." It doesn't matter if the person guesses incorrectly, whomever has the button holds it up and says, "Button, button, I have the button." The person with the button becomes "it."

3. Demonstrate the game once by being "it." Then, begin the game with one of the less popular children.

Something to think about—
The teacher can usually tell who has the button by the expression on the child's face. By controlling when the music starts and stops and who guesses, the teacher can be certain that all children participate.

TEDDY BEARS AND OTHER BEARS

THIS IS THE BEAR

By Sarah Hayes

Illustrated by Helen Craig

THIS IS THE BEAR is the story of how Fred, a teddy bear, gets lost when a dog pushes him into a garbage can. The events leading to his eventual rescue from the garbage dump are the scenes of the story. Fred's owner never gives up. He takes a bus to the dump, persuades the garbage man to search for Fred, and finally the dog who pushed Fred into the garbage can is the one who sniffs around and finds him. The story is told in rhyme and Helen Craig's brightly colored drawings, with effective use of white space, her attention to detail and the emotional expressions of the characters add drama to the search for the lost teddy bear.

Circle Time Presentation

Discuss losing favorite toys and how we feel. Show the cover and ask the children to tell you which toy is lost. Point out the end paper pages of the book where a checkerboard pattern is created with the teddy bear in one square followed by a garbage can in the next and alternating on each row. From the checkerboard pages, ask the children to predict what they think a teddy bear and a garbage can together might mean. Read THIS IS THE BEAR. Confirm the children's predictions. They were correct; the teddy bear was accidentally put in the garbage can.

STORY STRETCHER

For Art: Talking Pictures

What the children will learn—
To use the cartoonist bubble to show people are talking

Materials you will need—
Comic strips from the newspaper, paper, crayons and markers

What to do—

1. Point out the way the illustrator of THIS IS THE BEAR showed us what the characters were saying by drawing a bubble with a tail and pointing the tail towards the character who is speaking. Also, show how cartoonists use this technique in the newspaper comic strips.

2. Ask the children to draw pictures where someone is talking.

3. After the pictures are drawn, have each child tell you what the characters are saying, and write the dictation in a bubble over the characters' heads.

Something to think about—
For older preschoolers, you might emphasize the talking pictures even more by taking pictures of the children or by having them draw self-portraits. Then, cut out little bubbles and tape them on top of the pictures with quotes of what you heard the child say during the day. For example, you snap Michael eating applesauce at snack and on his picture he is saying, "I like it with cinnamon." Or, Caroline draws a picture of herself with barrettes in her hair and you tape a bubble to her picture saying, "My mommie bought me these new barrettes."

ANOTHER STORY STRETCHER

For Art: Hidden Pictures

What the children will learn—
To create a picture with hiding places

Materials you will need—
Two pieces of construction paper per child, one white and another color, crayons, scissors, stapler

What to do—

1. Demonstrate a "hidden" picture. Take a child's drawing from a previous day, place a piece of construction paper over it, staple together on the left side only and then cut a door or doors into the cover to match the spot where a main part of the picture is. For example, if a child drew a picture of a truck with a driver, cut a small door to show the driver's face, another shows the wheels and another the trailer.

2. Ask the children to draw a picture of anything they choose.

3. Select a different colored construction paper, and with a pencil, lightly mark the spot which corresponds to a main part of the picture.

4. Cut several windows or doors to match the main parts. Make a fold so that the windows or doors open easily.

5. Staple the cover sheet of construction paper and the picture together along the left hand side of the paper only.

Something to think about—
When the hidden pictures are finished, the artists can have their friends guess what the picture is by opening the doors. After the guessing is finished, the friend can check for correctness by opening up the entire cover.

S T O R Y   S T R E T C H E R
For Library Corner: Telling A Lost Teddy Story

What the children will learn—
To tell a story with a similar plot, but with a different setting or ending

Materials you will need—
None needed

What to do—
1. Discuss with a small group of children the story of THIS IS THE BEAR. Have them recall losing their favorite toys.

2. Tell them that we are going to make up a story about a lost teddy bear or another favorite toy which gets found.

3. Have them brainstorm ideas about what might happen.

4. Select an idea which seems to excite them and have a child begin telling the story. At your signal, the storyteller stops, and another child continues telling the story where the first teller left off.

Something to think about—
For younger preschoolers, keep the same main character of Fred and pretend he is lost in their house or at preschool. Also, younger preschoolers may have difficulty linking to other children's parts of the story and you may want to simply have each child tell her own story, varying the setting. When older preschoolers have become adept at the turn taking storytelling, tape record some of the stories and have them illlustrate main scenes. Leave the tapes and illustrations in the library corner.

S T O R Y   S T R E T C H E R
For Mathematics And Manipulatives Center: CheckerBoard Patterns

What the children will learn—
To create a pattern

Materials you will need—
Checkerboard, poker chips or unifix cubes or counting blocks

What to do—
1. Start a pattern with the objects. For example, place red counting blocks on some of the red squares of the checkerboard. Have the child finish the pattern.

2. Other patterns might be to fill in every square with a long sequence of colors, a red block, a blue one, a yellow one, a green one, a purple one, an orange one. Fill in the top line and the child repeats the pattern on the line below it. Vary the patterns by using different objects and by filling alternating squares.

3. Also, try some incomplete repeated patterns with older preschoolers. For example, on one row, have red, yellow, blue and red. Then, have the child think what color would come next, yellow.

Something to think about—
For younger preschoolers, replicating a pattern gives them a sense of accomplishment. Older preschoolers will enjoy making up their own patterns for the top row, and then having a friend duplicate it on the next row. The level of difficulty can be varied easily.

The pattern possibilities are endless just using everyday classroom items.

S T O R Y   S T R E T C H E R
For Music And Movement: What's Missing?

What the children will learn—
To observe carefully and recall the missing toy

Materials you will need—
Small stuffed animals, 5 to 7, a large sheet of poster board, bag

What to do—
1. Ask the children to sit in a very tight circle with you.

2. Have all the little stuffed animals in a grocery bag. Bring them out one at a time and have the children describe them. For example, "This is a white dog with black ears and a black nose." Place them on the floor in front of you.

3. Then, place the piece of poster board over the animals. Take one away. Uncover them and have the children tell you which one is missing.

4 Add intrigue to the game by having the children close their eyes, then play some music and give the missing animal to the teacher's aide to hide behind one child's back.

5. Stop the music and without looking, the children guess where the missing animal is.

Something to think about—
To vary the activity, have the children close their eyes and while the music is playing, one child hides in the room. When the music stops, they look to see who is missing. Then someone goes and looks for the child while the music is playing and the teacher gives hints to the hiding place by saying, "You're getting hotter," as the searcher nears the hiding place.

11

TEDDY BEARS AND OTHER BEARS

JESSE BEAR, WHAT WILL YOU WEAR?

By Nancy White Carlstrom

Illustrated by Bruce Degen

This cheerful rhyming story follows a little bear from the beginning of his day when he is dressing for play until the night when he is tucked in tight with his teddy bear. Mother Bear begins each scene by saying, "Jesse Bear, what will you wear?" Then Jesse answers with a rhyme. She asks, "What will you wear?" in the morning, at noon and at night. Bruce Degen's illustrations are affectionate renderings of loving feelings between this humanized bear family. The bordered pictures are filled with everyday details. The colors are warm and bright, each scene is delightful enough for many browsings through the book.

Circle Time Presentation

Have the children tell you the color of something they have on. After a few children, begin phrasing your question in the following way, "Colin Bear, what did you wear?" "Jessica Bear, what did you wear?" Then read JESSE BEAR, WHAT WILL YOU WEAR? Some of the children will begin predicting when the text will contain the phrase, "Jesse Bear, what will you wear?" Encourage their participation. The rhymes also are easy for the children to hear. Reread the story and pause for the children to complete the rhymes, as "red and head," "pants and dance," "rose and toes," "sun and run," "sand and hand" and others.

STORY STRETCHER

For Cooking And Snack Time: Celery Crunchies

What the children will learn—
To prepare celery crunch snacks

Materials you will need—
Two or three stalks of celery, cream cheese or pimento cheese or peanut butter, knives and cutting boards, spreaders, vegetable brush if available

What to do—
1. Select several children to assist you in washing the celery and separating it into stalks.

2. At snack time, have each child cut her own slice from the stalk and fill it with one of the fillings. If possible, have a selection of cream cheese, pimento cheese or peanut butter.

3. Leave at least one stalk whole so that children can see how it looks when purchased.

Something to think about—
Choose some of the "picky" eaters to help with the snack preparation. They are more likely to try the snack if they are involved in the preparation. Do not force children to eat foods which they dislike, but encourage experimenting. Often young children lack experience with a variety of foods because their families do not serve them or the foods may be prepared differently at home.

STORY STRETCHER

For Housekeeping And Dress-up Corner: Jesse Bear, What Will You Wear?

What the children will learn—
To select clothes to fit the characters in the book

Materials you will need—
Blue shorts, red shirt, bib, light blue pajamas, white apron, necktie and vest

What to do—
1. Place the copy of JESSE BEAR, WHAT WILL YOU WEAR? in the dress-up corner.

2. Place a red shirt in the dress-up corner. Have the blue shorts, the pajamas and the bib also available.

3. Ask the children to see if they can find what Jesse Bear has to wear.

4. After the discoveries, leave them to play Jesse Bear, but also have hidden Mother Bear's white apron, Father Bear's tie and vest.

5. When someone dresses up in Mother Bear's and Father Bear's clothing, go over and say, "Mother Bear, what will you wear?," and "Father Bear, what will you wear?"

Something to think about—
Changing the dress-up clothes to fit a story helps children who are

less imaginative to improvise in their roles. Also, recycling the clothing helps children find a few surprises for the improvisations of their own stories they create through play.

STORY STRETCHER

For Library Corner, Flannel Board: Jesse's Clothes

What the children will learn—
To retell JESSE BEAR, WHAT WILL YOU WEAR by dressing Jesse appropriately

Materials you will need—
Flannel board, felt pieces of Jesse, underwear with stars on it, blue pants, red shirt, a bib, light blue pajamas and a tiny teddy bear, Mother Bear and Father Bear (optional)

What to do—
1. Reread JESSE BEAR, WHAT WILL YOU WEAR in the library corner during free play and have the children in the library corner place the flannel board pieces on at the appropriate times in the story.

2. Leave the children to retell the story on their own. Someone may want to "pretend read" by being the teacher.

Something to think about—
Retelling stories helps children to internalize the structure of the story. Because Jesse's play, dressing and undressing is something which also happens to them, children relate well to the story and can predict what he will have to do to get ready for lunch and for bed. The rhyming and recurring phrase also helps them to build a "scaffold" of how the story is told. On a long car trip, one child amazed her family by telling numerous stories. When her father asked her how she could remember so many, she said she closed her eyes and thought about the pieces she put on the board.

STORY STRETCHER

For Sand Table: Jesse's Sand Toys

What the children will learn—
To manipulate the dump trucks hauling loads of sand

Materials you will need—
Sand table or sand box outside, dump trucks, shovels, pails

What to do—
1. Show the children who choose the sand table during free play the picture of Jesse Bear in his sand box. Ask them what they would need so they can play what Jesse played.

2. Have them collect the dump trucks, sand pails and shovels.

3. Leave them to their own play.

Something to think about—
Revitalize interest in the sand table by moving it to a different location in the classroom, placing different items in it and varying the moisture content in the sand. Also, regularly connect the sand table with books you read. Children learn as they construct, excavate, fill, weigh, compare and control the flow and form of the sand. Cooperation develops naturally as the children see how their actions affect others.

STORY STRETCHER

For Science And Nature Center: Blowing Bubbles

What the children will learn—
To blow bubbles with a variety of tools

Materials you will need—
Liquid soap or baby shampoo, plastic containers, bubble wands made of bent wire, spools, straws, large-holed strainer or sieve, posterboard, marker, tape, squares of construction paper

What to do—
1. Mix the bubble solution by diluting clear liquid soap or baby shampoo.

2. Demonstrate how to put the solution onto the blowing tools and how to blow gently.

3. Encourage experimentation with different sizes of bubble wands, spools, straws and sieves.

4. Make a simple graph by asking the children which blowing tools are their favorites for blowing bubbles. Draw columns on a sheet of posterboard, at the top of each column tape a tool or a draw a picture of the tool. Then let the children attach a small block of construction paper under their favorite tools. They can easily see which tool is the favorite by looking at the graph.

Something to think about—
Many science and mathematics concepts can be experienced even before children can count. The simple graph can be a pre-number or a number chart. For children who do not yet know how to count, the visual comparison makes the answer apparent.

11

TEDDY BEARS AND OTHER BEARS

JAMBERRY

By Bruce Degen

This book is a happy verse of a boy and a bear celebrating finding berries, blueberries, strawberries, blackberries and raspberries. The rhyme and illustrations tease and delight the young children so much that after a few readings they are chanting and singing the poem. It begins with, "One berry, Two berry, Pick me a blueberry," and continues to a joyous climax of boy and bear buried in berries. Bruce Degen's illustrations are slapstick humor at its best. Children will enjoy looking at the pictures many times to see all the "hidden" berry-related details, as a mouse eating toast with raspberry jam while floating in a tiny boat.

Circle Time Presentation

Ask the children to tell you their favorite kind of jam or jelly and their favorite kind of berries. Have one child look at the cover of the book and tell whether the book will be a funny book or not. Read JAMBERRY at least twice. Encourage the children to join in as they recall the rhyming lines. Announce all the berry activities you have planned for the day.

STORY STRETCHER

For Art: Silly Berry Jamberry Pictures

What the children will learn—
To draw a happy and silly picture with many berries in it

Materials you will need—
Paper, crayons or chalks

What to do—
1. Talk about the illustrations in JAMBERRY and how they make us feel happy and silly when we see them.
2. Ask the children to think of happy and silly pictures with lots of berries in them. JAMBERRY had a canoe filled with berries, a goose driving a train load of blackberries and elephants skating on raspberry jam.
3. Encourage the children as they are getting started with their silly pictures, then leave them to work on their own.
4. Display the silly berry JAMBERRY pictures on the bulletin board.

Something to think about—
If you have a child who doesn't want to draw a silly berry picture, encourage him to draw a picture where he is eating one of his favorite berry foods.

STORY STRETCHER

For Cooking And Snack Time: Tasting Berries

What the children will learn—
To compare the tastes of blueberries, strawberries, blackberries and raspberries

Materials you will need—
Fresh or frozen blueberries, strawberries, blackberries and raspberries, large bowls and serving bowls, spoons, whipped cream (optional)

What to do—
1. Have several children assist you in washing the berries and preparing them for the snack table.
2. At snack time, let the children serve themselves a few of each berry.
3. Taste the berries and compare the tastes. Discuss some of the foods we prepare with berries, jams, pies or cobblers, fillings for pastries.

Something to think about—
Add the whipped cream topping only after the children have tasted the berries in their natural forms. If you use frozen berries, select those which do not have sugar added.

(Adapted from Nancy Robbins' classroom.)

STORY STRETCHER

For Music And Movement: Berryland Marching Band

What the children will learn—
To march while playing rhythm band instruments

Materials you will need—
Rhythm band instruments, recording of march music, record or tape player

What to do—
1. Have all the children seated on the circle time rug. Distribute the rhythm band instruments.

2. Ask the children to place their instruments on the rug in front of them.

3. Start the recording of the march music and have the children clap their hands in time with the music.

4. Let the children pickup their instruments and play them in time with the music while they are seated on the rug.

5. Then, lead the children in a march around the room while they play their rhythm band instruments.

Something to think about—
Some of the rhythm band instruments are more popular than others. Invariably, many children want to play the drum and few want to play the triangle. We suggest you have all the instruments in a large box and distribute them around the circle without asking children for their choices. On some days, have smaller marching bands during free play and then the children can choose their instruments.

ANOTHER STORY STRETCHER

For Music And Movement: Dancing In The Meadow

What the children will learn—
To move and dance with streamers

Materials you will need—
Crepe paper streamers or scarves, recording of light, happy music, cassette or record player

What to do—
1. Show the children Bruce Degen's illustration of the bear, the boy, the ponies and the lambs dancing in the meadow with the paper streamers.

2. Have the children sit on the circle time rug and play some light, happy music. Have them

move their arms in a swaying motion to feel the rhythm of the music.

3. Then, play the recording again and move rhythmically around the room with the children in response to the music.

4. Place the crepe paper streamers across a table and let the children select a streamer.

5. Play the recording again and have the children move in response to the music. Tell them they are happy like the boy and the bear dancing in the meadow with the ponies and the lambs.

Something to think about—
At the first of the year, some children feel too inhibited to move with abandon. Encourage their participation gently without pressuring them or calling attention to their non-participation.

(Adapted from Debbie Phillips' classroom.)

STORY STRETCHER

For Science And Nature Center: Berry Plants And Berry Bushes

What the children will learn—
To recognize how berries grow

Materials you will need—
Strawberry plants, small blueberry, blackberry and raspberry bushes from a garden center

What to do—
1. If possible, visit a garden or farm where some berries are grown and let the children pick fresh berries from the vine or bush.

2. Ask a gardener or garden center owner to bring in plants for the children to see and talk with the children about the care the plants need to grow.

3. Place the plants in the science and nature center for the children to examine and care for.

Something to think about—
Create a display of berries, juices, jams and jellies for the children to associate with their plants. If possible, add pictures of the plants at various stages of development.

11

TEDDY BEARS AND OTHER BEARS

THE TEDDY BEAR'S PICNIC

By Jimmy Kennedy

Illustrated by Alexandra Day

All the teddy bears have their picnic in the woods on a special day. And if boys and girls want to know what happens the author tells them, they'd "better go in disguise." At the beginning of the book, we see a little boy dressing in a teddy bear's costume followed by scenes of teddy bears of all sizes and descriptions marching to the picnic in a line that covers the hillside. The teddy bears have lovely things to eat, they play hide-and-seek and basketball, have sack races and other games. The last scene is a surprise, when we see that not only was the little boy in teddy bear disguise, but so were his mother, father and little sister. Included with the book is a 7" long-playing record of Bing Crosby and the Bearcats singing the song. Alexandra Day's illustrations are appealing full-page tempera paint pictures which depict the teddy bears and those who visit the picnic in disguise.

Circle Time Presentation

Ask the children to bring their teddy bears to school with them on the day you plan to read the book. Have the children sit with their teddy bears in their laps as you read THE TEDDY BEARS' PICNIC. Have one child retell the surprise at the end of the book. Then, play the record which accompanies the book. Tell the children all the teddy bear activities you have planned for the day.

(Adapted from Perrie Weedon's classroom.)

STORY STRETCHER

For Art: Decorating For The Teddy Bears' Picnic

What the children will learn—
To decorate their classroom for a party

Materials you will need—
Crepe paper, balloons, tape, poster board, markers

What to do—
1. Blow-up the balloons before the children arrive and have them hidden in a closet.

2. Show the cover of the book to the children who come to the art center during free play and have them tell how the teddy bears have decorated for their picnic.

3. Place the balloons and the decorating supplies in the art center. Ask the children to think of ways they might decorate the classroom to make it look festive for a picnic.

4. After the children have brainstormed for a few minutes, have them work in pairs, placing the decorations around the room.

Something to think about—
If the weather permits, decorate the playground outside and have most of the daily activities outside.

STORY STRETCHER

For Cooking And Snack Time: Picnicking With Our Teddy Bears

What the children will learn—
To picnic with their teddy bears

Materials you will need—
Picnic baskets, picnic food, brightly colored tablecloths, plates, napkins, cups, knives, forks, spoons, food

What to do—
1. Pack picnic baskets of some of the children's favorite picnic foods or have the food service workers pack individual picnic lunches and carry them to the picnic area in large baskets.

2. Have the children set the picnic tables with tablecloths, plates, napkins and eating utensils.

3. Ask the children to bring their teddy bears with them and eat their picnic lunches while taking care of their teddy bears.

Something to think about—
Young preschoolers may not be able to manage to eat their lunch while holding a stuffed animal. Include the teddy bears by seating them on the grass nearby in full view of the picnickers.

STORY STRETCHER

For Housekeeping And Dress-up Corner: Dressing Teddy Bears

What the children will learn—
To dress their stuffed animals

Materials you will need—
Baby clothes, shirts, pants, dresses, hats, scarves, ribbons

What to do—

1. During free play, show the children who select the housekeeping and dress-up corner the pictures of the many ways the teddy bears dressed for their picnic. Some wore hats, others wore shorts and tee shirts, still others wore ribbons, streaming scarves and capes.

2. Have the children dress their teddy bears in special clothes for the march to the picnic and playing deep in the woods.

3. After their teddy bears are dressed, let the children dress in any special clothes they want from the collection in the dress-up corner.

Something to think about—
Alert the parents through the newsletter that for this week's activities, the class needs many baby clothes to dress their teddy bears. After clothes have been donated, rotate them in and out of the housekeeping and dress-up corner so that the area is kept interesting. The children will be more inventive in their play if the props are changed with some degree of regularity.

STORY STRETCHER

For Music And Movement: Marching To The Teddy Bears' Picnic

What the children will learn—
To march holding their teddy bears

Materials you will need—
Record which accompanies the book, record player, teddy bears

What to do—

1. Have the children sit in a circle on the floor with their teddy bears in their laps.

2. Play the "Teddy Bears' Picnic" record and have the children sing along with you.

3. Start the record again and have the children move their teddy bears like they are marching to the song.

4. Then, ask the children to march around in a circle with their teddy bears in their arms.

Something to think about—
Younger preschoolers may have difficulty marching in step to the music and holding the teddy bears. Have them place their teddy bears in a tight circle in the middle of the circle time rug and let the children march around the teddy bears while the record is playing.

ANOTHER STORY STRETCHER

For Music And Movement: Teddy Bears' Picnic Games

What the children will learn—
To play a variety of games

Materials you will need—
Pillow cases for a non-competitive sack race, hula hoops, basketball and goal, soft baseball and large bat

What to do—

1. Set up the games at different stations around the playground.

2. Show the children how to jump in the pillowcases, hold them up and jump to the finish line.

3. Do not place children in competition. Instead line the children up with their sacks and have them jump from one area to another. When a child crosses the finish line, then another one begins at the starting line.

Something to think about—
Involve parents in the picnic play activities. Also, set up a refreshment stand and a rest area.

REFERENCES

Carlstrom, Nancy White. (1986). Illustrated by Bruce Degen. **JESSE BEAR, WHAT WILL YOU WEAR?** New York: Macmillan Publishing Company.

Degen, Bruce. (1983). **JAMBERRY.** New York: Harper and Row.

Freeman, Don. (1968). **CORDUROY.** New York: The Viking Press.

Hayes, Sarah. (1986). Illustrated by Helen Craig. **THIS IS THE BEAR.** New York: J.P. Lippincott.

Kennedy, Jimmy. (1983). Illustrated by Alexandra Day. **THE TEDDY BEARS' PICNIC.** San Diego: Green Tiger Press.

Additional References for Teddy Bears and Other Bears

Alborough, Jez. (1985). **RUNNING BEAR.** New York: Alfred A. Knopf. *The hilarious comedy of Polar Bear who parties too much and decides to put himself on an exercise program.*

Bunting, Eve. (1983). Illustrated by Jan Brett. **THE VALENTINE BEARS.** New York: Clarion Books. *Mrs. Bear plans a surprise Valentine's Day celebration for Mr. Bear despite their usual hibernating habits at that time.*

Douglass, Barbara . (1982). Illustrated by Patience Brewster. **GOOD AS NEW.** New York: Lothrop, Lee and Shepard Books. *When Grady's young cousin ruins his teddy bear Grandpa promises to fix the toy.*

Freeman, Don (1978). **A POCKET FOR CORDUROY.** New York: The Viking Press. *A toy bear wants a pocket for himself and searches for one in a laundromat.*

Gretz, Susanna. (1987). Illustrated by Alison Sage. **TEDDY BEARS STAY INDOORS.** New York: Four Winds Press. *The five Teddy Bears amuse themselves on a rainy day playing that they go into space, and, mostly, eating.*

CLASSIC STORIES

The Runaway Bunny
Caps for Sale
Curious George
The Three Billy Goats Gruff
Where the Wild Things Are

THE RUNAWAY BUNNY

By Margaret Wise Brown

Illustrated by Clement Hurd

Margaret Wise Brown's classic story and Clement Hurd's classic illustrations have reassured many young children that even when they feel like running away, their mothers will always be near-by. The imagination of the little bunny is seen when he tells his mother that he will runaway and become a trout and she replies, "If you become a fish in a trout stream, I will become a fisherman and will fish for you." Many children enjoy the scene where he says he will become a sailboat and the mother replies, "If you become a sailboat and sail away from me, I will become the wind and blow you where I want you to go." After all his imaginings, the little bunny decides if he can't run away from his mother, then he might as well stay home.

Circle Time Presentation

Read THE RUNAWAY BUNNY. Draw a line down the center of a chart tablet or of the chalk board. On one side write, Little Bunny, and on the other side, write Mother Bunny. Write or draw pictures of what the children recall Little Bunny said he would run away and become, a fish, a rock, a crocus, a bird, a sailboat, a flying trapeze artist, a little boy. Then, have the children recall what Mother Bunny will become, a fisherman, a mountain climber, a gardener, the wind, a tight rope walker and a mother.

STORY STRETCHER

For Art: Bunny's Imaginings

What the children will learn—
To extend their imaginations about other things the Runaway Bunny could become

Materials you will need—
Construction paper, crayons or marker, old magazines and catalogs, scissors, glue

What to do—
1. Have the children imagine some other things the Runaway Bunny could become. For example, an airplane, then Mother Bunny would become a pilot. One child told us, ice cream and Mother Bunny would become the ice cream cone. Another child said, a boy at preschool and Mother Bunny would become his teacher.

2. Ask the children to draw a tiny bunny anywhere they would like on the sheet of paper, then look through magazines and cut out pictures of other things the Runaway Bunny could become and glue them on to make a collage of Bunny's Imaginings.

Something to think about—
Some children may prefer to simply draw all the things that Runaway Bunny could become. After the children have finished with their collages, encourage them to discuss the counterparts of what Mother Bunny would then become.

STORY STRETCHER

For Cooking and Snack Time: Raw Carrot Crunch

What the children will learn—
To use a vegetable peeler

Materials you will need—
Carrots, several vegetable peelers, two paring knives, small cutting boards if possible, small bowls

What to do—
1. Have some children assist in washing the carrots.

2. Demonstrate how to use a vegetable peeler.

3. Allow the children to scrape the outside of the carrots.

4. Assist them in slicing the carrots. Have only two paring knives used at once so that you can supervise.

5. Prepare enough raw carrots for snack time.

Something to think about—
Try to find the carrots which are not packaged and still have their green tops because many children are not use to seeing them. Describe how the carrots grow with the greens on top of the ground and the carrot underneath the ground.

STORY STRETCHER

For Creative Dramatics: Dressed For The Part

What the children will learn—
To respond to cues in the reading of the story

Materials you will need—
A grocery bag with fishing gear, a grocery bag with boots and ropes for mountain climbing, a grocery bag with a gardener's hoe or spade, hat and gloves, a grocery bag with a small tree branch, a grocery bag with a sailboat, a grocery bag with rope and umbrella for the imaginary tight rope walker, a rocking chair and a carrot

What to do—

1. Place the clothing and props for each part in a grocery bag.

2. Give the props out and let the children get dressed.

3. Have the dressed actors hide behind a screen or bookshelf.

5. Read THE RUNAWAY BUNNY and each time the bunny says what he will become have an actor appear and walk across the front of the circle time area representing what Mother Bunny will become.

6. When it is time for the little bunny to become a little boy, simply have a girl walk out without any props and then go and sit in the rocking chair representing that she is the mother.

7. For the last scene where the little bunny decides to be himself, have a child walk over and you give him a carrot.

Something to think about—
Alternate the characters and let other children participate. Role-play for several days and soon the children will organize their own presentation. Also have a Father Bunny.

For Library Corner, Flannel Board: Runaway Bunny And Running After Mother

What the children will learn—
To retell the story of THE RUNAWAY BUNNY

Materials you will need—
Flannel board pieces of Little Bunny, Mother Bunny, a fish, fishing pole, a rock, a mountain climber's ropes, a flower, a gardener's hat and hoe, some wings to add to the bunny's back, a tree, a sailboat, a flying trapeze, an umbrella, a striped shirt, a rocking chair, a carrot

What to do—

1. Make the bunny and his mother quite large. Place the bunny on one side of the flannel board and his mother on the other side.

2. As you tell the story, place the rock on the Runaway Bunny's side, then place the mountain climber's ropes on Mother Bunny's side and continue this pattern throughout the story.

3. When you get to the part where Runaway Bunny says he will become a little boy, place the stripped shirt over the bunny, and place the Mother Rabbit in the rocking chair.

4. For the ending, place the carrot between the two, connecting them.

Something to think about—
Flannel boards allow the story to be retold more often and bring the story a new visual impact. Construct the felt pieces large enough for little fingers to manipulate them easily. Also, leave the flannel board story out with the book in the library.

For Water Table: Runaway Sailboats

What the children will learn—
To move the sailboats in the water by creating wind currents

Materials you will need—
Water table or tubs of warm water, blue food coloring or tempera paint, small sail boats purchased or made at school, two or three large sheets of cardboard

What to do—

1. Fill the water table with warm water and color it light blue with either food coloring or a very watery mixture of blue tempera paint. The water should look blue like Clement Hurd's scene where the Little Bunny is running away to become a sailboat.

2. Leave the sailboats near the water table waiting for some sailors.

3. Watch to see how the sailors make their sailboats move across the water. Some will blow like Mother Bunny who said she would become the wind and blow the bunny where she wanted him to go.

4. Introduce the cardboard and see if the sailors can think of how to make a wind to move their sailboats.

Something to think about—
Water play is a relaxing activity and one which requires little preparation. Limit the number of children who can be at the water table to two or three at a time, and there should be few problems.

CAPS FOR SALE

By Esphyr Slobodkina

CAPS FOR SALE is an old folktale of a peddler who walked up and down the streets balancing a stack of caps, his own checkered cap, then bunches of gray, brown, blue and red caps. As he walked he shouted, "Caps! Caps for sale! Fifty cents a cap!" When he stopped to rest, he leaned against a tree with all of his caps balanced on this head and took a nap. When he awoke, all the caps except his own checkered one were gone. Then he spotted the monkeys up in the tree, and each one had on one of his caps. He shouted at them repeatedly to give him the caps until in anger he threw his own cap on the ground. Then the monkeys imitated him and threw their caps on the ground. The peddler restacked the caps and walked on shouting, "Caps! Caps for sale! Fifty cents a cap!"

Circle Time Presentation

Begin circle time by shouting, "Caps! Caps for sale! Fifty cents a cap!" Even though some of the children will already know the story, they will be eager to hear it again. Read the book and pause for the children to join you in saying the peddler's lines. Let them tell you the order the peddler stack his caps. Read, "first his own checkered cap," then the children will complete the sequence. Discuss all the things the children can choose to do during free play which are CAPS FOR SALE activities.

STORY STRETCHER

For Art: Cap Pictures

What the children will learn—
To paint a picture with a cap in it

Materials you will need—
Easel, construction paper, tempera paints, brushes, stapler

What to do—
1. Cut large cap shapes from gray, brown, blue and red construction paper, at least four of each color.

2. Tell the children that you are going to make a bulletin board about the book, CAPS FOR SALE.

3. Staple a large checkered cap that you have made onto the base of the bulletin board and show them that the next caps you are going to put up are gray caps and so on just like the peddler stacked his caps.

4. Attach a large construction paper cap on the easel when each child is ready to paint. Tell them, "You may paint anything you like, but please include at least one cap in the picture you are painting on your cap shaped paper."

5. After the paintings are dry, have several children arrange them in the order by color on the board.

Something to think about—
The peddler has sixteen caps for sale. If you have more than sixteen children, make extra red ones, which are the peddler's favorite. The children often like the red caps best, too.

STORY STRETCHER

For Creative Dramatics: Caps And Monkeys

What the children will learn—
To role-play scenes from CAPS FOR SALE

Materials you will need—
Caps

What to do—
1. Ask parents to contribute caps.

2. Sort the caps by color. Substitute other colors if you do not have gray and brown ones donated.

3. Select one child to be the peddler and the other children can be the monkeys.

4. The child peddler probably will not be able to balance all the caps, so just stack a few on the peddler's head.

5. Read the book and pause for the peddler to carry out the actions and the monkeys to put on the caps, tease the peddler and finally throw the caps down for the peddler to restack.

Something to think about—
Once is not enough. The children will want to dramatize the story again. For variety have them change their cap colors and encourage more improvisations of the monkeys' antics as they tease the peddler.

For Housekeeping And Dress-up Corner: Caps And Hats

What the children will learn—
To associate the variety of caps and hats with the jobs or activities to which they relate

Materials you will need—
Variety of types of caps and hats, caps with advertisements on them, sports caps, tennis hats, rain hats, western hats, hat rack

What to do—
1. In your parent newsletter, request caps and hats for the dress-up corner.

2. Discuss with the children which adults might wear the hats or caps.

3. Ask the children to think of the people they know who wear caps and hats. For examples, people who make deliveries to the center, baseball players, mother playing tennis, grandfather going fishing and children when dressed to play outside in the winter.

4. Rotate the caps and hats in and out of the dress-up corner. Place a variety of types out at once.

Something to think about—
Have a cap or hat day and the children can wear their caps and hats all day except for snack time. Explain that it is good manners to take off one's cap when eating.

For Mathematics And Manipulatives Center: From Concrete To Abstract Caps

What the children will learn—
To sort, sequence and represent the caps by color

Materials you will need—
Variety of caps, several of the same color, construction paper caps of the same colors and crayons of the same colors, scissors

What to do—
1. Place the caps in random order on the table in the mathematics and manipulatives center. Ask the children to sort them by color.

2. Recall the peddler's hats and the order he balanced them.

3. Decide which order they would like to place their hats.

4. Cut construction paper caps of the same colors as the real caps and have the children pair the paper caps with the real ones.

5. Remove the real caps from the table and discuss the fact that these paper caps represent the real ones. Ask the children to tell you some other ways they could remember the real caps without them being on the table, as draw pictures of them.

6. Begin removing the paper caps one at a time and place a crayon of the same color in its place. Let the children finish the pattern across the table.

Something to think about—
To extend the activity further have the children make marks across the top of their papers in order representing the crayons and discuss how they can recall the caps we had on the table in many different ways.

For Music And Movement: Balancing Caps

What the children will learn—
To use their arms for balance as they balance caps on their heads

Materials you will need—
Many caps, cassette tape or record, tape player or record player

What to do—
1. Sit in a chair and let a child place several caps on top of your head. Slowly get up from the chair, stretch out your arms for balance and walk around the circle time rug with the caps on your head. Call out, "Caps! Caps for sale! Fifty cents a cap!"

2. Select three or four children to balance caps and let the other children place the caps one at a time on the children's heads.

3. After a few practice rounds, exchanging peddler's roles, start the music and the peddler's walk about the circle time area until the music stops.

4. Stop the music and select new peddlers. Start the music and the children placing the caps on the peddlers' heads must get the caps balanced before you stop the music again.

5. Restart the music for the new peddlers to parade with their caps.

Something to think about—
Observe the children who are less coordinated at balancing the caps and plan some special balance or walking board activities with them.

CURIOUS GEORGE

By H. A. Rey

This first book of the CURIOUS GEORGE stories has become a classic. In it we are introduced to the man in the yellow suit and learn how he and George began their adventures. We also learn how George became known as Curious George. The book is divided into five distinct sections, George's capture, the voyage and his shipboard antics, learning about his new home including accidentally telephoning the fire department, his being caged and escaping and his new home in the zoo. The style of drawing George and the illustrations of his surroundings have become as identifiable as the Curious George stories themselves.

Circle Time Presentation

Ask the children, "Who is a famous animal we know named George? Who is the man in the yellow suit? Where does George live?" With these brief questions, you can quickly tell which children know Curious George. Tell the children you want them to listen to try and find out how George became known as Curious George. Read the sections on George's capture and his problems aboard ship. Continue reading George's adventures at another circle time.

S T O R Y   S T R E T C H E R

For Art: Telephone Books

What the children will learn—
To decorate the covers of their own telephone books

Materials you will need—
Construction paper, typing paper, crayons, markers, stapler, list of children's telephone numbers

What to do—
1.   Ask the parents' permissions to distribute their telephone numbers.

2.   Make a list of emergency numbers from your community.

3.   Discuss with the children that Curious George was playing with the telephone when he called the fire department by mistake. Emphasize the importance of not playing with the real telephone.

4.   Print the list of names, addresses and telephone numbers of the class members, one complete list for each child.

5.   Fold or cut a sheet of construction paper so it makes a front and back cover for the paper lists.

6.   Ask the children to brainstorm some pictures they might draw so that whenever they see this book they will know it is their telephone book.

7.   Accept all the children's ideas and tell the artists they can use the ideas discussed or design their own cover.

Something to think about—
For kindergartners, list names and addresses and they can fill in each class member's telephone number.

S T O R Y   S T R E T C H E R

For Block Building: Fire Trucks

What the children will learn—
To role-play the actions of fire fighters

Materials you will need—
Toy fire trucks, fire helmets, boots, safety gear

What to do—
1.   Ask the fire fighters at a fire station to donate old boots, helmets, safety belts. If this option isn't possible, improvise by making fire fighters hats of construction paper, use old fishing boots, a rain slicker and a man's wide belt for the safety belt.

2.   While a visit to a real fire station is the best way for children to learn about the different pieces of fire fighting equipment, another way is to have fire fighters visit with their truck. The fire fighters have many requests during fire prevention week. Call well in advance of the date you want the fire fighters to visit.

3.   After the visit, provide toy fire trucks and equipment.

4.   When the children are engaged in play, ask them to tell you some of the fire safety rules by having them pretend to be a fire fighter speaking to a group of children.

Something to think about—
Children internalize much of what they have heard when they choose to play those roles. We provide the props, the motivation to play the roles and the support as they clarify what it really means to be fire fighters. Read other books on the topic.

For Cooking and Snack Time: George's Banana Treats

What the children will learn—
To make their own banana treats

Materials you will need—
One banana per child, knife, granola, raisins and other dried fruit and nuts, bowls, napkins, spoons, juice

What to do—
1. Tell the children that Curious George became tired of just plain bananas, so he decided to make banana treats.

2. Place small serving bowls of the granola, raisins, other dried fruits and nuts on the snack tables.

3. Cut the bananas in half. Cut a slice in the banana peel to make it easy for the children to start peeling.

4. Give each child a little bowl and tell them to place their banana in the bottom of the bowl, then choose an ingredient to sprinkle on top of it.

5. Show the children how to cut through their bananas with the side of the spoon.

Something to think about—
Ask a small group of older preschoolers to help with the preparation of the snack with one child assisting you in cutting the bananas into two pieces. Slice the bananas in the bottom of the bowls for younger preschoolers.

For Housekeeping And Dress-up Corner: A Curious George Visitor

What the children will learn—
To improvise some Curious George adventures

Materials you will need—
Curious George stuffed animal or monkey stuffed animal, large hat, yellow shirt

What to do—
1. Place the Curious George stuffed animal at the table in the housekeeping corner. Also, place the yellow shirt and large hat in a prominent place in the dress-up corner.

2. Tell the children who come to the dress-up corner during free play that there is a special visitor there today who is always curious and often in trouble.

3. Watch the play develop. After a lull in the play, ask the children to tell you the ways they played that George was curious.

4. If the children do not begin playing with the hat and shirt to be "the man in the yellow suit" who is George's owner and rescuer, then you briefly take on the role until a child seems ready to assume it.

Something to think about—
Often young children will simply incorporate Curious George into their on-going pretending to be a family in the housekeeping corner. They will make Curious George the baby or a brother. Older preschoolers often design their play with one of them being Curious George with all of his antics.

For Science And Nature Corner: Zoo Animals

What the children will learn—
To recognize zoo animals

Materials you will need—
Picture cards, reference books on zoos and zoo animals

What to do—
1. Show the illustration of Curious George at the zoo and ask the children to identify all the animals in the picture with George.

2. Explain that if they went to the zoo they would see monkeys, but not Curious George.

3. Show pictures of real monkeys and other zoo animals.

4. Discuss how the zoo animals need humans to feed them, build their shelters and provide them with water and medical care.

5. If you live in a city where there is a zoo, have a zoo keeper visit the classroom and discuss his or her job. Often the zoo keeper will bring an animal to your classroom.

Something to think about—
If you have already studied farm animals, extend the activity by having children sort picture cards by whether the animals are zoo or farm animals.

The Three Billy-Goats Gruff

Pictures by ELLEN APPLEBY

THE THREE BILLY GOATS GRUFF

By Ellen Appleby

This book is a Norwegian folktale familiar to many children in this country. The folktale begins like many with, "Once upon a time." The characters are the youngest, the second and bigger billy-goat, the third and biggest billy-goat and the troll. When the youngest billy-goat "trip, traps" across the bridge that the troll lives under, the troll proclaims he is going to gobble up the little goat, but the smart little goat convinces him to wait for his bigger brother. When the second billy-goat arrives, he convinces the troll to wait for the biggest one, who butts the troll off the bridge. The billy-goats then graze on the green hillside and get nice and fat.

Circle Time Presentation

Begin by saying the phrase, "Trip, trap, trip, trap." Some of the children will recognize it and reply, "Who's that tripping over my bridge?" Read THE THREE BILLY-GOATS GRUFF and encourage the children to join you when they know what comes next. Reread the short story if the children ask you. If not, retell the story in your own words and let the children provide the repeated lines. Ask a child who has shown little interest in books to take the book to the library corner. Tell the children that you made a flannel board story of the book and invite them to try it out during free play.

STORY STRETCHER

For Art: Playdough Characters

What the children will learn—
To associate their playdough sculptures with the story

Materials you will need—
Playdough, plastic knives for sculpting, index cards, marker

What to do—
1. Discuss the troll and how silly he looked. Ask the children to sculpt at least one of the characters from the story.

2. Display the sculptures for at least a day at the art center. Place an index card with the child's name on it under the sculpture.

Something to think about—
Many of the young preschoolers who are not yet able to sculpt the billy-goats or the troll can shape the hill the goats climbed, the bridge they crossed, or will just enjoy taking small lumps of playdough, shaping it and "trip, trapping" across the table representing the bridge.

STORY STRETCHER

For Creative Dramatics: The Three Billy-Goats Gruff

What the children will learn—
To act out the roles of the billy-goats in the story

Materials you will need—
Large hollow blocks

What to do—
1. Have some children construct a bridge of large hollow blocks.

2. Ask the children who are most familiar with the story to be the first set of billy-goats. You be the troll.

3. Read the story for the first set of characters, pausing for the actors and their audience to say the familiar lines.

4. At the end of the story where the biggest billy-goat butts the troll off the bridge, have the biggest billy-goat just push you lightly down into your chair. Emphasize pushing lightly.

5. Re-enact the story with three different billy-goats.

Something to think about—
Some young children do not like to play the villain. We suggest that the teacher play that role.

STORY STRETCHER

For Library Corner, Flannel Board: Trip, Trapping Goats

What the children will learn—
To retell the folktale

Materials you will need—
Flannel board, felt characters or shapes for the bridge, hill, three billy-goats and troll

What to do—
1. Have one of the children who has shown less interest in stories help you retell the story in the library corner.

2. Invite the child to retell the story after you have modeled it.

3. Suggest that pairs of children work together and retell the story. One child is the teller and the other child places the flannel board pieces on at the right time.

Something to think about—
Researchers have found that children internalize story structure and recall more of a story when they think about a story in more than one form. Folktales for the flannel board are excellent stories for children to retell and to figure out the sequence from the smallest billy-goat to the largest one.

STORY STRETCHER

For Mathematics And Manipulatives Center: Sets Of Three

What the children will learn—
To make sets of three, ordering by size

Materials you will need—
Ordinary classroom items — pieces of paper, crayons, pencils, cars, books, dolls, plates

What to do—
1. Have several children help collect the items from around the room. You need three of everything, but each must be a different size. For example three different sized dolls, three different lengths of crayons, a saucer and two plates of different sizes.

2. Randomly place all the items on the table.

3. Ask the children to sort the things that go together.

4. Discuss the three billy-goats and how there was a little one, a bigger one and the biggest one.

5. Then assign a child per set and ask the children to place their

items in order from the smallest to the largest.

6. Mix the object up again and let the children place different sets of three items in order.

Something to think about—
Make the task easier by using fewer sets of items. Complicate it by using objects which are not the same, as a spoon, fork and knife for one set; a little car, larger van and big truck for another and differing sizes of dolls and stuffed animals.

STORY STRETCHER

For Sand Table: Hills And Bridges

What the children will learn—
To mold hills and construct bridges

Materials you will need—
Sand table, sand, watering can, small manipulative blocks

What to do—
1. With the children who choose the sand table at free play time, discuss the story of THE THREE BILLY-GOATS GRUFF.

2. Ask them how they could fix the sand so that it looked like the bridge and hills of the story. Accept their ideas and collect any additional pieces they recommend from around the room.

3. Let them construct the terrain of the story, then ask some of the children from the art center if they would like to display their playdough sculptures at the sand table.

Something to think about—
You may want to extend the play for the original sand table players and have them sculpt their own playdough goats and troll. Young preschoolers may lose sight of the original story while playing in the sand, or sometimes they will just play for a while and then you will hear periodically, "Trip, trap, trip, trap," and realize they have not forgotten their story.

WHERE THE WILD THINGS ARE

By Maurice Sendak

This exciting, yet reassuring tale, has won the author critical acclaim for both text and illustrations, but for the children it is Max's story. It is the story of a child sent to bed without his supper for making a "smart" remark to mother. Max dreams a most adventuresome tale of a faraway land where there were wild things. Max was able to tame them by staring into their yellow eyes and then even to enjoy them as playmates in a "wild rumpus." But Max grew hungry and homesick and sailed back through his dreams to awaken to supper on a tray in his room. Maurice Sendak's illustrations in WHERE THE WILD THINGS ARE won him the Caldecott Medal.

Circle Time Presentation

Many children will already know the book, but part of the delight of circle time for an individual child is discovering that other children enjoy the book also. Read the book with much suspense, then reassurance in your voice. After the reading, ask a few of the children which part of the story they liked best. Look at the pictures of the "wild things" again and talk about Max's trick for calming the creatures.

STORY STRETCHER

For Art: Monster Posters

What the children will learn—
To paint giant, but friendly monsters

Materials you will need—
Butcher paper, tempera paints, brushes, stapler, string or yarn

What to do—

1. Give each child a long sheet of butcher paper, about three feet long.

2. Double over the top edge of the paper two or three times and staple together to create a sturdy edge.

3. Staple a piece of yarn or string to the top of the butcher paper so that the large poster can be hung up easily.

4. Ask the children to paint a "wild thing," one from the story or one they imagine.

Something to think about—
Display the "wild thing" posters around the room. Invite other children from the building to see the posters. Many of them will be familiar with the book and will appreciate your children's art work.

ANOTHER STORY STRETCHER

For Art: Wild Thing Masks

What the children will learn—
To make a paper bag mask of a "wild thing"

Materials you will need—
Paper bags, crayons or markers, scissors, yarn or ribbon, stapler

What to do—

1. With the children who come to the art center during free play, look at Maurice Sendak's illustrations of the "wild things."

2. Place all the materials you have collected on the table.

3. Ask the children how they would make a paper bag mask of a "wild thing." Emphasize that theirs should be different than the ones in the book. Those drawings are just to give us ideas, start us thinking.

4. Assist the children in making the holes for the eyes and mouth. Have the children place the paper bags over their heads and then with a pencil make a dot where the eyes should go. Remove the paper bag from the child's head and cut the eyes. It doesn't matter if the mouth is far below where it should be. Let the child draw the mouth and assist with the cutting if needed.

5. Have the children wear their masks during the "wild rumpus" for music and movement time.

Something to think about—
We want the children to use their imaginations and create their own versions of the "wild things," but they will be inspired by Maurice Sendak's drawings.

For Library Corner, Listening Tape: Max And The Wild Things

What the children will learn—
To tell the story in their own words

Materials you will need—
Cassette tape and recorder

What to do—

1. Ask the children who come to the library corner during free play to help you make a tape of WHERE THE WILD THINGS ARE for the listening station. Tell the children this tape will be different because the story will be in their own words.

2. Start the tape and talk directly to the listeners for whom you are making the tape. Introduce the book by stating the title and explaining that this story is being told by children. Tell their names. Then, tell the listeners the page turning signal. For instance, tell them whenever they hear this sound (a fork tapped lightly against a glass) to turn the page.

3. Continue by telling the listeners where to open the book. You might say, "Boys and girls, open the book to the picture of Max using a large hammer."

4. Then say, "Brian, tell what Max is doing." Brian will begin telling the story, but will pause for you to make the page turning signal.

5. Repeat this routine for each page of the book.

6. Record the book in its original version on the other side of the cassette tape.

Something to think about—
Vary the activity by having older preschoolers take turns. One child may tell the beginning, another the middle and another the end.

WHERE THE WILD THINGS ARE is an excellent book for children to tell in their own words because it is already familiar, and the illustrations capture the essence of the story so well.

For Housekeeping And Dress-up Corner: Wild Things Costumes

What the children will learn—
To dress in costumes

Materials you will need—
Old Halloween costumes, tent or card table with long cloth

What to do—

1. With the children who come to the housekeeping and dress-up corner during free play, show the pictures of Max in his costume and the monsters or wild things.

2. Bring out the costumes and let the children enjoy dressing in them and playing out the story. Do not direct them, but let their play emerge from the costumes.

3. Max retreated to a tent when he was tired of the "wild rumpus." Provide the tent or the card table with a long cloth over it to hide under as a retreat when children are tired of being "wild things."

Something to think about—
For young preschoolers, dressing in the costumes will become the focus of their play. The older children will seize the costumes and combine them with the story for inventive variations on Max's adventure with the "wild things."

For Music And Movement: Wild Rumpus

What the children will learn—
To move like "wild things"

Materials you will need—
Recording of some lively instrumental music, tape or record player

What to do—

1. With the children seated on the circle time rug, read again the part of the book which follows Max's controlling the "wild things" by staring them down, and then the examples of the "wild rumpus," as they played together.

2. Ask the children to think about what a "wild rumpus" might be like. Discuss that the "wild things" and Max jumped, ran, swung through the trees.

3. Tell the children they can be "wild things" when the music is playing, but as soon as you stop the music, they must act like tired monsters and fall on the floor to relax.

4. Have several sessions of the "wild rumpus."

Something to think about—
Control the level of activity of the children. Stop the music before they are out of control, but let it play long enough that they have a sense of moving for the fun of moving.

REFERENCES

Appleby, Ellen. (1984). **THREE BILLY-GOATS GRUFF: A NORWEGIAN FOLKTALE.** New York: Scholastic, Inc.

Brown, Margaret Wise Brown. (1942). **THE RUNAWAY BUNNY.** Illustrated by Clement Hurd. New York: Harper and Row.

Rey, H.A. (1941). **CURIOUS GEORGE.** Boston: Houghton Mifflin Company.

Sendak, Maurice. (1963). **WHERE THE WILD THINGS ARE.** New York: Harper and Row.

Slobodkina, Ephyr. (1940). **CAPS FOR SALE.** New York: Harper and Row.

Additional References for Classic Stories

Galdone, Paul. (1975). **THE GINGERBREAD BOY.** Boston: Clarion Books. *The Gingerbread Boy eludes the hungry grasp of everyone he meets until he happens upon a fox more clever than he.*

Galdone, Paul. (1968). **HENNY PENNY.** New York: Clarion Books. *Henny Penny's cry of alarm, "The sky is falling," is believed by Cocky Locky, Ducky Lucky, Goosey Loosey, Turkey Lurkey, but not Foxy Loxy. An old tale retold with a fresh ending.*

McGovern, Ann. (1968). Illustrated by Winslow Pinney Pels. **STONE SOUP.** New York: Scholastic, Inc. *The story of a young hungry man who tricked an old woman into making him a delicious soup starting with a smooth round stone.*

Potter, Beatrix. (1986). **THE COMPLETE TALES OF PETER RABBIT AND OTHER FAVORITE STORIES.** Illustrated by Charles Snatore. Philadelphia, PA: Courage Books, Running Press. *The story of Peter Rabbit who manages to get into mischief in Mr. McGregor's garden, in spite of his mother's warning. This edition includes the five most treasured tales of Beatrix Potter.*

Williams, Margery. (1984). Illustrated by Michael Green. **THE VELVETEEN RABBIT.** Philadelphia, PA: Courage Books, Running Press. *The little velveteen rabbit learns from the other nursery toys what it means to be real.*

COUNTING

Roll Over: A Counting Song
Have You Seen My Duckling?
Ten, Nine, Eight
The Doorbell Rang
Over in the Meadow

ROLL OVER:
A Counting Song
Illustrated by Merle Peek

Peek illustrates this favorite counting song by showing a little boy who keeps rolling over in bed. Each time he rolls over, he imagines an animal falling out of the bed. By the time he counts backwards from ten to one, all the animals are out of the bed. "Alone at last," he falls asleep, with all the animals on the floor around his bed. Peek's bedtime illustrations are blue and white with the candle light casting a yellow glow.

Circle Time Presentation

Have the children count with you from one to ten, and then have them count backwards from ten to one. Read ROLL OVER! A COUNTING SONG without singing the words. Some children will recognize the words and suggest you sing it. The music to the tune is located on the last pages of the book. Sing the song with the children and do the hand motions, holding up ten fingers and then with your hands do a rolling action. Continue the countdown. Sing the song several times throughout the day for practice.

STORY STRETCHER
For Art: A Light In My Picture

What the children will learn—
To create the effect of lights using yellow chalk

Materials you will need—
Blue and white construction paper, colored chalks, extra pieces of yellow chalk

What to do—
1. Show the children Merle Peek's illustrations in ROLL OVER! ROLL OVER! A COUNTING SONG. Call attention to the way the artist used soft yellow to show how the candle was lighting up the room.

2. Ask the children to draw a picture they want which has light in it, sunlight, moonlight, light from a lamp or a candle. They can highlight the rays of the light with yellow chalk.

Something to think about—
For older children who are in the stage of representational art, also point out how the illustrator showed the shadows of the animals. Have them notice how the shadows changed when the animals moved. Also, show the page where the little monkey's shadow is on the floor as the moonlight shines across his back.

STORY STRETCHER
For Housekeeping And Dress-up Corner: Alone At Last

What the children will learn—
To count backwards from ten to one

Materials you will need—
Nine stuffed animals, one doll, doll bed

What to do—
1. Place the doll in the middle of the doll bed. Line up the stuffed animals on both sides of the doll. If there isn't enough room, place them lengthwise on the bed. Ask the children how many they think are in the bed.

2. Have a child count them, then begin singing the song. Point to the children and let them take an animal out of the bed when the song says, "one fell out."

3. Let the last child shout, "Alone at last," as the voice of the doll.

Something to think about—
This book is also a good selection for a naptime reading. However, instead of the lively tune and hand motions, sing it as a slow gentle lullaby.

STORY STRETCHER
For Mathematics And Manipulatives Center: Guesstimate What's Left

What the children will learn—
To estimate how many are left

Materials you will need—
Ten interesting objects, quite different from each other, as three

pretty seashells, two blue blocks, one strangely shaped puzzle piece, two photographs of children, two small cars, paper bag; any ten interesting objects will do

What to do—

1. Ask one child to take the items from the paper bag and place them on the table in the mathematics center.

2. As the child is lining up the objects, have the other children take turns describing them. This is to focus their attention on each object.

3. Have another child group the like items together and re-emphasize that there were three seashells, two photographs, etc.

4. Then, ask the children to "guesstimate" how many things are on the table. After a guess or two is given, let them count.

5. Have the children close their eyes while you remove one set of objects, then the children try to think which set is missing, and recount to see how many are left. Continue down to zero.

Something to think about—
Simplify the task for younger children by using five objects instead of ten. Complicate it for older youngsters by having more groups or sets of items.

STORY STRETCHER

For Music And Movement: Singing Roll Over!

What the children will learn—
To sing this favorite childhood counting song

Materials you will need—
None needed

What to do—

1. Sing the song with the hand movements signifying the numbers and the rolling motion.

2. Change the words of the song from, "and the little one said, Roll Over! Roll Over!," to the "big one said."

3. Continue making changes throughout the song by changing little to "short one," then "tall one," then "fat one," then "thin one." Use your hands to signal when to sing short, tall, fat and thin.

Something to think about—
Children enjoy singing and love the pleasure of sharing the experience with their friends. "Roll Over!" is a song they can sing with gusto. Try to select a variety of songs which create different moods. If you have some favorites you enjoy, sing them often, whenever you feel like it. Also, include the words to many of the children's favorite songs in the parent newsletters.

STORY STRETCHER

For Sand Table: Digging For Dinosaurs

What the children will learn—
To practice counting backwards from ten.

Materials you will need—
Sand table or tubs of sand, plastic dinosaurs

What to do—

1. Have two children who are interested in the sand table bury the plastic dinosaurs in the sand. Then they invite two friends to come and find them. Each time a dinosaur is found, help the children count backwards from ten to find out how many are left.

2. When the first team of excavators have found ten dinosaurs, then they hide them from the other two and stay nearby to count backwards as each one is found.

Something to think about—
For younger preschoolers who are not yet sure of their counting, use only five dinosaurs and the children count from one to five. For older preschoolers, try combinations of animals, as five wild animals and five dinosaurs. Keeping track of two sets is a more difficult thinking process.

13
COUNTING

HAVE YOU SEEN MY DUCKLING?

By Nancy Tafuri

There are only two phrases in this book, yet the story is complete. The story begins with one adventurous baby duckling swimming away from the nest while the seven other babies watch. In the next scene, the seven left behind have their beaks open and seem to be telling mother duck what happened. The remainder of the story is mother duck and her brood of seven visiting the various inhabitants of the pond, a crane, a turtle, a beaver, a catfish and another mother duck to ask the question, "Have you seen my duckling?" In each scene, the adventurous one is barely visible, but is somewhere in the picture. Tafuri's texturing of the feathers, expressions of the animals, and simple, yet interesting view of pond life create a reassuring counting adventure in this Caldecott Honor Book.

Circle Time Presentation

Have the children count to eight and tell them in this book they will help to create the story by counting. At first, show the entire book from beginning to end without speaking, but allow enough time for the children to spot the barely visible little duck. Select one child to be the special "see-er," the one who stands beside you and points out the barely visible duck. Then, read and tell the story of the actions seen in the pictures. At each new scene, have the children count to see if the eighth little duck has returned.

STORY STRETCHER
For Art: Pond Pictures

What the children will learn—
To use watercolors

Materials you will need—
Watercolors, small brushes, watercolor paper if available, paper towels

What to do—
1. Point out the pond pictures in the book.
2. Demonstrate how much water to use, how to put paint on the brush and how to dry some of the water on it.
3. Ask the children to create watery pictures with the watercolors, and if they want to add some pond inhabitants, they may. Watercolors require much experimentation before the children are able to paint small objects in their paintings. Encourage the children to make their paintings look like water.

Something to think about—
Children who are already painting realistic pictures find watercolors a new challenge. They expect to control the colors like crayons.

Young children enjoy the experimentation and watching the colors mix. Leave the watercolors out at the art table for several days so the children can gain some control of the medium.

STORY STRETCHER
For Library Corner: Dictated Stories

What the children will learn—
To compose a story to go with the illustrations

Materials you will need—
Paper, pencil or chart tablet, markers

What to do—
1. Have some of the children who are in the library corner tell the story of HAVE YOU SEEN MY DUCKLING? Most of the pages do not have words on them, but the children can see the story in the illustrations.
2. Let one child tell you a story in her own words. You write what she says on paper, then read it back to her. After reading her story, ask if she wants to change anything.
3. Print the edited version of the child's story on the chart tablet.
4. Repeat this series of steps with several children. Let them illustrate their story, if they wish.

Something to think about—
When children become experienced storytellers, tape record several versions of the story and place them at the listening station. Be certain to include some "lively" ones to inspire other children. Also, bind some of their dictated stories into published books. Directions for an easy binding process are included in the appendix of this book.

For Music And Movement: Quack! Quack! Quack!

What the children will learn—
To sing the "Hand Rhymes" song of five little ducks from Marc Brown's HAND RHYMES, published in 1985 by E.P. Dutton of New York

Materials you will need—
None needed

What to do—
1. Teach the children the familiar song and hand motions to "Quack! Quack! Quack!"

"Five little ducks that I once knew,
Big ones, little ones, skinny ones, too.
(Refrain)
But the one little duck with the
Feather on his back,
All he could do was, 'Quack! Quack!
   Quack'
All he could do was, 'Quack! Quack!
   Quack'

Down to the river they would go,
Waddling, waddling, to and fro.
(Repeat refrain)

Up from the river they would come
Ho, ho, ho, ho, hum, hum, hum.
(Repeat refrain)

Something to think about—
Sing the song with eight ducks to match the story.

For Science And Nature Center: Who Lives In The Pond?

What the children will learn—
To name some of the pond birds, animals, fish and insects

Materials you will need—
Pictures of pond birds, animals, fish and insects to supplement the ones found in HAVE YOU SEEN MY DUCKLING?, posterboard, marker

What to do—
1. If possible, visit a pond and observe the inhabitants first-hand.

2. On the posterboard, draw four columns and title the poster, "Who lives at the pond?"

3. Review the pictures in HAVE YOU SEE MY DUCKLING? and place pictures of the animals in the right column. Count all of the pond's inhabitants.

4. Classify the inhabitants the children list under the categories of birds, animals, fish or insects.

Something to think about—
If you have some crafts people in your community who paint duck decoys, have them bring in some of their collection. If there is a wild life refuge near your school where ducks can be seen easily, consider a short field trip. Many of the wild life preserves by their nature are in isolated areas where it is difficult to see the waterfowl. An alternative is to have ducks visit the school. If you have farms in your community, have someone bring in some baby ducks for the children to see.

For Water Table: Water Table Pond

What the children will learn—
To create a pond environment

Materials you will need—
Water table, small buckets or pails, clumps of grasses with soil attached (optional), tempera paint of blue and green, any plastic models of pond inhabitants

What to do—
1. Fill the water table with clean water. Have some children add some blue and green watery tempera paint to the water to give it a pond color.

2. Place some clumps of grasses in the pails and add water until the grasses are floating.

3. Put the grasses in their buckets in the corners of the water table.

4. Supply any plastic ducks or other models of pond birds, animals, fish or insects you can find.

5. Hide a little duck behind some tall grasses.

Something to think about—
Remember that the water table simulation of a pond will inspire much imaginative play. Reinacting the story in the book isn't necessary; however, to get the play started it may be helpful to recall the book and the inhabitants of the pond.

TEN, NINE, EIGHT

By Molly Bang

This Caldecott Honor book is the poem a father says to his little girl to get her ready for bed. It starts with "ten small toes all washed and warm" and continues counting down to "four sleepy eyes which open and close" to finally, "one big girl all ready for bed." The text is printed on the left page and the full-color illustrations face it. The father and daughter are dressed in up-to-date clothing and the house and toys, including a doll, are warmly and realistically illustrated.

Circle Time Presentation

Have the children count with you from one to ten. Hold up fingers to help them count. Encourage them to count their fingers, too. Then ask a confident counter to count backwards. Have the child come to you and put down one of your fingers for each number.

Ask the children to listen to how a father helps his daughter get ready for bed by counting backwards. Read TEN, NINE, EIGHT. The story is a reassuring one for young children and their response may be a nice calm, "Ah, ah," after the story. Read this story as a naptime selection also.

STORY STRETCHER

For Art: Window Pane Pictures

What the children will learn—
To draw a picture representing what they see out a window

Materials you will need—
Drawing paper, construction paper, scissors, crayons

What to do—
1. Show the children the picture in TEN, NINE, EIGHT where the father is counting window panes and the cat is looking out.

2. Have the children go to a window in the classroom and count the number of window panes. Are there as many as in TEN, NINE, EIGHT? In the book, there was a picture of two windows with four panes in each window.

3. Have the children look at the scene outside the classroom window and imagine what it would look like as a picture. Also, have them close their eyes and remember what it looks like outside their bedroom windows at home.

4. Ask the children to draw a real or imaginary scene.

5. Cut window frames and panes from construction paper by taking a whole sheet and cutting out four squares.

6. Let the child staple the window pane over his picture.

Something to think about:
Drawing often becomes too routine and a time filler when the teacher simply provides paper but no motivation. Associating the drawing with a book and displaying the sketches in a different manner will inspire the artists to draw again.

STORY STRETCHER

For Library Corner, Listening Station: Magnetic Counting Tape

What the children will learn—
To count backwards from ten by listening to the tape of the book

Materials you will need—
Tape recording of book, magnetic board, magnetic numerals

What to do—
1. Record Molly Bang's story, TEN, NINE, EIGHT.

2. Have two children work as partners while listening to the tape. One is the page turner, and the other uses the magnetic board. As each number word is said, the child places the numeral on the board.

Something to think about—
This activity can also be used with a group of four or five children at the listening station. In addition, the children can help with the tape recording. After a few readings, the children know the rhymes and can read along. Invite some "less interested counters" and "less interested in books" children to participate in the taping. It may be the extra motivation they will need.

For Mathematics And Manipulatives Center: Counting Forwards And Backwards

What the children will learn—
To practice counting

Materials you will need—
Magnetic numerals, interesting items to count, magnetic board

What to do—

1. Set up a display of interesting items to count. You may select some from the book, nine stuffed animals, seven shoes, six seashells, five buttons or choose items from your classroom.

2. Have the children who need practice counting to come to the table and count the objects. As the child counts, you place the magnetic numeral on the board. For example, as the child says, "One," you place the magnetic 1 on the board and continue. Extend each child's learning by at least one number beyond where they stopped.

3. For the more proficient counters, ask them to count the objects in a set, as seven shoes, and to place the 7 on the board.

4. For other proficient counters, have them count up to ten and back again to one. However, always have them associate the counting with real objects, not just rote counting.

Something to think about
Avoid grouping by ability, simply change the requirement based on what you know the child can do, but use the same materials. Allowing slower children to participate with faster ones helps the child to see what she will be learning next.

For Music And Movement: Shoe, Shoe, Who Has The Shoe?

What the children will learn—
To find the missing shoes

Materials you will need—
Four pairs of shoes from the dress-up corner, lively music

What to do—

1. Have the children sit in a circle. Show them the picture of the "7 empty shoes in a short straight row," from TEN, NINE, EIGHT.

2. Place four pairs of shoes from the dress-up corner in a short straight row. Then, ask the children to close their eyes and to keep them closed while the music is playing. Place one of the shoes on someone's foot and return to your chair.

3. Have them open their eyes, and count the shoes. Repeat the phrase, "Shoe, shoe, who has the shoe? You, you, you have the shoe," (Raines). Then point to the child who has it.

4. The child who has the shoe then returns it to the row and he gets to be the one who says, "Shoe, shoe, who has the shoe? You, you, you have the shoe," when the music stops again.

Something to think about—
It may be too difficult for young preschoolers to wait their turn through all the participants. Vary the game by putting several shoes on several children at once. Instead of having one child say the shoe, shoe phrase, when the music stops they all point around the circle to the children who have the dress-up corner shoes on.

For Science And Nature Center: Counting Seashells

What the children will learn—
To count seashells and to group them by their shapes

Materials you will need—
A collection of seashells, boxes or plastic tubs for sorting

What to do—

1. During free play, ask some of the children in the science and nature center to help you arrange the seashells.

2. As the children are arranging them, they will naturally begin grouping or sorting them according to some attribute. Young children may simply say, "This one is like that one." Older preschoolers may comment, "I've found five this shape."

3. After the display is arranged attractively, have one child invite a friend to come to the center and see the shells.

4. When the friend is there, ask one of the arrangers to select her favorite shell. Have her friend find others which are similar in shape to the favorite shell. Then ask the two friends to count how many shells they have.

5. Continue with other friends finding and counting shells.

Something to think about—
This activity can be as simple or as complicated as the ability levels of the children require. For quite young children, there may be three beautiful shells to count as they are three years old. For some kindergartners, the sorting by shape and counting may reach twenty or more. The important point to remember is to accept the child's level of understanding and to extend her learning where possible.

The Doorbell Rang
by Pat Hutchins

THE DOORBELL RANG

By Pat Hutchins

One afternoon Ma made cookies for Victoria and Sam, and they complimented her on her baking. To which she replied, "No one makes cookies like Grandma." As Victoria and Sam are counting out the cookies to share, the doorbell rings and their friends Hannah and Tom arrive. While recounting the cookies to share with the two new arrivals, the doorbell rings again, and it's Peter and his little brother. While recounting the cookies again, the doorbell rings once more, and it's Joy and Simon and their four cousins. Finally, when there is only one cookie per child, the doorbell rings one last time. It's Grandma with more cookies. The illustrations are very brightly colored with many patterns in the checkered tablecloth, the tiled floor, bordered rug, the children's clothes and Ma's skirt.

Circle Time Presentation

Ask the children what their favorite kinds of cookies are. Where do they get them? Who bakes them? Read THE DOORBELL RANG. Have the children count how many times the doorbell rang. Have them count the number of children who came to Victoria's and Sam's house. Have them count again to know how many children there were in the story. See if they remember to count Victoria and Sam. Discuss how willing the children were to share their cookies with their friends. Have them guess what they will have for snack.

STORY STRETCHER

For Art: Weaving Patterns

What the children will learn—
To make a pattern by weaving alternating colors

Materials you will need—
Large sheets of construction paper, one to two inch wide strips of construction paper in a contrasting color, scissors

What to do—
1. Before giving the supplies to the children, take a sheet of construction paper and cut long straight slits in it from about an inch from the top to about an inch from the bottom. Six or seven slits equally spaced is usually enough.

2. Cut strips of construction paper from a contrasting color.

3. Demonstrate for the children how to lace the strip over and under the slit in the whole sheet of paper to create a checkerboard pattern.

Something to think about—
This activity is more of a craft and a small muscle activity than an art

activity because the child is following directions and there is no creative expression involved. The only decision the child may make is the color of the paper. However, to add a little creativity, once the pattern is all finished, the children can decorate the squares with their own designs. A test of whether an activity is an art activity is to determine how different each child's project is. If they look very similar, then there was was little creativity involved.

STORY STRETCHER

For Clean-up Time: Mopping The Floor

What the children will learn—
To clean the floor properly

Materials you will need—
Small plastic bucket, mild detergent, sponge mop with a squeeze handle

What to do—
1. Point out to the children the way the illustrator in THE DOORBELL RANG shows more muddy tracks on the floor everytime more children come into kitchen.

2. Have them notice that their clean-up mop and bucket are like the ones in the story.

3. Demonstrate how to wring the water from the mop by lifting the lever on the handle.

4. Have the children practice squeezing the water from the mop several times. Ask them to take turns cleaning areas of the floor.

Something to think about—
Children enjoy being helpers and learning how to do ordinary household tasks. To help them manage more easily, shorten the handle of the mop and partially fill the bucket.

For Cooking And Snack Time: Baking Grandma's Cookies

What the children will learn—
To follow directions in preparing a recipe

Materials you will need—
Two packages of chocolate chip cookie dough, two cookie sheets, two spatulas, two knives, serving platters, posterboard, marker

What to do—

1. Tell the children the directions and then demonstrate the steps.

2. Divide the class in half, one group works with the aide and one with the teacher.

3. Have each child participate in some step of the preparation.

Something to think about—
Make a rebus chart of the directions from the package of cookie dough. For example, draw a long roll of dough. Draw a knife cutting the dough and then draw the pinwheels which are cut for the roll. Show the knife cutting the pinwheels into four sections. Draw a cookie sheet with some cookies on it. (See the Appendix for a sample rebus chart.) For some snacks, bake cookies from scratch. Work in smaller groups and enlist the assistance of a parent or a grandparent.

For Mathematics And Manipulatives Center: Counting Cookies

What the children will learn—
To divide by counting

Materials you will need—
Playdough, cookie cutters, rolling pins, spatulas

What to do—

1. For the children who need extra practice counting, have them make cookies from their play dough.

2. After they have made a batch of cookies and counted them, have them invite a friend over to share the cookies.

3. Ask the cookie maker to divide the cookies by counting, "one for you and one for me," until all the cookies are gone.

4. Count the number of cookies each person has.

Something to think about—
Practicing counting will become routine for young children if they have something interesting to count. Counting cookies, real or imaginary ones, is more interesting than counting by rote.

For Science And Nature Center: How Does A Doorbell Ring?

What the children will learn—
To take apart and reassemble a doorbell

Materials you will need—
A simple doorbell mechanism, non-electric

What to do—

1. Mount a simple buzzer door bell onto a piece of plywood with screws.

2. With a few children watching, begin taking apart the doorbell.

3. Start unloosening the screws and let a child finish it.

4. Take off the cover, turn the knob, and watch how the buzzer works to make the doorbell ring.

5. Have the children describe the mechanics of how the doorbell operates by observing it.

Something to think about—
Write their observations on paper and leave them at the science and nature center. When other children are examining the doorbell and someone asks how it works, read a child's description. Then, invite the new observer to describe how the doorbell operates. If you think of yourself as having a poor mechanical mind, you may want to invite someone else to be in charge of the dismantling of the doorbell. However, this simple device might just be the confidence builder you need to get over your fear of mechanical things.

13
COUNTING

OVER IN THE MEADOW

By Olive A. Wadsworth

Illustrated by Mary Maki Rae

Mary Maki Rae illustrates this favorite counting rhyme which includes both counting and sounds to create a rhythm. We count turtles, fish, owls, rats, bees, crows, frogs, lizards, ducks and beavers. The children will enjoy making the animal and insect sounds. The bright illustrations are wonderful for large group circle times.

Circle Time Presentation

Discuss that a meadow is a field of grasses. Sometimes it has a stream flowing through it. Ask the children to think what animals or insects they might find in a meadow or in a stream. Read OVER IN THE MEADOW and see if any of their insects or animals are mentioned. The patterned language and the easy rhythm of the book make it a natural for rereading. During the second reading, encourage the children to say the rhymes along with you. Recall whether the children mentioned some animals or insects not written about in the book. Make up a rhyme for one of their insects. Their butterfly might be number eleven and flitter about.

STORY STRETCHER

For Creative Dramatics: "We Move," Said The Children

What the children will learn— To dramatize the insects' and animals' movements

Materials you will need— None needed

What to do—

1. Think of movements or sounds for each of the animals or insects mentioned. Make digging motions for the one turtle, swim like the two fishes, hoot like the three owls, gnaw like the four rats, buzz like the five bees, caw like the six crows, jump like the seven frogs, lie flat with arms outstretched to bask like the eight lizards, quack like the nine ducks and build a dam like the ten beavers.

2. Demonstrate the movements and sounds. Rehearse a few at a time until everyone knows the motions for each animal or insect.

3. Read OVER IN THE MEADOW allowing enough time for the children to dramatize the movements and sounds during and after each part.

Something to think about— Creative dramatics is often done in large groups where children feel less self-conscious. Also, when they see their teacher doing the motions, it signals that it is alright for the child to try them. Encourage participation, but ignore non-participants. Do not stop everything and call attention to a child who isn't participating, it often makes the child less willing to be involved.

STORY STRETCHER

For Library Corner, Flannel Board: Counting Baby Animals And Insects

What the children will learn— To listen to the counting rhyme and place the corresponding number of animals or insects on the flannel board

Materials you will need— Enough felt or construction paper to make mother turtle and one baby turtle, mother fish and two baby fishes, mother owl and three baby owls, mother rat and four baby rats, mother bee and five baby bees, mother crow and six baby crows, mother frog and seven baby frogs, mother lizard and eight baby lizards, mother duck and nine baby ducks, mother beaver and ten baby beavers; flannel board, cassette tape of OVER IN THE MEADOW

What to do—

1. Construct the flannel board pieces of colorful felt, or of construction paper and laminate them; glue a piece of an old emery board on the plastic to make them hold in place on the flannel board.

2. Provide a cassette tape of you reading OVER IN THE MEADOW for the child to listen to while placing the animals and insects on the board. Be sure to pause long enough between the scenes for the child to count and place the babies on the flannel board.

Something to think about—
If your children do not need practice with counting, they still will enjoy the flannel board and the listening tape because they can chant the rhymes as they place the pieces on the board.

STORY STRETCHER

For Mathematics And Manipulatives Center: Magnetic Numerals With Rhymes

What the children will learn—
To associate the numeral with its number words

Materials you will need—
Magnetic board, magnetic numerals, pictures of the mother animals and insects, pictures of the sets of baby animals and insects from OVER IN THE MEADOW, magnetic strips

What to do—

1. Working with small goups of children at a time, have them match the pictures of mother animals or insects and their babies.

2. Ask a child who can count from one to five to arrange the numerals in order on the magnetic board.

3. Have another child arrange the numerals from six to ten.

4. Remove the numerals and put them back up one at a time as you read the book.

5. Mix up the pictures of the mothers and the babies and give each child several.

6. Read OVER IN THE MEADOW and when you say the name and number of an animal or insect the child with the picture of the mother attaches it to the magnetic board and the child with the picture of the set of baby animals attaches it along side.

Something to think about—
Through this activity, children practice counting, recognizing numerals, associating number names, matching sets and, in addition, they practice their listening skills.

STORY STRETCHER

For Music And Movement: Fireflies

What the children will learn—
To move in response to the music

Materials you will need—
Flashlights, slow swaying music, record or tape player

What to do—

1. Tell the children that fireflies alson live in meadows.

2. Discuss how fireflies shine their lights.

3. Darken the room and slowly turn a flashlight on and off.

4. Begin the music and gently move the flashlight across the ceiling of the classroom, occassionally turning it off and then back on like the firefly.

5. Have the children sway gently back and forth either seated or standing while the music is playing.

6. After they seem to have the rhythm of the music, give flashlights to three or four children and let them move their lights in response to the music.

7. Stop the music and give the flashlights to other children or keep the music playing and gently take the light from one child and pass it to another.

Something to think about—
Place colored tissue paper over the flashlights to create the effects of a misty summer night.

STORY STRETCHER

For Science And Nature Center: Insect Habitats

What the children will learn—
To observe insects and plants in their environments

Materials you will need—
Terrarium with living plants, whatever insects are available at the season of the year, grasshoppers in the spring, fireflies in the summer or crickets in the fall, magnifying glasses

What to do—

1. Solicit the children's and their families' help in finding insects for the terrarium.

2. Ask the children to try to remember where the insect was when it was captured, behind a blade of grass, on a twig or hiding in a dark place.

3. Discuss the needs of the insect, food, water, a place to sleep hidden from its predators.

4. Create a habitat in the terrarium, providing food, water and hiding places.

5. Have the children observe the insects through the magnifying

glasses and compare the different varieties and sizes.

Something to think about—
Children learn a respect for living things by the way we treat the animals and insects in our classrooms. After your nature study is finished, return the living insect to a habitat similar to the one where it was found.

REFERENCE

Bang, Molly. (1983). **TEN, NINE, EIGHT**. New York: Greenwillow Books.

Hutchins, Pat. (1986). **THE DOORBELL RANG**. New York: Greenwillow Books.

Peek, Merle. (1981). **ROLL OVER! A COUNTING BOOK**. New York: Clarion Books.

Tafuri, Nancy. (1986). **HAVE YOU SEEN MY DUCKLING?** New York: Penguin Puffin.

Wadsworth, Olive A. (1986). Illustrated by Mary Maki Rae. **OVER IN THE MEADOW**. New York: Penguin Puffin.

Additional References for Counting

Anno, Mitsumasa. (1975). **ANNO'S COUNTING BOOK**. New York: Thomas Y. Crowell Company. *Introduces counting and number systems by showing mathematical relationships in nature.*

Crews, Donald. (1986). **TEN BLACK DOTS**. New York: Greenwillow Books. *A counting book which shows what can be done with ten black dots — one can make a sun, two a fox's eyes, or eight the wheels of a train.*

de Brunhoff, Laurent (1986). **BABAR'S COUNTING BOOK**. New York: Random House. *Babar's three children go for a walk and count what they see with numbers up to twenty.*

Gretz, Susanna. (1969). **TEDDY BEARS 1 TO 10**. New York: Four Winds Press, Macmillan Publishing Company. *As teddy bears are washed, dried, take the bus, and have tea they introduce the numbers one to ten.*

Lionni, Leo. (1960). **INCH BY INCH**. New York: Astor Honor, Inc. *A clever inchworm talks the Robin out of eating him by measuring, counting the inches, until he inches out of sight of the Robin.*

COLORS

Red Is Best
Mary Wore Her Red Dress and Henry Wore His Green Sneakers
Green Eggs and Ham
Is It Red? Is It Yellow? Is It Blue?
Brown Bear, Brown Bear, What Do You See?

14
COLORS

RED IS BEST

By Kathy Stinson

Illustrated by

Robin Baird Lewis

A little girl says her mother does not understand about red. She likes her red barrettes, mittens, boots and her red cup. She even likes red paints the best because they "put singing in her head." Children sympathize with the little girl and understand her logic and love of the color red. Robin Baird Lewis' illustrations match the text beautifully with splashes of red. The book is printed in Canada and contains pajamas spelled "pyjamas" and mittens are called "mitts."

Circle Time Presentation

Wear a red sweater or blouse for this special red day. Ask children to tell you their favorite colors. List them on a chart tablet writing the color names in matching colors of markers. Decide which color is the class favorite. Read RED IS BEST. Children often request you to read this book again. Reread and pause for the children to say with you, the "Red is best" phrase. At the end of circle time, announce the "red" activities for the day.

STORY STRETCHER

For Art: Painting With Red And Music

What the children will learn—
To express their feelings about red

Materials you will need—
Easel, white paper, tempera paints, brushes, painting shirts or smocks, cassette tape of lively music

What to do—
1. Set up the easel for free play time with red tempera paint available.

2. Play a cassette tape of lively, energetic music.

3. Ask children if they want any other colors.

4. After the paintings are dry, have the children take their pictures to the writing area of the library corner.

Something to think about—
Change the paint the second day and have red paper with white tempera paints and a choice of colors. Whenever the easel-painting becomes an infrequently chosen activity, vary the paper color, paper texture or choice of paints and watch for the increased interest.

(Adapted from Linda Patton's classroom.)

STORY STRETCHER

For Cooking And Snack Time: Red Party

What the children will learn—
To make an everyday occasion festive by decorating

Materials you will need—
Red napkins, red paper cups, red gelatin mix, mixing bowl, mixing spoon, rebus chart of directions for making gelatin (optional), red construction paper

What to do—
1. Early in the morning's activities, have three or four children assist you in mixing a package of gelatin.

2. After one package has been prepared, gather another group to mix a second batch.

3. Let children who have not assisted with making the gelatin decorate the tables for snacks by placing red objects from around the classroom onto red construction paper for red centerpieces.

Something to think about—
Ask the children to bring something red from home for the centerpieces for the following day. Follow the same procedure and have other colors featured on other days.

STORY STRETCHER

For Housekeeping And Dress-up Corner: Dressing Red

What the children will learn—
To practice putting on different pieces of clothing mentioned in the story

Materials you will need—
As many different pieces of red clothing as you can find, including the one's mentioned in the story — red socks, red mittens, red jacket,

red boots, red barrettes, red pajamas — full length mirror

What to do—

1. Place the red clothing out in an interesting arrangement in the dress-up center.

2. Add a few new items of red clothing each day.

3. Place the RED IS BEST book in the dress-up area.

Something to think about—
Always have both boys and girls clothing available. At the end of the playtime, encourage the children to arrange the clothing in an interesting way (like in store windows) for the next children who choose that area.

S T O R Y S T R E T C H E R

For Library Corner: Red Is Best Caption

What the children will learn—
To associate their spoken words with written words

Materials you will need—
Writing materials, paper, crayons, red markers

What to do—

1. Ask children to draw or paint a picture with something red in it in the art center.

2. Have the children bring their RED IS BEST pictures to the library corner and let them dictate a caption for their pictures. If they are older preschoolers, they may have an entire story to dictate, or they may wish to write own caption using their own invented ways of spelling the words or even scribbled lines.

Something to think about—
Discuss briefly the child's picture by asking "Tell me about your picture." Then, ask the child to tell you what he or she would like to have you write at the bottom or on the back of the picture. As you print each word, say it aloud. Then reread the caption fluently, maki ng it sound like a whole thought, rather than emphasizing individual words. Encourage the child to say it or read it aloud after you. Don't be concerned if the child does not recall it exactly. The idea is to begin associating spoken words with written words, not exact word for word reading.

S T O R Y S T R E T C H E R

For Mathematics And Manipulatives Center: Sorting By Color Attributes

What the children will learn:
To sort objects by their attribute

Materials you will need—
Variety of small red objects, including blocks and poker chips, small tubs or boxes for sorting

What to do—

1. Place the variety of objects on a table in the mathematics and small manipulatives center.

2. Invite the children to think of the ways they can use red to sort the blocks and attribute pieces. For example, large red things, small red things, round red things, red rectangular things.

Something to think about—
Young preschoolers may need boxes or bins to sort like objects. Older preschoolers can use yarn or twine and make a circle on the table for their sorting.

MARY WORE HER RED DRESS AND HENRY WORE HIS GREEN SNEAKERS

Adapted and Illustrated by

Merle Peek

Based on the popular children's song, Merle Peek draws animal characters and dresses them in different colors. "Katy wore a yellow sweater. Ben wore his blue jeans. Amanda wore her brown bandana. Ryan wore his purple pants. Stacy wore her violet ribbons. Kenny wore his orange shirt. Katy wore her pink hat." All the animal characters go to a birthday party for Katy and the pink hat is her party hat, which she forgets she has on and wears it to bed. The tune to "Mary Wore Her Red Dress" is printed at the back of the book. The illustrations are cleverly printed using only the colors which have been named. As colors are added, the pictures become more colorful, ending with full-color pages showing the birthday party.

Circle Time Presentation

Sing "Mary Wore Her Red Dress" and other verses with two or three of your children's names. Then read MARY WORE HER RED DRESS AND HENRY WORE HIS GREEN SNEAKERS. After reading the book, sing the song again using the names of the animals and the colors they wore.

STORY STRETCHER

For Art: Making Party Hats

What the children will learn—
To decorate party hats

Materials you will need—
Construction paper, newspaper, glitter, glue sticks, scissors, stapler, hole puncher, yarn, tape

What to do—
1. Place newspaper down on table tops.

2. Roll a sheet of pink construction paper into a cone shape and staple in place. Put the party hat on and mention that it is like Katy's party hat from the story.

3. Show the children how to add decorations.

4. From scraps of construction paper cut tiny irregular pieces to decorate the hat. Also, punch holes in scraps of paper and glue the holes and the tiny scraps onto the hat with dots of glue.

5. After all the tiny shapes are glued in place, let the children draw designs with their glue sticks, then shake some glitter over the glue for the finishing touches.

6. Make straps to tie the hats on by stapling a piece of yarn to each side of the hat. To reinforce the straps, place a piece of tape on the outside and inside of the hat where the staple is.

Something to think about
Create a party box to encourage children not to waste paper. Whenever they have scraps left from projects, ask them to put the paper in the party box. Keep the box handy and when it is filled tell the children it is time to make more decorations.

STORY STRETCHER

For Cooking and Snack Time: Party Cupcakes

What the children will learn—
To decorate their own cupcakes

Materials you will need—
Cupcakes, frosting, sprinkles, raisins, nuts, bowls, spoons, plastic knives, milk

What to do—
1. Tell the children that you want to celebrate Katy's birthday, but you will need help preparing for the party.

2. If possible, bake cupcakes with the children assisting from the beginning, or have the cupcakes already baked.

3. Fill small bowls with water and show the children how to wet their plastic knives then scoop out some frosting and spread it on the cupcake. Wetting the knife makes the frosting spread more smoothly.

4. Clear away the frosting supplies and place several sets of bowls of the decorating toppings on the snack table so the children can reach them easily.

5. After the cupcakes are frosted and decorated, let the children admire each other's work, before eating their decorations.

Something to think about—
If possible, serve two cupcakes per child so the children can take one home to show their decorations for Katy's birthday party.

For Creative Dramatics: Dressing For Katy's Party

What the children will learn—
To dress like the animals at Katy Bear's birthday party

Materials you will need—
Red dress, green sneakers — spray paint some old ones — yellow sweater, blue jeans, brown bandana, purple pants or substitute purple shirt, violet ribbons, orange shirt, pink hat made as an art project

What to do—
1. Select children to dress like the characters.

2. Have them get dressed and hide behind a bookcase or screen.

3. When it is their character's time to appear in the story, have the children come and sit in a special chair beside you.

4. Select other children to get dressed for the story. Let the children who presently have the clothes on help the new characters get dressed quickly.

5. While the other children are waiting for the new characters to finish dressing, sing about the colors of clothes they are wearing.

Something to think about—
Have the children wear the party hats they made for the art project during the time you are dramatizing the book.

For Library Corner, Flannel Board: Katy Bear's Party Guests

What the children will learn—
To place the flannel board pieces on at the right cue

Materials you will need—
Flannel board, felt pieces for Mary Squirrel in her red dress, Henry Raccoon in his green sneakers, Ben Bear in his blue jeans, Amanda Rabbit in her brown bandana, Ryan Fox in his purple pants, Stacy Fox in her violet ribbons, Kenny Porcupine in his orange shirt and Katy Bear in her pink hat

What to do—
1. Have the children recall all the animals who came to Katy's birthday party. As a child says an animal, place the animal on the board and say what the character's name is.

2. Ask if the animals are in the same order they appear in the story. Turn the pages of the book and let the children place them in order.

3. Then, give each child a different flannel board character to place on the board as the group sings the song.

4. Read the story-song backwards by having Kenny Porcupine be first and continue back through Mary Squirrel in her red dress. Then end with all the characters at Katy's birthday party.

Something to think about—
Do not be concerned if your animals do not look like the illustrations in the book. Having an outline of the animals' shapes and the color of clothing will make them recognizable.

For Music And Movement: Singing What My Friend Is Wearing

What the children will learn—
To vary the words to "Mary Wore Her Red Dress"

Materials you will need—
Index cards, marker

What to do—
1. Print all the children's names on index cards. Shuffle them and let each child take a card.

2. With the children sitting on the circle time rug, start with the child nearest you and tell him whose name he has. The child then goes and gets the person whose name he has. They both come and stand near you. The child with the card tells you what color he wants the group to sing about that his friend is wearing.

3. Sing the song using the color the child selected.

4. Have the first child sit down and his partner now looks at her card. You tell the child the name she has.

5. Repeat the process.

Something to think about—
Using the cards to call on children helps avoid the problem of children making the selections, and then some children are always last to be selected. Also, to vary the activity for older preschoolers, include patterns, checks and plaids in your songs, as well as descriptions of clothes, as tank tops, sweat shirts and jogging pants.

GREEN EGGS AND HAM

By Dr. Seuss

Theodor Seuss Geisel

The main character emphatically states through a pattern of rhythm and rhyme that he does not like Sam-I-am or green eggs and ham. Sam-I-am pursues the narrator offering him green eggs and ham while in a car, on a train and in a boat. Finally, exasperated he tries the green eggs and ham, and much to his surprise, he likes them. The recognizable illustrations in this much loved book are characteristically Seuss. While the book is quite long, it reads quickly because the rhyming leads the reader through a fast-paced story.

Circle Time Presentation

Just the mention of the title may bring applause from your listeners. Read GREEN EGGS AND HAM and ask the children which pictures they think are the funniest. Then ask them, "Would you, could you, eat green eggs and ham?" After several children give their opinions, tell them today you are going to be Sam-I-am and offer them green eggs and ham. Repeat, "Would you, could you eat green eggs and ham?" to end the circle time.

STORY STRETCHER

For Art: Silly Cars, Silly Trains, Silly Boats

What the children will learn—
To create silly cars, trains and boats

Materials you will need—
Playdough, plastic knives

What to do—
1. Show the children at the art center the illustrations of the funny looking car, train and boat in GREEN EGGS AND HAM.

2. Suggest that they might like to make some silly cars, silly trains and silly boats to show to the other children.

3. Ask the playdough sculptors to place their creations in the center of the snack tables as the Dr. Seuss centerpieces for the green eggs and ham they will have for snack.

Something to think about—
Because the Seuss illustrations are such flights of fantasy, the children enjoy making the car, train and the boat look like the Seuss ones from the story, but also encourage them to make their own versions of silly cars, trains and boats.

(Adapted from Marcia Gideon's classroom.)

STORY STRETCHER

For Cooking and Snack Time: Green Eggs And Ham

What the children will learn—
To try tasting something, even if it looks very different than what they are accustomed to eating

Materials you will need—
Eggs, egg beater, mixing bowl, food coloring, dash of salt and pepper, vegetable oil, electric skillet, ham, orange juice, toast, knives, forks, plates, napkins

What to do—
1. Slice the pre-cooked ham, make the toast, and turn the skillet on to be warming before the children come to assist you.

2. With small groups of children at a time, prepare green eggs by letting them break their own eggs into a mixing bowl. Show the children how to scramble the eggs with the egg beater. Then, put just a drop of green food coloring in the eggs and let them take turns beating the eggs and watching the color change.

3. Place a small amount of vegetable oil in the skillet and scramble the eggs.

4. Pour the scrambled eggs into a bowl and let the children serve themselves, as well as get their toast, ham and orange juice.

Something to think about—
Discuss whether the green eggs taste any different than most eggs. Have the children close their eyes and ask them if the eggs taste different when they are not looking at them. Of course, if some children do not want the eggs, do not insist.

For Housekeeping And Dress-up Corner: Funny Seuss Hats

What the children will learn—
To decorate their hats and make them look like Seuss hats or clown hats

Materials you will need—
A variety of hats, plastic flowers, pipe cleaners, ribbons, stapler, full-length and hand mirrors

What to do—

1. Show the illustrations from GREEN EGGS AND HAM and have the children notice the funny looking, squashed down, big hat the main character is wearing. If you have other Dr. Seuss books in the classroom, look at the funny looking hats he draws on many of his characters.

2. Ask the children if they could make some of the hats in the dress-up corner look funny like Dr. Seuss hats or like clown hats. Show them the supplies you have collected and tell them they can make any funny hats they want.

3. Assist the funny hat makers in getting started, stapling on plastic flowers or tying ribbons, but encourage them to improvise on their own.

4. When the hat makers are thoroughly involved, leave them to their own creations and check back with them periodically.

Something to think about—
Assist younger preschoolers until the hats are completed and they begin pretending their funny roles.

For Library Corner, Listening Station: Sam-I-am Convinced Me

What the children will learn—
To listen to the story through earphones and stay on the correct page while looking at the book

Materials you will need—
Listening station with earphones, cassette tape of the story, tape recorder, stapler

What to do—

1. Tape record yourself reading GREEN EGGS AND HAM. Use the clicking of a stapler to signal when to turn the page. You want to have a signal which will not interfere with the rhythm and rhyme of the story.

2. Have only three or four children at a time at the listening station.

3. Select someone as book holder who is good at manipulating the pages for the group listening of the story.

4. Adjust the volume on the listening station and wait for the tape and the book holder to get synchronized, then leave the children to operate the listening station on their own.

5. Assign a tape rewinder to prepare the listening station for the next group of children.

Something to think about—
Stay with the younger preschoolers at the listening station and hold the book and turn the pages for them.

For Music And Movement: Name-I-am

What the children will learn—
To clap the rhythm of the chant

Materials you will need—
None

What to do—

1. With all the children on the circle time rug, begin clapping rhythmically the syllables of the children's names. For example, Maria is three claps, Ma-ri-a, pausing longer on the second syllable. Brian is two short claps, Bri-an. Then ask the children to clap Sam-I-am, one long, followed by two quick claps.

2. After clapping many of the children's names, extend the activity by choosing children whose names have not yet been clapped and teach them to say "I-am" after their names. For example, Michael-I-am, Kendra-I-am or Denise-I-am.

3. Then add this little chant, point to the child, clap and say,

Teacher: Your name-I-am?
Child: Jaime-I-am
Teacher: Do you like Green eggs and ham?
Child: Yes, I like Green eggs and ham." (Raines based on Dr. Seuss)

Something to think about—
Notice the children having difficulty with the clapping and design extra listening and coordination activities for them.

IS IT RED? IS IT YELLOW?
IS IT BLUE?

By Tana Hoban

This wordless picture book only contains the words used in the title. It is a collection of photographs of everyday objects found mostly in the city. Under the pictures are circles showing the main colors in the photographs. Some of the photographs we see are a striped golf umbrella, balloons, a child in a striped shirt drinking from a water fountain. This concept book is a visual pleasure where the child is invited to continue answering the question, "Is it red? Is it yellow? Is it blue?"

Circle Time Presentation

Tell the children you will be reading them a different book, one where they must read the pictures to answer a question about colors. Review the primary and secondary colors by having children who are wearing those colors stand in a row near you. Then ask, "Is this a red sneaker? Is this a yellow shirt? Is this a blue jacket?" Show the pictures from the book and ask different children to tell you what they see. Some will just say they see red, but encourage the children by saying, "You are right, the picture does have red in it. What is the thing that is red?" For these pictures, let the children count how many different colors they see. Go back through the book and count how many different photographs were of red things, of yellow objects and of blue items.

STORY STRETCHER

For Art: Circle Color Keys

What the children will learn—
To associate their red, yellow and blue pictures with Hoban's photographs and color keys

Materials you will need—
Easel, paper, primary color paints, clothespin

What to do—
1. Show children Tana Hoban's photographs. Talk about the way Hoban uses the circles at the bottom of the page as color keys. Discuss the photographs they like best and the circle color keys on the bottom.

2. Place the paper on the easel and fold under one or two inches along the bottom. If necessary, hold it in place with a clothes pin.

3. Have the children paint their pictures the way they normally do, but when they have finished, turn down the inch or two of paper you folded under and say to them, "What circle color keys do you need to show the colors in your painting?"

4. Show the child how to twirl the brush so it makes a circular motion and paints a color key at the bottom of the painting.

Something to think about—
Some children will have mixed the primary colors and come out with others. They may paint the color keys as the colors they started out with or their mixed versions.

STORY STRETCHER

For Cooking and Snack Time: Red, Yellow And Blue Snacks

What the children will learn—
To taste blue gelatin with red and yellow apples in it

Materials you will need—
Plain gelatin, mixing bowl, wooden spoon, water, gelatin mold or bowl, blue food coloring, red and yellow apples, two paring knives, cutting boards, lemon juice, plastic wrap

What to do—
1. With a few children assisting at a time, prepare the gelatin and the apples. Follow the package directions for mixing the gelatin, but add blue food coloring to the mixture.

2. Pour the gelatin into the mold or a clear glass bowl and place it in the refrigerator to begin setting.

3. Show the children how to wash the apples thoroughly.

4. Demonstrated how to core and slice the apples.

5. Allow two children at a time to work with the paring knives and cutting boards to slice the apples. Supervise them.

6. Place the sliced apples in a bowl and squeeze lemon juice over them to keep them from turning dark. Cover with plastic wrap and store in the refrigerator.

7. Add the apples to the gelatin before it is completely set.

8. Serve the "Is it red? Is it yellow? Is it blue?" snack.

Something to think about—
Be certain to include both boys and girls in your food preparation activities.

STORY STRETCHER

For Mathematics And Manipulatives Center: Patterns Of Beads

What the children will learn—
To repeat a color pattern

Materials you will need—
Beads, yarn or string, colored unit blocks

What to do—
1. Show the children who come to the mathematics and manipulatives center, a pattern of stringing beads that you have begun. Ask someone to finish it by following your pattern.

2. Give beads and strings to the other children, and ask them to create their own patterns.

3. After the children are started and they have understood how to repeat the pattern, tell them you want to see if you can make a pattern of blocks like their beads.

4. Line up unit blocks in the same pattern of colors the child has created.

5. Demonstrate the process once more and then when the children finish their beads, have them work with each other to replicate the color pattern with the unit blocks.

Something to think about—
Some teachers choose to color macaroni or pasta shapes with food coloring and string those.

ANOTHER STORY STRETCHER

For Mathematics And Manipulatives Center: Our Favorite Colors Chart

What the children will learn—
To construct a simple graph

Materials you will need—
Sheet of typing paper, primary and secondary colored crayons

What to do—
1. Ask the children who come to the mathematics and manipulatives center to select the crayon that is their favorite color from a box of primary and secondary colors

2. With each selection, ask the child to make a mark on the sheet of typing paper.

3. Then ask the children from the center to conduct a poll of the other children. Tell them to ask each child to pick his or her favorite color from the crayon box. After each selection the pollster returns to the table to indicate the child's choice by making a mark on the paper. Continue until all the children have been asked for their favorite color.

4. Now have the pollsters look at the sheet of paper and count the number of marks for each color. You write the totals in the color of crayon. For instance, if five children selected red, then write the numeral 5 with the red crayon. Announce the favorite color of most of the children.

Something to think about—
Extend the activity by making a simple graph of the results, an enlarged poster of the typing paper tallies.

STORY STRETCHER

For Science And Nature Center: Mixing Colors

What the children will learn—
To mix the secondary colors by combining the primary colors

Materials you will need—
Tempera paints in the primary colors, baby food jars and lids, coffee stirrers

What to do—
1. With the children who come to the science and nature center during free play, demonstrate how to mix primary colors to make secondary colors.

2. Mix a tiny drop of blue into the lid of a jar containing yellow tempera paint, and ask the children to observe what is happening. Then let them mix the colors, but control the amount by mixing in the lids of the containers.

3. Next mix a tiny drop of blue into the lid of the red paint, and ask the children to observe what is happening. Then let them mix their own purple color in the lids of the baby food jars.

4. Mix a tiny drop of red into the lid of the yellow paint, and ask the children to observe what is happening and to predict what color we can make if we mix in more red. Let them continue the process of mixing in only a few drops at a time until they have orange.

Something to think about—
The excitement of their color discoveries will entice other experimenters to come to the science and nature center.

14

COLORS

BROWN BEAR, BROWN BEAR, WHAT DO YOU SEE?

By Bill Martin, Jr.

Illustrated by Eric Carle

"Brown Bear, Brown Bear, what do you see?" is one of the most famous questions in literature for young children. The text is a series of animals asking the same question, "What do you see?" The brown bear answers the question. The other characters are a redbird, a yellow duck, a blue horse, a green frog, a purple cat, a white dog, a black sheep, a goldfish, a mother and children. The book is also available as a "big book" with some extra animals. Eric Carle's bold and clever illustrations are of a single animal covering two pages. In typical Carle fashion, even the end paper pages are colorfully decorated.

Circle Time Presentation

Show the children the cover of the book and tell them in this book the bear asks a question that all the other animals repeat. Read BROWN BEAR, BROWN BEAR, WHAT DO YOU SEE? Whenever the children begin to hear the rhythm of the language, the question and the reply, they will begin to predict what comes next and will join in with, "What do you see? I see a yellow duck looking at me. Yellow duck, yellow duck, what do you see?" Read the book again. Have a child who was eager to hear the book again place it in the library corner. Tell the children you have made a flannel board story of BROWN BEAR, BROWN BEAR, WHAT DO YOU SEE?

STORY STRETCHER

For Art: Strangely Colored Animals

What the children will learn—
To imagine and draw or paint a large animal of an unexpected color

Materials you will need
A choice of either tempera paints or crayons, easel, paper

What to do—
1. Look again at Eric Carle's illustrations and have the children tell you what they notice about the animals. They are quite large, covering two full pages, and some are strangely colored. The children will easily recall the blue horse and the purple cat.

2. Ask the children what would be a funny color for some other farm animals, as a green cow, a pink rooster, an orange pig. Also have them think of some wild animals and some strange colors.

3. Tell the children that you would like them to draw or paint a big animal, one that almost covers the whole paper like Carle's animals.

4. Extend the story by having the children dictate the patterned language question for you to write on their picture. For example, the child who painted a red goat dictated, "Red goat, red goat, what did you see?"

Something to think about—
Repeat the activity another day because the children will think of other animals they want to paint. For the second day, have the children paint or draw on typing paper and bind the pictures into a class book. Directions for book binding are included in the appendix of this book.

STORY STRETCHER

For Library Corner, Flannel Board: Brown Bear Saw

What the children will learn—
To match the patterned language questions in sequence to the flannel board characters

Materials you will need—
Flannel board pieces of a brown bear, redbird, yellow duck, blue horse, green frog, purple cat, white dog, black sheep, goldfish, surprise animal, mother or teacher, children

What to do—
1. Read the book again to the children who come to the library corner during free play.

2. Distribute the flannel board pieces among the children and start with Brown Bear and ask his question. See if the children can remember the sequence the animals appear in the story.

3. Just for fun, add a strangely colored animal that was not mentioned in the story, as an orange pig, insert it just after the goldfish and before the mother.

Something to think about—
Usually the children will have the sequence and the lines of the book memorized with just a few sessions with the book and the flannel board. When someone says to you, "I can read this book," reply, "Yes, I'm sure you can. Would you like me to listen to you read it?" Children's first attempts at reading, even though it may be memorization, should be praised. Pretend reading and reading parts of a book are confidence builders for the young child.

ANOTHER STORY STRETCHER

For Library Corner, Listening Tape: Group Chanting

What the children will learn—
To say the words to BROWN BEAR, BROWN BEAR, WHAT DO YOU SEE?

Materials you will need—
Cassette tape, tape recorder

What to do—
1. Tell the children they have remembered the words to BROWN BEAR, BROWN BEAR, WHAT DO YOU SEE? so well that you want to make a tape recording of their saying the words along with your reading.

2. Read the book and keep the rhythm of the language flowing as they join in with you for one practice session before you record.

3. Record the tape without any page turning signal; it is built in by the way the pictures and text are organized. The children all know when to turn the page.

4. When another group of children come to the library corner during free play, have them listen to the first group's tape and ask if they want to make a tape.

Something to think about—
Extend the listening tape idea by focusing on the colors of the animals. Give each child pieces of construction paper which are the same colors as the animals mentioned in the book. For the younger children, you show the pictures as they listen to the tape and have them then hold up the color of paper which matches the pictures. For older children, listen to the tape and do not show the pictures, just have them hold up the colors as they listen.

STORY STRETCHER

For Mathematics And Manipulatives Center: Patterns Of Colors

What the children will learn—
To sequence colors in a predictable pattern

Materials you will need—
Beads, stacking blocks, construction paper in one inch wide and two or three inch long strips in the colors of brown, red, yellow, blue, green, purple, white, black and gold, yarn or shoe strings

What to do—
1. With the children who come to the mathematics and manipulatives center during free play, recall all the animals in BROWN BEAR, BROWN BEAR. When a child says an animal, place that colored square of construction paper on the table. For example, when a child says frog, place the piece of green paper on the table.

2. Then ask if the colors are in the right order. Often they do

recall the bear first so they have the beginning color.

3. Have the children sequence the pieces of paper. Someone will decide they need to check the book, so have it available.

4. When the colors are in order, give the children beads or blocks of those colors and let them choose which they will use to make a Brown Bear string of beads or a Brown Bear stack of blocks.

Something to think about—
Extend the activity by making a yarn necklace of the paper strips. Punch holes in one end of the construction paper strips and the children string them in the order they appear in the book.

STORY STRETCHER

For Music And Movement: Old Mac Martin Had A Farm

What the children will learn—
To adapt a song to match the animals in the book

Materials you will need—
None

What to do—
1. Have the children recall all the animals in BROWN BEAR, BROWN BEAR, WHAT DO YOU SEE? If needed, bring the flannel board out with all the animals placed in sequence across the board.

2. Tell the children the author of BROWN BEAR is Bill Martin, Jr. and these are the animals he thought of for the book. Ask them to pretend that Bill Martin has all these animals on a farm and begin singing, "Old Mac Martin Had a Farm." If your children are young preschoolers, continue singing Old Mac Donald.

3. Think of sounds for each of the characters, a roar for the bear, a chirp for the redbird, a quack for the yellow duck, a nay for the blue horse, a rivet for the green frog, a meow for the purple cat, a bow wow for the white dog, a baa baa for the black sheep, a glub glub for the goldfish, a "love you" for the mother and a hurray for the children.

4. Sing the song several times throughout the week.

Something to think about—
After learning the song, let children volunteer to sing the different animal parts. The other children who did not volunteer will sing the mother's and children's parts together as a group.

REFERENCES

Geisel, Theodor Seuss (1960). **GREEN EGGS AND HAM.** New York: Random House.

Hoban, Tana. (1978). **IS IT RED? IS IT YELLOW? IS IT BLUE?** New York: Greenwillow Books.

Martin, Bill, Jr. (1983). Illustrated by Eric Carle. **BROWN BEAR, BROWN BEAR, WHAT DO YOU SEE?** New York: Henry Holt and Company.

Peek, Merle. (1985). **MARY WORE HER RED DRESS, AND HENRY WORE HIS GREEN SNEAKERS.** New York: Clarion Books.

Stinson, Kathy. (1982). Illustrated by Robin Baird Lewis. **RED IS BEST.** Toronto: Annick Press, Ltd.

Additional References for Colors

Johnson, Crockett. (1955). **HAROLD AND THE PURPLE CRAYON.** New York: Harper and Row Publishers. *The story of a little boy who draws himself an adventure, complete with escape back to his own bed.*

Lionni, Leo. (1959). **LITTLE BLUE AND LITTLE YELLOW.** New York: Ivan Obolensky, Inc. *Story of how green is made when blue and yellow become friends.*

Lionni, Leo. (1975). **A COLOR OF HIS OWN.** New York: Pantheon Books. *The sad chameleon has a problem — unlike all the other animals, he has no color of his own.*

Rossetti, Christina. (1971). Illustrated by José Aruego. **WHAT IS PINK?** New York: Macmillan Company. *Christina Rossetti's poem describes the primary and secondary colors by associating them with things in nature.*

Wylie, Joanne & David. (1983). **A FISHY COLOR STORY.** New York: Children's Press. *A child introduces the colors while answering questions about a beautiful fish.*

CATS AND OTHER PETS

Cat Do, Dogs Don't
Where Does My Cat Sleep?
Amelia's Nine Lives
Hi, Cat!
Millions of Cats

15

CATS AND OTHER PETS

Cats Do, Dogs Don't

Norma Simon pictures by Dora Leder

CATS DO, DOGS DON'T

By Norma Simon

Illustrated by Dora Leder

Norma Simon contrasts the many differences between dogs and cats as pets. A child is used as a narrator for the contrasts with pictures of a dog on one page and a cat on the facing ones. Dora Leder's colorful illustrations include both boys and girls playing with and caring for their pets. The children of different ethnic backgrounds are dressed in up-to-date clothing and their actions and facial expressions are realistic accompaniments to the text.

Circle Time Presentation

Have the children who have cats as pets raise their hands. Have children who have dogs as pets raise their hands. Ask a cat owner to tell something about how a cat acts. Then, ask a dog owner to tell if a dog acts like that. Invite children who do not have pets to join in the discussion by telling about pets they know. Continue the contrasting discussion with other children's information about pets' behaviors. Read CATS DO, DOGS DON'T. After the reading, ask the children to tell you whether or not the pets in the story acted like their pets at home or like pets they know.

STORY STRETCHER

For Cooking And Snack Time: Choose Your Fruit

What the children will learn—
To select a nutritious snack for you and one for your pet

Materials you will need—
Variety of fruits — oranges, apples, pears, bananas, white and purple grapes, tangerines — large fruit bowls

What to do—
1. Show the illustration of the child seated at his kitchen counter eating grapes while watching his pet play. Discuss people snacks and pet snacks, as chew biscuits. Mention that people food is not always good for pets and they should check with their parents before giving people food to their pets.

2. Before snack time, have several boys and girls wash the fruit and arrange it attractively in a large fruit bowl for each snack table.

3. At snack time, have the children choose the snack they want from the fruit bowl.

Something to think about—
Encourage parents to help their young children make choices. In busy family life, it is often quicker and easier to make decisions for children, but we want our children to be independent thinkers and giving them choices helps the youngsters to realize that it is important to think for themselves. Discuss with parents the many decisions young children can make. Mention choices about snacks; the fruit bowl forces them to choose.

STORY STRETCHER

For Music And Movement: Catching Frisbees

What the children will learn—
To throw and catch a frisbee

Materials you will need—
Three small frisbees or heavy paper plates turned upside down

What to do—
1. During outside play, or inside if you have a room designed for large muscle activity, begin throwing a frisbee with one child.

2. As other children become interested, have the teacher aide begin throwing and catching with another child.

3. Assist some of the less coordinated children or those inexperienced with frisbees by holding their hands and arms and practicing the movement.

Something to think about—
Young children are eager to develop motor skills. The ones who are quite coordinated enjoy showing off their skills on the climbing equipment. Often the playground noise is punctuated

with children shouting, "Teacher, look at me, I can . . . ." Early childhood educators can assist less coordinated children by starting special motor activities with those youngsters, but then let them go off to play on their own. End the play session by having those children come back and do the activities again.

For Sand Table: Cats' And Dogs' Hidden Treasure

What the children will learn—
To search for hidden objects, count them and decide whether they are for cats or dogs

Materials you will need—
Sand table, or large plastic tubs with sand, dog bones, biscuits or chew sticks, cat toys mentioned or pictured in the book — toy mouse, bell, piece of string — digging spoons and paper cups, boxes

What to do—
1. Share your idea for the sand table with some of the pet owners. Have them bring in the treasures which cats and dogs would like.

2. Let the children who brought in the objects hide them in the sand, and then they go and get their friends to become the first diggers for the pet treasures.

3. Have shoe boxes near the sand table, one for cat treasures and one for dog treasures. Count to make certain all the treasures are found.

Something to think about—
Vary the activity by having other pet owners bring in objects their pets enjoy on other days. Let children who do not have pets help friends who do have pets bury the treasures.

For Water Table: Shampooing Imaginary Pets

What the children will learn—
To soap and rinse a pretend pet

Materials you will need—
Water table, dirty stuffed animals, no-tears baby shampoo, a pitcher, soft scrub brushes

What to do—
1. Have some children assist you in filling the water table with warm water.

2. Select the stuffed animals which really need a bath. Place a few of them at a time near the water table. Save a few for the next crew of pet washers.

3. Add enough shampoo to the water to make it nice and bubbly.

4. Demonstrate with the scrub brush how to wash the pet gently so it does not hurt, but hard enough to clean. Also, demonstrate how to pour water over the pet to rinse.

Something to think about—
You will probably have to rerinse the stuffed animals to get out the shampoo. Place them in the dryer in a laundry bag so they do not bounce around too much causing the stitching to come apart. Place a sheet of fabric softner in the laundry bag as well.

For Work Bench: Plumber's Tool Chest

What the children will learn—
To associate certain tools and supplies with plumbing

Materials you will need:
PCV pipes and fittings, wrenches, putty, a plumber's helper, a tool chest

What to do—
1. Open the book, CATS DO, DOGS DON'T, to the page where the father and the little girl are trying to fix the overflowing sink when the plumber arrives on the scene. Place it on display at the work bench.

2. If possible, have a plumber visit the class and demonstrate the tools. If not, the maintenance person for your school or center usually has some of these tools and supplies. Invite the maintenance worker to do the demonstration.

3. Place the pipes and fittings on the work bench with the wrenches.

4. Allow only two or three children at a time to use the workbench so that each can explore, experiment and pretend with the tools and equipment.

Something to think about—
Often in our units on careers, or what I want to be when I grow up, we choose the usual fire fighter, doctor or nurse themes. Be certain to include many of the service occupations as well. During the pets unit is also a good time to emphasize veterinarians.

CATS AND OTHER PETS

Norma Simon *pictures by* Dora Leder

WHERE DOES MY CAT SLEEP?

By Norma Simon

Illustrated by Dora Leder

A preschool girl tells where she goes to bed, sleeps, and wakes up and then compares where her cat sleeps. As she narrates the story, she shows us where Mommy and Daddy sleep, where baby sleeps and two places where Grandpa sleeps. Throughout the story, Rocky the cat is shown in some usual and unusual sleeping places throughout the house. Dora Leder's charcoal drawings are detailed and expressive. The family members' clothing, the furniture and room arrangements are realistic and create a warm sense of security.

Circle Time Presentation

Discuss all the places that we sleep, at home in our beds, at school on our cots, on the couch watching tv, in a sleeping bag, in the car on a trip. Ask the cat owners to tell where their pets sleep. Read WHERE DOES MY CAT SLEEP? Let the children who do not have cats for pets add any places Rocky sleeps that the cat owners did not mention. Recheck the book for reference if needed. Discuss any places which surprised the children, as in the sink, in the mixing bowl, in a paper bag and on top of a cabinet way up high.

STORY STRETCHER
For Art: Rocky's Chair Collage

What the children will learn—
To cut out and name the types of chairs

Materials you will need—
Furniture ads, catalogs, magazines, paper, scissors, glue

What to do—
1. Display the picture in WHERE DOES MY CAT SLEEP? which shows the three different types of chairs where Rocky sleeps.

2. Place the collage materials out on the art table and ask the children to find as many different types of chairs as they can for Rocky to sleep on, cut out the pictures and glue them onto the paper.

3. While the children are working and showing you the pictures they have found, mention the types of chairs. "That one is a ladder back." "You're cutting out a wing backed chair." "That recliner is like the one in the book, the one where Grandpa and Rocky slept after lunch."

Something to think about—
Young preschoolers need much practice handling scissors. Creating collages gives them a purpose for their cutting and pasting. Their initial attempts will often be rounded ovals around the pictures, rather than following the lines of the chairs. Accept their level of development, but give them many activities using scissors. Purchase good quality scissors and clean off the glue and paste often so that they cut easily. Never recut for a child; with practice, you will see improvement.

ANOTHER STORY STRETCHER
For Art: Charcoal And Chalk Drawings

What the children will learn—
To use charcoal and chalk to create shaded pictures

Materials you will need—
White construction paper, variety of thicknesses of charcoal, black construction paper, chalk, tissues

What to do—
1. Show the children Dora Leder's illustrations in WHERE DOES MY CAT SLEEP? Explain that charcoal makes the pictures look so soft.

2. Let the children experiment with the charcoal on white paper by making lines of various thicknesses. Have them draw circles and shapes, then using the tissues, smudge the lines to make them look softer.

3. Also, experiment with the white chalk on the black paper following the same steps.

4. After the experimentation stage is over, ask the children to make charcoal drawings and chalk drawings.

Something to think about—
When a new medium or new materials are introduced, always allow time for exploration and experimentation. Have the new medium available throughout the week. Some young ones will not progress to the drawing picture stage, but will enjoy exploring the possibilities of the lines and the smudges.

For Library Corner: Cat Owners' Talks

What the children will learn—
The responsibilities of cat owners

Materials you will need—
None needed

What to do—
1. Ask a group of children to join you which includes both cat owners and those who wish they had a cat.

2. Show the pictures in WHERE DOES MY CAT SLEEP which show the little girl playing with or feeding her cat.

3. Have the cat owners tell about their pets by describing the cat and telling what they do to help take care of the cat.

4. Let children who do not have cats, tell about a cat they know, or about a kind of cat they wish they could have.

5. Display both fiction and reference books on cats in the library corner for later browsing and discussion time.

Something to think about—
Extend the idea of responsibility for a pet by having a veterinarian, a vet's assistant or a humane society volunteer come to class to talk about pets. Help the children understand that pet ownership can not be taken lightly and because

some families do not have the space or travel too much, then it is best for them not to be pet owners. They can enjoy their friends' or relatives' pets.

For Mathematics And Manipulatives Center: Cat Calendars

What the children will learn—
To count the pictures of cats

Materials you will need—
Posterboard, markers, glue, old magazines, cat food coupons and ads, and if possible, a cat fancier's calendar

What to do—
1. Have the children who come to the mathematics center help you to make a cat calendar for this month.

2. If possible, show a calendar which has pictures of cats on it.

3. Have the squares for the days of the month already drawn off.

4. Ask the children to look through the magazines, cat food coupons and ads you have brought and to cut out small pictures for your calendar. Then, each day of the week, at calendar time, we will add a cat's picture to the calendar.

5. After the children have found and cut out several pictures, count the number of pictures and ask if you have enough.

Something to think about—
For young preschoolers, you might place a star on the square indicating how many you need. For example, if today is the 20th, then place a star on the 20. Then, even before they know how to count, they can match a picture to a square and see that they either have enough or need more.

For Music And Movement: Cat Chant

What the children will learn—
To echo chant the lines about a cat

Materials you will need—
Cue card of the chant if you haven't memorized it

What to do—
1. Say the entire poem all the way through in a rhythmic chant. Pretend to be holding a little cat next to you and stroking its' fur.

"I have a cat
So warm and furry
And when he sleeps
All he does is
purrrr, purr, purry
My little cat,
My very little cat
My little cat
So furry." (Repeat first stanza.) (Raines)

2. Have the children echo chant each line with you. You say the line with expression and the children repeat it after you.

3. Practice saying the entire chant together several times throughout the day and during your unit on pets.

Something to think about—
Print a copy of the cat chant for the children to take home. Also, if you are musical, feel free to make up a tune and sing the chant to the children, or add your own verses.

CATS AND OTHER PETS

AMELIA'S NINE LIVES

By Lorna Balian

Nora's cat, Amelia, disappeared. Nora looked everywhere for her, but when she couldn't be found, Nora started crying. She cried for days, even though Mama kept reassuring her that cats have nine lives and Amelia would come home. Mama placed a lost pet ad in the newspaper; Papa painted a lost cat sign for the front lawn, and Ernie went to all the neighbors looking for Amelia. Soon black cats began showing up from everywhere but those cats were not Amelia. Finally Nora is thrilled by Amelia's return—along with her four newborn kittens. The clever illustrations have the background as black and white line drawings and the characters are warmly colored with modern family dress and stylized round faces.

Circle Time Presentation

Ask cat owners to tell the names of their cats. Ask where they got their cats, from an animal shelter or as a special gift? Read AMELIA'S NINE LIVES and pause before the Tuesday scene to ask the children what else the family might do to find Amelia. At the end read Papa's new sign which isn't mentioned in the text, "Free Cats to a Good Home." Discuss what a good home would be.

STORY STRETCHER
For Art: Cat Collage

What the children will learn—
To cut out cat pictures and arrange them in a collage

Materials you will need—
Magazines, cat food cents-off coupons, old cat calendars, crayons

What to do—
1. Place the variety of sources of cat pictures on the art table. Ask the children to find at least one cat which looks like Amelia for their collages. If they can't find one, ask them to draw Amelia and surround her with pictures of other cats.

2. While the children are looking for cat pictures, have them tell you whether the cats in the pictures look like their cats at home or their friends' cats.

3. As you discuss the cat pictures, tell the children the proper and common names for the types of cats as Siamese, Burmese, Persian, Tabby and Calico.

Something to think about—
The cat pictures can be arranged on a bulletin board entitled, "Amelia and Her Friends," hung from a clothes lines stretched across a wall, strung as mobiles to hang from the ceiling or stapled together and inserted between two sturdy covers for a class scrapbook of cat pictures. Also, invite cat owners to bring in photographs of themselves and their cats for the display of cat artwork and the pet projects all around the room.

STORY STRETCHER
For Creative Dramatics: Nora's relatives and neighbors

What the children will learn—
To guess the identities of Nora's relatives and neighbors

Materials you will need—
Dress-up clothes for Nora, Mama, Papa, Ernie, Grandma, Mrs. Perkins, Uncle George, the letter carrier, Aunt Lucy, Mr. Olson and Cousin Jake, grocery bags

What to do—
1. Place each character's clothing in a separate dress-up bag.

2. Show the children their character's pictures in AMELIA'S NINE LIVES. Have them get dressed and wait behind a screen or out in the hall. Let the aide assist with the dressing.

3. While the characters are dressing, review the pictures in AMELIA'S NINE LIVES and point out who each person is. Also, have the children try and remember which characters came on which day to give Nora a cat they thought was Amelia.

4. Have each character knock on the door and then say, "Who am I?"

5. After the child says, "Who am I?" you tell something about this person, as I came to see Nora on the same day as Cousin Jake, or I was the only person to come to see Nora on Wednesday.

Something to think about—
Older children may be able to tell their own identity clues. For

younger preschoolers, getting dressed appropriately, remembering to knock and say, "Who am I?" is enough to recall

For Mathematics And Manipulatives Center: Counting Amelias

What the children will learn—
To practice counting the cats and kittens

Materials you will need—
None needed

What to do—

1.   Count the number of cats on the cover of AMELIA'S NINE LIVES.

2.   Turn each page and have the children count the number of cats they see. On some pages, there will be zero because Amelia is lost and the neighbors and relatives have not started bringing black cats to Nora.

3.   Continue counting the cats on each page. After all the relatives and neighbors bring black cats, there are nine. Then, Nora finds Amelia and there are ten. Then, Nora brings in Amelia's four kittens and there are fourteen.

4.   Discuss with the children what their parents might say if they had ten cats and four kittens.

Something to think about—
Zero is not an easy concept for young children. Practice counting zero in a lot of concrete ways. For example, before snack time before placing anything on the table, ask the children how many glasses are on the snack table. They will say none and you should reply, "You are right; there are zero glasses." Count empty sets equalling zero by asking how many crayons are in this empty box? How many felt pieces are on this empty flannel board?

For Music And Movement: Looking For Amelia

What the children will learn—
To search for an object based on a clue

Materials you will need—
Stuffed animal cat, record or tape, cassette player or record player

What to do—

1.   Reread the part of AMELIA'S NINE LIVES where Nora and her family are searching all over the house for Amelia.

2.   Show the children your pretend Amelia and have them close their eyes while Amelia runs away. Play a record or cassette of some music. Ask the aide to hide the stuffed animal.

3.   Stop the music and ask a child to go search for Amelia, but give her clues, as Amelia's hiding near the same place you hang your coats. Or Amelia's hiding where Kevin always chooses to play.

4.   When Amelia is found, then the child who was searching becomes the one to hide the cat. Play the music while the cat is being hidden and have the children close their eyes.

Something to think about—
Older children may be able to take over your role and also give the clues. However, it is best for you to retain calling on children to find Amelia so that all children participate.

For Science And Nature Center: Caring For A Kitten

What the children will learn—
To recall the important points about how to care for a kitten as a new pet

Materials you will need—
None needed:

What to do—

1.   Invite a cat enthusiast, a veternarian's assistant or a volunteer from the local humane society to talk about caring for a new pet.

2.   After your speaker has left, discuss with the children some main points they should remember when a kitten is given to them as a pet. All pets need love and attention, but baby kittens also need to sleep a lot. They need special food, a water bowl and their food served in the same place every day. They need a litter box which must be changed often and a special stratching pole or surface. And, cats need a special place to sleep with a soft blanket which they can associate as theirs. Many pet owners also provide toys to entertain cats.

Something to think about—
Encourage parents to tell you when they plan to give pets to their children as gifts. You can reinforce pet ownership at school, but parents must remember that preschoolers are not yet old enough for sole responsibility of meeting all of the pet's needs.

CATS AND OTHER PETS

HI, CAT!

By Ezra Jack Keats

Archie was on his way to see his friend, Peter, when he saw a cat sitting on top of a garbage can. Little did Archie know, but the cat followed him. Archie entertained the little kids on the street corner by pretending to be an old man and then a clown with a huge paper bag over most of his body. Peter called him Mister Big Face. Just as Archie had them all in stitches, the cat jumped inside the bag and started shaking and scratching. It scared all the little children so much they ran away. Then the bag tore apart with the cat going one way and Archie the other. When Archie got home, he told his mother the whole story, ending with, "You know what, Ma? I think that cat just kinda liked me!" The illustrations are in the wonderful Keats' style with paint and a bit of collage.

Circle Time Presentation

Not all children can have pets. Discuss some of the reasons why children might not be able to have pets. If we live in apartment buildings, or travel a lot, or have allergies, or just do not have enough space right now, then we probably will have to wait until we are older to have pets. Read and discuss HI, CAT!

STORY STRETCHER

For Art: Fabric Collages

What the children will learn—
To use fabrics in a collage design

Materials you will need—
Swatches of fabric, scissors, paper, glue, crayons or tempera paints

What to do—
1. Point out Keats' effective use of fabric to show Archie's shirt and his painting to show the stripes on Peter's shirt.

2. Look at some of the swatches of cloth and decide what piece of clothing this fabric could make in a picture.

3. Encourage the children to either glue on fabric and make a design around it, or to draw a picture and then cut out fabric for one of the character's clothing.

4. Ask everyone to make a tiny cat in the scene.

Something to think about—
For young preschoolers, pre-cut pieces of fabric to look like shirts, pants, dresses, blouses, skirts. They can glue on the clothing pieces and draw the characters in the clothes. Five year-olds will enjoy doing the entire project themselves. After their collages are complete, let the children dictate a caption for the picture. If one child makes a collage about

Archie and one makes a collage about Peter, place the collages side by side and have the children decide what Archie and Peter would say to other.

ANOTHER STORY STRETCHER

For Art: Silhouettes

What the children will learn—
To recognize each other by their silhouettes

Materials you will need—
Overhead projector or bright flashlight, white butcher paper, black and white construction paper, tape, scissors, rubber cement

What to do—
1. The teacher does all of the following steps to create the silhouettes. Tape a sheet of butcher paper onto a flat wall.

2. Shine the light from an overhead projector or a bright flashlight onto the wall. Have the child stand between the light and the paper creating a shadow on the wall.

3. Trace around the shadow creating a pattern.

4. Place the white butcher paper pattern onto black construction paper and trace around it.

5. Cut out the silhouette from the black paper and glue it with rubber cement onto heavy white construction paper.

Something to think about—
Making the silhouettes is a teacher art project. Children appreciate their own silhouettes and try identifying the ones of other children. Do not send the silhouettes home immediately, but let the children enjoy making the comparisons.

For Cooking And Snack Time: Pistachio Ice Cream Or Lime Sherbet

What the children will learn—
To eat a new flavor of ice cream

Materials you will need—
Pistachio and vanilla ice cream, lime sherbet, cones, scoop

What to do—

1. Ask the children what flavor of ice cream they think Archie is eating, the one which Willie, Peter's dog, jumped up and started licking. We are not told in the story; we just see that it is green.

2. Serve the children tastes of both pistachio ice cream and lime sherbet. Have them practice saying the names of the ice cream.

3. Let them choose which green cone they want, pistachio ice cream or lime sherbet. If you have some child who will not eat either, then serve the vanilla ice cream.

Something to think about—
Food preferences may be idiosyncratic or may be learned from family preferences. Expand their experimenting with tastes and have them try frozen yogurt or tofu ice cream. Most children are willing to experiment if they know they can honestly state their preferences. Try to have familiar substitute flavors whenever serving something which may be unfamiliar. Also, never use food as a reward for good behavior, and never withhold food as punishment for bad behavior.

For Creative Dramatics: Mister Big Face

What the children will learn—
To make a paper bag puppet for a costume

Materials you will need—
Large paper grocery bags, scissors, markers, crayons, full-length mirror, small stuffed black cat

What to do—

1. Look at the scenes of Mister Big Face in HI, CAT!

2. Brainstorm some other faces which would be good for a paper bag puppet as other clown faces, a jack-o-lantern face, a witch, a lion. If they like, let the children make all the faces clown faces, then any design is alright.

3. Cut out eyes before you begin by placing the bag over the child's head, and with a crayon draw about where the eyes should be cut. Mark the sides at the top of the shoulder for armholes.

4. Remove the bag from the child's head, cut out the eyes and the armholes from the paper bag, and give the bag to the child to decorate. Cut the mouths after they are decorated.

5. After the Mister Big Faces are made, have a parade of paper bag puppets.

Something to think about—
Place the full length mirror near by the art table so the children can see themselves. Place a small stuffed black cat nearby to watch the performers. Have only four or five clowns performing at once so they will have an audience.

For Library Corner: Extend The Story

What the children will learn—
To suggest extensions to the story, HI, CAT!

Materials you will need—
Chart tablet or drawing paper, markers or crayons

What to do—

1. Often young children are disappointed that the story ends without Archie getting to have the cat as a pet. Invite a small group of children to the library corner. Tell the children we do not know whether Archie ever saw the cat again. What do you think? What would you like to happen to Archie and the cat?

2. Reread HI, CAT! and then ask the children to tell you what could have happened the next day. Write their dictations onto a chart tablet, or let them draw pictures showing the next day and you write what they dictate about their drawings.

3. Reread their dictations from the pictures or the chart tablet.

4. Ask the children to keep their new ending to the story a secret. Then, invite another small group to dictate their new ending to HI, CAT!

5. At another group time, read all the new endings to the book.

Something to think about—
Young children who learn to love books often add expressions to their own retelling of the stories. After listening to a group of older fours and fives retell HI, CAT!, we noticed children adding their own endings to be certain Archie kept the cat.

199

MILLIONS OF CATS

By Wanda Gag

This 1929 Newberry Honor book is a classic in children's literature. A little old man and a little old woman were very lonely and longed for a cat. The old man set out to find a sweet little fluffy cat. He walked until he saw a hill where there were, "Cats here, cats there, cats and kittens everywhere, hundreds of cats, thousands of cats, millions and billions and trillions of cats." He tried to pick out the prettiest one, but he couldn't decide so he took them all. When they arrived home, the old woman insisted that there was no way they could keep all the cats. So they decided to let the cats decide who was the prettiest. They began to scratch and claw and quarrel. There was such a terrible noise that the old man and old woman went inside. When the noise stopped, they could not see a single cat, except for one tiny little scrawny kitten hidden in some grass. It knew it wasn't the prettiest one so it didn't get in the fight. They took the kitten for their pet and were lonely no longer.

Circle Time Presentation

Children enjoy chanting the recurring phrase, "Hundreds of cats, thousands of cats, millions and billions and trillions of cats." Teach them the phrase before reading the book and tell them whenever you start saying it, they should join in. Read MILLIONS OF CATS. Decide the type of kitten which is prettiest to them.

STORY STRETCHER

For Art: Cat Sculptures

What the children will learn—
To shape their playdough to look like a cat

Materials you will need—
Playdough in a variety of colors, plastic knives

What to do—
1. Mix a recipe of playdough. Color the dough with food coloring to achieve the cat colors. If available, also mix up some black playdough for the black cat. Ask the cake decorator at a supermarket what colors to use to achieve the grey and black.

2. Have the children recall the many different cats they heard about in MILLIONS OF CATS. The little old man chose the white one first, then the fuzzy grey kitten, the black shiny one, the brown and yellow striped kitten that looked like a baby tiger, and finally the thin scraggly one who was left at the end of the story.

Something to think about—
Do not model how to sculpt a cat from the playdough. If the children have been playing with playdough throughout the year, many will already be sculpting animals. They usually start by rolling long snakes, then they make birds' eggs and nests, then

cups and saucers. Soon, they branch out into sculpting people and animals. They will associate the variety of colors of playdough with the cats mentioned in the story, and even if their sculpture does not look like a cat, they can describe it as the white cat or the yellow cat.

STORY STRETCHER

For Library Corner, Listening Tape: Cat Sounds

What the children will learn—
To recite the recurring phrase and make cat sounds on cue

Materials you will need—
Cassette tape, tape recorder

What to do—
1. With the children who choose the library corner during free play, make a tape of MILLIONS OF CATS with them saying the recurring phrase, hundreds of cats, thousands of cats, millions and billions and trillions of cats." Also, select three children to make cat sounds, one to purr, one to meow and one to hiss.

2. Read the story and where the recurring phrase appears have the children say it together.

3. Use the cat sounds as page turning signals and also record them where the story indicates those sounds might be made.

4. When the tape is completed, replay it for the children. Also share it during one of the circle times. Place the tape permanently in the library corner with the copy of MILLIONS OF CATS.

Something to think about—
Some children become upset at the end of the story. We are not told what happened to the cats except for the little old woman's conjecture, "I think they must have eaten

each other all up." Emphasize that this is not a real story. Also, you may say, "I think the cats just got tired of fighting and ran away."

For Mathematics And Manipulatives Center: Voting For Our Favorite Cat

What the children will learn—
To cast their ballot for their favorite cat calendar picture

Materials you will need—
Pictures from a cat calendar or magazine, posterboard, marker, construction paper, library book pockets or envelopes, scissors, glue or stapler

What to do—
1. Cut cat pictures from a cat calendar or a magazine. Let the children discuss which ones they like best, then eliminate all but the four or five top favorites.

2. Construct a poster of the top favorites by gluing them straight across the top of the posterboard. Glue on the library card pockets or envelopes. Place one under each cat picture.

3. Cut strips of construction paper about the size of a library card and give to each child.

4. Explain the voting procedure. Select the cat picture which is your favorite and place the card in that pocket.

5. After the voting, count the cards and declare the favorite cat picture. Staple the cards end to end and hang them under the pictures for a simple graph. With a marker in a contrasting color, make a frame around the winning picture.

Something to think about—
Select some of the least opinionated children to express their votes first. Also, try

numerous versions of these simple graphs.

For Sand Table: Hills And Valleys

What the children will learn—
To construct the countryside where the old man looked for the kitten

Materials you will need—
Sand table, sand, watering can or sprinkler, bowls, trowels, any instruments the children like to use for shaping

What to do—
1. Show the children who come to the sand table during free play the illustrations in MILLIONS OF CATS of the hills, valley and pond.

2. Have them brainstorm what they would need to turn the sand table into the countryside scenes.

3. Ask them to collect their tools from around the room, from any center they choose.

4. Leave the book for their future reference and leave the earth movers to their task.

Something to think about—
The sand table should be available for children to use on a regular basis so that they can experiment with a variety of tools, with the wetness of sand they need for sculpting and with quantities needed. After this experimentation and exploration of the properties of the sand, you will begin to see role-playing and stories created at the sand table. Creating a landscape of a story they have just heard is a natural extension.

For Science And Nature Center: Observations Of Cats

What the children will learn—
To report their close observations of cats

Materials you will need—
Index cards, pencil

What to do—
1. Discuss the point that scientists are keen observers. Recall some of the animals and plants you have observed in class and what you learned by the close observations. Mention that sometimes we forget to observe the animal behaviors of our very own pets.

2. Through the discussion, recall that when we studied other animals we wanted to know what they ate, where they lived and slept, their habitat, what they liked to do, what they looked like and what sounds they made.

3. Ask children to bring in pictures of their cats for the science and nature corner display.

4. Interview the children about their pets by answering all the questions they think are important about animal behaviors.

5. Write their answers on index cards and leave them in the science display area. Whenever children come to the science area, you can read some of the cards or ask the child pictured with the cat to retell their observations of the pet.

Something to think about—
Apply this same study to other household pets — dogs, birds, even fish. Let children who do not have pets observe a friend's pet.

REFERENCES

Balian, Lorna. (1986). **AMELIA'S NINE LIVES**. Nashville: Abingdon Press.

Gag, Wanda. (1928). **MILLIONS OF CATS**. New York: Coward, McCann, (Putnam Publishing Group.)

Keats, Ezra Jack. (1970). **HI, CAT**. New York: Macmillan Publishing Company

Simon, Norma. (1986). Illustrated by Dora Leder. **CATS DO, DOGS DON'T**. Niles, IL: Albert Whitman.

Simon, Norma. (1982). Illustrated by Dora Leder. **WHERE DOES MY CAT SLEEP?** Niles, IL: Albert Whitman.

Additional References for Cats and Other Pets

Chalmers, Mary. (1986). **SIX DOGS, TWENTY-THREE CATS, FORTY-FIVE MICE, AND ONE HUNDRED SIXTEEN SPIDER**S. New York: Harper and Row. *Annie tries unsuccessfully to keep her 190 pets out of the company room to avoid frightening her friend Priscilla.*

Gackenbach, Dick. (1984). **WHAT'S CLAUDE DOING?** New York: Clarion Books. *A dog refuses all the neighborhood pets' invitations to come out to play, not admitting that he's generously keeping his sick master company.*

Keats, Ezra Jack. (1964). **WHISTLE FOR WILLIE.** New York: The Viking Press. *Peter wants to whistle and finally does when he is able to whistle for his dog, Willie.*

McPhail, David. (1985). **EMMA'S PET**. New York: E.P. Dutton. *Emma, a girl bear, wants a cuddly pet other than her cat which is not so cuddly. She searches for a pet and finds a bug, a bird, a mouse, a frog, a fish, a turtle, and then brings home someone else's dog. Finally, she runs home and cries in the soft, cuddly lap of her father and decides she doen't need another pet.*

Noble, Trinka Hakes. (1980). Illustrated by Steven Kellogg. **THE DAY JIMMY'S BOA ATE THE WASH.** New York: The Dial Press. *Jimmy's boa constrictor wreaks havoc on the class trip to a farm.*

TRANSPORTATION

The Car Trip
Truck Song
The Train to LuLu's
The Train
Flying

TRANSPORTATION

The Car Trip

by Helen Oxenbury

THE CAR TRIP

By Helen Oxenbury

The book opens with the family preparing for a trip. The little boy is buckled in his car seat in the back. They stop along the way for gas and to eat in a cafeteria. After they stop for gas, the little boy gets car sick. Then the car will not start. Their long car trip turns into a short one. However, the trip was one of the best for the little boy because he was able to ride up front next to the truck driver who towed their little red car home. Helen Oxenbury's illustrations are colorful and realistic, especially the cafeteria scene, the gas station and the traffic jam.

Circle Time Presentation

Ask the children what their families do to prepare for a long trip in the car. Then read THE CAR TRIP. The children will identify with the little boy's getting car sick and will want to tell you their car sickness stories. Move on to discuss the sequence of the story. First, the little boy got in his car seat and his mother buckled his seat belt. Recall his entertaining himself by pretending to be a lion. Decide whether the cafeteria or the gas station came first. Then, next comes Dad's trying to repair the car and the scenes of the tow truck's taking them home. Discuss the surprise in the final scene. Instead of the little boy being upset about the cancelled trip, he was happy about the tow truck experience.

STORY STRETCHER

For Art: Car Window Pictures

What the children will learn—
To remember what they see when they go on car rides

Materials you will need—
Paper, large markers and crayons

What to do—
1. Ask the children who come to the art table to tell you what color car they have, then with the same color marker draw a border around the edge of their paper. The border represents their car window.

2. Have the children pretend that they are looking out the window of their car and draw what they see.

Something to think about—
If your children are young preschoolers, you might cut out car or truck shapes from large pieces of construction paper and let them decorate their vehicles. Older pre-schoolers may enjoy making several views seen from their car window. For example, they could draw a scene from the beginning of the trip, where they stopped overnight and from the end of the trip.

STORY STRETCHER

For Block Building : Traffic Jam

What the children will learn—
To construct a highway system with connecting roads

Materials you will need—
A strip of butcher paper long enough to stretch across the floor of the block building area, marker, yardstick, toy trucks, cars and buses

What to do—
1. Ask some of the block builders to help you make a highway. Draw a highway on the butcher paper by marking parallel lines down the middle using the yard stick to guide your markings.

2. Have the children create a traffic jam by lining up all the vehicles from end to end.

3. Discuss what is needed to clear up this traffic jam. Help the children discover that they need some on and off ramps and side roads so that the vehicles will have a place to turn.

4. Stay nearby to supervise the road builders if needed. When the system looks complete, the drivers can enjoy their highway system.

Something to think about—
On another day create another traffic jam and help the children to see that they need traffic signals to control the flow of traffic. Add the signals and help the drivers obey them.

For Cooking and Snack Time: Making Sandwiches

What the children will learn—
To prepare a peanut butter and jelly sandwich

Materials you will need—
Peanut butter, jelly, bread, spreading knives, plastic wrap or sandwich bags

What to do—

1. Mention that when the family went for their trip in the car, they prepared sandwiches to take with them. Tell the children that they are going to prepare sandwiches and then wrap them to keep them fresh for snack time.

2. With a small group of children at a time, demonstrate how to take a small amount of peanut butter and spread it on one slice of bread, then a small amount of jelly and spread it on the other slice. Show the children how to put the slices together and then how to wrap them.

Something to think about—
Children are often frustrated in their first attempts to make peanut butter and jelly sandwiches because the bread usually tears. Purchase a hearty whole grain bread instead of white bread and it will tear less easily. Also, peanut butter and jelly will spread more easily if they are at room temperature. In addition, for young preschoolers, the sandwich bags are easier to handle than tearing the plastic wrap from a roll.

For Creative Dramatics: A Bus Ride

What the children will learn—
To ride the bus safely

Materials you will need—
A steering wheel or a pretend one of a paper plate, a bus driver's hat, chairs arranged to represent the aisles of the bus

What to do—

1. If your children are experienced bus riders, simply remind them of the rule that the bus cannot start until everyone is seated.

2. If you have inexperienced bus riders, have the experienced bus riders discuss what happens when they ride the bus. First, they wait at the bus stop and look for the bus. When the bus comes, they get in line. If the bus is a city bus, they pay their money, and then move slowly down the aisle of the bus and find a seat. The bus driver watches them in the mirror until all the riders are seated before taking off.

3. Let an experienced bus rider be the first one to hold the steering wheel, wear the hat and be the driver.

Something to think about—
If you have a number of children who have never ridden a bus, consider taking the class on a bus ride. Phone the bus company and find a short, but interesting, trip. Tell them of your plans in case any special preparation is needed.

For Mathematics And Manipulatives Center: Counting Cars, Vans, Trucks, Buses

What the children will learn—
To practice counting

Materials you will need—
A variety of small toy vehicles

What to do—

1. For your transportation unit, invite the children to bring their little toy cars, trucks, vans and buses to school.

2. Label the toys on the morning that they are brought in so that there will be no confusion about who the owners are.

3. Create a display of all the vehicles at the mathematics table.

4. Have the children put the vehicles into categories, cars, several different types of trucks from paneled trucks to eighteen wheelers, vans for pleasure and those for deliveries, school buses and city buses.

5. Practice counting by counting the vehicles in each category.

Something to think about—
Recall that counting is one way we entertain ourselves when we have a long car ride. We count the number of red cars we see, or big trucks, or cars like ours, or trucks like Grandpa's.

TRUCK SONG $3.95

TRUCK SONG

BY DIANE SIEBERT PICTURES BY BYRON BARTON

TRUCK SONG

By Diane Siebert

Illustrated by Byron Barton

TRUCK SONG is a poem discribing how trucks move through country roads, city highways and long hauls on the interstates. Drivers are described and the feeling of moving on is conveyed in the rhythm of each stanza. While young children may not understand all the lingo and imagery in the words, the illustrations and their basic curiosity about trucks will sustain their interest. The narrator is a trucker who described all types of trucks, the truck stop, the traffic jam, the loading dock and the feeling of getting ready for tomorrow and another run. Byron Barton's pictures of trucks will invite comparisons with models in the classroom. The trucks are up-to-date versions with decorations and ads painted on.

Circle Time Presentation

If you have children whose fathers or mothers are truck drivers, ask them to bring their trucks to school for circle time. Or have a child who enjoys trucks drive one of the eighteen wheelers over to the circle time rug. Then read TRUCK SONG and let the children think of all the different descriptions of trucks that were mentioned in the poem. There were eighteen. Look back through the pictures again so the children can identify some of the trucks, eighteen wheelers, panel trucks, cement mixers, dump trucks

STORY STRETCHER

For Art: Painting Trucks

What the children will learn—
To decorate the shape of a truck

Materials you will need—
Construction paper, tempera paints, brushes

What to do—

1. From a whole sheet of construction paper, cut the side view of a tractor trailer truck.

2. Show the children Byron Barton's illustrations in TRUCK SONG.

3. Brainstorm with the children what their trucks might be hauling.

4. Ask them to paint the sides of their trucks but to try and make them different from the ones in the book.

Something to think about—
Print the name of the child on the front door panel, or the name of the school. Children who are interested in trucks may already be aware of the interesting designs painted on them or the advertisements on the sides, while others may not yet associate that the ads let you know what the driver is

hauling in the truck. Call attention to the trucks which make deliveries to the school or center, and ask the children how they know what is being delivered. When a study of community helpers is planned, be sure to include truck drivers in the study.

STORY STRETCHER

For Block Building: Loading Docks

What the children will learn—
To build a loading dock

Materials you will need—
Large hollow blocks, small blocks, big trucks, smaller vans and trucks

What to do—

1. Show the children Byron Barton's illustration of all the big trucks lined up at the loading docks. Explain that this is where they unload their cargo and pick up something new to haul.

2. To demonstrate, place a large hollow block lengthwise on the floor representing the loading dock. Place two smaller blocks at opposite ends of the block area to represent two schools. Have a child fill the trailer of one big truck with small blocks. Ask the driver to deliver the blocks to the dock and unload them. Have two other drivers come with their smaller trucks, fill them with blocks from the dock and deliver the blocks to the two preschools.

3. Substitute new drivers for the big trucks and the smaller trucks so that other children will understand the process and the function of the loading docks.

4. Leave the children to play on their own, building loading docks, making deliveries and redistributing their loads.

Something to think about:
Discuss other cargo the trucks might need to deliver to the schools, as food, toys, paper, paints and furniture.

For Library Corner, Listening Station: Truck Sounds

What the children will learn—
To make the sound effects of a truck

Materials you will need—
Tape recorder, cassette tapes

What to do—
1. Read the TRUCK SONG and ask the children to make some of the sound effects they make when they are playing with the trucks in the block building area. They can make engine noises, the sounds of warning when trucks are backing up, the screeching of brakes and the beeping of horns. Look at the illustrations of the truck driving through rain and think of sound effects, the swishing of the water under the tires and the slapping of the windshield wipers.

2. Practice the sounds a few times.

3. Tape record yourself reading TRUCK SONG with the children providing the sound effects.

4. Add the tape and the book to the collection for the listening station. You'll find the children's favorite selections are the ones they helped to record.

Something to think about—
If you have access to a real truck from one of the parents, tape record the sound of the brakes, the air horn, the backing-up warning sound, the windshield wipers slapping and some CB messages.

For Mathematics And Manipulatives Center: How Much Is Too Much?

What the children will learn—
To estimate capacity

Materials you will need—
Toy trucks with open trailers or beds, random items as small manipulative blocks, crayons, paper clips, and odd sized items from around the room as puzzle pieces, plastic cups

What to do—
1. Involve some children in helping you collect all the materials.

2. Ask some of the children playing with trucks to assist you in the activity.

3. Have the small blocks loosely piled up, not stacked neatly, and ask the children whether these blocks will fit into the truck.

4. Get one child to pile up how many blocks she thinks would fit into the truck. Then, have her fill the truck and see if she is right. Continue the process using other materials.

5. Then try a combination of items, blocks and puzzle pieces, sheets of paper and crayons, and so forth.

6. Leave the children to manipulate the trucks and their loads on their own, but insist that before they load, they estimate the capacity for each haul.

Something to think about—
The physical manipulation of the items for the loads and loading the trucks will help the children improve their estimates.

For Music And Movement: The Wheels On The Truck Go

What the children will learn—
To vary "The Wheels on the Bus" song to apply to trucks

Materials you will need—
None

What to do—
1. Have the children recall the song, "The wheels on the bus go round and round. Round and round. Round and round. The wheels on the bus go round and round. All through the town." (Source unknown)

2. Sing the song by changing the words to the wheels on the truck.

3. Add another verse, "The horn on the truck goes, honk, honk, honk. Honk, honk, honk. Honk, honk, honk. The horn on the truck goes, honk, honk, honk. All through the town."

4. Sing a third verse, "The driver in the truck says, mov-ing on, mov-ing on. Mov-ing on. Mov-ing on. The driver in the truck says, mov-ing on. All through the town." (Variation Raines)

Something to think about—
Add other verses to the song, "The wipers on the truck go swish, swish, swish." "The brakes on the truck go screech, screech, screech." "The loader of the truck says hurry back, hurry back, hurry back." "The boys and girls say blow your horn, blow your horn, blow your horn." "The driver of the truck says buckle up, buckle up, buckle up."

THE TRAIN TO LULU'S

By

Elizabeth Fitzgerald Howard

Illustrated by Robert Casilla

Beppy is responsible for her little sister, Babs, for a nine hour train trip from Boston to Baltimore where they will stay the summer with Lulu. The Travelers' Aid lady tells their mother and father that only Lulu can take them away once they arrive. Reassured, the parents send their two little girls, with suitcases, paper dolls, crayons, a teddy bear and lunch boxes off on the train ride to Lulu's. In Baltimore, there are aunts and uncles waiting to greet them, but only Lulu can take the girls. Finally, they see her white hair and hugs and kisses start their summer with great-aunt Lulu. Robert Casilla's watercolor illustrations are beautiful and capture the mood and emotions of the two young travelers.

Circle Time Presentation

Ask the children if they have been on a train. Also, ask if any of the children take care of their little brothers or sisters, or maybe older ones are instructed to take care of them. Show the picture of Beppy and her little sister, Babs, at the beginning of the story. Tell the children to listen to what Beppy's mother and father tell her about taking care of Babs. Read THE TRAIN TO LULU'S. After reading, ask the children to tell all the ways Beppy took care of Babs on the train trip.

STORY STRETCHER
For Art: Watercolor Scenes

What the children will learn—
To paint with watercolors

Materials you will need—
Watercolor paints, paper, brushes, sponges, small bowls with water

What to do—
1. Show the children Robert Casilla's beautiful watercolor illustrations in THE TRAIN RIDE TO LULU'S. Point where the water makes the colors run together. Show the pictures of the train racing by and the colors running together in a blur.

2. Demonstrate how to use just a little water on the brush, dry it on the sponge and dip the brush in the paint.

3. Let the children paint anything they choose.

Something to think about—
Leave the watercolors in the art center for several days for the children to experiment. On another day, float the paper in water to wet it, instead of using the dry paper method.

ANOTHER STORY STRETCHER
For Art: Milk Carton Train

What the children will learn—
To construct and paint an engine and train

Materials you will need—
Empty milk cartons from snack servings, tempera paint, liquid soap, brushes, scissors, pipe cleaners

What to do—
1. Mix dry tempera paint and liquid soap to the desired consistency. If you have premixed tempera, add liquid soap to the mixture. The soap makes the paint stick to the waxy surface of the milk cartons. Leave the tops on the milk cartons while the children are painting so that they have a place to hold the carton.

2. Have the children paint the milk carton train cars.

4. Cut the tops off most of the cartons, leaving a square open painted box. Holding the open side up, punch a hole in the front and back of the carton and insert a pipe cleaner on each side. On the inside of the carton tie each end of the pipe cleaners into large hard knots.

5. To make the engine, insert a pipe cleaner in the center of the bottom of a milk carton which does ***not*** have the top cut off. Tie the pipe cleaner in a large hard knot on the inside of the milk carton. Then, staple the top of the milk carton closed and turn it on its side so that the point from the top is the front of the engine. Connect the other cars with the pipe cleaners.

Something to think about—
The teacher should make the engines for the younger children.

For Library Corner, Listening Station: Two Sisters Travel Alone

What the children will learn—
To listen to the adventure of the two girls on their long train ride

Materials you will need—
Cassette tape, recorder, stapler

What to do—
1. Record yourself reading THE TRAIN RIDE TO LULU'S.

2. Tell the children which picture they should be looking at to begin the reading. It is the one where Babs has her teddy bear propped against a suitcase.

3. As a page turning signal, click the stapler together.

Something to think about—
THE TRAIN RIDE TO LULU'S is a confident, comforting book for children who must travel without their parents.

For Music And Movement: The Wheels On The Train

What the children will learn—
To sing a variation of the song, "The Wheels on the Bus"

Materials you will need—
None

What to do—
1. With the children seated on the circle time rug, sing the first verse of "The Wheels on the Bus." "The wheels on the bus go round and round, round and round, round and round. The wheels on the bus go round and round, all through the town." (Source unknown)

2. Ask the children how they could make this a train song instead of a bus song. "The wheels on the train go clickety-clack, clickety-clack, clickety-clack. The wheels on the train go clickety-clack all down the track."

3. Have the children think of the verse about the driver in the song, "The Wheels on the Bus." "The driver on the bus says, 'Move on back, move on back, move on back.' The driver on the bus says, 'Move on back,' all through the town."

4. Ask the children how they could sing a verse about a train conductor instead of a bus driver. "The conductor on the train says, 'All aboard, all aboard, all aboard.' The conductor on the train says, 'All aboard, we're leaving town.'" (Variation Raines)

Something to think about—
Many children will know little about what conductors actually do until you read THE TRAIN RIDE TO LULU'S and other train books.

For Science And Nature Center: Physics Experiment

What the children will learn—
To observe the extra force needed to pull heavy loads

Materials you will need—
Wagons, wheelbarrows, open train cars, large hollow blocks

What to do—
1. Ask the builders to build a steep hill or mountain train track.

2. Have the children pull or drive their wagons, wheelbarrows and open train cars around empty on the floor. Ask them if it is easy or hard to move the vehicles. Ask the observers how they can tell it is easy. The children moved quickly.

3. Have other children load the wagons, wheelbarrows and train cars with heavy blocks. Then have the children move them around the floor loaded down with blocks. Ask the children if it is harder to pull or drive than when empty. Have the observers tell how they know it was harder to move the loaded vehicles.

4. Then have the children push their loaded vehicles up the steep hill or mountain train track. Ask them if it is harder to push their loaded vehicles uphill or to drive them loaded on the floor. Have them compare the hardest and the easiest. Ask the observers what they saw that made them think it was hard to push the loaded vehicles up the steep train track.

Something to think about—
If you do not have open train cars which can be loaded, substitute large trucks, instead. Change roles and let the observers become the engineers and the drivers.

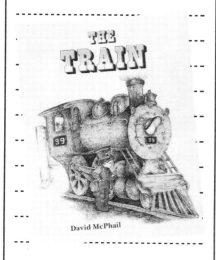

David McPhail

THE TRAIN

By David McPhail

Matthew is a little boy who loved trains. He even had a train set in his room. When his baby brother played with the train, he made it go too fast and it jumped off the track. Matthew was trying to repair it with his tools when his father told him he had to go to bed. Matthew fell asleep and dreamed of repairing a real train, of being a station master helping with the luggage, the conductor taking the tickets, the fireman shoveling the coal and finally the engineer driving the train. David McPhail's colorful illustrations have a dream-like quality.

Circle Time Presentation

If possible, have a small train set already assembled on a table near the circle time area. Turn it on and discuss how easy it is for a toy train to go off the track. Read THE TRAIN. Ask the children if they can tell you what part of the story was real and which part was the dream. Discuss how they know the differences. Compare this small train set to what a big train must be like. Reinforce any special rules for playing with the train set, but be careful not to make the children overly cautious.

STORY STRETCHER
For Art: Dream Pictures

What the children will learn—
To experiment with layering colors

Materials you will need—
Crayons, paper, plastic knives

What to do—
1. Show the children David McPhail's illustrations in THE TRAIN. Ask them to notice how there seems to be colors on top of colors.

2. With some small scraps of paper, demonstrated layering colors by taking one crayon and completely covering a section and then take another crayon and color over that same area.

3. Let the children experiment with the technique using a variety of color combinations.

4. Then, with a plastic knife, demonstrate how to lightly scrape the area and notice how the colors blend together even more.

5. Ask the children to draw a dream picture or use the technique to draw anything they choose. Encourage them to use the layered colors for at least part of their pictures.

Something to think about—
Threes and young fours will enjoy making the layered crayon colors and may not get to the stage of drawing a picture, but many of the older fours and fives will create elaborate dreams scenes. These children may want you to write a caption for their dream pictures or even a whole story. Let them dictate it, and you write it.

STORY STRETCHER
For Block Building : Toy Trains

What the children will learn—
To set-up and operate a simple train set

Materials you will need—
For younger preschoolers, a wooden train set with tracks, not electric; for kindergartners, a simple electric train set, easy to control

What to do—
1. Through the parent newsletter, ask for a volunteer to bring in a train set. Describe the simple type you want.

2. Request that the parent set up the trains and give you any special instructions, then disassemble the train set.

3. Have a special table set up for the train set so that it doesn't have to be moved often. Place all the parts of the train set on the table.

4. With a few helpers, assemble the train set.

5. Leave the children to enjoy the train set and to recall Matthew's set in THE TRAIN.

Something to think about—
Almost every community has a train enthusiast who will have pictures and models of many different types of trains. Invite the collector to tell the class about trains, but ask the speaker to only bring those

models that the children can handle.

For Creative Dramatics: The Train Ride

What the children will learn—
To imagine the roles needed for the train ride

Materials you will need—
Chairs, luggage, tickets, engineer's hat, hole punch

What to do—

1. Arrange the chairs so that there are seats on each side of an aisle, like seats on a train.

2. Select children for the roles of passengers, station master, ticket seller, conductor and engineer.

3. Have the station master supervise the loading of the luggage in the baggage compartment.

4. Select someone to sell the tickets to the passengers.

5. Ask the conductor to shout, "All aboard, all aboard for _____." Choose the name of a neighboring town.

6. Have the engineer say the sound, "Clickety-clack, clickety-clack" when the train is moving. The passengers can join him.

7. Give the conductor a hole punch to punch the passengers' tickets while passing up and down the aisle.

8. When the pretend train arrives, have the conductor shout, "All passengers off for _____."

Something to think about—
Few children will have experienced train rides, except for subway trains or commuter trains. Therefore, you will need to stay nearby to assist in the role playing for the first few attempts.

For Housekeeping And Dress-up Corner : Packing For Our Train Trip

What the children will learn—
To fold clothes

Materials you will need—
Dress-up clothes, child-sized suitcases, backpacks

What to do—

1. Simply bringing in the extra dress-up clothes and suitcases will prompt a discussion of taking a trip.

2. Start the children planning a train trip. Pretend to be a parent and instruct the children about packing and folding their clothes nicely.

3. After the children become engaged in play, leave them on their own.

Something to think about—
Open up a suitcase you have packed neatly with folded clothes. Include toiletries, pajamas and a change of clothes. Ask the children for suggestions of what you might need to entertain yourself on the trip, and add those items to the suitcase.

For Work Bench: Matthew's Tool Box

What the children will learn—
To use simple tools

Materials you will need—
The tools mentioned in the story, wrenches, hammer, paint, brushes, a cloth for cleaning, tool box, engineer's cap, index card, marker, tape, pieces of wood with screws and nails started

What to do—

1. Ask some of the children to help you prepare a tool box for Matthew. Reread the part of the story where his tools are mentioned. Then bring out the empty tool box. Print a label which reads Matthew's tool box and tape it to the tool box.

2. Have the children find the tools mentioned in the story from the classroom supply. Place them inside.

3. Then, ask for a volunteer who wants to be Matthew. Give the child the engineer's hat and Matthew's tool box.

4. Have the work bench supplied with screws that need tightening into blocks of wood, and nails that need to be hammered in.

Something to think about—
Whenever possible, have some real jobs to do with the tools. There are always toys which need a screw tightened or a bolt which needs a turn of the wrench. Matthew's tool box can be supplied with just the right size of screw driver and wrench.

16
TRANSPORTATION

FLYING
By Donald Crews

Crews' full color book follows an airplane from the point of people boarding to their arrival at their distination. The scenes are of the plane taxiing, taking off, and the many sights it flies over, including flying through and over the clouds. The few words are descriptions of the actions of the plane. There are no scenes of the inside of the plane or of the pilot, navigator and flight attendants. The last scene is the people getting off the plane.

Circle Time Presentation

If you know some of your children have flown, ask one or two to tell you about the flight. Read FLYING and ask other children to tell you about the pictures. For example, when the text reads, "flying across the country," discuss what the plane was flying over, as fields and farms and forests. Discuss the city picture also. Compare the beginning of the book where the sun is shining, and then turn to the back of the book and ask the children what time of day it is. Also, show the end pages of the book where Donald Crews has white planes flying in a blue sky at the beginning, and the end pages at the back of the book have black planes flying in a dark blue sky.

STORY STRETCHER

For Art: Cloud Pictures

What the children will learn—
To use cotton balls to create the effect of clouds

Materials you will need—
Light blue and dark blue construction paper, cotton balls, glue sticks, crayons

What to do—
1. Open FLYING to the illustrations showing the plane flying up to the clouds, through the clouds and on top of the clouds.

2. Ask the children to create a cloud picture. It can be them looking up at the clouds or, like the illustrator's pictures, of an airplane and the clouds.

3. Demonstrate how to stretch the cotton balls to make them look like clouds. Also, demonstrate how to use the glue stick and make several dots of glue where you want to make the clouds stick.

Something to think about—
To further extend the idea of flying and the view from up so high, have children who have flown describe how the houses and cars looked liked toys from the window of their airplane. Also use the cotton balls and glue sticks to create winter scenes.

STORY STRETCHER

For Block Building : Model Airport

What the children will learn—
To work together to create an airport of small and large blocks

Materials you will need—
Plastic building blocks, large wooden blocks, plastic airplanes, helicopter, cars, markers, paper, instant print film, camera

What to do—
1. Show the children Donald Crews' illustration of the plane flying over the airport.

2. Ask them if they could create an airport in the block corner by using both the small building blocks and the large ones.

3. Let them brainstorm some ways to get started.

4. After the builders seem to have a plan in mind, retreat from the area, but stay close enough to encourage participation.

5. Take pictures of the beginning, construction-in-progress, and the finished airport.

6. Display the pictures on a bulletin board where parents can view them easily. Add captions to the pictures about the children working together to build an airport.

Something to think about—
The children who often choose the small building blocks and those who usually build with the large

hollow blocks may not be accustomed to working together. Encourage new partnerships by helping the children see how Donald Crews shows some small buildings in the illustration and some large ones.

For Cooking And Snack Time: Snacks In Flight

What the children will learn—
To spread a soft cheese onto crackers

Materials you will need—
Cheese spreads, crackers, plastic knives, assorted juices

What to do—
1. Explain that when you fly, the flight attendants serve you a choice of beverages and a snack.

2. Have the last children who were in the dress-up corner pretend to be flight attendants to pour the juice.

3. The passengers have a choice of orange juice, apple juice or pineapple juice.

4. Also have the attendants give each child a plastic knife and each table two or three tubs of soft cheese spread.

5. Have the adult at the snack table demonstrate how to spread the cheese. Do not hold the cracker in your hand, but place it flat on the table. It is less likely to break that way.

6. Let each child spread crackers with the soft cheese spread.

Something to think about—
On other days during your transportation unit, let other children be the flight attendants and serve the snacks. Be certain you have both male and female attendants and male and female

pilots, baggage handlers and ticket agents.

For Housekeeping And Dress-up Corner: Pilots And Flight Attendants

What the children will learn—
To dress in the uniforms of pilots and flight attendants

Materials you will need—
Captain's hat from a commercial airline or a military one, blazers, scarves, aprons, plastic flight wings, serving cart, full length mirror

What to do—
1. Ask for donations to the dress-up corner in the parent newsletter announcing your transportation unit.

2. Encourage children who have not flown to play in the dress-up area with those who have.

3. Assist with dressing the flight attendants and have them model their outfits in front of the full length mirror.

4. Leave the flight attendants and pilots to manage the airplane on their own.

Something to think about—
Some dress-up clothes can serve double duty. The pilot's hat can also be a police officer's hat. The blazers can belong to flight attendants or be the dress-up clothes for the office. Parents are eager to help when they know why you need items. Grandparents often have some of the best items to donate. Take pictures of the children in the dress-up clothes and post them on the parent bulletin board or send the picture to the grandparent who donated the items.

For Sand Table: River Traffic

What the children will learn—
To create their version of the river flowing through the city

Materials you will need—
Sand table or large plastic tubs filled with sand, a wallpaper pan — long narrow pan for wetting wallpaper— small plastic building blocks, small plastic boats, pitcher for pouring water

What to do—
1. Show the interested children Donald Crews' illustration of the plane flying over the river which flows through the city.

2. Ask the children to think of how they could construct the city with a river flowing through it by using the supplies you have collected for them. The wallpaper pan becomes the river.

3. After they seem to have a clear plan, leave the book open and in view and leave the builders to their design.

Something to think about—
Often it is said that young children have short attention spans; however, when there is an interesting activity which requires some thoughtful action, preschoolers continue their projects for a long time. We have seen some four year-olds who sustained a block building project for three days with basically the same plan in mind, to build a castle. They began adding construction paper people and flags on the third day.

REFERENCES

Crews, Donald. (1986). **FLYING.** New York: Greenwillow Books.

Howard, Elizabeth Fitzgerald. (1988). Illustrated by Robert Casilla. **THE TRAIN TO LULU'S.** New York: Bradbury Press.

McPhail, David. (1977). **THE TRAIN.** Boston: Atlantic Little Brown Company.

Oxenbury, Helen. (1983). **THE CAR TRIP.** New York: Dial Books for Young Readers.

Siebert, Diane. (1984). Illustrated by Byron Barton. **TRUCK SONG.** New York: Harper and Row.

Additional References for Transportation

Burningham, John. (1972). **MR GUMPY'S MOTOR CAR.** New York: Thomas Y. Crowell. *Mr. Gumpy's human and animal friends squash into his old car and go for a drive — until it starts to rain.*

Crews, Donald. (1984). **SCHOOL BUS.** New York: Greenwillow Books. *Follows the progress of school buses as they take children to school and bring them home again.*

Maestro, Betsy and Giulio. (1986). **FERRYBOAT.** New York: Thomas Y. Crowell. *A family crosses a river on a ferryboat and observes how the ferry operates.*

Rockwell, Anne. (1986). **THINGS THAT GO.** New York: E. P. Dutton. *Trains, tow trucks, sailboats, buses, sleds, jeep, bicycles, and other things that go can be seen in the city, in the country, on the water, in the park and many other places.*

Ross, Pat and Joel (1981) Illustrated by Lynn Wheeling. **YOUR FIRST AIRPLANE TRIP.** New York: Lothrop, Lee and Shepard. *An account of what ordinarily happens when you travel on a commercial airplane.*

POEMS, JINGLES, CHANTS & RHYMES

Read-Aloud Rhymes for the Very Young
Hand Rhymes
Out and About
Honey, I Love and Other Love Poems
Sing a Song of Popcorn: Every Child's Book of Poems

POEMS, JINGLES, CHANTS & RHYMES

READ-ALOUD RHYMES FOR THE VERY YOUNG

Selected by Jack Prelutsky

Illustrated by Marc Brown

The book is a collection of more than 200 verses, some familiar and some delightful new discoveries. There are counting rhymes, silly verses, weather poems, jump rope chants, celebrations of holidays and connections with young children's emotions. Teachers will want to keep this collection nearby and select poems to go with all the units of study we selected to feature in STORY STRETCHERS: ACTIVITIES TO EXPAND CHILDREN'S FAVORITE BOOKS. The 8 1/2 by 11 sized book is large enough for viewing the pictures in a group at circle time, yet there is enough detail in the drawings that children will want to look at the book on their own. Marc Brown's illustrations are warmly colored and add dimension to the rhymes.

Circle Time Presentation

Choose five selections a day to read. Then end each day's reading with the rhyme you want to teach the children to say. Five good ones to teach preschoolers are: "Teddy Bear, Teddy Bear," "The Little Turtle,""Singing-Time," "Five Little Chickens" and "The Star." Read each line of the rhyme and have the children repeat it after you. Say the lines together several times throughout the day when the children are together for group activities. Each day repeat the ones you learned earlier in the week. Also, send copies of the poems home in the parent newsletter.

STORY STRETCHER

For Art: Animal Squares

What the children will learn—
To draw pictures of animals whose movements they can imitate

Materials you will need—
Paper, crayons or markers

What to do—
1.   Fold a sheet of typing paper or construction paper into four squares.

2.   Have the children mark lines down and across the paper following the fold lines.

3.   Show Marc Brown's illustrations of "Good Morning" where he has painted one animal in each square.

4.   Ask the children to draw four animals they can imitate.

Something to think about—
Do not fold the paper for the younger preschoolers to draw in the smaller squares, but do request that they draw animals whose movements they can imitate.

STORY STRETCHER

For Library Corner: The Story In The Pictures

What the children will learn—
To tell a story based on a picture

Materials you will need—
Paper, pencil

What to do—
1.   Show the illustrations which go with the following poems, "The Gold-Tinted Dragon," "Picnic Day," "Bedtime" and "Somersaults."

2.   Let each child select a picture they would like to tell a story about. Ask the child to tell you what is happening in the picture.

3.   Discuss what they think would happen next if there were other pictures about this poem.

4.   After the discussion, ask the children to think of a story to go with the picture. Have one child begin and the other children can add sentences.

5.   Write down the children's story as it unfolds.

6.   When their story is completed, read it back to them and compliment them on their storytelling abilities.

Something to think about—
Giving specific compliments takes practice. Instead of simply saying, "Good story" say, "Tina, your description of how the dragon felt helped us to get started telling the story." Compliment all the children for their individual contributions. For younger preschoolers, let each child tell individual stories.

For Mathematics And Manipulatives Center: Counting Rhymes

What the children will learn—
To repeat the counting rhyme with motions

Materials you will need—
None

What to do—
1.   Read the rhyme through in its entirety, and show the illustrations for "Ten to One."

2.   Repeat the rhyme and have the children hold up their fingers to show the number in the verse.

3.   After the children know the verses and can coordinate holding up the right number of fingers, have a child with blocks count out the right number of blocks for each verse of the rhyme.

Something to think about—
Make the illustrations into flannel board pieces and the children can see the "five fluttering fireflies" and "two tall tailors."

For Music And Movement: Animal Moves

What the children will learn—
To move like a rabbit, frog, duck, dog, bird and fish

Materials you will need—
None

What to do—
1.   Ask the children, "Can you move like a rabbit?" Let them move like they think a rabbit moves.

2.   Continue with the questions and let the children show you their movements for the other animals — frog, duck, dog, bird and fish.

3.   Read "Good Morning" and ask the children to do the accompanying body motions of waddling and quacking like a duck, hiding and squeaking like a mouse, running and barking like a dog, and flying and cheeping like a bird.

4.   Repeat the rhyme and movements.

Something to think about—
Finger plays and body movements have some standard moves we can expect as "flapping arms for flying like a bird" and "waddling like a duck," but these are motions young children may not have learned yet. Many of the favorite finger plays and jump rope chants which are passed down from generation to generation incorporate these movements.

For Science And Nature Center: Poetic Insects And Animals

What the children will learn—
To compare the behaviors of real animals to the ones in poems

Materials you will need—
Pictures of any of the following insects or animals which are available: ants, crickets, grasshoppers, caterpillars, squirrels, rabbits, mice, donkeys, ducks, chickens, pigs, polar bears, lions, giraffes, monkeys, elephants

What to do—
1.   Select a few of the pictures of real insects and animals which you have available in the classroom.

2.   Ask the children who come to the science and nature center to describe an insect or animal from viewing the picture.

3.   Also, have the children tell other information they know about the insect or animal. For example, "The giraffes live in a zoo."

4.   Then, read the poem "Giraffes Don't Huff." Ask the children to tell if the information in the poem is correct. Karla Kuskin's poem does provide accurate information. Some poems are funny and meant to entertain, as "Polar Bear," but do not provide a true picture of the insect or elephant.

5.   Continue the process of alternating descriptions of pictures, reading the poem and determining if the poem is true or not.

Something to think about—
The same process can be used for poems about the seasons and weather or about birds.

HAND RHYMES

Collected and Illustrated by

Marc Brown

Young children will enjoy the fourteen familiar hand games, finger plays, which Marc Brown has illustrated. The detailed hand motions for each rhyme are drawn on a vertical strip in the left margin. The directions are easy to follow. Bright colorful illustrations face the pages where the hand rhymes are printed.

Circle Time Presentation

Select hand rhymes which go along with a unit you have planned. For example, chant "The Caterpillar" (p. 28) during your study of "Growing Things." Teach "Snowflakes" (p. 17) and "The Snowman" (p.18) for your study of "Winter." Learn "Kittens" (p. 24, 25) for the unit on "Pets." Repeat the hand rhymes several times throughout the day and at the circle time for the following day.

STORY STRETCHER

For Art: Sponge Painting

What the children will learn—
To create background designs

Materials you will need—
Sponges, scissors, tempera paint, bowls, construction paper, crayons or markers

What to do—
1. Cut the sponges into small pieces, two or three inches in size.
2. Show the children Brown's illustrations which look like sponge painting in the background.
3. Demonstrate how to use the sponge to paint by pressing the sponge into the paint, then onto the paper. It leaves a light, airy print which can be used to paint background greenery, flowers and other designs.
4. Encourage the children to draw pictures or animals in the foreground.

Something to think about—
Young preschoolers will enjoy the sponge painting and may not choose to add anything in the foreground.

STORY STRETCHER

For Creative Dramatics: The Snowman

What the children will learn—
To imagine what the snowman would do if he came to life

Materials you will need—
None

What to do—
1. Teach the children the words and motions to Marc Brown's hand rhyme, "The Snowman."
2. The hand rhyme ends with, "He'll stand there all night, while we go to bed." Show the illustration and ask the children to think of a name for the snowman. Have them decide whether or not he needs a snow family.
3. Ask the children to imagine what the snowman might say to the rest of his family.
4. Have a few of the more verbal and imaginative children pretend to be the snow family. Get them started with some dialogue and let the children improvise.
5. Ask for volunteers to play the children who wake up the next morning and instead of one snowman, there is a whole family. What would the children say when they saw the snow family?

Something to think about—
Read other snowman and winter books to stimulate the drama.

STORY STRETCHER

For Library Corner, Flannel Board: Little Bunny

What the children will learn—
To chant the hand rhyme while placing the felt pieces on the flannel board

Materials you will need—
Flannel board, felt pieces for the bunny, squirrel, tree, duck

What to do—

1. Teach the children the chant and the hand motions.

2. Echo chant each line until the children know the hand rhyme.

"There was a little bunny who lived in the wood.
He wiggled his ears as a good bunny should.
He hopped by a squirrel.
He wiggled by a tree.
He hopped by a duck.
And he wiggled by me.
He stared at the squirrel.
He peeked round the tree.
He stared at the duck.
But he winked at me! (Brown, p. 21)

3. Select four children to place the felt pieces of the bunny, squirrel, duck and tree on the flannel board as each line is said.

Something to think about—
Instead of using Marc Brown's motions for the hand rhymes, ask the children for ways to show what the little bunny is doing. Use the hand motions they suggest and chant "Little Bunny."

STORY STRETCHER

For Mathematics And Manipulatives Center: Kittens Hand Rhyme

What the children will learn—
To subtract by one by chanting the hand rhyme

Materials you will need—
None

What to do—

1. Teach the children the words and motions to "Kittens."

"Five little kittens, sleeping on a chair.
One rolled off, leaving four there.

Four little kittens, one climbed a tree
To look in a bird's nest. then there were three.

Three little kittens, wondered what to do.
One saw a mouse. Then there were two.

Two little kittens, playing on a wall.
One little kitten, chased a red ball.

One little kitten, With fur soft as silk,
Left all alone, To drink a dish of milk.
(Brown, p. 24, 25)

Something to think about—
Add another verse to the hand rhyme, "No little kittens. None do we see. Zero kittens, Where could they be?" (Raines)

STORY STRETCHER

For Science And Nature Corner: The Caterpillar

What the children will learn—
To compare what happens to the caterpillar in the hand rhyme with what they know about real caterpillars

Materials you will need—
None

What to do—

1. Read the hand rhyme, "The Caterpillar," as if it is a poem.

2. Reread the rhyme in a chant fashion, emphasizing the rhyming words.

3. Chant the hand rhyme with the hand motions.

4. Teach it to the children by breaking it into smaller sections.

5. Ask the children how the caterpillar in the rhyme is like a real caterpillar. It spins a cocoon, sleeps in a cocoon and becomes a butterfly. Ask if there is anything in the rhyme which a real caterpillar does not do? Real caterpillars do not say, "I think I'll take a nap." (Brown, p. 28)

Something to think about—
Read non-fiction and fiction books about caterpillars. FROM EGG TO BUTTERFLY by Marlene Reidel is a good non-fiction selection, and THE VERY HUNGRY CATERPILLAR by Eric Carle is a popular fiction choice.

219

OUT AND ABOUT

By Shirley Hughes

A little girl and her baby brother play their way through each season of the year and its accompanying weather. Shirley Hughes' eighteen poems describe young children and their escapades, but they remind adults of the discoveries of childhood. Hughes' illustrations are wonderfully detailed, warm and affectionate looks at the play of children and the love of family and neighborhood. Unlike many poetry books, OUT AND ABOUT has illustrations which are large and can easily be seen in a large group circle time.

Circle Time Presentation

Show one of the double page illustrations which best suits the weather of the day. Ask the children to tell about the pictures. Then, read the poems which fit the weather. Show the other double page illustrations, and ask the children to tell you what season is pictured. Select an opposite weather poem to read. For example, if you read "Cold," a winter poem, then read, "Squirting Rainbows," a summer poem.

STORY STRETCHER

For Art: Weather Pictures

What the children will learn—
To draw what is happening because of the weather

Materials you will need—
Paper, crayons or markers

What to do—
1. Allow the children at the art center to look through all of Shirley Hughes' double page illustrations of the weather.

2. Discuss what the weather is like today and what people are doing because of the weather.

3. Request that the children draw weather pictures.

4. Display the pictures on a weather bulletin board.

Something to think about—
Onto a sheet of construction paper, print one of Shirley Hughes' poems which describes the present weather. Center it in your display of the children's weather drawings.

ANOTHER STORY STRETCHER

For Art: Sand Pictures

What the children will learn—
To add texture to their paintings

Materials you will need—
Paper, crayons or markers, white glue, brushes, newspaper, large bowl of sand

What to do—
1. After reading Shirley Hughes' poems, "Sand" and "Seaside," ask the children to draw a picture of a day at the beach or of themselves playing in the sand box.

2. Cover the art table with newspapers to clean up the sand more easily.

3. Demonstrate on one child's picture how to make the sandy area. Have the child point out where the sand is, and then have him paint that area with a thin layer of white glue. Shake some sand over the glue and it will stick in place.

4. Have the children complete their sand pictures and place them flat until the glue and sand is thoroughly dried.

Something to think about—
Have the children compare their sand pictures to sand paper.

STORY STRETCHER

For Housekeeping And Dress-up Corner: Dressing For The Season

What the children will learn—
To sort clothing according to the season when it would be worn

Materials you will need—
Four grocery bags, boys and girls clothing for all seasons of the year, marker, full-length mirror

What to do—
1. With a small group of children, go through the clothing in the housekeeping corner and separate it by what we need for cold winter weather and hot summer weather.

2. After the clothes are in two groups, go through them again and decide what lightweight clothing would be appropriate for spring and for fall.

3. Print the names of the four seasons on the grocery bags. Place one outfit in each grocery bag. Have the children decide what clothing could go together to make an outfit for that season.

4. Let the clothes sorters try on the clothing.

Something to think about—
Place the clothing in the bags and insert one piece of clothing which does not belong. For example, put a swimsuit in with the winter coats and gloves. Or put earmuffs in with the shorts and tee shirts. Let the children decide what does and does not belong in each bag.

STORY STRETCHER

For Library Corner: Action Pictures

What the children will learn—
To describe the actions in the pictures

Materials you will need—
None, except a copy of the book

What to do—
1. Show the children the double page pictures in Shirley Hughes' book, OUT AND ABOUT. Select a scene of the present season and have the children talk about what they see in the picture.

2. Ask the children to complete the sentence, "I see _____ _____." Encourage the children to be specific. For example, if a child says, "I see a lady with flowers." Ask what kind of flowers. Or, if a child says, "I see a car," ask what color car. Soon the children will begin incorporating more specifics into their descriptions.

Something to think about—
The child's picture book tells the story and inspires the imagination. By encouraging children to look closely at the pictures, we lead them to even more interpretations of the story. Show the children other Shirley Hughes books to enjoy.

STORY STRETCHER

For Sand Table: Sand Poem And Sand Castles

What the children will learn—
To make sand castles

Materials you will need—
Sand table, variety of sizes of plastic containers, watering can, shovels and scoops

What to do—
1. Read Shirley Hughes' poem, "Sand." Ask the children to recall what they like about playing in the sand, then reread the poem.

2. One of the phrases in the poem is, "The build-it-into-castles kind." Request the children build sand castles.

3. Help the children get started by watering down the sand and teaching them how to pack it tightly to make it retain its shape for castle building.

4. Leave the sand builders to their task and check back with them periodically to admire their castles.

Something to think about—
Young children enjoy filling and packing the containers with sand. Older children may become more involved in building connected forms that look like castles.

17
POEMS, JINGLES, CHANTS & RHYMES

HONEY, I LOVE
AND OTHER LOVE POEMS

By Eloise Greenfield

Illustrated by

Diane and Leo Dillon

HONEY, I LOVE is a collection of fifteen poems by Eloise Greenfield beginning with the poem which is the title of the book. "I Look Pretty," the third poem in the collection celebrates how the little girl feels when she dresses up in Mama's clothes. Although advertised for 7 to 11 year olds, the sentiments and clarity of expression make the poems lovely choices for younger preschoolers. As with many poetry selections, the feelings transcend the age lines. Diane and Leo Dillon's illustrations are a creative combination of realistic charcoal drawings of the little girl whose feelings are featured, and child-like etchings in a smaller size are overlaid at either the top or the bottom of each page and express the content of the poems.

Circle Time Presentation

Begin by telling the children some of the things you love, as bright sunshine streaming through the windows in the morning, violets on a window sill, running through the woods with your little dog. Then ask the children to tell you some of the things they love. After ideas have been shared, read the title poem, "Honey, I Love." If more children appear eager to tell things they love, continue the discussion. Read "I Look Pretty" and ask several children to tell how they feel when they are in the dress-up corner.

STORY STRETCHER
For Art: Charcoal Drawings

What the children will learn—
To experiment with using charcoals

Materials you will need—
Variety of sizes of charcoals, paper, tissues, hair spray

What to do—
1. Show the children who come to the art center during free play the lovely shading in the charcoal drawings from HONEY, I LOVE.

2. Have the children experiment with making marks with the thin pieces, the fat round pieces and other shapes of the charcoal. Use the sides of the charcoal and make wide, light marks. Press down hard on the pieces and see the differences in shading. Smudge some of the lines with tissue.

3. After the experimentation, leave the children on their own to make any drawing they please or continue experimenting.

4. Spray the drawings lightly with hair spray to keep them from smudging as the children take them home.

Something to think about—
Have the children look back through the charcoal illustrations and tell what they think the little girl is thinking or feeling on each page.

STORY STRETCHER
For Housekeeping And Dress-up Corner: We Look Pretty

What the children will learn—
To enjoy dressing like grown-ups

Materials you will need—
Usual dress-up clothes for both males and females, full-length mirror, instant-print camera (optional)

What to do—
1. Tell the children who select the housekeeping and dress-up corner during free play that they look pretty, and ask them if they feel like the little girl in the poem, "I Look Pretty."

2. Have the children admire themselves in the mirror and pose like they would to have their pictures taken. Recall with them that at the end of the poem, the little girl posed.

3. Take instant print pictures of the children pretending to be grown-ups.

Something to think about—
Children delight in the freedom to dress-up and pretend. Send the pictures of the children home to the parents, but include a message about the importance of play and pretending. Remind the parents that problem-solving techniques and a rich vocabulary develop through play.

For Library Corner: Things We Love Tape

What the children will learn—
To extend the idea inspired by the poem, "Honey, I Love"

Materials you will need—
Cassette tape, tape recorder

What to do—
1. With the children who come to the library corner during free play reread the title poem, "Honey, I Love."

2. Remind them of some of the things other children said they love when the poem was discussed during circle time.

3. Ask the children to tell you some things they love.

4. Make a tape recording of "Honey, I Love," and at the end, have each child tell you something they love.

5. Leave the tape at the listening station for other children to hear.

Something to think about—
On another day, record another poem, as "I Look Pretty," and have the children share their feelings about when they feel pretty.

For Music And Movement: I Get Down

What the children will learn—
To think about how music makes they feel

Materials you will need—
Recording of some lively music with a strong bass sound, tape or record player

What to do—
1. With all the children on the circle time rug, play the recording and let the children move any way they feel like moving, clapping hands, stopping feet, standing and moving, dancing around.

2. Stop the music and have the children put into words how the music made them feel.

3. Read "Way Down in the Music."

4. Start the music again at a much lower volume and read the poem again with the music playing in the background.

5. Turn the volume up again and let the children move as they feel the music.

Something to think about—
Help children celebrate the joy of their feelings by appreciating their individual responses to the music. Some children may lightly tap fingers while others dance and romp around the room. Try to give each child the freedom of responding as individuals, while still celebrating with friends the feelings they share.

For Music And Movement: Jump Rope Chants

What the children will learn—
To say some of the jump rope chants

Materials you will need—
Jump ropes

What to do—
1. Invite some older children who are good at jumping rope to come to the playground and demonstrate.

2. Have them do several jump rope routines and say the chants which go with them, as "Teddy Bear, Teddy Bear, Turn around."

3. Encourage the children to say the verses as the children jump in time to the chant.

4. After the jumpers have gone, let the younger children practice the chants by jumping without the ropes.

5. Complete the session by having the children sit in a circle and rest while you read "Rope Rhyme."

Something to think about—
Rarely can preschoolers coordinate jumping in time with the rope, but they can jump over a rope that is swung back and forth, rather than around and overhead. Swing the rope in time to the music and quite low to the ground. Have the child jump over it.

17
POEMS, JINGLES, CHANTS & RHYMES

SING A SONG OF POPCORN:
Every Child's Book of Poems

Edited by

Beatrice Schenk de Regniers

Illustrated by nine

Caldecott Medal Artists

The collection contains 128 poems representing a full range of contemporary poets and ones from the past. The volume contains hilarious poems and sentimental ones, spooky ones and pretty ones. The illustrations are also varied in style. The nine Caldecott Medal artists are: Marcia Brown, Leo and Diane Dillon, Richard Egielski, Trina Schart Hyman, Arnold Lobel, Maurice Sendak, Marc Simont and Margot Zemach. The "Mostly Nonsense" section is filled with entertaining selections sure to delight young children.

Circle Time Presentation

Read the "Good Morning" poem by Muriel Sipe. We are introduced to a downy duck that quacks, a timid mouse that squeaks, a dog that bow-wows and a bird that cheeps. Ask the children what they say, when someone says, "Good morning." Tell the children one of the favorite things you like to hear them say when you first see them is, "Good morning." Then read "My Favorite Word" by Lucia and James L. Hymes, Jr. Ask the children if their favorite word is the same as the one in the poem, "Yes." Read "My Favorite Word" again.

STORY STRETCHER
For Art: Watercolor Weather

What the children will learn—
To experiment with watercolor paints

Materials you will need—
Watercolor paper or construction paper, watercolor paints, brushes, paper towels

What to do—
1. Show the children several of Marcia Brown's illustrations from the "Mostly Weather" section of the book.

2. Ask the children what the poems on those pages probably are about based on what they see in the illustrations.

3. Tell the children that Marcia Brown used watercolors to paint the pictures in the book.

4. Demonstrate how to load the watercolor brushes with paint and water and how to dry it by dabbing the brush lightly on paper towels.

5. Let the children experiment with the paints.

6. Ask them to paint some weather pictures using their watercolors.

Something to think about—
Leave the watercolor paints out for several days. Young children need time to experiment and explore the possibilities of a medium.

ANOTHER STORY STRETCHER
For Art: Funny Pictures

What the children will learn—
To make a funny picture to accompany a poem

Materials you will need—
Construction paper, old magazines or catalogs, scissors, glue

What to do—
1. Read the following three poems from the "Mostly Nonsense" section of SING A SONG OF POPCORN: "If We Walked on Our Hands" by Beatrice Schenk de Regniers, "A Funny Man" by Natalie Joan and "The Folk Who Live in Backward Town."

2. Show the funny illustrations and talk about the lines from the poems that the children like best. Reread any one of the poems they request.

3. Ask the children to cut out and paste pictures of people or things in funny positions like what was described in one of the poems.

Something to think about—
At circle time, read the three silly poems again. After each poem is read, let the children who made funny pictures for that poem show their illustrations.

STORY STRETCHER
For Library Corner, Listening Station: Funny Pictures Tape

What the children will learn—

To enjoy the poems and pictures with a group of friends

Materials you will need—
Cassette tape, tape recorder, listening station, earphones, construction paper, stapler

What to do—

1.   Make a cassette recording of the three funny poems the children illustrated with their funny pictures: "If We Walked on Our Hands," "A Funny Man" and "The Folk Who Lived in Backward Town."

2.   Construct books of pictures which illustrate the three poems by stapling the pictures for each poem together. Make a construction paper cover or follow the directions for making a bound book which appear in the appendix.

3.   On the tape, instruct the children to turn off the recorder after each poem and look at the book of pictures which goes with that poem.

Something to think about—
This same activity is appropriate for other poems as well. You could record weather poems or spooky poems and make books illustrating them.

STORY STRETCHER

For Music And Movement: The Little Turtle

What the children will learn—
To sing the poem as a finger play

Materials you will need—
None

What to do—

1.   Read the poem "The Turtle" (p. 74) through once.

2.   Reread the poem, and this time add the hand motions. When the turtle is snapping, hold your fingers together and open and close them against your thumb.

Make the motion for "caught the mosquito" by clapping your hands. For the line, "But he didn't catch me," shake your head no and point to yourself.

3.   Say each verse and have the children practice it.

Something to think about—
After the children know the poem and motions well, have them pair off, face each other and say the poem. Instead of ending with "But he didn't catch me," have the children say, "But he didn't catch you" and point to their partners. You lead them, but they face each other for an audience. Expect a lot of giggles, and do the poem more than once.

STORY STRETCHER

For Science And Nature Corner: Nature Poems

What the children will learn—
To appreciate nature through the words of poets

Materials you will need—
Index cards, construction paper, marker

What to do—

1.   Select poems to go with your science displays and activities. For example, when mixing colors, read Christina G. Rossetti's "What is Pink?" For your live insect collection, read Rossetti's "Hurt No Living Thing." For the dinosaurs unit, read "Pachycephalosaurus" by Richard Armour. In the collection, there is an entire section devoted to animals and another on weather.

2.   Print the poem onto a large index card or construction paper and leave it in the science and nature center. When you are in the center interacting with the

children, read the poem when it seems appropriate.

Something to think about—
Placing a copy of the poem in the science and nature displays should become so routine that the exhibits do not look complete without the poem.

REFERENCES

Brown, Marc. (1985). **HAND RHYMES**. New York: E.P. Dutton.

de Regniers, Beatrice, (Ed.) (1988). **SING A SONG OF POPCORN: Every Child's Book Of Poems**. New York: Scholastic, Inc.

Greenfield, Eloise. (1978). Illustrated by Diane and Leo Dillon. **HONEY, I LOVE**. New York: Harper and Row, Publishers.

Hughes, Shirley. (1988). **OUT AND ABOUT**. New York: Lothrop, Lee and Shepard Books.

Prelutsky, Jack. (1986). Illustrated by Marc Brown. **READ-ALOUD RHYMES FOR THE VERY YOUNG**. New York: Alfred A. Knopf.

Additional References for Poems, Jingles, Chants and Rhymes

Allen, Roach Van. (1985). **I LOVE LADYBUGS**. Allen, TX: DLM Teaching Resources. *A poem about feelings and "hugs," which is one book in a series of patterned language books.*

Amoroso, Lisa. (1987). **OLD MOTHER HUBBARD AND HER DOG.** New York: Alfred A. Knopf, Inc. *Old Mother Hubbard runs errand after errand for her remarkable dog.*

dePaola, Tomie. (1985). **TOMIE DEPAOLA'S MOTHER GOOSE.** New York: G.P. Putnam's Sons. *An illustrated collection of over 200 Mother Goose nursery rhymes.*

Little, Lessie Jones. (1988). Illustrated by Jan Spivey Gilchrist. **CHILDREN OF LONG AGO**. New York: Philomel Books. *Poems reflecting simpler days, with grandmothers who read aloud and children who walk barefoot on damp earth and pick blackberries for their paper dolls to eat.*

Lobel, Arnold. (1986). **THE RANDOM HOUSE BOOK OF MOTHER GOOSE**. New York: Random House. *Selections from Mother Goose, 306 timeless nursery rhymes.*

TALL AND FUNNY TALES

If You Give a Mouse a Cookie
The Giant Jam Sandwich
Cloudy With a Chance of Meatballs
Teeny Tiny
The Bear's Toothache

IF YOU GIVE A MOUSE A COOKIE

By Laura Joffe Numeroff

Illustrated by Felicia Bond

The funny consequences of giving a mouse a cookie lead to preposterously delightful scenes. "If you give a mouse a cookie, he's going to ask for a glass of milk. When you give him the milk, he'll probably ask for a straw." The story continues on with whatever is given requiring something else to go with it. The scene of the little mouse trimming his hair with nail scissors always brings lots of giggles. The children also like the scene where the little mouse wants the boy to tape the picture he just finished drawing to the refrigerator door. Felicia Bond's illustrations are bright, colorful and cartoon-like. The little mouse's facial expressions are particularly endearing.

Circle Time Presentation

Show the children the first scene in the book of the little boy sitting outside on the grass offering a cookie to a tiny mouse dressed in blue overalls. Read the first line, "If you give a mouse a cookie," and then let the children think of what might happen if they gave a mouse a cookie. If the children answer realistically, ask them to imagine that the mouse could talk, then what do they think might happen. Encourage their imaginative, tall tale type of responses. Read IF YOU GIVE A MOUSE A COOKIE.

STORY STRETCHER

For Art: Mouse Pictures

What the children will learn—
To draw a picture they think the mouse might draw

Materials you will need—
Paper, crayons, markers

What to do—
1.   Look at Felicia Bond's illustrations where the little mouse is drawing a picture.

2.   Ask the children to think of other pictures the little mouse might draw. Have the children brainstorm a few ideas.

3.   Tell the children they may draw a picture the little mouse might draw, their favorite part of the book, or something the little mouse might see if he came to their house for a cookie.

Something to think about:
Cover the children's pictures in clear contact paper or laminate them to make a place mat for snack time. Another good art project for the story is playdough. Very young preschoolers can make the cookies for the mouse, while older preschoolers can sculpt the little mouse.

STORY STRETCHER

For Cooking And Snack Time: Chocolate Chip Mouse Cookies

What the children will learn—
To bake chocolate chip cookies

Materials you will need—
Recipe ingredients and mixing utensils or prepackaged roll of cookie mix, knife, cookie sheet, oven, spatula, plates, napkins, cups, milk to drink

What to do—
1.   During free play time, let the children come in small groups to the snack area and help prepare the cookies for baking.

2.   Ask the children what kind of cookie the boy gave the little mouse in IF YOU GIVE A MOUSE A COOKIE.

3.   Read the recipe or the directions on the roll of cookie mix to the children.

4.   Let each child assist in several steps of the preparation.

5.   Serve the cookies warm, if possible, with cold milk to drink.

Something to think about:
While eating the chocolate chip mouse cookies, discuss what the children thought was funny about the story. Ask them what other kinds of cookies they think the mouse might like to eat.

STORY STRETCHER

For Creative Dramatics: Pantomiming Mouse

What the children will learn—
To act like the mouse in IF YOU GIVE A MOUSE A COOKIE

Materials you will need—
None, except the book

What to do—

1. With all the children seated on the circle time rug, look at the scenes of the story and have different children tell you what the mouse is doing or feeling.

2. Ask the children to think of ways we could move to show the mouse's feelings and actions. For example, we could act like we are drinking milk, dab our lips with a "napkin," hold up our hair and pretend to cut it with fingers.

3. Continue with other scenes letting different children think of ways to show the mouse's actions and feelings until ideas have been given for all the scenes.

4. Then read the story and let the children pantomime mouse's part.

Something to think about—
For young preschoolers, demonstrate the actions and have them practice them, then tell the story and pantomime with them.

STORY STRETCHER

For Library Corner: If Mouse Came To Our Classroom

What the children will learn—
To imagine a variation of the story IF YOU GIVE A MOUSE A COOKIE

Materials you will need—
Chart tablet, markers

What to do—

1. With the children who come to the library corner during free play, discuss IF YOU GIVE A MOUSE A COOKIE. Ask the children to imagine what would happen if the mouse came to their classroom.

2. Have the children visualize the little mouse knocking on the door of their classroom. Say, "Scott hears a knock on the door, opens the door, looks down and

there is a little mouse asking for a chocolate chip cookie. What would Scott say?"

3. Let the children talk through a bit of the dialogue and a few scenes until you can hear a good storyline developing. If necessary, lead the discussion a bit longer. Then tell them, "This is such an interesting story. I want to write it down so I can read it to other children who come to the library corner."

4. Print what the children dictate on the chart tablet. Reread the story and make any changes they request.

Something to think about—
Consider leaving the top half of the chart tablet blank and after the story is finished have the children draw pictures. If the stories are good ones, also tape record them and use the chart tablet stories at the listening station.

STORY STRETCHER

For Mathematics And Manipulatives: If Then Sequence

What the children will learn—
To let objects represent the sequence of the story

Materials you will need—
Cookies, glasses, straw, mirror, scissors, broom or dust pan, mop, little box with cotton ball, book, paper, crayon, pen, tape,

What to do—

1. Review the sequence of events in IF YOU GIVE A MOUSE A COOKIE by looking at the illustrations and asking, "If we want something to remind us of this picture, what could we use?" For the first scene the children will say, "A cookie." The next would be a glass of milk and so on.

2. If you have older preschoolers, send different children to find the object reminders for each picture. If you have younger children, have the items already collected on the table and ask them to arrange the objects in order.

3. After all the items are collected and arranged from one end of the table to the other in sequence, ask the children to tell the story by looking at the objects. Get them started by saying, "If you give a mouse a cookie, he's going to want a glass of milk." The children will continue on, "When you give a mouse a glass of milk, he'll probably ask for a straw."

Something to think about—
Leave the objects which represent the story out on the table and ask other children to tell the story by what they see.

18

TALL AND FUNNY
TALES

The Giant Jam Sandwich

Story and pictures by John Vernon Lord
with verses by Janet Burroway

THE GIANT JAM
SANDWICH

By John Vernon Lord

Verses by Janet Burroway

The residents of Itching Down had a serious problem; they were invaded by four million wasps. The nasty wasps harassed the picnickers, drove the farmers from their fields, stung Lord Swell's bald head, buzzed and dived and ate everything in sight. The townspeople had a meeting and thought up the plan of making a giant jam sandwich to capture the wasps. The story ends with what happened to the giant jam sandwich. The illustrations are witty, inventive and invite several perusals for a few extra giggles per reading.

Circle Time Presentation

Tell the children you are going to read a tall tale. Then read THE GIANT JAM SANDWICH. After reading the story, discuss the townspeople's good ideas. Ask the children what they thought were the silliest parts and the best ideas. Look at the illustrations again just for the fun of it and discuss what a tall tale is.

STORY STRETCHER

For Art: Tall Tale Pictures

What the children will learn—
To associate exaggeration with tall tales

Materials you will need—
Paper, crayons or markers

What to do—

1. Discuss that a tall tale is one which uses exaggeration. Ask the children to show you with their hands how big a sandwich really is. Then, ask them how big the sandwich was in THE GIANT JAM SANDWICH. Continue the discussion until the children have a sense of what exaggeration means.

2. Show some of the children's drawings from a previous day and ask them what they could have drawn that would make their pictures tall tales. For example, if a child drew a picture of her family and her dog, she might draw a huge dog bigger than the house. Another child who drew a car might draw huge wheels on it.

3. Have the children think of pictures they might draw which use exaggeration, making something bigger, taller, fatter than we usually expect to see it.

4. During the children's drawing, ask them to tell you about their pictures.

Something to think about—
If some children do not understand the exaggeration point, do not be concerned. New concepts often need to be expressed in several different forms before they are internalized.

STORY STRETCHER

For Block Building: The Town Of Itching Down

What the children will learn—
To build a town which could be Itching Down

Materials you will need—
Small interlocking building blocks

What to do—

1. Ask the block builders to look at the illustrations in A GIANT JAM SANDWICH. Mention that most of the buildings in Itching Down are made of bricks. Have them think of how they might make a model of the town of Itching Down.

2. Leave the builders to work on their own, but periodically check back with them to encourage their building. Ask them to be sure and include the huge bakery and the town hall.

3. When the buildings are finished, see if the builders can think of ways to show the funny vehicles the people made to move the giant loaf of bread. Leave them to invent on their own with the book near by for reference.

4. After the block builders have finished, ask them to invite children over to see their version of the town of Itching Down.

Something to think about—
Leave the block town up for more than one day and the children may think of other items to add. They probably will make their own giant jam sandwich of playdough and

haul it on the bed of a toy eighteen wheeler. Longer involvement with projects often leads to more creative responses.

For Cooking And Snack Time: Giant Jam Sandwich

What the children will learn—
To spread jam for a large sandwich

Materials you will need—
Unsliced loaves of bread, bread knife, cutting board, margarine, jam, cups, milk, plates, plastic knives, napkins, toaster oven (optional)

What to do—
1.   If possible, purchase loaves of bread which just need to be baked. Bake them in the classroom so the children can smell the aroma of the bread baking.

2.   Show the children the difference in sliced and unsliced bread. Slice the loaves at the table for the children to see how you must saw back and forth with the knife, just like the townspeople of Itching Down sawed through their giant loaf of bread.

3.   Cut one loaf of bread lengthwise and open it up like a hoagie sandwich bun.

4.   Let the children each spread some of the bread with margarine and jam for their version of the giant jam sandwich.

5.   Cut their giant jam sandwich into servings and serve with milk.

Something to think about—
If you want to avoid sweets for your snack time, try a giant toasted cheese sandwich served with orange juice, or a giant loaf spread with peanut butter and served with apple juice.

For Housekeeping And Dress-up Corner: Bakery

What the children will learn—
To dress-up like bakers and pretend the roles in a bakery shop

Materials you will need—
Construction paper, tissue paper, scissors, stapler, small paper bags, napkins, aprons, baking pans, playdough, rolling pins, cash register, scales, table and kitchen area of the housekeeping corner

What to do—
1.   Make chef's hats by cutting a two inch wide strip of construction paper to fit each child's head. Then staple sheets of white tissue paper onto the strip for the crown of the chef's hat.

2.   The hats will draw attention to the housekeeping corner where the baking equipment is and will invite children to become bakers. The cash register, scales and paper bags will prompt the children to role-play customer and cashier.

3.   Near the end of free play, ask some children to make a giant loaf of bread with playdough to represent the one in THE GIANT JAM SANDWICH. Place it on the snack table for other children to see.

Something to think about—
When you see a play idea appealing to more children than usually use that center, add an extra table and a few more prompts, but contain the size of the group to the number of children who can play together cooperatively.

(Idea adapted from Sally Warren's classroom at the Project for the Study of Young Children at George Mason University.)

For Music And Movement: The Flight Of The Wasps

What the children will learn—
To move and buzz like wasps

Materials you will need—
None

What to do—
1.   With the children seated on the circle time rug, start a buzzing sound, changing the tempo from fast to slow, and back again. Ask the children what they think the wasps might be doing when you are buzzing fast (flying), and when you are buzzing slowly (circling over the town).

3.   Buzz really fast and stretch one hand up high and then dive it into your lap. Ask the children what was happening, the wasps were diving into the giant jam sandwich. Then, stop the buzzing and the dive and say, "Kersplat." Ask the children what that means; the wasps were stuck in the jam and the other giant slice of bread fell on top.

4.   Tell the children to pretend they are wasps and use one hand to buzz through the air doing the three types of buzzing. First, fly and buzz fast, then slow down and circle the town and finally, dive into the jam, "Kersplat." Repeat the buzzing using two hands.

5.   Finish the activity by having the children move around the room, buzzing and flying, and end by falling on the floor, "Kersplat."

Something to think about—
If you have a recording of fast-paced violin music, play it for the children to buzz and fly as the music indicates.

TALL AND FUNNY TALES

CLOUDY WITH A CHANCE OF MEATBALLS

By Judi Barrett

Illustrated by Ron Barrett

Grandpa's accidental flipping of a pancake which landed on Henry's head at breakfast time prompted Grandpa to tell an exaggerated bedtime story of a town where it rained food. In the town of Chewandswallow, there were no grocery stores because the weather provided all the food. But a terrible disaster struck. It rained and snowed and flooded too much food, more than the people and animals could eat, more than the sanitation department could clean up, so the people made boats of stale bread and sailed away to a new land. Fortunately, there the weather was ordinary and food came from the grocery stores, but whenever they saw snow they thought of mashed potatoes. Ron Barrett's illustrations begin with detailed black and white line drawings until the children begin imagining Grandpa's bedtime story. Then the pictures are colorful with all the foodstuff in its wildest form, as the tomato tornado and the spaghetti tying up the town.

Circle Time Presentation

Mention that you have another story which is a tall tale; it is an exaggeration. Read CLOUDY WITH A CHANCE OF MEATBALLS. Be prepared to pause often to show the pictures and allow for "giggle time." Immediately, the children will want you to read the story again. Reread it and then ask the children what they would like to have it rain if they lived in the town of Chewandswallow.

STORY STRETCHER

For Art: Raining Food Pictures

What the children will learn—
To draw silly weather pictures

Materials you will need—
Paper, crayons, markers

What to do—
1.   With the children who come to the art center during free play, look at Ron Barrett's hilarious illustrations in CLOUDY WITH A CHANCE OF MEATBALLS.

2.   Ask the children what food they would like it to rain if they lived in the town of Chewandswallow. Suggest that the children draw their silly weather pictures of it raining a food they like.

3.   When the pictures are completed, let the children dictate a caption or sentence for their story, and you print whatever the children tell you on the back or the bottom of their drawings.

Something to think about—
At a later circle time, let the children share some of their "raining food" pictures. Have the children who did other art projects tell what they think would be funny weather pictures.

STORY STRETCHER

For Block Building : A New Town

What the children will learn—
To build a new town for the people from Chewandswallow

Materials you will need—
Variety of sizes of boxes, masking tape, tempera paints, liquid soap, brushes, crayons, building blocks

What to do—
1.   Discuss how the people from Chewandswallow had to sail across the sea to a new land and build a new town.

2.   Ask the block builders to construct a new town for the people. Bring out the different sizes of boxes and have the children assist you in taping some of them closed. Stand them on end and ask the children what types of buildings the boxes could be.

3.   Have the children paint the boxes with tempera paint into which you have mixed some liquid soap. The liquid soap helps the paint adhere to the surfaces.

4.   Allow the boxes to dry for a day, then have the children draw windows and doors onto the boxes.

5.   Ask them to construct the town with the boxes, and then if they need other buildings, use the small building blocks and add more houses and stores.

Something to think about:
Allow several days for this project and encourage road construction and landscaping on other days.

STORY STRETCHER

For Cooking and Snack Time: Snowy Mashed Potatoes

What the children will learn—
To mix instant mashed potatoes

Materials you will need—
A package of instant mashed potatoes, hot plate, liquid and dry measuring cups and spoons, mixing bowl, mixing spoon, milk, butter or margarine, bowls, spoons, napkins, raw vegetables, vegetable peeler, knife, cutting board, serving plate

What to do—
1. Have a small group of children assist you in washing, peeling, slicing and arranging raw vegetables on a serving plate.

2. With a few children at a time, prepare single servings of instant mashed potatoes as directed on the package. Let each child mix his own mashed potatoes in individual serving bowls.

3. Have the children who prepared their potatoes together sit together at a snack table and eat raw vegetables with the potatoes.

Something to think about—
If one serving of mashed potatoes is too much per child, half the recipe, or have two children work together preparing the potatoes then divide their serving. If you think mashed potatoes are too unusual a snack, then serve ice cream to remind the children of snow. Also, in one illustration a golden Jell-O mold is seen as the colors of a sunset. Consider apple Jell-O to remind the children of CLOUDY WITH A CHANCE OF MEAT-BALLS.

STORY STRETCHER

For Library Corner: Grandpa's Tall Tale

What the children will learn—
To listen for Grandpa's exaggerations in the bedtime story he tells

Materials you will need—
Cassette tape, recorder, stapler

What to do—
1. With a small group of children, record yourself reading CLOUDY WITH A CHANCE OF MEATBALLS and pause for their laughter throughout the story.

2. Ask the children to help think of a page turning signal to record on the tape so that when other children listen they will know when to turn the page. When we tried this with children, one boy suggested, "Say pancake." A little girl said to say, "You're teasing." We finally decided to say, "Uh-oh." For young children, click the stapler for the page signal.

3. At the end of the tape, let each child describe a favorite scene from the book.

4. Leave the tape and the book at the listening station for other groups of children to hear throughout the week.

Something to think about—
Some teachers select different groups of children to be "tape recording assistants" each week. As soon as circle time is over each day, the "tape recording assistants" go with the teacher to the library corner and prepare a tape. Afterwards, they are free to choose any other centers for the remaining time.

STORY STRETCHER

For Water Table: Houseboats

What the children will learn—
To construct houseboats for the people of Chewandswallow

Materials you will need—
Flat styrofoam, half gallon paper milk cartons, tempera paint, liquid soap, crayons or permanent ink markers, brushes, glue, bowls

What to do—
1. With the children, think of ways to construct houseboats. Accept a variety of ideas. Tell them this is a three day project.

2. Paint the milk carton houses with a mixture of tempera paint and liquid soap. The liquid soap makes the paint stick to the waxy surface of the milk carton. After painting, let the houses for the boats dry overnight.

3. Ask the children to draw cabin doors and portholes with their crayons or permanent ink markers.

4. To seal the paint so that it doesn't come off in the water, mix thin white glue with a little water and paint it on. Allow the glue to dry overnight. Wash the brushes and bowls immediately.

5. On the third day, staple the houses onto the styrofoam to make the houseboats and sail them in the water table.

Something to think about—
Encourage children to try different materials, plastic containers glued on styrofoam, wooden constructions from the work bench, two large milk cartons for a cruise ship.

18
TALL AND FUNNY TALES

TEENY TINY

Retold by Jill Bennett

Illustrated by Tomie dePaola

Jill Bennett has retold this old tale of a teeny tiny woman who happens upon a teeny tiny bone while out walking. She decides to take the bone home with her to make into a soup. When she returns from her walk, she places the bone in her otherwise empty cupboard and lies down to take a nap. Then she hears a tiny voice say, "I want my bone." She pulls the covers over her head and lies trembling in her bed. But the voice grows louder and louder, and the teeny tiny woman grows more and more frightened. When the voice screams at it's loudest, "Give me my bone," the teeny tiny woman throws back the covers and yells, "Take it!" Tomie de Paola's drawings of the teeny tiny woman and her dog and cat are charming. A clever technique is that the print is larger and larger as the voice grows louder and louder.

Circle Time Presentation

TEENY TINY is an excellent book for a not-too-scary Halloween or just for an ordinary day. Read TEENY TINY in your suspense voice. Often when the book is read the first time, the children do not spot the tiny ghosts. Show the illustrations again and reread the book with the children joining you in repeating the "teeny tiny" phrases, the "Give me my bone" phrases and the ending, "Take it!"

STORY STRETCHER

For Art: Teeny Tiny Puppets

What the children will learn—
To make tiny puppets

Materials you will need—
Construction paper, stapler, colored pencils, scissors

What to do—
1. Ask the children to draw pictures of Teeny Tiny, a ghost, the dog and the cat. Draw a short line on one edge of the construction paper to show the children how tall to make their drawings of the characters. For older preschoolers make it four inches high, for younger preschoolers, six inches high.

2. Let the children cut out their pictures. It doesn't matter if the pictures are not trimmed exactly. Accept whatever level of cutting skills they have.

3. Cut four inch long and one inch wide strips of construction paper. Staple the ends together to make a tab for the children to hold by pinching their thumb and index fingers together.

4. Staple each picture onto a separate holding strip.

5. Let the children play with their Teeny Tiny puppets and listen for their telling of the story.

Something to think about—
Finger puppets for young children's hands are often just too tiny to manage. This variation of finger puppets, tab puppets, is more appropriate. The diminutive size of the puppets also adds to the drama of the TEENY TINY story. The tiny ghosts are tiny frights.

STORY STRETCHER

For Creative Dramatics: Pantomiming Teeny Tiny

What the children will learn—
To pantomime the actions of the little woman in the story

Materials you will need—
None

What to do—
1. Ask the children to think of ways to show the different things Teeny Tiny did. If you have young preschoolers, show them the actions, as opening a door, putting the bone in the pocket, placing it in the cupboard, pulling covers up to her chin, then over her head.

2. Read TEENY TINY and have the children act out the movements.

3. Vary the activity by dividing the group in half. Ask one group to pantomime the actions while the other group says Teeny Tiny's lines with you.

4. At the end, have everyone shout together, "Take it!"

Something to think about—
Read the book in almost a whispering voice to get the mood of the story and create the illusion of the teeny tiny world.

For Housekeeping And Dress-up Corner: Filling Teeny Tiny's Cupboard

What the children will learn—
To sort and put away groceries

Materials you will need—
Empty cans and boxes, masking tape, grocery bags

What to do—
1. Invite parents to send in empty canned vegetables, fruits and soup cans, empty boxes from cereals, baking mixes and crackers. Ask them to open the cans from the bottom.

2. When the cans come in, check the edges for rough spots and place masking tape over any edge which might scratch a child.

3. Place the empty cans and cartons into grocery bags. Leave the grocery bags on the kitchen table in the housekeeping area.

4. Ask the children who come to the housekeeping area to fill Teeny Tiny's cupboard so she will not have to go out looking for a bone to make soup.

5. Ask the children how they might sort the items. Then help them decide where to store the groceries before they continue with their play.

6. Let the children play in the housekeeping corner on their own.

Something to think about—
Replenish your grocery items often. Freshly filled grocery bags on the table will encourage the children to play supermarket or a family cooking together.

For Library Corner, Flannel Board: Teeny Tiny's Story

What the children will learn—
To retell the story in sequence

Materials you will need—
Flannel board, felt pieces of Teeny Tiny, her dog and cat, bone, cupboard, covers, tiny ghosts

What to do—
1. Make the felt characters and pieces for the flannel board.

2. Tell the story and let the children who are in the library corner during free play place the pieces on the board.

3. Select someone to be the voice of Teeny Tiny and someone to be the voice of the ghosts asking for the bone. If you have young preschoolers, let them say their lines along as you read. Older preschoolers may not need your assistance.

4. Leave the flannel board and the book in the library corner for children to practice the story on their own.

Something to think about—
Encourage a child who is less verbal to practice TEENY TINY with you. Then leave him to play with the flannel board pieces. Ask him to come and get you if he wants you to hear him tell the story again.

For Library Corner, Listening Station: Teeny Tiny Frights

What the children will learn—
To anticipate the ending of the story

Materials you will need—
Cassette tape, tape player, listening station, earphones

What to do—
1. With a group of children who come to the library corner during free play, tape record the story of TEENY TINY.

2. Have the children practice for the recording by joining you in saying the "teeny tiny" phrases. Click your tongue in the roof of your mouth as the page turning signal.

3. Record the story remembering to pause and have the children finish a phrase. For example, read, "When the teeny tiny woman had gone a teeny tiny way, she came to a teeny tiny _____." Point to the gate in the picture and the children will complete the phrase.

4. Have all the children together say the phrase, "Give me my bone." Help them remember to say it loud, louder and loudest by your hand motions and facial expressions.

5. Let everyone shout together the last phrase, "Take it!"

6. Set up the listening station with earphones to hear the tape the children helped you make.

Something to think about—
Hearing the tiny frights in TEENY TINY is more exciting over the earphones.

18
TALL AND FUNNY TALES

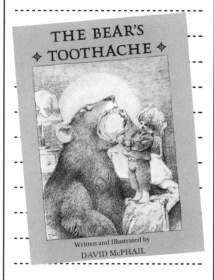

THE BEAR'S TOOTHACHE

Written and Illustrated by
DAVID McPHAIL

THE BEAR'S TOOTHACHE
By David McPhail

A little boy dreams a huge bear is moaning in pain outside his bedroom window. After inviting him in, the boy examines his teeth with a flashlight and tries several maneuvers to pull the bear's aching tooth. Finally, he finds the solution. He ties one end of his cowboy rope around the tooth, has the bear stand on the window ledge and jump. The tooth pops out and the bear is relieved. As a reward for helping, the bear gives the boy his giant tooth to place under his pillow. McPhail's tall tale is illustrated in layered colors with line drawings on violet and charcoal backgrounds to create the dreamy night mood.

Circle Time Presentation

Discuss tall tales as outrageous stories which are fun to think about. They often make us giggle because something happens which is unbelievable, but which we like to thing about anyway. Read THE BEAR'S TOOTHACHE. Discuss the scenes the children thought were the funniest or most outrageous. Ask a good storyteller to retell the story to the group by looking at the pictures.

STORY STRETCHER
For Art: Night Pictures

What the children will learn—
To combine coloring and painting to create a mood

Materials you will need—
Crayons, black, dark gray, lavender or purple tempera paints

What to do—
1. At the art table, show the children David McPhail's illustrations in THE BEAR'S TOOTHACHE. Ask them how they think he made it look like night time for his tall tale dream.

2. Demonstrate how they can make their pictures look like night pictures, also. The art process is crayon resist. With crayons, ask the children to draw a picture of something that happens at night, or a scene from THE BEAR'S TOOTHACHE, or anything they like.

3. Then, have the children paint lightly over their pictures with the night color they select, black, gray, lavender or purple. The paint will not stick to the wax crayon, but will soak into the paper where it is not colored with crayon.

Something to think about—
Even if you have preschoolers who are still at the scribble stage and who can not draw a realistic picture, use the crayon resist technique with them anyway. They will enjoy the process. Young preschoolers also need more paper and paints because they want to try things several times. It is almost as if they want to do it more than once to prove to themselves that it is reliable, that the results will be the same again.

STORY STRETCHER
For Housekeeping And Dress-up Corner: Cowgirl And Cowboy Clothes

What the children will learn—
To associate certain items of clothing with western clothes

Materials you will need—
Western hats, leather tooled belts, jeans, denim skirts, western shirts or blouses, some with fringes, cowboy or cowgirl boots

What to do—
1. Place at least one obvious western dress item in the dress-up corner for the children to find.

2. Have the children who are in the dress-up corner help you unpack the western clothes, and discuss with them that these are things that cowboys and cowgirls wear to work on the farms and ranches and to dress up, too. Ask them to look through the other clothes in the dress-up corner and see if there are some other pieces which also might be considered western clothes.

3. After the associations have been made, leave the children to enjoy dress-up and playing cowgirls and cowboys like the little boy in THE BEAR'S TOOTHACHE.

Something to think about—
If you are a Southwesterner, your children may be very familiar with western clothes, but they will still enjoy trying on a belt with a huge buckle, an over-sized ten-gallon hat and adult-sized cowboy boots. Avoid adding toy guns which may come with some children's cowboy and cowgirl outfits, if you ask for donations of clothing from home.

STORY STRETCHER

For Library Corner: Story Lamp

What the children will learn—
To recognize that when the story lamp is turned on the teacher is in the library corner ready to read a story

Materials you will need—
Inexpensive lamp, teddy bear with a cloth tied around his jaw

What to do—
1. During circle time one day, explain that anytime the children see the story lamp turned on, it means the teacher is in the library corner and anyone can come to hear a special story. (The teacher will read any story the child chooses.)

2. For several days, turn on the story lamp for a part of free play. Also, use special props, as the teddy bear with a cloth tied around his jaw to emphasize which story you will begin with before reading their selections.

3. Reread THE BEAR'S TOOTHACHE under the glow of the story lamp and with one child holding the bear. In your pocket hide a big tooth of clay or white playdough which has hardened. Give the tooth to a child to place in the science and nature center.

Something to think about—
Don't overuse the story lamp during free play. Make it special and turn it on only when you are free to spend uninterrupted time in the library corner. Children often request that we read funny stories and tall tales over and over again, so make tapes of these books.
(Adapted from an idea from Dr. Mary Montebello, George Mason University.)

STORY STRETCHER

For Music And Movement: Who's Hiding?

What the children will learn—
To observe closely for who is missing

Materials you will need—
Tape or record of some lively music, tape or record player

What to do—
1. Mention the huge bear who was hiding in the little bear's room. Show the two funny pictures of the bear hiding.

2. Tell the children that there is someone hiding in their room and have them try and guess who it is. Have the teacher's aide hide with a piece of clothing showing, as an edge of a sleeve poking outside the closet door or feet seen below a room divider.

3. Describe how to play the Who's Missing? game. While the music is playing, all the children keep their eyes closed, no peeking. The teacher will tap someone on the head to go and hide. The music will keep playing until the person is in a hiding place. When the music stops, everyone can open their eyes and see who is missing.

4. Then, the teacher will select a child to go and find the missing

one. Play the music all the time the searcher is searching. Give hints, by saying, "You're getting hot, or you're cold."

Something to think about—
Simplify the game for younger children, by stopping after the children guess who is missing. Then, the child who is in hiding pops out of the hiding place. The music starts again for someone else to hide.

STORY STRETCHER

For Science And Nature Center: Animal Teeth And People Teeth

What the children will learn—
To observe the differences in the teeth of various animals and recall the main points about good dental health

Materials you will need—
Animal teeth, real or clay models, dentist's model of teeth, speaker, toothbrush

What to do—
1. Ask parents to send in any animal teeth they or their older children have collected. If there are none available, set up the display with the clay model of the bear's tooth from the story lamp presentation in the library corner and with the dentist's model of human teeth.

2. Invite a dentist, dental assistant or a volunteer from the local medical society to make a presentation on dental care.

3. After the visitor leaves, reemphasize the presentation by creating a posterboard of pictures of the main points. Emphasize healthy snacks, as well as care of the teeth and gums.

4. Reinforce how to brush teeth by using the dentist's model and by brushing teeth at school.

Something to think about—
Dentist's models of a set of teeth can be ordered from school supply stores or local dentists will donate them. Sales people from medical companies often give them to dentists as promotional items.

REFERENCES

Barrett, Judi. (1978). Illustrated by Ron Barrett. **CLOUDY WITH A CHANCE OF MEATBALLS.** New York: Macmillan Publishing Company.

Bennett, Jill. (1986). Illustrated by Tomie dePaola. **TEENY TINY.** New York: G.P. Putnam's Sons.

Lord, John Vernon. (1972). Verses by Janet Burroway. **THE GIANT JAM SANDWICH.** Boston: Houghton Mifflin.

McPhail, David. (1972). **THE BEAR'S TOOTHACHE.** Boston: Little, Brown and Company.

Numeroff, Laura Joffe. (1985). Illustrated by Felicia Bond. **IF YOU GIVE A MOUSE A COOKIE.** New York: Harper and Row, Publishers.

Additional References for Tall and Funny Tales

Eagle, Mike (1985). **THE MARATHON RABBIT.** New York: Holt, Rinehart and Winston. *A rabbit wants to run with the people in a marathon race around the city.*

Lobel, Arnold. (1979). **A TREEFUL OF PIGS.** New York: Greenwillow Books. *A farmer's wife uses drastic measures to get her husband to abandon his lazy ways.*

Noble, Trinka Hakes. (1980). Illustrated by Steven Kellogg. **THE DAY JIMMY'S BOA ATE THE WASH.** New York: The Dial Press. *Jimmy's boa constrictor wreaks havoc on the class trip to a farm.*

Steig, William. (1982). **DOCTOR DESOTO.** New York: Scholastic, Inc. *Doctor Desoto is a mouse dentist who takes care of small and large animals' teeth. He is afraid one patient, a fox, may be his last until he comes up with a plan to trick the hungry animal.*

APPENDIX

Steps in Binding a Book

 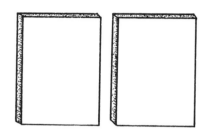 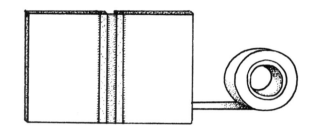

1. Cut two pieces of heavy cardboard slightly larger than the pages of the book.

2. With wide masking tape, tape the two pieces of cardboard together with ½-inch space between.

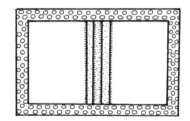 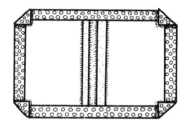

3. Cut outside cover 1½ inches larger than the cardboard and stick to cardboard (use thinned white glue if cover material is not self-adhesive.)

4. Fold corners over first, then the sides.

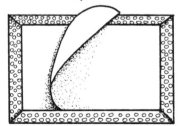 

5. Measure and cut inside cover material and apply as shown.

6. Place stapled pages of the book in the center of the cover. Secure with two strips of inside cover material, one at the front of the book and the other at the back.

Sample Rebus Chart

Directions for Making Muffins

1. Preheat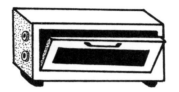

2. Place  in

3. Empty  into

4. Add 1 and ½  water

5. Stir

6. Pour into

7. Bake in

8. Serve and

BASIC ART DOUGH

the best and easiest uncooked dough

MATERIALS:
4 cups flour
1 cup iodized salt
1¾ cups warm water
bowl

PROCESS:
1. mix all ingredients in bowl
2. knead 10 minutes
3. model as with any clay
4. bake 300° until hard
5. or air dry for a few days

INDEX

Authors And Illustrators

A

Alborough, Jez	154
Allen, Roach Van	226
Aliki	46
Amoroso, Lisa	226
Anno, Mitsumasa	178
Appleby, Ellen	162, 166
Archambault, John	90, 94
Arnold, Tedd	76, 82
Aruego, José	28, 34, 190

B

Balian, Lorna	118, 196, 202
Bang, Molly	172, 178
Bennett, Jill	234, 238
Bennett, Rainey	58
Barrett, Judi	232, 238
Barrett, Ron	232, 238
Barton, Byron	206, 214
Bassett, Jeni	130
Berger, Barbara	78, 82
Bond, Felicia	228, 238
Bonners, Susan	140, 142
Bourgeosis, Paulette	82
Branley, Franklyn M.	104, 106
Brett, Jan	154
Brewster, Patience	70, 154
Brown, Margaret Wise	72, 82, 156, 166
Brown, Marc	216, 218, 226
Bunting, Eve	154
Burningham, John	214
Burroway, Janet	230, 238

C

Carle, Eric	58, 96, 112, 188, 106, 118, 190
Carlstrom, Nancy White	148, 154
Carter, Kathy	73
Carter, Peter	130
Casilla, Robert	208, 214
Chalmers, Mary	202
Cherry, Lynne	116, 118
Chorao, Kay	56, 58
Clark, Brenda	82, 124, 130
Clem, Penny	80
Clifton, Lucille	142
Cobb, Darlene	81

Cohen, Miriam	42, 44, 46
Craig, Helen	146
Crews, Donald	178, 212, 214

D

Dantzer-Rosenthal, Marya	54, 58
Dabcovich, Lydia	134, 142
Day, Alexandra	152, 154
Degen, Bruce	148, 150
de Brunhoff, Laurent	178
dePaola, Tomie	20, 34, 226, 234, 238
de Regniers, Beatrice Schenk	224, 226
Dillon, Diane	222, 226
Dillon, Leo	222, 226
Douglass, Barbara	70, 154
du Bois, William Pène	50, 58
Durrett, Kathryn	61

E

Eagle, Mike	238
Eckert, Mary	113
Ehlert, Lois	84, 94
Elam, Janice	62

F

Fernandes, Eugenia	34
Flack, Marjorie	48, 58
Freedman, Sally	82
Freeman, Don	144, 154

G

Gackenbach, Dick	202
Galdone, Paul	166
Gag, Wanda	200, 202
Geisel, Theodor Seuss, Dr. Seuss	184, 190
George Mason University	105, 127
Gibbons, Gail	114, 118
Gideon, Marcia	184
Gilchrist, Jan Spivey	118
Goss, Janet L.	118
Gray, Suzanne	127
Green, Michael	166
Greenfield, Eloise	222, 226
Gregory, Valiska	130
Gretz, Suzanna	154, 178
Goffstein, M.B.	130

H

Harste, Jerome C.	118
Hayashi, Akiko	138
Hayes, Sarah	146, 154
Heine, Helme	38, 46
Heller, Ruth	102, 106
Hines, Anna Grossnickle	34, 68, 70, 94
Hoban, Lillian	24, 34, 42, 44, 46, 142
Hoban, Russell	24, 34
Hoban, Tana	94, 187, 190
Hoffman, Hilde	136, 142
Hook, Frances	142
Howard, Elizabeth Fitzgerald	208, 214
Hubbard, Pat	85
Hughes, Shirley	40, 46, 220, 226
Hurd, Clement	156
Hurd, Edith Thacher	64, 70
Hutchins, Pat	32, 34, 66, 70, 174, 178

I

Iwamuro, Kazuo	46

J

Johnson, Crockett	86, 94, 190
Johnston, Tony	34
Jonas, Ann	52, 58

K

Kantrowitz, Mildred	154
Keats, Ezra Jack	130, 198, 202
Keller, Holly	58, 104, 106
Kellogg, Steven	202, 238
Kennedy, Jimmy	152, 154
Koide, Tan	82
Koide, Yasuko	82
Kline, Suzy	58
Kraus, Robert	28, 34
Krauss, Ruth	86, 94
Kroll, Steven	70

L

Leder, Dora	58, 192, 194, 202
Legan, Mary	64
Le Tord, Bijou	94
Lewis, Lisa	114
Lewis, Naomi	118
Lewis, Robin Baird	180, 190
Lionni, Leo	108, 118, 178, 190

Little, Lessie Jones 226
Lobe, Mira 130
Lobel, Anita 238
Lobel, Arnold 238
Lord, John Vernon 230, 238
Lloyd, Megan 118

M

Maestro, Betsy 214
Maestro, Giulio 214
Malone, Nola Langner 46
Marshall, James 36, 46
Martin, Jr., Bill 90, 94, 188, 190
Mayer, Mercer 26, 34, 70, 74, 82
McCrady, Lady 70
McCully, Emily Arnold 64, 70, 130
McGovern, Ann 166
McMillan, Bruce 142
McPhail, David 202, 210, 214, 236
Miller, Edna 118
Mitgutsch, Ali 88, 94
Moncure, Jane Belk 142
Montebello, Mary 237
Morgan, Allen 124, 130
Munsinger, Lynn 82
Murphy, Jill 30, 34

N

Nerlove, Miriam 54, 58
Noble, Trinka Hakes 202, 238
Numeroff, Laura Joffe 228, 238

O

Opgennoorth, Winfried 130
Oxenbury, Helen 204, 214
Oz, Robin 82

P

Parker, Nancy Winslow 154
Patterson, Penny 97
Patton, Linda 180
Pearson, Susan 110
Peek, Merle 168, 178, 182, 192
Pels, Winslow Pinney 166
Phillips, Debbie 151
Plaster, Ruth M. 69
Potter, Beatrix 166
Powell, Korey 79
Prelutsky, Jack 216, 226
Preston, Edna Mitchell 58
Project for the Study of
    Young Children 105, 127

Q

Quilan, Patricia 34

R

Ragsdale, Linda Larmon 85
Rand, Ted 90, 94

Rae, Mary Maki 176, 178
Reidel, Marlene 106
Rey, H.A. 160, 166
Rice, Eve 82
Robbins, Nancy 150
Rockwell, Anne 62, 70, 122, 130, 132, 142, 214
Rockwell, Harlow 62, 70, 122
Romney, Steve 118
Ross, Joel 214
Ross, Pat 214
Rossetti, Christina 190
Ryder, Joanne 116, 118
Rylant, Cynthia 80, 82, 94

S

Sage, Alison 15
Siebert, Diane 206, 214
Sendak, Maurice 126, 130, 164, 166
Seuss, Dr. 184, 190
Simon, Norma 192, 194, 202
Simont, Marc 106
Sindle, Virginia 98
Slobodkina, Esphyr 158, 166
Smith, Mavis 34
Soya, Kiyoshi 138
Stanovich, Betty Jo 60, 70
Steig, William 238
Stinson, Kathy 180, 190
Stock, Catherine 120, 130
Stoddard, Sandol 82
Szilagyi, Mary 80, 92, 94

T

Tafuri, Nancy 142, 170, 178
Testa, Fulvio 118
Thompson, Richard 34
Tresselt, Alvin 128, 130
Tuder, Lisa L. 94
Turkle, Brinton 142

UV

Udry, Janice May 106
van Kampen, Vlasta 34
Viorst, Judith 56, 58

W

Wadsworth, Olive A. 176, 178
Wallner, John 110
Warren, Sally 231
Weedon, Perrie 152
Wheeling, Lynn 214
Wildsmith, Brian 106
Wilhelm, Hans 46, 58
Williams, Linda 118
Williams, Margery 166
Williams, Vera B. 70
Wright-Frierson, Virginia 60, 70
Wylie, David 190

Wylie, Joanne 190

XYZ

Yabuuchi, Masayuki 92, 94
Yaroslava 128, 130
Yoshi 100, 106
Zeifert, Harriet 34, 140
Zolotow, Charlotte 50, 58, 120, 130

Titles

*This * indicates titles of the books used as the foundation for the S T O R Y S-T-R-E-T-C-H-E-R-S. If only one name is listed, the author also is the illustrator.*

A

All By Myself 94
    by Anna Grossnicke Hines
Air Is All Around You* 104–106
    by Franklyn M. Branley, illustrations by Holly Keller
Alfie Gives A Hand* 40, 41, 46
    by Shirley Hughes
Amelia's Nine Lives* 196, 197, 202
    by Lorna Balian
Anno's Counting Book 178
    by Mitsumasa Anno
Ask Mr. Bear* 48, 49, 58
    by Marjorie Flack

B

Babar's Counting Book 178
    by Laurent de Brunhoff
Baby Sister For Frances, A* 24, 25, 34
    by Russell Hoban, illustrations by Lillian Hoban
Bear's Toothache, The* 236–238
    by David McPhail
Bedtime For Bear 82
    by Sandol Stoddard, illustrations by Lynn Munsinger
Best Friends* 42, 43, 46
    by Miriam Cohen, illustrations by Lillian Hoban
Big And Little 46, 91, 94
    by Ruth Krauss, illustrations by Mary Szilagyi
Big Boy, Little Boy* 60, 61, 70
    by Betty Jo Stanovich, illustrations by Virginia Wright-Frierson
Big Ones, Little Ones 94, 171
    by Tana Hoban
Boy Who Didn't Believe in Spring 142
    by Lucille Clifton, illustrations by Brinton Turkle
Brown Bear, Brown Bear, What Do You See?* 188–190
    by Bill Martin, Jr., illustrations by Eric Carle

C

Caps For Sale* 158, 159, 166
by Esphyr Slobodkina
Car Trip, The* 149, 204
by Helen Oxenbury
Carrot Seed, The* 86, 87, 94
by Ruth Krauss, illustrations by Crockett Johnson
Cats Do, Dogs Don't* 192, 193, 202
by Norma Simon, illustrations by Dora Leder
Chair For My Mother, A 70
by Vera B. Williams
Chicken Soup With Rice* 126, 127, 130
by Maurice Sendak
Chickens Aren't The Only Ones* 102, 103, 106
by Ruth Heller
Children Of Long Ago 226
by Lessie Jones Little, illustrations by Jan Spivey Gilchrist
Chipmunk Song* 116–118
by Joanne Ryder, illustrations by Lynne Cherry
Cloudy With A Chance Of Meatballs* 232, 233, 238
by Judi Barrett, illustrations by Ron Barrett
Color Of His Own, A 140
by Leo Lionni
Come To The Meadow* 68, 70
by Anna Grossnickle Hines
Corduroy* 144, 145, 154
by Don Freeman
Counting Wildflowers 142
by Bruce McMillan
Curious George* 160, 161, 166
by H. A. Rey

D

Daddy Makes The Best Spaghetti 34
by Anna Grossnickle Hines
Day Jimmy's Boa Ate The Wash, The 202, 238
by Trinka Hakes Noble, illustrations by Steven Kellogg
Devin's New Bed 82
by Sally Freedman, illustrations by Robin Oz
Doorbell Rang, The* 174, 178
by Pat Hutchins
Dr. Desoto 238
by William Steig

E

Emma's Pet 202
by David McPhail

F

Ferryboat 214
by Betsy and Giulio Maestro
First Comes Spring* 132, 133, 142
by Anne Rockwell
First Snow 122, 130
by Emily Arnold McCully
First Snowfall, The* 122–124, 130
by Anne and Harlow Rockwell
Fishy Color Story, A 190
by Joanne and David Wylie
Five Minutes Peace* 30, 31
by Jill Murphy
Flying* 212, 214
by Donald Crews
Foo 34
by Richard Thompson, illustrations by Eugenia Fernandes
Franklin In The Dark 82
by Paulette Bourgeosis, illustrations by Brenda Clark
Frederick* 108, 109, 118, 166
by Leo Lionni
Friends* 38, 46
by Helme Heine
From Seed To Pear* 88, 94
by Ali Mitgutsch

G

George And Martha One Fine Day* 36, 37, 46
by James Marshall
George And Martha Back In Town 46
by James Marshall
Geraldine's Blanket 58
by Holly Keller
Giant Jam Sandwich, The* 230, 231, 238
by John Vernon Lord and verses by Janet Burroway
Gingerbread Man 166
by Paul Galdone
Good As New 70, 154
by Barbara Douglass, illustrations by Patience Brewster
Goodnight, Goodnight 72, 73, 82
by Eve Rice
Goodnight Moon* 72, 83, 82
by Margaret Wise Brown
Grandfather Twilight* 78, 79, 82
by Barbara Berger
Green Eggs And Ham* 184, 185, 190
by Theodor Seuss Geisel, Dr. Seuss
Green Grass Grows All Around, The* 138
by Hilde Hoffman
Grouchy Ladybug, The 58
by Eric Carle
Growing Vegetable Soup* 84, 94
by Lois Ehlert

H

Hand Rhymes* 171, 218, 219, 226
by Marc Brown
Happy Birthday, Sam* 66, 67, 70
by Pat Hutchins
Harold And The Purple Crayon 190
by Crockett Johnson
Have You Seen My Duckling?* 170, 171, 178
by Nancy Tafuri
Henny Penny 166
by Paul Galdone
Here Are My Hands* 90, 94
by Bill Martin, Jr. and John Archambault, illustrations by Ted Rand
Hi, Cat!* 198, 199
by Ezra Jack Keats
Home, A 46
by Nola Langner Malone
Honey, I Love And Other Love Poems* 222
by Eloise Greenfield, illustrations by Diane and Leo Dillon
House Of Leaves* 138–140, 142
by Kiyoshi Soya, illustrations by Akiko Hayashi
Hurry Up, Jessie 34
by Harriet Ziefert, illustrations by Mavis Smith

I

I Dance In My Red Pajamas* 64, 70
by Edith Thacher Hurd, illustrations by Emily Arnold McCully
I Love Ladybugs 226
by Roach Van Allen
If I Could Be My Grandmother 70
by Steven Kroll, illustrations by Lady McCrady
If You Give A Mouse A Cookie* 228, 229, 238
by Laura Joffe Numeroff, illustrations by Felicia Bond
I'll Always Love You 58
by Hans Wilhelm
Inch By Inch 178
by Leo Lionni
Is It Red? Is It Yellow? Is It Blue?* 186, 187, 190
by Tana Hoban
It Didn't Frighten Me 118
by Janet L. Goss and Jerome C. Harste, illustrations by Steve Romney

J

Jamberry* 150, 154
by Bruce Degen
Jesse Bear, What Will You Wear?* 148, 154

by Nancy White Carlstrom, illustrations
by Bruce Degen
Just Grandpa And Me   70
  by Mercer Mayer

K L

Leaves   118
  by Testa Fulvio, English translation by
  Naomi Lewis
Let's Be Friends Again   46
  by Hans Wilhelm
Little Blue And Little Yellow   190
  by Leo Lionni
Little Old Lady Who Wasn't Afraid Of
Anything   118
  by Linda Williams, illustrations by
  Megan Lloyd

M

Marathon Rabbit   238
  by Mike Eagle
Mary Wore Her Red Dress And Henry
Wore His Green Sneakers*   182
  by Merle Peek
May We Sleep Here Tonight?   82
  by Tan Koide, illustrations by Yasuko
  Koide
Me Too!*   26, 27, 34
  by Mercer Mayer
Millions Of Cats*   200–202
  by Wanda Gag
Mitten, The*   128–130
  by Alvin Tresselt, illustrations by
  Yaroslava
Mousekin's Thanksgiving   118
  by Edna Miller
Mr. Gumpy's Motor Car   214
  by John Burningham
My Dad Takes Care Of Me   34
  by Patricia Quilan, illustrations by
  Vlasta van Kampen
My Favorite Time Of The Year*   110
  by Susan Pearson, illustrations by
  John Wallner
My Mama Says There Aren't Any
Zombies, Ghosts, Vampires, Creatures,
Demons, Monsters, Fiends, Goblins,
Or Things*   56, 58
  by Judith Viorst, illustrations by
  Kay Chorao

N

No Jumping On The Bed!*   76, 82
  by Tedd Arnold
Now One Foot, Now The Other   70
  by Tomie dePaola
Night In The Country*   80, 82
  by Cynthia Rylant, illustrations by
  Mary Szilagyi

O

Old Mother Hubbard And Her Dog   226
  by Lisa Amoroso
Our Snowman   130
  by M.B. Goffstein
Out And About*   220, 221, 226
  by Shirley Hughes
Over In The Meadow*   176–178
  by Ezra Jack Keats

P

Pocket For Corduroy, A   154
  by Don Freeman

Q

Quilt Story, The   34
  by Tony Johnston, illustrations by
  Tomie dePaola

R

Rabbit Seeds   94
  by Bijou Le Tord
Rabbit's Morning   142
  by Nancy Tafuri
Random House Book Of Mother
Goose, The   226
  by Arnold Lobel
Read-aloud Rhymes For The Very
Young*   216, 226
  selected by Jack Prelutsky, illustrations
  by Marc Brown
Red Is Best*   180, 181, 190
  by Kathy Stinson, illustrations by
  Robin Baird Lewis
Riddle Soup   130
  by Valiska Gregory , illustrations by
  Jeni Bassett
Roll Over! A Counting Song*   168
  by Merle Peek
Running Bear   154
  by Jez Alborough
Runaway Bunny, The*   81, 156, 157, 166
  by Margaret Wise Brown, illustrations
  by Clement Hurd

S

Sadie And The Snowman*   124, 130
  by Allen Morgan, illustrations by
  Brenda Clark
Sarah's Questions*   140–142
  by Harriet Ziefert, illustrations by
  Susan Bonners
School Bus   214
  by Donald Crews
Seasons Of Arnold's
Apple Tree, The*   114, 118
  by Gail Gibbons

Shhhh!   58
  by Suzy Kline, illustrations by
  Dora Leder
Silly Tilly And The Easter Bunny   142
  by Lillian Hoban
Sing A Song Of Popcorn: Every
Child's Book Of Poems*   224, 226
  edited by Beatrice de Regniers, illustra-
  tions by Nine Caldecott Medal Artists
Six Dogs, Twenty-three Cats, Forty-five
Mice, And One Hundred
Sixteen Spiders   202
  by Mary Chalmers
Sleepy Bear*   134, 135, 142
  by Lydia Dabcovich
Snowman Who Went For
A Walk, The   130
  by Mira Lobe, illustrations by Winfried
  Opgennoorth, translated by Peter Carter
Snowy Day, The   130
  by Ezra Jack Keats
Spring Is Here!   142
  by Jane Belk Moncure, illustrations by
  Frances Hook
Some Things Are Different, Some Things
Are The Same*   54
  by Marya Dantzer-Rosenthal, illustra-
  tions by Miriam Nerlove
Something Is Going
To Happen*   120, 121, 130
  by Charlotte Zolotow, illustrations by
  Catherine Stock
Sometimes Its Turkey—Sometimes Its
Feathers   118
  by Lorna Balian
Stone Soup   166
  by Ann Mcgovern, illustrations by
  Winslow Pinney Pels

T

Tale Of Peter Rabbit, The   166
  by Beatrix Potter
Teddy Bears 1 To 10   178
  by Suzanna Gretz
Teddy Bears Stay Indoors   154
  by Suzanne Gretz, illustrations by
  Alison Sage
Teddy Bears' Picnic*   152–154
  by Jimmy Kennedy, illustrations by
  Alexandra Day
Teeny Tiny*   234, 235, 238
  retold by Jill Bennett, illustrations by
  Tomie dePaola
Temper Tantrum Book, The   58
  by Edna Mitchell Preston, illustrations
  by Rainey Bennett
Ten Black Dots   178
  by Donald Crews
Ten, Nine, Eight*   172, 173, 178
  by Molly Bang

There's An Alligator Under
My Bed*   74, 75, 82
  by Mercer Mayer
Things That Go   163, 214
  by Anne Rockwell
This Is The Bear*   146, 147, 154
  by Sarah Hayes, illustrations by
  Helen Craig
This Year's Garden   94
  by Cynthia Rylant, illustrations by
  Mary Szilagyi
Three Billy-goats Gruff, The* 162, 163, 166
  by Ellen Appleby
Tiny Seed, The*   112, 113, 118
  by Eric Carle
Titch*   32–34
  by Pat Hutchins
Tomie dePaola's Mother Goose   226
  by Tomie dePaola
Ton And Pon, Big And Little   46
  by Iwamuro, Kazuo
Train, The*   210, 211, 214
  by David McPhail
Train To Lulu's, The*   208, 214
  by Elizabeth Fitzgerald Howard,
  illustrations by Robert Casilla
Treeful Of Pigs, A   238
  by Arnold Lobel, illustrations by
  Anita Lobel
Truck Song*   206, 207, 214
  by Diane Siebert, illustrations by
  Byron Barton

U V

Valentine Bears, The   154
  by Eve Bunting, illustrations by
  Jan Brett
Velveteen Rabbit, The   166
  by Margery Williams, illustrations by
  Michael Green
Very Busy Spider, The*   98, 99, 106
  by Eric Carle
Very Hungry Caterpillar, The*   96, 97,
  by Eric Carle   106, 219

W

We Are Best Friends   46
  by Aliki
What's Claude Doing?   202
  by Dick Gackenbach
What Is Pink?   190
  by Christina Rossetti, illustrations by
  José Aruego
When I Go Visiting*   62, 64, 70
  by Anne and Harlow Rockwell
Where Can It Be?*   52, 53, 58
  by Ann Jonas
Where Does My Cat Sleep?*   194
  by Norma Simon, illustrations by
  Dora Leder

Where The Wild Things Are*   164, 166
  by Maurice Sendak
Whistle For Willie   202
  by Ezra Jack Keats
Who's Hiding Here?*   100, 101, 106
  by Yoshi
Whose Baby?*   92, 94
  by Masayuki Yabuuchi
Whose Mouse Are You?*   28, 29
  by Robert Kraus, illustrations by
  José Aruego
Will I Have A Friend?*   44, 46
  by Miriam Cohen, illustrations by
  Lillian Hoban
William's Doll*   50, 51, 58
  by Charlotte Zolotow, illustrations by
  Wiliam Pène du Bois
Willy Bear   154
  by Mildred Kantrowitz, illustrations by
  Nancy Winslow Parker

XYZ

Your First Airplane Ride   214
  by Pat and Joel Ross, illustrations by
  Lynn Wheeling

Activities Or Centers

Art Activities

Add-on pictures   134
Alligator paw prints   74
Animal squares   216
Birthday cards for friends   48
Birthday party masks   40
Blossoms   88, 89, 114, 132, 134
Blue t-shirts   32
Brushes and feathers   56
Bunny's black and white pictures   72
Bunny's imaginings   156
Button pictures   144
Cap pictures   158
Car window pictures   204
Cat collage   196
Cat sculptures   200
Chalk drawings   24, 90, 194
Charcoal and chalk drawings   194
Charcoal drawings   194, 222
Circle color keys   186
Class mural   44
Cloud pictures   212
Crayon etching   80
Decorating eggs   102
Decorating soup bowls   126
Decorating vests   128
Dream pictures   210
Envelope for Ask Mr. Bear card   48
Fabric collages   198

Fabric painting   100
Fish pictures   104
Flower arranging   114
Flower posters   140
Friendship collage   42, 43
Funny falling pictures   76
Funny pictures   76, 224, 225, 237
Gadget printed wrapping paper   66
Green leaf pictures   138
Group mural   26, 134
Hidden pictures   146, 147
Hiding pictures   52
Knock, knock   54
Leaf rubbings   110
Light in my picture   168
Milk carton train   208
Monster posters   164
Mouse pictures   28, 228
My house, your house   54
Night pictures   236
Painting trucks   206
Painting with red and music   180
Paper bag masks   136
Party hats, making   182, 183
Pastel twilight pictures   78
Photo album, class   62
Pictures and compliments   42
Pictures we paint in our minds   108
Plaster of paris hand prints   90
Playdough characters   162
Playdough snowmen   124
Pond pictures   170
Raining food pictures   232
Rocky's chair collage   194
Sand pictures   220
Shape that clay   44
Silhouettes   198
Silly berry Jamberry pictures   150
Silly cars, silly trains, silly boats   184
Snowflake pictures   122
Soft pictures   52
Spider webs   98, 99
Sponge lift-off   116
Sponge painting   112, 218
Spring photographs   132
Stamp pictures   36
Strangely colored animals   188
Talking pictures   146
Tall tale pictures   230
Teeny Tiny puppets   234
Telephone books   160
Tissue paper designs   96
Watercolor scenes   208
Watercolor weather   224
Watercolors   38, 60, 92, 112, 120,122,
   170, 208, 224
   220, 224, 232
Weather pictures   220, 224, 232
Weaving patterns   174
Wild thing masks   164
Window pane pictures   172
Wish collage,   50

Yellow and orange design   28
Yellow, green and spring   68

Block Building

Bucket of blocks   55
Building dream houses   76
Building in progress   45
Fire trucks   160
Gathering wood   128
Loading docks   206
Model airport   212
New town, A   232
Old stone wall   108, 109
Tent play   124
Town of Itching Down   230
Traffic jam   204, 206
Train like William's   50
Train set   50, 210
Trains, pegs and things   60
Tree house   26, 27, 114, 115
Wheelbarrow lift   86

Cooking And Snack Time

Alligator bait salad   74
Baby apple pies   114
Baking a cake   24
Baking Grandma's cookies   175
Bernard's birthday lunch   40
Breakfast muffins   120
Carrot and raisin salad   86, 87
Caterpillar snack week   96
Celery crunchies   148
Chocolate chip mouse cookies   228
Choose your fruit   192
Clean-up time (mopping the floor)   174
Cooking chicken soup with rice   126
Country apples   80
Cream cheese and jelly sandwiches   56
Egg in a hole   102
Fredrick's granola log   108
Friends share cherries, The   38
George's banana treats   161
Giant jam sandwich   230, 231, 238
Green eggs and ham   184, 185, 190
Making sandwiches   205
Marmalade toast   30
No cooking picnic   68
Orange air   104
Party cupcakes   182
Pear treats   88
Picnicking with our teddy bears   152
Pistachio ice cream or lime sherbet   199
Pumpkin bread   110, 111
Raw carrot crunch   156
Red party   180
Red, yellow and blue snacks   186
Snack with Josh and Stephan   55
Snacks in flight   213
Snowmen and snowwomen cookies   125
Snowy mashed potatoes   232

Squeezing orange juice   45
Sunflower seeds   84, 112, 113
Sweet honey   134
Tasting berries   150
Tasting blueberries   64
Winter snacks   122

Creative Dramatics Activities

Acting like Sleepy Bear   135
Bus ride   205
Caps and monkeys   158
Dressed for the part   156
Dressing for Katy's party   183
Frederick tab puppets   109
Hiding place   25, 147, 237
It won't come up!   87
Mister big face   198, 199
Nora's relatives and neighbors   196
Pantomime   27, 229, 234
Pantomiming mouse   228
Pantomiming Teeny Tiny   234
Pretending to be chipmunks   116
Show what we feel   29
Skip, hop, gallop, trot   49
Snowman, The   114, 122-125, 130, 218
Three Billy-Goats Gruff   162, 163, 166
Tight rope walking   36
Train ride   208, 209, 211

Housekeeping And Dress-up Corner

Alone at last   168
Astronauts   104, 105
Bakery   120, 230, 231
Bunny's bedroom   72, 73
Caps and hats   43, 159
Cowgirl and cowboy clothes   236
Curious George Visitor, A   161
Dolls and stuffed animals   50, 55, 72, 163
Dressing bears   132
Dressing for the season   220
Dressing red   180
Dressing teddy bears   145, 152
Farmers' clothes   98
Filling Teeny Tiny's cupboard   235
Fruit stand   89
Funny Seuss hats   185
Getting ready for work   121
Hanging up clothes   66
Here are my hands to button,
   zip and snap   90
Jesse Bear, what will you wear?   148, 154
Mrs. Large's household   30
Packing for a visit   62
Packing for our train trip   211
Pilots and flight attendants   213
Pretend picnicking   68
Rain wear   138
Setting the table   64
Wagon ride   55
We look pretty   222

What gardeners wear   84
Wild thing costumes   165

Library Corner : Dictated Stories, Chart Stories

Cat owners' talks   195
Composing a sequel   78
Dictated stories   170
Favorite spring things   133
Friendship chart   43
If mouse came to our classroom   229
New family members   29
Our diaries   37
Telling a lost teddy story   147
We feel big when we   91

Library Corner: Flannel Board Stories

Brown Bear saw   188
Counting baby animals and insects   176
How many animals can get inside?   129
Huge carrot, THE CARROT SEED   87
Jesse's clothes   149
Katy Bear's party guests   183
Little bunny   72, 73, 156, 157, 218, 219
I can tell a story   39
Max and the wild things   165
Mr. Bear and friends   49
Parts of a tree, the   136
RUNAWAY BUNNY and running
   after Mother   157
Sarah's visitors   138
Story retelling   57, 67, 97
THE TINY SEED grows   113
Trapping goats   162

Library Corner: Listening Station

A listening birthday calendar   127
A quiet retreat   81
Alfie gives a hand   40, 41, 46
Camouflage riddles   100
Cat sounds   200
Eggcitement tape   103
Follow the bees   135
Funny pictures tape   225
Grandpa's tall tale   233
Group chanting   189
Household noises   121
I want a brother   29
Listening for cracking ceiling   77
Listening with CORDUROY   144
Magnetic counting tape   172
Missing blanket   52
Peaceful ending   117
SADIE'S SNOWMAN   125
Sam-I-am convinced me   185
Sarah asks a lot of questions   140
Surprise, George!   37

Tape of WILLIAM'S DOLL with
   character voices 51
TEENY TINY frights 235
Things we love tape 223
TITCH tape 32
Truck sounds 207
Two sisters travel alone 209
WHOSE BABY? riddle tapes 92

Library Corner: Storytelling, Retelling, Riddles, Poems

Action pictures 221
Frederick's poem 109
Hey, Diddle, Diddle 73
Mothers' Day/Fathers' Day Poem 48, 49
Riddle pictures 93
Rhyming words 73, 219
Story lamp 237
Story retelling 57, 67, 97
Tell me a story 57
The story in the pictures 216
Warning, story inside 75

Mathematics And Manipulative Activities

Animal family puzzles 93
Cat calendars 195, 196
Checkerboard patterns 147
Circles, squares, rectangles 122
Comparisons, big and little 91
Counting Amelias 197
Counting cars, vans, trucks, buses 205
Counting cookies 175
Counting eggs 103
Counting forwards and backwards 173
Counting rhymes 216, 217
Counting seeds 113
Counting Walter's floors 77
Easter egg mathematics 133
Five lost 53
From concrete to abstract caps 159
Guesstimate what's left 168
How much is too much? 207
If then sequence 229
Kittens hand rhyme 219
Magnetic numerals with rhymes 177
Making sets by touch 145
Matching mittens 129
Missing crayons 57
Our favorite colors chart 187
Pairing by color 101
Patterns of beads 187
Patterns of colors 189
Sets of three 33, 163
Sorting by color attributes 181
Stringing pretend pearls 79
The alligator ate it! 75
Threes, threes, threes 33
Voting for our favorite cat 201

Weighing seeds 84
Winter wonderland village 121
Would you let a caterpillar crawl on
   your hand? 96, 97

Music And Movement Activities

Animal moves 217
Balance beams 75
Balancing an egg 57
Balancing caps 159
Berryland Marching Band 150
Button, button, who has the button? 145
Cat chant 195
Catching frisbees 192
Dancing in imaginary red pajamas 65
Dancing in the meadow 151
Falling leaves 111
Fireflies 176, 177, 217
Frances' sad song becomes a happy song 25
Friendship song 45
Growing plants 85
Here We Go 'Round the Apple Tree 115
Hide the blanket 53
I get down 223
Ice cream clouds 69
Ice skater's waltz 127
It's Snowing Song 123
Jump rope chants 216, 217, 223
Looking for Amelia 196, 197
Marching to The Teddy Bears' Picnic 153
Mitten, mitten, who has the mitten 129
Musical follow the leader 39
Musical I spy 141
Name-I-Am 185
Old Mac Martin Had a Farm 189
Parade, A 132, 133, 199
Pass the pearl 79
Playing basketball 51, 152, 153
Quack! Quack! Quack! 171
Reaching, Stretching, Growing, Knowing 91
Relaxing to music 31
Ring-A-Ring-O'-Roses 41
Sarah and the flying insects 139
Singing Roll Over! 169
Singing The Green Grass Grows All
   Around 136
Teddy Bears' Picnic Games 152
Ten Little Monkeys Jumping on the Bed 77
The flight of the wasps 231
The Little Turtle 216, 225
The Pear Tree 89
The Wheels on the Train Go 209
The Wheels on the Truck Go 207
Walking the spider web 99
What's missing? 147
Who's hiding here? 100, 101, 106
Who's hiding? 237
Wild rumpus 164, 165

Naptime, Transition Time

Clean-up time 31, 45, 66, 108, 128, 174
David takes a nap 60
Saying goodnight 72, 73

Sand Table Activities

Cats' and Dogs' hidden treasure 193
Country geography 81
Digging for dinosaurs 169
Digging for potatoes 85
Hills and bridges 163
Hills and valleys 81, 201
Jesse's sand toys 149
River traffic 213
Sand poem and sand castles 221
Snow plowing 123
Underground tunnels and burrows 117

Science And Nature Activities

Animal babies 81, 92, 93
Animal teeth 237
Berry plants and berry bushes 151
Bird nests 137
Blowing bubbles 41, 149
Camouflage in season 101
Caring for a kitten 197
Carrot tops 87
Carving a pumpkin 111
Caterpillar 37, 96, 97, 100, 106, 218, 219
Caterpillars in a terrarium 97
Cloud watching 69
Counting seashells 173
Display of eggs 103
Earth watching 69
Farm babies 93
Fishy water 105
Hatching baby chicks 43
Hives and honeycombs 135
How does a doorbell ring? 175
I spy walks 141
Insect habitats 177
Insects 100-102, 111, 112, 128, 134, 138,
   139, 142, 171, 176-178, 217
Inverted glass experiment 105
Like a chipmunk 116, 117
Magnetic rice 127
Mixing colors 187, 225
Nature poems 225
Nature walk 37, 68, 101, 111, 141
Nursery trees 89
Observations of cats 201
Observing a bird feeder 61
Oysters and pearls 79
Paper airplanes 27
People teeth 237
Physics experiment 209
Pictures of real spider webs 99
Pinwheels 34, 175
Planting seeds 33, 85
Poetic insects 217

249

Recognizing flowers	141
Seed pods	113
Seeing seashells	63
Sequencing the seasons	115
Water in all its forms	125
Who lives in the pond?	171
Wild animal babies	93
Zoo animals	161

Water Table Activities

Blowing bubbles	41, 149
Floating on the village pond	39
Houseboats	233
Runaway sailboats	157
Sailing birthday boats	67
Shampooing imaginary pets	193
Toys and bottles	31
Water table pond	171

Work Bench Activities

Hammer and saw	65
Matthew's tool box	211
Our tool chest	61
Plumber's Tool Chest	193

Terms

Acorns	37, 111, 113, 116, 117
Baby clothes	50, 122, 132, 145, 152, 153
Bakery	120, 230, 231
Balloon	132
Bananas	68, 84, 110, 161, 192
Baseball	43, 142, 153, 159
Basketball	50, 51, 152, 153
Beanbag	126
Bears	11, 73, 94, 132, 133, 144-146, 148, 150, 152-154, 178, 217
Berry	150, 151
Bicycle	38, 39, 132
Birdhouse	132
Birthday	40, 41, 48, 49, 66, 67, 70, 127, 182, 183
Boat	38, 39, 66, 67, 150, 184
Breakfast	120, 121, 132, 232
Bubble wands	149
Bulletin board	43, 72, 98, 138, 150, 158, 196, 212, 213, 220
Bus ride	205
Butterfly	96, 97, 100, 106, 138, 139, 176, 219
Button	90, 144, 145
Calendar	43, 92, 126, 127, 195, 201
Camouflage	100, 101
Carrot	86, 87, 94, 110, 156, 157
Cat	28, 65, 73, 78, 81, 82, 98, 100, 172, 188, 189, 192-202, 234, 235

Catalogs	42, 50, 54, 75, 76, 115, 140, 156, 194, 224
Chalk	24, 33, 72, 90, 101, 127, 134, 156, 168, 194
Chant	25, 91, 123, 141, 177, 185, 195, 218, 219, 223
Charcoal	194, 222, 236
Chart tablet	43, 61, 62, 72, 73, 75, 78, 79, 91, 117, 133, 136, 144, 156, 170, 180, 199, 229
Checkerboard	146, 147, 174
Clear contact paper	64, 139, 228
Clothespin	186
Collage	36, 42, 43, 48, 50, 52, 78, 108, 112, 140, 156, 176, 194, 196, 198
Community helpers	206
Cookie	66, 68, 75, 125, 174, 175 228, 229, 238
Crayon etching	80
Cream cheese	30, 56, 110, 148
Cupcakes	182
Difficulty napping	72, 73
Dinosaurs	74, 102, 169, 225
Doorbell	174, 175, 178
Easel	28, 42, 56, 62, 68, 76, 104, 116, 138, 158, 180, 186, 188
Eggs	24, 42, 43, 48, 56, 57, 102, 103, 109, 132, 133, 136, 137, 184, 185, 190, 200
Exaggeration	230, 232
Farm animals	81, 93, 98, 161, 188
Fine muscle control	48
Finger play	225
Fishing pole	69, 157
Flannel board	10, 39, 49, 75, 87, 97, 99, 113, 129, 136, 138, 139, 149, 157, 162, 163, 176, 177, 183, 188, 189, 197, 217, 218, 219, 235
Flashlight	177, 198, 236
Folk costumes	128
Fresh fruit	89, 120
Frisbee	192
Gardener	85, 88, 94, 151, 156, 157
Glitter	182
Granola logs	109
Graph	80, 97, 149, 187, 201
Hair spray	24, 134, 222
Halloween	37, 110, 165, 234
Hand motions	77, 115, 168, 171, 218, 219, 225, 235
Hats	43, 84, 98, 124, 152, 153, 159, 160, 182, 183, 185, 231, 236
Hide and seek	53
Honey	108, 109, 134, 135, 222, 223, 226
Humane society	195, 197
Ice skaters	127
Insect	69, 141, 176-178, 217, 225
Jam	150, 204, 206, 230, 231, 238
Jelly	30, 38, 56, 103, 133, 150, 205
Kite	32, 36, 68, 69, 132, 133
Lacing cards	115

Liquid soap	66, 149, 208, 232, 233
Magazines	42, 54, 76, 92, 93, 115, 140, 156, 194-196, 224
Magnet	127
Masks	40, 136, 164
Meadow	68-70, 98, 108, 142, 151, 176-178
Mirror	27, 29, 115, 121, 125, 181, 185, 199, 205, 213, 220, 222, 229
Mitten	128-130
Monster	56, 164
Muffins	55, 64, 120
Mural	26, 44, 134
Nuts	61, 65, 86, 88, 108, 109, 112, 116, 117, 127, 161, 182
Nuts and bolts	61, 65, 127
Outside-inside pictures	52
Pajamas	30, 62, 64, 65, 70, 148, 149, 180, 181, 211
Paper bag	128, 136, 164, 169, 194, 198, 199
Parent newsletter	159, 210, 213, 216
Patterns	49, 52, 53, 129, 147, 174, 183, 187, 189
Peanut butter	56, 74, 109, 148, 205, 231
Pet ownership	195, 197
Photographs	62, 92, 132, 139, 140, 142, 169, 186, 196
Picnic	11, 68, 69, 152-154, 216
Pilot	156, 212, 213
Pipe cleaners	76, 185, 208
Playdough	10, 44, 76, 79, 81, 89, 91, 103, 124, 137, 162, 163, 184, 200, 228, 230, 231, 237
Poem	49, 89, 90, 100, 109, 127, 150, 172, 190, 195, 206, 216, 217, 219, 220-226
Pond	38, 39, 140, 170, 171, 201
Primary colors	32, 186, 187
Pumpkin	110, 111, 113, 118
Puppets	109, 199, 234
Puzzle pieces	53, 66, 93, 103, 127, 207
Rain	85, 124, 138, 139, 159, 160, 207, 214, 232
Raisins	86, 88, 125, 161, 182
Raw vegetables	30, 233
Rebus chart	55, 175, 180
Recurring sentence patterns	53
Rhythm band	133, 150, 151
Riddles	7, 92, 93, 100
Rocking chair	157
Role-play	25, 29, 30, 38, 68, 72, 89, 121, 132, 138, 157, 158, 160, 231
Sandwiches	56, 68, 205, 208
Scarves	151-153, 213
Seashells	63, 169, 173
Secondary colors	186, 187, 190
Sequel	78
Sequence	39, 49, 67, 74, 87, 97, 115, 129, 136, 147, 158, 159, 163, 188, 189, 204, 229, 235
Shaving cream	120, 121

Silhouette 198
Snaps 90, 98, 145
Snow 112, 113, 120-125, 128, 130, 218, 232, 233
Snowman 114, 122-125, 130, 218
Sponge painting 112, 218
Stream 156, 176
Stuffed animals 50, 55, 72, 144, 145, 147, 152, 163, 168, 173, 193
Teeth 66, 164, 236-238
Tempera paints 28, 42, 66, 68, 76, 92, 104, 112, 116, 122, 158, 164, 180, 187, 188, 198, 206, 232, 236
Terrarium 97, 139, 177
Tissue paper 28, 96, 177, 231
Tool box 61, 211
Tools 56, 61, 65, 84, 149, 193, 201, 210, 211
Tow truck 204
Train set 50, 210
Troll 162, 163
Trucks 55, 121, 123, 149, 160, 204-207, 209, 214
Tunnel 69, 117, 141
Twigs 76, 77, 81, 101, 111, 114
Umbrella 36, 54, 138, 157, 186
Vegetables 30, 74, 75, 84, 85, 87, 127, 233, 235
Verse 45, 49, 90, 123, 150, 207, 209, 217, 219, 225
Vest 128, 148
Wagon 55, 128, 129
Watercolor 60, 88, 100, 170, 176, 208, 224
Western clothes 236, 237
Wheelbarrow 86, 87, 128
Wild life 92-94, 160, 171
Yarn 27, 40, 45, 79, 99, 101, 115, 164, 181, 182, 187, 189